D1011441

Social Security

Social Security

The Inherent Contradiction

Peter J. Ferrara

Studies in Public Policy

Library of Congress Cataloging in Publication Data

Ferrara, Peter J   1956–
   Social security.

   Includes bibliographical references and index.
   1. Social security—United States.   I. Title.
HD7125.F47   368.4'3'00973   80-18949
ISBN 0-932790-24-0

Printed in the United States of America.

CATO INSTITUTE
747 Front Street
San Francisco, California 94111

The art of government consists in taking as much money as possible from one class of citizens to give to another.

Voltaire

Experience should teach us to be most on our guard to protect liberty when the Government's purposes are beneficient. Men born to freedom are naturally alert to repel invasion of their liberty by evil-minded rulers. The greatest dangers to liberty lurk in insidious encroachment by men of zeal, well-meaning but without understanding.

Justice Louis Brandeis
Olmstead v. *United States*
277 U.S. 479 (1927)

Contents

Acknowledgments

Special thanks are due to many individuals who made extremely valuable contributions to the effort to produce this book. To begin with, I would like to express my appreciation to Mark Frazier of the Sabre Foundation whose entrepreneurial imagination, foresight, and encouragement initiated this effort. Special thanks are also due to David Ranson of H. C. Wainwright and Co. who is so brimming with knowledge that he has mastered the art of teaching by osmosis and who greatly enhanced my ability to perform the empirical research necessary to complete this book. An immeasurable degree of credit is due to Steven Alexander of Amdahl Corporation whose awesome actuarial and computer skills and unique ability to apply those skills imaginatively were invaluable aids in completing some of the most important sections of this book. I would also like to express special thanks to Robert Nozick of Harvard University for his comments and his example.

Special thanks are also due to Martin Feldstein of Harvard University for his comments, patience, and enthusiasm. I would also like to thank Colin D. Campbell of Dartmouth College and the American Enterprise Institute, Mitchell Polinsky of Harvard Law School, Edgar K. Browning of the University of Virginia, and Charles Meyer for their advice, suggestions, and insightful comments. Thanks also to Mark Weinburg, Frank Arnold, Robert Case, and Alvin Joran for their comments on the original manuscript.

I would also like to thank the employees of the Social Security Administration for their generally courteous and competent responses to my many questions. Thanks also to typists Micki and Ruth for their special abilities and to Cathe, Sandy, Doug, Lisa, Joanne, Donna, and Maryann for general support. Thanks also to Chris and Dean for proofreading and general services.

Of course, I owe a special debt of thanks to those at the Cato Institute who helped to produce this book, especially Edward Crane and Robert Formaini.

Part One

The Defects of the
Social Security System

1

The Inherent Contradiction

Social security is the showpiece of America's welfare state. It is by far the largest of all government programs, constituting one-fourth of the federal budget. It has been touted as the most successful government program in the nation's history. It has enjoyed widespread popularity and support, despite its controversial beginnings. It is the one program offered with confidence as an example of how government can improve the common good. It was the most important legislative act of the New Deal, and in the minds of many people it has come to stand for the New Deal itself.

Because it is the showpiece of the welfare state, social security has been virtually immune from serious criticism. Most economists have uncritically accepted the program's basic structure and method of operation. The program's many ardent supporters have refused to acknowledge any serious defects in the current system and have denounced the program's critics as enemies of the elderly and the poor. Some of the country's most respected public policy analysts have even labeled the program as one of "the most effective and successful institutions ever developed in the United States."[1]

But the time for this Pollyanna approach to social security is over. In recent years, prominent economists and analysts have advanced many valid and powerful critiques of the program based on its numerous serious shortcomings. The most sophisticated econometric studies show that the program is needlessly costing Americans hundreds of billions of dollars annually because of its negative impacts on the economy. Other studies show that young people entering the

[1]Joseph A. Pechman, Henry J. Aaron, and Michael K. Taussig, *Social Security: Perspectives for Reform* (Washington, D.C.: Brookings Institution, 1968), p. 1.

3

system today will never receive a fair return on all the social security taxes they will pay into the program over the course of their lives. The program is fundamentally coercive, forcing all Americans to participate regardless of their desires. It imposes on all Americans a single insurance plan with a particular set of provisions instead of allowing a system of diverse options that would permit individuals and their families to choose a specific plan suited to their needs. The inequities and negative economic impacts of the system fall most heavily on some of the most vulnerable groups in society—blacks, the poor, women, the elderly, and the young. The program is financed by a regressive payroll tax that causes economic inefficiency and imposes a hardship on the poor. Despite recent tax increases and official assurances, the danger that the system will become bankrupt remains real. These and other shortcomings of the social security system will be described in more detail in this book.

These problems have been compounded by the tremendous growth of the program in recent years. Social security has ballooned into what is probably the largest social welfare program in the world. Total expenditures under the program have grown from $10 million in 1938 to $8.9 billion in 1958, $30.3 billion in 1968, and $114.2 billion in 1978.[2] The program's total expenditures in 1978 constituted 24.8% of the total federal budget. Social security has now grown too big, and its many serious negative impacts have become too severe, for its defects to be ignored.

Many of the negative impacts of the program have grown more severe in recent years not only because the program has grown so large, but also because it has become so outdated. Social security was enacted in the depths of the Great Depression over forty years ago, and many of its features were structured to fit the economic and social circumstances of those times. Despite the changes in these circumstances that have occurred over the years, however, there have been no fundamental changes in the basic structure of the program. Many economic and social impacts that might have been thought desirable then are no longer desirable now. The Great Depression is over. It is time for social security to be reevaluated and fundamentally reformed.

---

[2]Social Security Administration, *Social Security Bulletin, Annual Statistical Supplement,* 1975, p. 66; Board of Trustees, Federal Old-Age and Survivors Insurance and Disability Insurance Trust Funds, *1978 Annual Report,* p. 73; Board of Trustees, Federal Hospital Insurance Trust Fund, *1978 Annual Report,* p. 27.

An additional factor exacerbating the problems of social security is that the program has just recently begun to enter an entirely new stage of development. Social security operates on a pay-as-you-go basis. The tax money currently paid into the program is not saved and invested but immediately paid out to recipients. A crucially important but poorly understood characteristic of any pay-as-you-go system is that it has two distinct stages of development: a start-up phase and a mature phase. Many of the most serious problems and shortcomings of a pay-as-you-go system appear in a powerful way only in the mature stage. The American social security system has only recently begun to pass from the start-up phase to the mature phase, and most of the serious, widely publicized malfunctions of the program are due to this development. The problems arising from the maturing of the social security system will be explored in more detail later, especially in chapters 4 and 5.

In addition, the social security program has long been misrepresented and deceptively described by politicians and government officials in order to create a false impression among voters about the true nature and operation of the program. This false impression has been used to cover up many of the program's major shortcomings and to sell it to a public that would probably not buy it if it understood how it really worked. The nature, source, and purpose of these misrepresentations will also be discussed in more detail in later chapters.

The basic theme of this book is that the source of all the major defects of the social security program is an inherent conflict in its objectives. The current social security program tries to serve two contradictory functions: a welfare function and an insurance function. The program tries to fulfill these two functions at once but fulfills neither adequately. This attempt to serve two functions with one program results in all the serious, negative impacts mentioned above and discussed throughout this book.

In an insurance program, individuals are paid benefits after various contingencies occur. The amount of these benefits depends solely on how much the individual has paid into the program in the past, and the benefits are paid regardless of whether the individual really needs them. For example, if a millionaire buys a life insurance policy of $1 million and designates his sole heir as beneficiary, upon the millionaire's death the beneficiary will receive the million dollars, even though he also inherits his benefactor's other millions.

Social security serves an insurance function by paying benefits when a person retires, is disabled, dies, or is hospitalized. These benefits are paid under a formula that, in general, grants higher benefit amounts to those who have paid higher social security taxes. These benefits are, in general, paid regardless of whether the individual recipient needs them.

A welfare program pays benefits only to individuals who are in poverty or need. The amount of these benefits depends solely on the degree of need, and the benefits are paid regardless of how much the recipient has paid into the program in the past. A millionaire will never receive any welfare benefits even though he may pay thousands into welfare programs over the course of his life.

Social security serves a welfare function through the many provisions of the program's benefit structure, which pays benefits to some individuals solely because it is felt they are in need. These benefits are paid even though they cannot be justified on the basis of past tax payments into the program. The result is that the beneficiaries of these welfare elements receive far more than they have paid for on insurance grounds, while others receive far less. Social security also includes in its benefit structure welfare elements that deny benefits to individuals because it is felt they are not in sufficient need, even though these benefits can be justified on the basis of past tax payments into the system. The result is that these individuals receive less than they have paid for on insurance grounds.

The many ways in which the social security program serves these two functions will be discussed in more detail in chapter 2. The combination of these two conflicting objectives within the social security program has been noted often. For example, the conflict was explicitly recognized in a study published by the Brookings Institution in 1968 entitled *Social Security: Perspectives for Reform* by Joseph Pechman, Henry Aaron, and Michael Taussig. Recognition of this conflict was further developed in another Brookings study, published in 1977, entitled *The Future of Social Security* by Alicia Munnell.

The two objectives are often referred to in the literature as the goal of individual equity (insurance) and the goal of social adequacy (welfare). These two functions are fundamentally incompatible, and the result is very bad welfare and very bad insurance. Insurance pays benefits to individuals on the basis of what they have paid into the program in the past, regardless of their need. Welfare pays benefits to individuals based on their need, regardless of what they have paid into the program in the past.

The schizophrenic nature of the program has resulted in its fatal flaw—the social security taxes paid into the system now are not saved and invested through a trust fund as in private insurance, savings, or pension plans, but instead are paid out immediately to current recipients on a pay-as-you-go basis, like a welfare program. This method of operation began when the original funds paid into the system were immediately paid out as benefits to recipients who had paid little or nothing themselves. This was done in pursuit of the welfare objectives of the program. It was felt that these original recipients needed the benefits even though they had not paid for them. But the payment of benefits to these original nonpaying recipients required that all future recipients be paid out of current cash on a pay-as-you-go basis as well because there were no saved funds to pay for the benefits of these later recipients. Because social security has always pursued welfare objectives in addition to insurance ones, it operates on a pay-as-you-go basis.[3]

This fatal flaw causes social security to be a bad insurance program that has several major negative effects on the economy and the program's participants. For the economy as a whole, the operation of social security on a pay-as-you-go basis results in a serious decline in savings, which results, in turn, in a loss of capital investment. This loss of capital results in a decline in economic growth and national income. According to the econometric studies conducted by Harvard professor of economics Martin Feldstein, the operation of social security on a pay-as-you-go basis results in an annual loss of hundreds of billions of dollars in national income.

For the individual taxpayer, the fatal flaw means he loses the interest return he would get on his tax money if it were invested. Over the course of a lifetime this interest return would accumulate, and at retirement the individual taxpayer would receive in benefits much more than he would get under a mature pay-as-you-go transfer payment scheme like social security. It is true that a pay-as-you-go system generates its own internal rate of return on past tax payments

---

[3]It would be possible to operate a program with both welfare and insurance objectives on a fully invested basis rather than on a pay-as-you-go basis. The money from the invested trust fund could simply be paid out under a benefit structure with both welfare and insurance elements instead of according to to how much each individual paid in, as in insurance. Similarly, a pay-as-you-go system could have a benefit structure without any welfare elements but determined by the amount paid in. The pursuit of both welfare and insurance objectives in the same program does not in itself require that the program be funded on a pay-as-you-go basis. However, because the program also pursued the welfare objective of providing benefits to those in the start-up phase who had paid relatively little into the program, it was and is operated on a pay-as-you-go basis.

through naturally increasing taxes on future generations. But, as will be seen later, this rate of return is far below the return available on investments in productive private sector alternatives.[4]

The operation of social security on a pay-as-you-go basis also means that there is no trust fund to guarantee future benefit payments. The only guarantee of future benefits is the willingness of future taxpayers to continue to bear the program's tax burden. This leaves social security financially vulnerable to any factors that will tend to increase this tax burden or decrease the willingness of taxpayers to continue to pay. Pay-as-you-go financing thus leaves the program vulnerable to future threats of bankruptcy and makes it a financially insecure means for the program's participants to acquire insurance protection.

The presence of the welfare function in the social security system operates to the detriment of the insurance function in other ways. The program must be coercive and compulsory only because it pursues welfare objectives in addition to insurance ones. With a welfare element in the benefit structure, some beneficiaries get more than they pay for and others get less. If the program were not compulsory, those that got less than they paid for would voluntarily opt out, leaving only those entitled to more than they paid for. The program would thus become financially insolvent and could no longer continue.

If the program involved only insurance, however, it could give all participants exactly what they paid for and pay them a fair competitive return on their tax payments. If it were operated on a fully funded basis rather than on a pay-as-you-go basis, it could then be completely voluntary, allowing individuals who made alternative arrangements to leave the program. If some did choose to leave, the program could still continue because those remaining would be paying their own way.

Mixing a welfare program with an insurance system results in a coercive insurance system. Since in a free society voluntarism is preferable to coercion, this coercive element in social security is another reason why it is bad insurance.

---

[4]The concept of a rate of return naturally generated in a pay-as-you-go system was first advanced by Paul Samuelson. See "An Exact Consumption-Loan Model of Interest with or without the Social Contrivance of Money," *Journal of Political Economy* LXVI (December 1958): 467–82. As will be shown in chapters 4 and 9, the rate of return provided by the pay-as-you-go system is approximately 10–15% as great as the rate of return provided by private sector alternatives.

Furthermore, because the welfare element requires that the program be compulsory and coercive, the entire program must be run by the government since the government is the only institution empowered to employ such coercion. This subjects the program to various political influences and results in an inherently unstable program that tends to be run on a political rather than on an economic basis. Politicians become tempted to use the program for their own ends at the expense of the program's participants. They may, for example, seek to buy votes in the short run with unsound, extravagant, and unwarranted benefit increases that are to the detriment of the long-run interests of their constituents. Politically powerful special interest groups may also be able to gain special privileges or advance their favorite ideological causes through the program. The result is to make social security bad insurance because it is unnecessarily subjected to political pressures.

In addition, because the welfare element requires that virtually everyone participate in the government program, it requires that everyone accept one uniform insurance plan. Without the welfare element, people could be allowed to choose from a variety of insurance and investment options offered in the private market. Individuals and families could develop insurance plans suited to their particular circumstances and get greater value for their insurance dollars.

The sharpest conflicts between the welfare and insurance objectives of social security occur in the benefit structure. As we have seen, a good insurance program will pay beneficiaries a fair rate of return based on the amount they have paid into the program, regardless of their need. The more one pays for, the more he will receive. A good welfare program will pay beneficiaries based on their need, regardless of how much they have paid into the program; the more one needs, the more he will receive. A program that tries to pursue both insurance and welfare objectives is therefore faced with the hopelessly difficult problem of attempting to design its benefit structure so that the program will be both good welfare and good insurance.

The results of this dilemma can be seen in social security's current benefit structure. The inclusion of welfare elements with insurance elements in this structure has resulted in a disbursement of benefit payments that is widely perceived as unfair. With regard to insurance, this perception is entirely correct. Because of the welfare elements in the program, some benefits are paid on the basis of need rather than past tax payments. Some beneficiaries will therefore receive more than they have paid for in past taxes, while others will receive less than they have paid for. The result is to make social security an unfair insurance program because beneficiaries cannot count on getting full value for their tax dollars.

The clearest example of this inequity is the social security earnings test, which provides that an elderly social security recipient who earns more than a certain minimum amount annually will lose a proportional amount of old-age benefits. This provision is based on a welfare rationale: An elderly person who is still earning enough to support himself does not need old-age benefits and therefore should not be allowed to receive them. But it would be unfair for an insurance program to deny an elderly beneficiary benefits that he has paid for, after the program has collected money for years on the promise of those benefits, simply because the potential recipient would like to continue working or finds an additional source of income. A person who pays for insurance benefits over the course of his life should receive them regardless of whether he needs them. The earnings test makes social security an inequitable insurance program.

Similarly, many of the elements in the benefit structure that discriminate against women are based on welfare rationales, as we shall see. While these provisions may make sense from a welfare point of view, they also contribute to making social security an inequitable insurance program.

In addition, the presence of the welfare elements in the benefit structure makes the system economically inefficient. If benefits were paid solely on insurance grounds, each taxpayer would receive full value for his tax payments. Every dollar paid in taxes would bring an equal value in return, and the more each taxpayer paid in taxes the more he would receive in benefits. The taxpayer would think of his social security tax payments as if they were a charge for a good or service, not a tax. He would think of them as part of his after-tax income, which he has used to pay for insurance protection.

However, because a large portion of social security benefits is paid out in welfare, a taxpayer cannot count on receiving full value for his tax payments. A dollar paid in taxes will not necessarily bring an equal value in benefits, and paying more in taxes now will not necessarily result in higher benefits later on. Because the welfare elements make the connection so weak between what a taxpayer pays into the program and what he gets out of it, the taxpayer thinks of his social security payments as a tax rather than as a charge for a service. He will get his benefits later regardless of what he pays into the system, and more tax payments now do not "buy" him more insurance protection. The taxpayer will thus not think of his social security payments as part of his after-tax income, which he has used to pay for a service, but as part of his before-tax income that he must pay in taxes.

Under the present system, the social security payroll tax will reduce the employee's effective compensation by the full amount of the tax, creating a wedge between what the employer pays, which includes the tax, and what the employee receives, which does not. Because of this wedge, the employee receives less than his employer is willing to pay him and less than the full value of his work. This reduced compensation will tend to discourage employment and reduce the labor supply below the optimal amount, which is the amount of labor that would be supplied if workers were paid their full value. This reduced labor supply is a significant economic inefficiency that grows worse as social security taxes rise. The wedge exists only because of the welfare elements in the social security benefit structure. An insurance program without welfare would not have these defects.

Just as the pursuit of welfare objectives through social security makes it a bad insurance program, the pursuit of insurance objectives through social security makes it a bad welfare program. Because of the program's insurance objective, social security is financed by a payroll tax on wage income up to a certain maximum amount. The tax is a basic charge for insurance protection, like a charge for any other consumer item. This method is an appropriate way to finance an insurance program. If someone wants insurance protection he should have to pay the same charge as anyone else, just as if he were purchasing a loaf of bread, and if he makes higher payments in absolute terms, then he is entitled to more insurance protection and higher benefits later on.

But the payroll tax is an inappropriate way to finance a welfare program because the payroll tax is regressive. It takes a higher percentage of the incomes of the poor than of those with higher incomes, thus hurting most the very people a welfare program is supposed to help. Financing a welfare program with a regressive tax makes the program ineffective and counterproductive.

Similarly, the benefits in a welfare program should be paid solely on the basis of need. The purpose of such a program is to help the needy, and only the truly needy should receive benefits. But the presence of the insurance elements in social security requires that some benefits be paid to those who are not in need but who are entitled to benefits because they have paid social security taxes in the past. Because welfare benefits are passed out along with the insurance benefits, funds meant to help the poor are sometimes wasted on those who do not need them. For example, a wealthy retired couple with substantial investment income may still receive social security benefits, including large portions of welfare. Or those who have earned one pension in government employment may work the minimum number of years in the private sector to qualify for social security and get a second pension. These so-called double-dippers will often get the advantage of the welfare elements in the benefit structure meant to help those with a low earnings history who might not be able to qualify for adequate old-age benefits based on their past tax payments alone. As a result of these and similar practices, young persons—perhaps struggling to start their own families—are forced to pay substantial social security taxes to finance welfare benefits for many elderly recipients who are not in need. The insurance elements in social security serve to make it a wasteful and inefficient welfare program.

These shortcomings of the social security system, as well as many others, and the many ways in which the conflicting objectives of the program interact to produce them, will be discussed in detail throughout this book. The purpose of raising them here is to point out the inherent conflict between the welfare and insurance objectives of social security, a conflict that results in a program that is both bad insurance and bad welfare.

This book weaves all the major criticisms of the social security program into a unifying theme: The aims of the program are inherently contradictory. The program's conflict in objectives has been recognized throughout its history, but it seems that this conflict has never been made the major focus of a study and overall critique of the program that shows how the conflict creates all the program's major defects and concludes that the program is inherently and fundamentally unsound.

Many critics of social security have focused on one or another of the shortcomings of the program. Martin Feldstein has emphasized the program's negative effects on the economy through its impacts on savings and capital investment. Milton Friedman has emphasized the program's negative impact on the poor and its compulsory, coercive nature. Arthur Laffer and David Ranson have focused on the program's financial insolvency and its negative impact on the economy because of the effects of the payroll tax on the labor supply. Edgar Browning has noted the political instabilities associated with the program. Warren Shore has shown how individuals can get a better deal in the private sector. As we proceed through this book, we will discuss each of these critiques, as well as several others, noting how all of them ultimately base their criticisms of the program on its conflict in objectives. We will thus present a unified view of all the major shortcomings of the program.

This book presents an analysis of the program from a libertarian perspective, and, though an acceptance of basic libertarian principles is not necessary for an acceptance of most of the analysis presented here, the book is perhaps best judged as a contribution from that viewpoint.

It would seem that with all these shortcomings, the social security program is in need of basic, fundamental reform. As the above discussion should have made clear, the key to sensible reform is to split the welfare and insurance functions into separate programs or sets of institutions. (This suggestion has already been advanced in a Brookings Institution study by Pechman, Aaron, and Taussig in 1968 and a study by Munnell almost ten years later, both noted above.) The welfare function can then be performed by an entirely different program that could be more carefully adapted to fulfill the needs of the elderly poor. A move in this direction has already been made with the establishment of the Supplemental Security Income program (SSI) in 1974. SSI is a welfare program supplementing social security benefit payments to the elderly based on need. There is no reason why the entire welfare element of the present social security system could not be transferred to SSI.

It may be that an even better vehicle than SSI could be designed for the welfare portion of the present social security system. This welfare portion could be made part of a negative income tax in a general reform of all welfare programs, or, conceivably, private charitable institutions could be an even better alternative. From a libertarian perspective, private institutions are preferable. But the question of the ideal welfare system is beyond the scope of this book. The topic here is social insurance, and the important conclusion is that the welfare function needs to be separated from the insurance function and served by entirely separate institutions. Since we already have the SSI program and it serves a function closely paralleling the welfare function of social security, it seems ideal, at least in the short run, to shift the current welfare function entirely to this program. The question of further reform of SSI and America's general welfare system is left to others.

This leaves the question of what to do with the insurance portion of the present program. Feldstein has gone one step beyond the Brookings Institution and advocated that the insurance portion be financed on a fully funded basis with a self-supporting trust fund. Tax money currently paid into the program would be saved and invested by the government in a trust fund that would be used to pay benefits to current taxpayers when they retire or otherwise qualify for benefits. This program would solve many of the problems associated with pay-as-you-go financing.

This book will go one step beyond Feldstein's suggestion and advocate that the insurance portion of social security be turned over completely to the private sector. Individuals would be allowed to provide for their old age and other contingencies by investing in private insurance, savings, and pension plans the money they would have paid in social security taxes. Once the welfare and insurance functions of the current program are separated, many may feel that the welfare function would still have to be performed by the government, but there is no reason why the insurance function must be. If an invested system is superior to pay-as-you-go financing, as Feldstein argues, then there is no reason why the investments cannot be made through private rather than government mechanisms.

Such a private investment system is in fact quite likely to be superior to a government investment program. The major objection to Feldstein's proposal is that many feel uncomfortable with having the government invest huge sums of money in the private economy. Although Feldstein has some possible solutions to this problem, a private system would completely avoid it. Privatization would also reduce or eliminate the coercion and political instability associated with a government-operated program. It would allow greater diversity because individuals would be able to choose from a wide variety of plans and pick the one best suited to their needs. The forces of competition might lead to the development of new and superior plans. Privatization would in effect be a denationalization of the old-age insurance industry, which up until now has performed as badly as other nationalized industries in this country and elsewhere. The exact contours of a private system and a proposal concerning how to reform the present system into a private one will be discussed in detail later in this book.

Although the reform proposals suggested here are radical and fundamental, they are simple and logical extensions of the most sophisticated, recently advanced reform measures. They are the natural conclusions of the many sound critiques of the program that have been heard in recent years from many quarters. They hold the promise of changes that will make everyone better off and no one worse off.

Despite the unquestioning, uncritical attitude that many have taken toward the program in the past, social security is like all other human institutions: It has its shortcomings, but improvements can be made through reasonable reform. There is no reason to believe that social security, with the persistence of the Egyptian sphinx, must remain in its present form for all time to come.

2

Social Security: Myth and Reality

Most Americans believe what they have been told about social security, and consequently they have an erroneous view of the program's structure and method of operation. Most people think of social security as an insurance program analogous to private insurance. They believe that their tax payments are pooled in special trust funds where they accumulate interest and that the payments will be returned. They believe that the tax money paid into the trust funds guarantees their future security. They believe their future benefits will represent a fair return on their tax dollars and will be determined by the amounts they have paid into the program. They believe, in short, that the program operates just like private insurance.

These beliefs are false. Tax money currently paid into the program is not pooled in special trust funds but is immediately paid out to current recipients on a pay-as-you-go basis. It is not accumulated, and it accrues no interest. There are in reality no trust funds but merely cash flow accounts in which the money sits only long enough for benefit checks to be written. Tax money currently paid into the program, therefore, guarantees nothing about the future. All future benefit payments are dependent on the willingness of future taxpayers to continue to pay. The amount of these future benefits is also influenced by one's marital status and the number and ages of any children one may have. In short, even though the program pursues insurance goals, it operates more like a welfare transfer payment scheme because of the many welfare elements in the program.

These false impressions and beliefs have been created by the deceptive and misleading statements about and blatant misrepresentations of social security by politicians and government officials over the years. The true structure and operation of the program today, how it got that way, and where it is likely to go in the future will be described in this chapter. We will see how the program serves both welfare and insurance functions and examine the many welfare and insurance elements in the program. We will also examine some of the deceptions and misrepresentations surrounding the program and the roles they have played in the program's history. We will begin by examining the legislative history of the program's enactment.

Legislative History

Although the Social Security Act was the culmination of a long campaign stretching back into the nineteenth century, the legislative history of the act begins with President Roosevelt's message to Congress on 8 June 1934. In that message, Roosevelt outlined the broad objectives of his administration, focusing primarily on the goal of eliminating economic insecurity. Roosevelt promised to send a bill to Congress in the next year concerning this issue and created the Committee on Economic Security to study the matter and develop legislative proposals.

The committee's report was sent to Congress on 17 January 1935, and the Social Security Act was passed on 14 August. The bill established a wide range of programs that were meant to solve what was termed the problem of economic insecurity. The bill included provisions for unemployment insurance, aid to families with dependent children, as well as programs for the elderly.

We will focus only on the old-age portion of the bill, which established two major programs for the elderly. The first was the Old-Age Assistance program (OAA), which was primarily a welfare program providing immediate annuities and pensions to the elderly who were too poor to provide for themselves. This program will be described in more detail later in this chapter. The second was the Old-Age Insurance program (OAI), which has developed into the major social security program for the elderly.

The legislative history of the act makes clear that the social security program was intended to provide only a basic floor of income in old age, allowing individuals to build further income protection through private alternatives if they desired. Social security was never intended to become the sole means of support for the elderly or to provide all the old-age income that individuals might desire. People were expected and encouraged to provide additional support for their old age through the many private alternatives available.

The chief concern of the act's originators and major supporters was to provide basic security, freeing the elderly from dependency and poverty. Once this basic security was attained, however, they were quite content to allow each individual to provide whatever additional old-age protection he or she desired through the private sector. Their goal of security and freedom from poverty and dependency could be achieved by providing a basic income. The concept of security implies the need for a basic level of protection that will provide this security. The emphasis given the word "security" in the campaign for the act suggests that this basic level of protection was the legislators' goal. There was never any suggestion that the government was to go beyond this goal and provide all old-age support. In fact, many of the program's original authors felt that such an attempt by government would be far too expensive.

This concern with basic security is stated more than once in Roosevelt's 8 June 1934 message to Congress:

> Among our objectives I place the security of the men, women and children of the nation first. This security for the individual and for the family, concerns itself primarily with three factors. People want decent homes to live in, they want to locate them where they can engage in productive work, and they want some safeguards against misfortune, which cannot be wholly eliminated in this man-made world of ours. . . .
>
> The third factor relates to security against the hazards and vicissitudes of life. Fear and envy based on unknown danger contribute to social unrest and economic demoralization. . . .
>
> Next winter we may well undertake the great task of furthering the security of the citizen and his family through social insurance. . . .
>
> Hence I am looking for a sound means which I can recommend to provide at once security against several of the great disturbing factors in life—especially those which relate to unemployment and old age.[1]

The president emphasized that the government was not attempting to preempt the field and that private alternatives would still play a major role: "Ample scope is left for the exercise of private initiative. In fact, in the process of recovery, I am greatly hoping that repeated promises of private investment and private initiative to relieve the government in the immediate future of much of the burden it has assumed, will be fulfilled."[2]

[1]Franklin D. Roosevelt, *The Public Papers and Addresses of Franklin D. Roosevelt*, comp. Samuel I. Rosenman (New York: Random House, 1938), vol. 3, pp. 287–93.
[2]Ibid., p. 292.

The purpose of social security was to provide safeguards against misfortunes, to provide security against the hazards and vicissitudes of life, which implies a need for a basic income that will provide this security. Roosevelt said nothing to suggest that the program was to become the sole means of old-age support. In fact, he expressly reserved a major role for private alternatives.

This basic theme of Roosevelt's speech became the centerpiece of the campaign for social security. It was echoed throughout the act's legislative history, including the reports of the Committee on Economic Security and the House and Senate committees. The Report of the House Ways and Means Committee said of the bill that "While humanely providing for those in distress, it does not proceed upon the destructive theory that the citizens should look to the government for everything. On the contrary, it seeks to reduce dependency and to encourage thrift and self-support."[3]

The Committee on Economic Security stated in its report, "In considering the costs of the contributory system it should not be overlooked that old-age annuities are designed to prevent destitution and dependency."[4] The Senate report stated, "We think that children who are able to do so should continue to support their aged parents and the legislation we are preparing is framed with this thought in mind."[5]

Further legislative history can be found in a discussion of the enactment of social security by J. Douglas Brown, a member of the old-age security staff of the Committee on Economic Security in 1934 and 1935 and chairman of the Advisory Council on Social Security in 1937 and 1938. His account of the act's beginnings supports the view that social security was meant to provide only a basic floor of income in old age. In discussing the drive to win legislative approval of the act he wrote, "Outside of Washington hard work was necessary to convince industrial executives generally of the soundness of a single contributory national plan which could become a solid uniform floor for private supplementary pension

[3]Report from the Committee on Ways and Means, 74th Congress, 1st Session, April 5, 1935, report no. 615m, H.R. 7260, p. 16, in Walter L. Barlow, *Social Security 1935*, Harvard Law School Collected Documents, 1938.

[4]Report of the Committee on Economic Security, p. 17, in Walter L. Barlow, *Social Security 1935*, Harvard Law School Collected Documents, 1938.

[5]Senate Committee on Finance, 74th Congress, 1st Session, May 13, 1935, report no. 628 in H.R. 7260, p. 4 in Walter L. Barlow, *Social Security 1935*, Harvard Law School Collected Documents, 1938.

plans in contrast to any arrangements for contracting out from coverage."[6] Brown wrote that the act was meant to provide a solid, consistent, and integrated layer of protection undergirding all private mechanisms for the prevention of dependency in old age and suggested, "It is fortunate that a number of larger, more progressive companies saw that their interest in a common floor of contributory protection coincided with that of the government."[7]

In addition, the Social Security Act as passed provided for a minimum benefit of ten dollars per month and a maximum benefit of eighty-five dollars per month, suggesting further that the act's original intent was to provide only a basic minimum floor of income support for the elderly, leaving individuals free to provide for further income support as they desired.

A second important point made clear by the legislative history of the act is that social security was intended from the beginning to be self-supporting: The entire program was intended to be financed by the payroll tax without contributions from general revenues.

There are many who currently support financing social security partially or entirely from general revenues, arguing that this was the original intent behind the act. The legislative history, however, shows that the bill's originators explicitly rejected this method of financing, as is clearly explained by Edwin Witte in his account of the passage of the Social Security Act.[8] Witte was executive director of the Committee on Economic Security and played a major role in the formulation and the passage of the act, a role that included close consultation with President Roosevelt.

In his account, Witte describes a meeting he attended with the president and other key authors of the act. He reports that in the meeting the president "again stated that all forms of social insurance must be self-supporting, without subsidies from general tax sources, but the conversation developed that he understood that assistance from general tax revenues would have to be given to people already old and without means."[9]

Roosevelt reiterated these views in his message of 17 January 1935 when he presented his proposal to Congress, saying, "These princi-

[6]J. Douglas Brown, *An American Philosophy of Social Security* (Princeton, N.J.: Princeton University Press, 1972) p. 22.

[7]Ibid., p. 66.

[8]Edwin E. Witte, *The Development of the Social Security Act* (Madison, Wisc.: The University of Wisconsin Press, 1972), p. 22.

[9]Ibid., p. 18.

ples should be observed in legislation on this subject. In the first place, the system adopted, except for the money necessary to initiate it, should be self-sustaining in the sense that funds for the payment of insurance benefits should not come from the proceeds of general taxation."[10]

The Report of the Committee on Economic Security did originally recommend that the program eventually receive partial support from general revenues several decades in the future. The committee's proposed tax and benefit schedules provided for a deficit after 1965 to be financed by general revenues. The president, however, explicitly rejected this recommendation and forced the committee to change its report. Witte reported the president's views, saying:

> All troubles regarding the report of the Committee were not over even when it had been signed and delivered to the White House. On the afternoon of January 16, after the President had already notified Congress that he would, on the next day, submit a special message dealing with Social Security, and after press stories on the message and the Committee's Report had already been given out at the White House, the President discovered a feature in the old-age insurance part of the program which he did not like. This was the aspect that a large deficit (to be met from general governmental revenues) would develop in the old-age insurance after 1965, as was stated clearly in the press releases which were prepared by Mr. Fitzgerald of the Department of Labor. The President thereupon sent for Secretary Perkins, who, in turn, asked me to come over after the President had indicated that he could not support such a program. When I arrived, the President was still under the impression that there must be a mistake somewhere in the tables which appeared in our report. When advised that the tables were correct, the President insisted that the program must be changed. He suggested that this table be left out of the report and that the committee, instead of definitely recommending the particular tax rates and benefit schedules incorporated in the original bill, merely present them as one plan for meeting the problems which Congress might or might not adopt.
>
> Following this conference with the President, all members of the Committee were communicated with and all agreed that the President's wishes in that matter must be carried out. The report was again withdrawn from the President and the changes made which he had suggested. It was not filed in final form until the morning of January 17, although it bears the date of January 15, 1935.[11]

---

[10]Message of the President Recommending Legislation on Economic Security, Jan. 17, 1935, p. 6 in Walter L. Barlow, *Social Security 1935*, Harvard Law School Collected Documents, 1938.

[11]Witte, *The Development of the Social Security Act*, pp. 74–75.

Witte reported further:

As previously stated, when the President examined in detail the tables
included in the report of the Committee on Economic Security, immediately prior to his special message of January 17, he discovered that
the Tables in the Committee's report did not jibe with his understanding of the old-age security program. He noted that large deficits would
result in 1965 and thereafter, to be met from general taxes; also that
the benefit payments would exceed the combined contributions of
employees and employers not only for all workers past middle age but
for all younger workers and for all future workers entering employment prior to 1957. As has been recited, the President then insisted that
the plan must be revised to make it entirely self-supporting.

To satisfy the President, the Committee's report was altered at the
last minute, avoiding a definite commitment to the tax and benefit
rates recommended by the staff. The working out of new rates to make
the plan self-supporting, however, required time. So the rates recommended by the staff had to be included in the original bill. The Committee on Economic Security, however, had definitely told the President that it would revise these rates to accord with his views and would
suggest an amendment to the Ways and Means Committee which would
make the old-age insurance system self-supporting (assuming the cor-
rectness of the actuarial calculations and continuance of the plan without material amendments in future years).[12]

The amendment embodying the president's changes was presented to the House Ways and Means Committee by Secretary of the
Treasury Henry Morgenthau representing the entire Committee on
Economic Security. Although the media reported the presentation of
the amendment as if it were a proposal solely from Morgenthau,
Witte reports that it had the unanimous support and recommendation of the full committee.[13] The Ways and Means Committee
adopted the Morgenthau amendment unanimously, and it remained
in the bill.[14]

Thus, some of the original drafts of the bill did include provisions
for general revenue financing. These provisions were placed in these
drafts by some members of the old-age security staff working for the
Committee on Economic Security, but those drafts were explicitly
rejected by President Roosevelt, and the bill he sent to Congress,
which it adopted without change, contained no such provision. In
determining the original intent of legislation, it is the wishes of those
with the power to pass it into law—President Roosevelt and the

12Ibid., pp. 149–150.
13Ibid., p. 150.
14Ibid., p. 151.

Congress—which are relevant, not the opinions of low-level bureaucrats expressed in the first rough drafts of the legislation. Furthermore, the full Committee on Economic Security, which was responsible for drafting the original proposals, adopted Roosevelt's views without dissent. All the major originators of the bill intended that it should be self-supporting.

The third point brought out by the legislative history of the act is that the program was originally intended to be financed on a fully-funded rather than on a pay-as-you-go basis. Currently paid taxes were to be saved and invested in a trust fund large enough to guarantee all currently promised benefits. Future benefits would then be paid out of the accumulated trust fund assets. The program was to be operated on the same actuarial principles used by private insurance plans. The concept of pay-as-you-go financing (currently paid taxes are not saved and invested but immediately paid out in current benefits) was not originally adopted.

This original intent was implied by President Roosevelt in his 18 June 1934 message to Congress: "Above all, I am convinced that social insurance should be national in scope, although the several states should meet at least a portion of the cost of management, leaving to the Federal Government the responsibility of investing, maintaining and safeguarding the necessary insurance reserves."[15] Witte also contends that this was his original intent as well as that of the Committee on Economic Security in drafting the act and that this original intent was adopted by Congress. He notes, however, the considerable controversy over the principle of full funding and the efforts of many to undermine this principle soon after passage of the act.[16] Studies by the Brookings Institution have also recognized that this was the original intent behind the act.[17]

The act as finally passed by Congress expressly stated this original intent. Section 201(a) authorized an annual appropriation to a reserve account of "an amount sufficient as an annual premium to provide for the payments under this title, such amount to be determined on a reserve basis in accordance with accepted actuarial prin-

---

[15]Rosenman, *The Public Papers and Addresses of Franklin D. Roosevelt*, pp. 291–92.

[16]"A 1938 Warning Recalled," *Wall Street Journal*, November 22, 1976.

[17]Joseph A. Pechman, Henry J. Aaron, and Michael K. Taussig, *Social Security: Perspectives for Reform* (Washington, D.C.: Brookings Institution, 1968), pp. 22–23; Alicia H. Munnell *The Future of Social Security* (Washington, D.C.: Brookings Institution, 1977), p. 5.

ciples."[18] To allow for the accumulation of this trust fund, the original act delayed the payment of benefits until 1942 while the tax rate was supposed to start at 2% in 1937 and grow steadily to 6% in 1946. A trust fund large enough to support and guarantee future benefit payments on an actuarial, insurance basis was in fact accumulated and actually lasted until the end of the 1940s. This trust fund was originally named the Old-Age Reserve Account, but this was later changed to the Old-Age Insurance Trust Fund and a board of trustees was named to safeguard the funds.

While these statements and actions clearly indicate an original intent to have the program operate on a fully-funded rather than on a pay-as-you-go basis, it is also true that many of the program's original supporters and strongest advocates never intended to follow through on this original intent and hoped to change the program over to a pay-as-you-go basis as time went on. The first major steps taken in this direction were the Social Security Act Amendments of 1939, and the changeover was completed over the course of the next several years. Nevertheless, the concept of fully-funded as opposed to pay-as-you-go financing was an important part of the campaign to gain public support for the program, as was the whole private insurance analogy, and it was probably necessary to gain sufficient support to successfully achieve passage of the act.

A fourth and final point established by the legislative history is that the social security program was structured to fit the unique economic circumstances that prevailed at the time of the program's enactment.

The circumstances of the depression made it seem more difficult to rely entirely on private alternatives for old-age support. For the elderly at the time, private alternatives seemed largely unavailable. Many who had planned to continue working had lost their jobs and seemed to have little prospect of getting them back. Others who looked to their grown children for support found this avenue cut off when their children lost their jobs. Many also lost their savings, on which they may have relied heavily in planning for old age. The Social Security Act was therefore attempting to respond to an acute and unique problem: Great portions of the elderly population had lost their planned means of old-age support.

Young people also found providing for old age through private alternatives difficult. For many who had lost their savings it seemed

[18]"Social Security Funding" *The Wall Street Journal*, January 18, 1977, p. 24.

too late to start all over and reach a sufficient level of savings for adequate support in old age. The unemployed were uncertain when —or if—they would get their jobs back and be able to start accumulating savings. Finally, it may have seemed that there was little opportunity for private investment in the middle of a depression and that any such investment would be far too costly.

These problems were noted in the Report of the Committee on Economic Security:

> Children, friends and relatives have borne and still carry the major part of the cost of supporting the aged. Several of the state surveys have discovered that from 30 to 50 percent of the people over 65 years of age were being supported in this way. During the present Depression, this burden has become unbearable for many of the children, with the result that the number of old people dependent upon public or private charity has greatly increased.
>
> The Depression will inevitably increase the old-age problem of the next decades. Many children who previously supported their parents have been compelled to cease doing so, and the great majority will probably never resume this load. The Depression has largely wiped out the wage earner's savings and has deprived millions of workers past middle age of their jobs, with but uncertain prospects of ever again returning to steady employment. For years there has been some tendency towards a decrease in the percentage of old people gainfully employed. Employment difficulties for middle-aged and older workers have been increasing, and there is little possibility that there will be a reversal of this trend in the near future.[19]

Because of the persistently high unemployment during the depths of the depression, the Social Security Act was structured to discourage the elderly from continued employment, removing them from the work force and opening up their jobs for younger workers. The act therefore included an earnings test that stopped benefit payments if the recipient earned more than a certain amount. It also granted retirement benefits to those who had paid little or nothing into the system so that they would be encouraged to stop working.

Keynesian economics encouraged the belief that the solution to the depression was to increase consumption and to discourage saving. It was thought that the depression was caused by inadequate demand, and that saving only decreased this demand because it was not being offset by increased investment. One way of increasing consumption and lowering savings was to operate social security on a

---

[19]Report of the Committee on Economic Security, pp. 20-21, in Walter L. Barlow, *Social Security 1935*, Harvard Law School Collected Documents, 1938.

pay-as-you-go basis. Individuals would then be forced to save for their retirement through social security instead of saving on their own, and the money paid into the program would not be saved but immediately paid out to current recipients. These recipients would then increase consumption by spending the benefits.

In 1935 the program was enacted with the original intent that it be operated on a fully-funded basis, as noted above. But those who favored pay-as-you-go financing from the start, as a way of helping to end the depression, were strengthened by the publication of Keynes's *General Theory of Employment, Interest, and Money* in 1936. By 1939 advocates of this form of financing had gained sufficient strength to begin the process of changing the program to a pay-as-you-go basis. One of the primary reasons that the program was restructured in this way, therefore, was to suit the unique economic circumstances of the 1930s.

This is not to say that the social security program was the *correct* response to these circumstances. If the depression was caused and continued by mistaken government policies, as many have argued, then these problems were not an indication of the failure of the private sector to provide for the elderly. In this event, the best government policy may have been merely to reverse the policies that caused and perpetuated the depression in the first place. To the extent that it was necessary for the government to do something to alleviate the problems of dependency it had caused, it may have been far preferable to initiate a temporary welfare program, placing greater reliance on private alternatives for provision of old-age support after recovery.

In addition, the view that encouraging the elderly to leave the work force would help to reduce employment is a totally fallacious one based on the concept known in economics as the "lump of labor" fallacy. The premise is that there are only a fixed number of jobs in the economy and when one person takes a job one less job remains for the others. But there is no fixed number of jobs in the economy. The number of jobs depends on the number of workers available with sufficient productive skills to pay their own way. When a new worker enters an economy with or without unemployment he will find a job if his productive skills are sufficient to produce enough to earn the wages he demands. He in effect creates his own job. This does not change the circumstances of those who were unemployed before he came. When this worker leaves the economy, the circumstances of the unemployed again remain unchanged. His departure does not mean that a new job has opened up for them if they do not have the productive ability to earn the wages they demand. Discouraging the elderly from working therefore does not mean that there will be more jobs available for the young. It means only that there will be less total employment in the economy.

Finally, while the Keynesian interpretation of the Great Depression has been widely accepted, there are many who deny its validity and argue that Keynesian policies may have prolonged the depression.[20] It may be that policies to increase consumption and lower savings have merely resulted in a lower long-term growth rate.

Whether or not these policies were right for the period, the important point is that social security was structured to fit the unique economic circumstances of the 1930s. These economic circumstances have changed drastically, and many policies that may have been appropriate then are appropriate no longer. Private alternatives for old-age support are not only widely available now but are superior to social security, as we shall see. Discouraging the elderly from working does not open up jobs for the young, but merely lowers total employment, wasting the skills of the elderly and lowering the GNP. The economy is now perfectly capable of absorbing additional saving, and discouraging this saving through social security merely results in less capital accumulation and less national growth, as will be discussed in chapter 3. Given the enormous differences between the American economy of the 1980s and the American economy of the 1930s, a program the size of social security must be restructured and reformed to take those differences into account.

Our review of the legislative history of the social security program has thus established four basic points. We will refer back to these four points throughout this book. The structure and development of the program since its enactment is discussed below.

Amendments

The Social Security Act has been amended many times since it was first passed in 1935. One of the most important of these amendments was made in 1939 when Congress began to abandon the fully-funded

[20]See for example, Murray N. Rothbard, *America's Great Depression* (Kansas City; Sheed, Andrews and McMeel, 1963); Murray N. Rothbard, *Man, Economy and State* (Princeton N.J.: Van Nostrand, 1962).

method of financing it had adopted in 1935 and embrace the concept of pay-as-you-go financing. Originally legislated tax increases were delayed and originally legislated benefits were increased and accelerated so payment would begin earlier, all with the express purpose of slowing any further trust fund accumulation. Significant benefit payments were begun in 1940, and the 2% tax rate was continued until 1950. Benefits were added for dependents of retired workers, and the survivor's insurance portion of the program was begun with the addition of benefits for survivors of deceased workers (the OASI program). Congress had thus begun to adopt the concept of using current taxes to pay current benefits. The process of changing over to pay-as-you-go financing, however, was not completed for several more years.

Another major amendment passed in 1956 established disability benefits for workers under sixty-five and imposed an additional disability insurance payroll tax to finance them. In 1965 another set of amendments added health care benefits for those over sixty-five and established another payroll tax to pay for them.

In 1972 Congress amended the act to index benefits so that they would increase automatically with the rate of inflation and thereby remain constant in real terms. The indexing formula, however, mistakenly indexed benefit increases to both wages *and* prices, which meant that benefits would increase at twice the rate of inflation. This error threatened to bankrupt the entire system, and the 1977 amendments responded by "decoupling" the benefit formula so that benefits would increase at the rate of growth in wages before retirement and at the rate of growth in prices after retirement.

Financing

Since its inception, social security has been financed by a flat rate tax on payrolls.[21] Half of the tax is assessed against the employee and half against the employer, although, as will be shown, the employee

---

[21]As we discuss the separate social security programs throughout this book, we will refer to the Old-Age and Survivor's Insurance program as the OASI program, to the Disability Insurance program as the DI program and to the Hospital Insurance program as the HI program. We will refer to the combined OASI and DI programs as the OASDHI program. It should be remembered that the DI program did not begin until 1957, and the HI program did not begin until 1966. The OASI program constituted the

actually bears the full burden of the tax. The payroll tax is assessed only on wage income up to a certain maximum annual amount, and workers with incomes above the maximum pay no tax on that portion of their income. The self-employed pay a flat rate tax on their income that has varied from two-thirds to three-fourths of the combined employer-employee tax for hired workers. The tax on self-employed workers was not imposed until 1950.

The original social security tax rate (OASI) was 1% for both employees and employers for a combined rate of 2%, assessed against the first $3,000 of income. This rate continued until 1950, when the combined rate was raised to 3%. By 1957, with the addition of the DI (disability insurance) tax, the combined social security tax rate (OASDI) reached 4.5% assessed against the first $4,200 of income. In 1966, with the addition of the HI (health insurance) tax, the combined social security tax rate (OASDHI) reached 8.4% assessed against the first $6,600 of income. The OASDI rate, without the HI tax, in 1966 was 7.7%. Even more dramatic tax increases began in 1970. In that year the OASDI rate was 8.4% and the OASDHI rate was 9.6% assessed against the first $7,800. By 1974 the OASDHI tax rate reached 11.7% assessed against the first $13,200 of wage income. In 1979 the OASDHI rate reached 12.26% assessed against the first $22,900 (see tables 1 and 2 in Appendix B).

The phenomenal growth in social security taxes since the program's inception can be seen clearly by looking at the maximum tax payable in each year. In 1937 the maximum tax payable, including both the employee's and the employer's share, was $60. In 1950 this amount was raised to only $90. By 1958, the maximum OASDI tax payable was $189, and in 1965 it reached $348. In the very next year the OASDI maximum was raised sharply to $508.20, and with the new HI tax, the OASDHI maximum reached $554.40. These totals increased steadily to $655.20 for OASDI and $748.80 for OASDHI in 1970 and $1,306.80 for OASDI and $1,544.40 for OASDHI in 1974. By 1979, these figures had exploded to $2,326.64 for OASDI and $2,807.54 for OASDHI (see table 2 in Appendix B).

---

entire social security program, therefore, until 1956. From 1957 to 1965, the OASDI program constituted the entire social security program, and since 1966 the OASDHI program has constituted the entire social security program. Any reference to the OASDHI program before 1966 simply means the entire social security program existing at that time.

From 1970 to 1979, in other words, the OASDHI maximum tax increased 275% and the OASDI maximum increased 255%. From 1965 to 1979, a period of less than fifteen years, the maximum social security tax payable rose over 700%, an increase of more than eightfold. From 1958 to 1979, the increase was almost 1400%. In every five-year period from 1949 to 1979 except one, the maximum social security tax approximately doubled.

The tax increases are not over. The 1977 amendments provided for continued tax increases through 1990. In the year 1990 the OASDI tax rate will reach 12.4% and the OASDHI rate will reach 15.3%. Under present law these rates will continue indefinitely after that. The 1977 amendments also increased the maximum taxable income to $25,900 in 1980 and $29,700 in 1981. After 1981 this maximum will be increased automatically each year by the rate of increase in average wages in covered employment (see tables 4 and 5).

Under the new law, by 1984 the maximum social security tax (OASDHI) will climb to over $4,000 a year *in constant 1980 dollars!* This will be almost twice the maximum tax in 1978. In 1990 these figures will increase to $5,234, and by the year 2000 the maximum tax will be $6,259. This tax will be paid by everyone who is today under forty-four and who will be earning the maximum taxable amount just before retiring at sixty-five. As table 5 shows, these maximum taxes will increase by the year 2050 to almost $15,000 per year for OASDHI and $12,000 for OASDI. It should be remembered that these figures are in constant 1980 dollars, so these increases are not due to inflation. It should also be noted that these projected increases are not speculations. They are taxes already mandated under current law.

This expansion in social security taxes has made social security one of the federal government's largest sources of income. Total social security taxes amounted to only $1.7 billion in 1949, and this total had reached only $8.9 billion by 1959. This OASDI total doubled by 1965 to $17.2 billion and doubled again by 1970 to $39.7 billion. By 1975 it had almost doubled again to $75.9 billion, and by 1978 it had climbed to $106.2 billion (see table 3).

In 1979 total social security taxes reached $124.6 billion, about equal to all federal taxes collected in 1965 ($124.3 billion). In 1980 total OASDHI taxes will reach $141.8 billion, equivalent to all federal taxes collected in 1966 ($141.8 billion). The 1985 OASDHI total of $198.1 billion in constant 1980 dollars will be approximately equal to all federal taxes collected in 1971 ($198.6 billion).

By 1990 total OASDHI taxes in 1980 constant dollars were projected to reach $246.3 billion, and by the year 2000 total OASDHI taxes in 1980 constant dollars will reach $309.6 billion. By 2025, when young people entering the work force today will begin to retire, total OASDHI taxes in 1980 dollars will equal $509.9 billion, and by 2050, OASDHI taxes are projected to reach $825.7 billion, again in 1980 constant dollars (see table 6).

These figures do not tell the whole story. As will be noted in chapter 5, under the projections of the Social Security Administration even these revenues will probably not be enough by a wide margin to finance all promised benefits in the future. What's more, these projections by the Social Security Administration are based on assumptions that may be overly optimistic.

With such sudden and dramatic increases after years of relatively low and stable tax rates, one must ask if the American people really support a social security program as massive and expansive as we have today. It seems more reasonable to believe that after years of being lulled into complacency with minimal taxes, the American people have been taken by surprise by the overwhelming tax increases of recent years. As Americans begin to reel under the impact of these tax increases, they may begin to consider if the program has grown too big and if these tax increases are really worth it. A fully public national debate on these issues is just beginning. As a result, recent tax increases may become vulnerable to repeal and the program may become subject to cutback.

But that is not likely to be the only effect of a reappraisal of the recent tax increases. It is quite likely that the questioning will go beyond the recent tax increases themselves and lead to a reappraisal of the entire program. Now that the tax of $60 a year, which lasted for the first fifteen years of the program, has turned into a monster gobbling up between $3,000 and $4,000 a year and more over the next few years, taxpayers can be expected to look at the entire social security system with a critical eye. They may well seriously question the value of the program itself, ask whether it is worth its enormous cost, and consider whether it should be retained in its current form. Any such public reappraisal is quite likely to lead to more than merely cosmetic changes. It seems that the recent tremendous cost explosion in social security has gravely undermined the program's traditional popularity and support, and this support seems to be deteriorating further every day. The time seems ripe, therefore, for basic, fundamental reform of the entire social security program.

Benefits

Social security began paying benefits in 1937, sending out checks for $1 million in that year. From this modest beginning, social security has come to rival in total expenditures our entire annual budget for national defense.

Coverage The original act provided for compulsory coverage for all workers under sixty-five engaged in commerce or industry. There were exceptions for workers in agriculture, domestic service, federal, state, and local government, nonprofit institutions, railroad lines, and self-employment. Over the years most of these exclusions have been eliminated, and today virtually all employees are covered, including the self-employed and professionals. The only major remaining exceptions are federal government employees, covered by the federal civil service retirement system, and railroad workers, covered by the railroad retirement system. State and local government employees not under a retirement system can be covered only if their employer elects coverage. State and local government employees already covered by a retirement plan can be covered by social security only if both the employee and the employer request it. These state and local government units retain the option of leaving social security once they enter the system. In 1940 social security covered 58% of all workers in paid employment; by 1977 89% were covered (see table 7).

The social security system now also covers most of the aged population. In 1940 less than 1% of the population over sixty-five received OASDHI benefits. By 1950 this level reached 16.4%. By 1960, however, the percentage had reached 61.6%, and by 1965 it had climbed to 75.2%. In 1977 90.4% of the aged population was receiving OASDHI benefits (see table 8).

Calculation of Benefits The calculation of all benefits is based on a worker's primary insurance amount (PIA). The PIA is determined in two stages. First, a worker's average monthly earnings (AME) must be calculated. The AME is calculated by starting with earnings in covered employment up to the maximum taxable amount for each year after 1950 or the age of twenty-one, whichever is later, up to the year the worker dies, is disabled, or reaches sixty-two. The five years of lowest wages and all years of disability are then excluded. Years of higher earnings after sixty-two are then substituted for years of lower earnings before sixty-two. The earnings for these years are added together and divided by twelve times the number of years to determine the AME.

The AME is then used to calculate the PIA under the PIA formula for that year. In 1978 the PIA formula contained ten brackets:

155.38% of the first $110 of the AME
 56.51% of the next $290
 52.80% of the next $150
 62.09% of the next $100
 34.53% of the next $100
 28.78% of the next $250
 25.92% of the next $175
 24.01% of the next $100
 22.56% of the next $100
 21.30% of the next $100

Beginning in 1975 the PIA formula became subject to automatic adjustments to provide for cost of living increases. Under this automatic provision the PIA formula is updated each June by multiplying the percentage in each bracket of the formula by the increase in the consumer price index (CPI) over the prior year, if that increase was greater than 3%. If it was not, then no adjustment is made until the CPI has increased at least 3% over the last time there was a cost of living benefit increase. In each January another bracket is added to the PIA formulas. This last bracket will be 20% of an amount of the AME equal to one-twelfth of the increase in maximum taxable income for January of that year. This then becomes a permanent part of the PIA formula for all future years, and the 20% is increased by the automatic cost of living adjustments described above.

After the 1977 amendments the process of calculation has become considerably more complicated. The method described above will continue to be used to calculate retirement and survivor's benefits for all workers who reach age sixty-two before 1979 and to calculate disability benefits for all workers who become disabled before 1979. A transitional method of calculation will be used to calculate the retirement and survivor's benefits for all workers who reach age sixty-two from 1979 to 1983 inclusive. This method cannot be used to calculate disability benefits for those who become disabled in 1979 and after. A new "decoupled" method of calculation will be used for those who reach sixty-two after 1983 or become disabled after 1979. All workers who have their benefits calculated under the transitional method can choose to have their benefits calculated under the new decoupled method if the benefits calculated under this method are higher.

The transitional method is the same as the old method with two differences: First, in calculating the AME no years after age sixty-two may be used; second, the June 1978 PIA formula is used with no increases for cost of living until the worker reaches sixty-two.

Under the new "decoupled" method an average indexed monthly earnings figure, AIME, must be calculated instead of an AME. To calculate an AIME the entire earnings history is indexed to the year in which the worker reaches age sixty. This age was chosen because a two-year lag is necessary to collect the necessary average wage data before the worker becomes eligible for a retirement benefit at age sixty-two. If disability or survivor's benefits for death before age sixty-two are being calculated, wages are indexed for the year two years before the year of disability or death. To index the wage for a given year, the wage is multiplied by the ratio of (a), the average wage in covered employment in the year to which the wages are being indexed, to (b), the average wage in covered employment for the given year. After the earnings history is indexed, the AIME is calculated in the same way as the AME.

The AIME is then multiplied by an entirely new PIA formula. The 1979 PIA formula is

90% of the first $180 of the AIME
32% of the next $905
15% of the rest

This PIA formula will be automatically adjusted each year by the rate of increase in average wages, rather than by the rate of inflation. The adjustment is made by multiplying the dollar amounts rather than the percentages in each bracket of the PIA formula by the rate of increase in wages in covered employment two years prior. In other words, the 1980 PIA formula dollar amounts equal the amounts shown above increased by the growth in average wages in 1978.

In calculating benefits, the correct PIA formula to use is the one for the year in which the worker becomes eligible for benefits. For disability benefits, this is the year the worker becomes disabled. For survivor's benefits before age sixty-two, this is the year of death. For retirement benefits and survivor's benefits after age sixty-two, this is the year in which the worker reaches sixty-two. If the worker continues to work until the age of sixty-five, the benefits calculated under his age sixty-two PIA are increased by the annual CPI increases for the intervening years (sixty-three, sixty-four, and sixty-five).

The PIA is the basic figure used for determining the amount of disability, retirement, or survivor's benefits to be received. Once the amount of benefits in the initial year is calculated, it is increased each year by the amount of increase in the CPI, compensating for inflation.

Two important points emerge from this discussion of the methods for calculating benefits. First, one of the chief welfare elements in the social security benefit structure can be found in the PIA formula: The higher the PIA the higher the ultimate benefit amounts. The formulas used both before and after the 1977 amendments have been heavily weighted to give those with low earnings histories a higher percentage of their past incomes in benefits than those with high earnings histories. This is accomplished by decreasing the percentages of the AME that count toward the PIA for higher amounts of the AME. In 1978, for example, 155.38% of the first $110 of the AME was counted toward the PIA but only 56.51% of the next $290 was counted, and this percentage generally continued to decrease for higher amounts of the AME. Similarly, in the new 1979 PIA formula, 90% of the first $180 of the AIME is counted toward the PIA while only 32% of the next $905 is counted and only 15% of the rest. However, because all pay in taxes the same percentage of their past income that is counted toward benefits, the result of the weighted formulas is that those with low earnings histories receive more in benefits for each tax dollar paid into the system than those with high earnings histories.

This result is justified on the basis of a welfare rationale rather than an insurance rationale. It is felt that those with low earnings histories would not receive adequate old-age incomes if benefits were based solely on their past income and what they paid into the system. The PIA formula is skewed to their benefit, giving them more than they paid for and leaving those with higher incomes with less than they paid for, which cannot be justified on the basis of an insurance rationale. In a pure insurance program, the PIA formula would be strictly proportional to past earnings, which are strictly proportional to past social security taxes. In insurance, benefits are solely related to what one has paid in the past, regardless of need.

Higher past payments would therefore entitle the beneficiary to proportionally higher benefits. The skewed PIA formula thus serves a welfare function instead of an insurance function, subsidizing those with low incomes based on their need at the expense of those with higher incomes.

The second important point is the change in indexing techniques adopted by the 1977 amendments. These amendments corrected the mistake enacted by the 1972 amendments, which included a formula that raised benefits twice for the rate of inflation rather than once, as intended. In correcting this error, Congress chose to index benefits to the rate of increase in wages rather than prices. While a worker is still working, the benefits promised him upon retirement are increased each year by the rate of growth in wages. This is accomplished by indexing a worker's earnings to average earnings in covered employment and by multiplying the dollar amounts in the PIA formula by the rate of growth in wages. After retirement, however, benefits are price indexed, rising only at the rate of increase in the CPI. The difference between wage-indexed and price-indexed benefits is enormous. Under wage indexing, taxes in future years will rise rapidly and constitute a much heavier burden than under price indexing. Wage-indexed benefits will also far surpass levels necessary to provide an adequate floor of old-age income and reach levels that are likely to make social security the sole means of old-age support in future years, an extreme departure from the original intent of the program. Despite the great significance of this choice between indexing methods, the entire controversy surrounding the choice made in the 1977 amendments went largely unnoticed by the American people and instead was left to academics and lobbyists. As a result, Congress chose the substantially more expensive wage indexing alternative. The "decoupling" controversy and its importance will be discussed in more detail in later chapters.

Types of Benefits The original Social Security Act provided for retirement benefits for workers aged sixty-five or over. Benefits for dependents and survivors were added in 1939. In 1956 Congress enacted provisions for disability benefits, and in 1965 Congress provided for hospital insurance benefits. These benefits are described in detail below.

Retirement Benefits A worker becomes eligible for retirement benefits at the age of sixty-two. If he works until sixty-five and retires, his monthly benefit will equal 100% of his PIA. If he retires before sixty-five and starts receiving benefits, his monthly benefit amount is permanently reduced by five-ninths of 1% for each month before sixty-five in which the worker will be retired. If a worker retires at sixty-two, the earliest possible age, his benefit will be 80% of his PIA. If he retires after sixty-five, his benefit is increased one-fourth of 1% for every additional month of work until seventy-two.

The worker's wife is entitled to additional benefits on the record of her husband if (a) she is sixty-two or over, or has in her care a child or grandchild under eighteen, or over eighteen and disabled, who is entitled to benefits on her husband's social security record, and (b) has been married to her husband for at least one year or is the natural mother of the husband's child. If the wife is sixty-five or over or if she is caring for her husband's child, then her monthly benefit will equal 50% of her husband's PIA. If she elects to receive this benefit before sixty-five and is not caring for the husband's child, then the benefit is permanently reduced 25/36 of 1% for every month prior to sixty-five in which she will receive benefits. If she elects to receive the benefit at sixty-two, she will receive 37.5% of her husband's PIA.

A divorced wife who was married to the retired worker for at least ten years, is not married, and has reached age sixty-two is also eligible for benefits. If she waits until sixty-five, her monthly benefit will equal 50% of her former husband's PIA. If she elects to receive benefits earlier they will be permanently reduced 25/36 of 1% for every month prior to age sixty-five in which she will receive benefits. Her benefit will therefore total 37.5% of her former husband's PIA if she retires at age sixty-two, the earliest retirement age.

A husband of a retired female worker is now entitled to the same benefits on her earnings record that a wife is entitled to on her husband's record, except that there are no benefit provisions for a divorced husband.

A child of the retired worker is entitled to benefits if he is dependent on the parent, unmarried, and either under eighteen, or eighteen through twenty-one and a full-time student, or age eighteen or over and under a disability begun before age twenty-two. The amount of his monthly benefit is 50% of his parent's PIA. A grandchild is entitled to the same benefits as a child under the same conditions if the grandchild's natural or adoptive parents were deceased or disabled at the time the worker became entitled to retirement benefits.

Wives, divorced wives, and husbands must forgo their own retirement or disability benefits to accept the dependent's benefits on
their spouse's records as described here. For example, if a wife's own
PIA is less than 50% of her husband's PIA, she will choose the wife's
benefits on her husband's record and forgo her own. If her own PIA
is greater than 50% of her husband's, she will choose her own
benefits and forgo the wife's benefits.

The retired worker's benefits and the benefits of all his dependents
as described here terminate at his death. The benefits to any of these
dependents will terminate at their own deaths if it occurs before the
retired worker dies.

Survivor's Benefits A widow who is not married and who has
reached the age of sixty is entitled to a survivor's benefit if she either
(a) was married to the deceased worker for at least nine months
before he died or (b) is the mother of his son or daughter. The
amount of her monthly benefit is equal to 100% of her deceased husband's PIA if payments began at age sixty-five. If she elects to
receive benefits before then, they will be reduced by 19/40 of 1% for
each month before age sixty-five, thus leaving a benefit equal to
71.5% of the husband's PIA for a widow who retires at sixty. If a
widow is sixty-two or over and her deceased husband began receiving an old-age benefit before sixty-five, she can receive no more than
he would be receiving if he were alive, but no less than 82.5% of the
deceased husband's PIA. Under the 1977 amendments the widow
may remarry after age sixty without a reduction in benefits. A surviving divorced wife who was married to a deceased worker for at
least ten years, who is not married, and who has reached age sixty is
also entitled to these survivor's benefits on the same terms and conditions as a widow.

A widow or a surviving divorced wife who otherwise qualifies for
survivor's benefits and is disabled can be eligible for survivor's benefits between ages fifty and sixty. She must have become disabled (1)
before the death of her husband or (2) during a period of seven years
following the death of her husband or after the termination of her
benefit as a mother, whichever is later. The monthly benefit amount
is 71.5% of the worker's PIA, permanently reduced by 43/240 of 1%
for each month before the age of sixty that the wife elects to receive
the benefits. Thus, at age fifty the disabled widow would receive
50% of her deceased husband's PIA.

The widow of a deceased worker who is not married is entitled to a mother's benefit if she has in her care a child or grandchild of her deceased husband who is under eighteen or over eighteen and disabled and who is entitled to benefits on the deceased worker's earnings record. The amount of monthly payments to the widow is equal to 75% of the deceased husband's PIA. A surviving divorced mother is also entitled to these benefits on the same terms and conditions.

A widower is entitled to the same benefits on the same conditions as a widow, except that there are no benefit provisions for a surviving divorced widower.

Each unmarried dependent child of a deceased worker who is under eighteen, or eighteen through twenty-one and a full-time student, or eighteen or over and under a disability begun before age twenty-two, is entitled to a monthly survivor's benefit equal to 75% of the deceased parent's PIA. An unmarried dependent grandchild is also entitled to these benefits if he meets these conditions and if his parents are either deceased or disabled or if one of his parents is alive but he is adopted by the surviving grandparent spouse.

A parent of a deceased worker is entitled to survivor's benefits if the parent is over sixty-two, was dependent upon the deceased, and has not remarried since the death of the deceased. The amount of the monthly benefit is equal to 82.5% of the deceased worker's PIA if one parent is collecting and 75% of the PIA for each parent if both are collecting.

To accept these survivor's benefits, all these beneficiaries must forgo their own retirement or disability benefits. The benefit payments to each beneficiary will terminate at his death if not terminated sooner.

Disability Benefits A worker is entitled to disability benefits if he proves disability, undergoes a five-month waiting period, and is under sixty-five. To be disabled a worker must be unable to engage in any substantial gainful work existing in the economy by reason of any medically determinable physical or mental impairment that can be expected to result in death or to last for a continuous period of not less than twelve months. The monthly benefit amount is equal to 100% of the worker's PIA. If the worker also receives workmen's compensation and is younger than sixty-two, this benefit may be reduced. If the family's total social security benefits are higher than 80% of average earnings before disability, then the social security benefits are reduced by the entire amount of workmen's compensation. If the family's total social security benefits are below 80% of average earnings before disability, benefits are reduced until social security benefits plus workmen's compensation benefits equal 80% of those prior earnings.

Benefits for dependents based on the disabled worker's PIA are the same as dependent's benefits for retired workers. All disability benefits terminate when a worker recovers, reaches sixty-five, or dies.

Lump Sum Death Benefits On the death of an insured worker, a lump sum payment of $255 is made to the widow or widower.

Hosptal Insurance A person entitled to social security benefits is automatically entitled to hospital insurance protection beginning on the first day of the month that person reaches sixty-five. A disabled person entitled to disability benefits is automatically entitled to hospital insurance after twenty-four months of entitlement to disability benefits. A disabled widow fifty or older who is caring for the deceased worker's child will also qualify for hospital insurance protection when she has met all entitlement requirements for disabled widows for twenty-four consecutive months. A person between sixty and sixty-five receiving widow's or widower's benefits is also entitled to hospital insurance coverage if he or she meets all entitlement requirements, other than the age sixty limitation, for disabled widow's or widower's benefits during the previous twenty-four consecutive months.

The hospital insurance plan pays for hospital care and related expenses. It does not cover physician's and surgeon's services prescribed to individuals. These are covered under the medical insurance plan. The two plans are called Medicare.

Hospital insurance benefit payments may be paid for three types of hospital and related health care services. First, payments may be made for up to ninety days of in-patient hospital care during each illness. An illness is considered over when the patient has spent sixty consecutive days out of the hospital. In addition, each beneficiary has a sixty-day lifetime reserve that can be used after ninety days of hospitalization for one illness are used up. Each beneficiary, however, can use only sixty such days in his lifetime. Second, payments may be made for up to 100 days of extended care services in a skilled nursing facility after discharge from a hospital. Third, payments may be made for up to 100 home health-care visits by visiting nurses, after the beginning of one illness and before the beginning of the next, in the one-year period following the latest discharge from a qualifying stay in a hospital or skilled nursing facility.

The hospital insurance beneficiary is subject to deductible and coinsurance charges that are adjusted annually. In 1979 a covered patient had to pay a $160 deductible charge for in-patient hospital care for each illness. In addition, he had to pay forty dollars coinsurance for each day from day sixty to day ninety and eighty dollars coinsurance for each day after that. For skilled nursing care, the patient was responsible in 1979 for a coinsurance charge of twenty dollars per day after the first twenty days.

The medical insurance plan is available on a voluntary basis to all persons sixty-five or over and to those persons under sixty-five entitled to hospital insurance benefits on the basis of disability. These include disabled workers at any age, disabled widows and widowers between the ages of fifty and sixty-five, persons age fifty or older caring for the deceased worker's child and who for twenty-four months have met all the requirements for filing but have a disability claim, and persons eighteen or over who receive social security benefits because they became disabled before reaching age twenty-two.

The program is financed by premiums paid by each person who enrolls and through contributions from the general revenues of the federal government that are at least equal to the amount of premiums paid by beneficiaries. In 1979 this premium was equal to $8.70 per month.

The plan provides insurance protection for physician's and surgeon's services, treatments and supplies incident to these services, as well as certain out-patient hospital services and laboratory tests, and home health services and other types of health care. The beneficiary pays an initial deductible amount on the total covered expenses for the year, and the plan pays for 80% of the remainder. Expenses covered by the hospital insurance plan cannot be paid for under the medical insurance plan, even if these expenses were not paid for by the hospital plan.

Besides the different types of benefits described above, there are many important general benefit provisions—the minimum benefit, the maximum benefit, and the earnings test.

Minimum Benefit Congress provided for a $10 minimum monthly retirement benefit in 1939. This benefit amount was payable to a retired worker even if the amount derived from the standard benefit calculation was less. The minimum benefit has been increased steadily, reaching $107.90 in 1977. The 1977 amendments froze the minimum monthly benefit at $121 (see table 9).

Maximum Family Benefits Except for the benefits payable to a divorced wife or the additional benefits a retired worker receives because of delayed retirement, the total of the monthly benefits, unreduced for early acceptance, payable on the record of a worker is subject to a maximum amount known as the maximum family benefit (MFB). If the total of the unreduced individual benefits is greater than the maximum family benefit, the amount paid to each secondary dependent beneficiary must be reduced proportionately. No reduction is made in the benefit payment for the entitled worker.

The MFB is calculated through a special formula. In June 1978 the formula was 151.9% of the first $436 of the AME plus 75.9% of the next $191, but not less than 150% of the PIA. For AMEs over $628, the MFB was 175% of the PIA.

The 1977 amendments enacted a revised formula for calculating the MFB. The 1979 MFB formula is

  150% of the first $230 of PIA
 + 272% of the next $102
 + 134% of the next $101
 + 175% of the rest.

Each year the dollar amounts in this MFB formula are multiplied by the rate of increase of average earnings in covered employment two years prior. The correct MFB formula to use in calculating benefits is the one in force in the year the worker becomes eligible for benefits. If a worker continues working until age sixty-five, the MFB will be calculated under the formula in force at sixty-two, adjusted upward automatically for increases in the CPI over the intervening years. The MFB continues to be adjusted upward each year after that by the rate of increase in the CPI.

The MFB has increased from $85.00 in 1939 to $1045.80 in January 1977 (see table 9).

Earnings Test Under the earnings test benefits are withheld from an otherwise eligible beneficiary if his earnings exceed a certain limit. In 1977 a recipient's benefits were reduced $1 for every $2

earned over $3,000 in a given year. The earnings limit is increased each year by the rate of increase in the CPI. The test does not apply to beneficiaries over the age of seventy-two or those receiving benefits because of disability. Otherwise, the test applies to retired persons and their dependents who receive benefits and to all recipients of survivor's benefits except the disabled.

The excess earnings of a retired worker are applied to reduce the MFB, so his extra earnings reduce the benefits of his dependents as well as himself. The extra earnings of dependent beneficiaries or those receiving survivor's benefits, except the disabled, are applied to reduce only their own benefits.

The 1977 amendments made two important changes in the earnings test. First, the earnings limit was raised to $4,000 in 1978, with provisions for annual increases of $500 until the limit reaches $6,000 in 1982. Thereafter, the limit will be increased each year by the rate of increase in average wages. For beneficiaries under sixty-five, the old limits, increased each year by the increase in the CPI, will continue to apply. Second, in 1982 the age at which the earnings test no longer applies will drop from seventy-two to seventy.

According to the Social Security Administration, nearly 16% of retired workers lost some benefits in 1973 because of the earnings test. In 1971 1.5 million workers were affected by the test, losing approximately 70% of their benefits, or about $2.2 billion.[22]

Tax Exemption Social security benefits have always been exempt from the personal income tax, nor is the worker taxed on the share of his social security taxes paid by his employer. In all other pension plans, however, the worker is taxed on the money he pays in contributions as income received. He is then taxed on benefit payments in excess of contributions when received in retirement. This does not apply, however, to individual retirement accounts (IRA's) and Keogh plans, which will be discussed in more detail later.

Qualifications For Coverage To become eligible for benefits, one must first attain insured status. This insured status is determined on the basis of quarters of coverage, which, prior to 1978, were defined as calendar quarters in which a worker is paid $50 or more in wages for employment covered under the law. Starting in 1978 a worker was credited with a quarter of coverage for each $250 earned in

[22]Munnell, *The Future of Social Security*, pp. 66–67.

covered employment during the year up to a maximum of four quarters. In 1979 the qualifying amount was increased to $260 under a special formula provided for annual increases.

An individual is fully insured if he has at least one quarter of coverage for each year elapsing after 1950, or the year the worker attained twenty-one, whichever is later, until the year the worker otherwise becomes eligible for benefits. Quarters of coverage earned at any time can be counted, including those earned before 1950. If any part of a year has been included in a period of disability, that year is not included as an elapsed year. A minimum of six quarters of coverage is required, and the maximum number required is forty. Any worker who works ten years, therefore, becomes fully insured permanently.

Fully insured status entitles a worker to virtually all benefits except those for disability. To receive these benefits, the worker must also become disability insured. This status is attained when the worker is fully insured and has at least twenty quarters of coverage during the forty-quarter period ending with the quarter in which the worker became disabled. A worker disabled before the quarter in which he attains age twenty-one is insured for disability if half the quarters in the period beginning with the quarter after the one in which he reached twenty-one are quarters of coverage. A worker disabled before the quarter in which he reaches age twenty-four is insured if he has six quarters of coverage in the eleven-quarter period ending with the quarter of disablement. A worker disabled by blindness needs only fully insured status to be insured in the event of disability.

A worker is currently insured if he has at least six quarters of coverage during the thirteen-quarter period ending with the earliest of (1) the quarter in which insured status is determined; (2) the quarter in which the worker became entitled to retired worker benefits; or (3) the quarter in which the worker most recently became entitled to a disabled worker's benefit. The purpose of this classification is to allow the family of a young deceased worker to receive survivor's benefits without the worker being fully insured. Currently insured status, therefore, entitles both the child and a surviving spouse or divorced wife caring for a child or grandchild of the deceased worker to survivor's benefits.

Total Benefits and Beneficiaries Total benefits remained under $1 billion until 1951, when $1.9 billion was paid out. By 1958 the

OASDI program was paying out $8.6 billion. This had more than doubled by 1965 to $18.3 billion. By 1970, with the addition of the HI program, total social security benefits had doubled again, with $37 billion paid out under the OASDHI program in that year. By 1975 total social security benefits had doubled once more, with OASDHI payments increasing to $78.2 billion. Total benefits were expected to double yet again by 1981, with OASDHI benefits increasing to $155.9 billion. In 1978 OASDHI benefits already totaled $110.5 billion, representing an increase of 280% since 1968 and almost 500% since 1965. Since 1958 total social security benefits have increased almost thirteen times (see table 10).

The 1978 total benefit figure represented a 280% increase since 1968 and an increase of about 500% since 1965.

In 1978 total expenditures under the entire social security program (OASDHI), including administrative and other expenses, amounted to $114.2 bilion. This constituted 24.77%, or about one-fourth of the entire 1978 federal budget of $461 billion. The OASDI program alone, with total 1978 expenditures of $96 billion, constituted 20.83% of the total federal budget in that year. These total social security expenditures compared with total federal non-social security transfer payments in 1978 of $71.1 billion and total federal purchases of goods and services in that year of $154 billion (see table 11).

Again, social security has attained this prominent position in the federal budget only in recent years, although, as table 16 shows, it has represented a steadily increasing portion of the federal budget since World War II. From just over 1% of the budget in 1946 and 2.5% in 1950, the program grew to about 8% of the budget in 1956 and 12.7% by 1960. The program continued its dogged, steady growth throughout the next decade, consuming 15.5% of the budget in 1965 and 18.8% in 1970.

In 1979 total social security expenditures were $129.1 billion, more than the entire federal budget in 1965 ($123.8 billion). In 1980 these expenditures were expected to reach $146.3 billion, more than the entire federal budget in 1966 ($143.6 billion). Social security expenditures will continue to soar dramatically well into the future. By 1990, just ten years from now, OASDHI expenditures will total $228.8 billion in constant 1980 dollars, with OASDI expenditures alone at $172.3 billion in 1980 dollars. In nominal terms OASDHI expenditures in 1990 will be approximately equal to the entire federal budget for 1975. By the year 2000 OASDHI expenditures will total $315.1 billion with OASDI expenditures at $215.5 billion. In nominal terms, OASDHI expenditures in 2000, just twenty years from now, will be more than one and one-half times the entire federal budget for 1978. Official projections for the hospital insurance program, HI, stop in the year 2000, although expenditures under this program alone are expected to almost double between 1990 and 2000 and to be about as large in 2000 as total OASDHI expenditures in 1977. Nevertheless, by 2025, when young people now entering the work force will begin to retire, total OASDI expenditures alone will be $522.2 billion in constant 1980 dollars, and by 2050 these expenditures will total $871.6 billion in 1980 dollars (see table 12). It should be noted that these totals are official projections of the Social Security Administration itself.

Table 10 also presents a perspective on the distribution of total social security benefits among the different programs within the system. In 1967, OASI represented 78.6% of total benefits, with DI at 7.8% and HI at 13.5%. In 1972, OASI benefits constituted 77.5% of the total, DI benefits constituted 9.3%, and HI benefits totaled 13.2%. In 1978 73% of all benefits were paid under the OASI program, with 11% paid under the DI program and 16% paid under the HI program. Thus both HI and DI have increased at the expense of OASI benefits over the last decade, but OASI still accounts for almost three-fourths of all social security benefits.

The number of total beneficiaries receiving benefits under social security will also continue to grow. In 1970 the OASI program paid benefits to 22.6 million beneficiaries, and the DI program made payments to 2.6 million. By 1978 OASI beneficiaries totaled 29.1 million, and DI beneficiaries totaled 4.9 million. By 2050 these figures were projected to reach 68.9 million for OASI and 11.0 million for DI (see tables 13 and 14).

The amount of benefits typically paid to individuals is illustrated by tables 9, 15, and 16. As table 9 indicates, the maximum retirement benefit per month payable to an individual who has had the maximum income all his life and who retires single at age sixty-five was $41.20 in 1940, increasing steadily to $103.50 in 1956, $216.10 in 1972, $412.70 in 1977 and $503.40 in 1979. If the worker retired with a spouse, these figures would be multiplied by 1.5. The maximum family benefit similarly increased steadily from $85 per month in 1940 to $200 per month in 1956, $517.00 in 1972 and $1,045.80 in 1977. The minimum benefit follows the same pattern, increasing from $10 per month in 1940 to $30 in 1956, $70.40 in

1972, $107.90 in 1977 and $121.80 in 1979. For all these provisions, the biggest increase has come in the 1970s. In general, under all three, the increase from 1940 to 1956 was less than the increase from 1956 to 1972, which in turn was less than the increase from 1972 to 1977.

Table 15 shows the same general patterns for average monthly amounts paid to individuals and families in retirement, survivor, and disability benefits. In general the increase from 1940 to 1956 in absolute terms was less than the increase from 1956 to 1971, which was less than the increase from 1971 to 1977. Benefit payments were accelerating more rapidly in the 1970s. In 1977 average monthly benefits were $236.80 for a retired single worker, $404.40 for a retired worker with a spouse, $226.50 for aged widows, $546.60 for widowed mothers with two children, and $538.10 for a disabled worker with wife and two children.

Table 16 illustrates both typical benefit amounts payable in the past and how these benefits are expected to grow in the future. The benefit amounts shown in the table are for single workers retiring at age sixty-five without a spouse. Those who retire with a spouse receive a 50% increase until one of the spouses dies. Benefits for the average worker, who earned $10,487 in 1978, increased from $1,362 in 1953 to $3,444 in 1971 and $6,893 in 1978, assuming the worker retired with a spouse. By 1990 the annual social security pension for an average income worker who retires with a spouse will be $7,844, growing to $14,331 in 2025 and $21,750 in 2050. These figures for future years are all in constant 1978 dollars. For a worker with maximum income who retires with a spouse, annual social security retirement benefits have grown from $1,530 in 1953 to $3,836 in 1971 and $8,591 in 1978. The same worker with a spouse at retirement will receive $10,587 in 1990, $22,452 in 2025 and $34,080 in 2050. Again these figures for future years are in constant 1978 dollars.

The phenomenal expansion in total and individual benefit expenditures suggested by these figures again raises the question of whether the American people really support a social security system this massive. With projected annual pensions of over $22,000 in 2025 in 1978 constant dollars and over $34,000 in 2050, the program has strayed far from its original intent, which was to provide a basic floor of retirement income in old age. The annual pensions described here will buy far more than the basic necessities of life for an elderly couple. The main focus of the program now seems to be to provide the sole means of old-age support, leaving little room for private alternatives. Why force individuals to pay so much into social security to acquire such high retirement benefits? It is not unreasonable to think that many between the ages of twenty and thirty, who are raising families, holding down new mortgages, and starting careers, would prefer to keep some of the $4,000 to $5,000 in annual taxes they will pay in the 1980s and forgo some of the $20,000 to $30,000 in annual pensions they are currently promised. Other individuals may have alternative investments opportunities that will provide them with greater returns than social security. In fact, as will be shown later, young people currently entering the program can do much better financially by investing in private alternatives outside of social security and help the economy besides. In short, there seems to be no justification for requiring people to provide for such huge pensions through social security.

Again it seems reasonable to conclude that the American people have been taken by surprise by the recent explosion in the size of the social security program and the shift in emphasis from providing a basic floor of old-age income to providing all retirement income. A major factor in the future expansion of the program and the shift in emphasis was the 1977 amendments, in which Congress chose to index benefits to wages rather than prices. Yet the significance of this choice was not widely understood by the American people, and the issue was not publicly debated. As the American public comes to fully appreciate the recent changes in social security, a strong public debate over the appropriate size and structure of the social security system is likely to begin, and the possibilities for fundamental reform of the entire program will be greatly enhanced.

The tremendous explosion in taxes and benefits in recent years and their continued growth bring out another important point: The program has now grown so large that its impacts on the economy and social life are enormous. Any negative impacts from the program which may have been tolerable in the 1950s and early 1960s are now devastating. The program is now too large and too powerful for its defects to be ignored.

The Trust Fund and Pay-As-You-Go Financing

The federal government maintains a separate account for each of the major social security programs which is designated as the trust fund for that program. The Old-Age and Survivor's Insurance program (OASI) has a separate OASI trust fund, the Disability Insurance program (DI) has a separate DI trust fund, and the Hospital Insurance program (HI) has a separate HI trust fund. We will refer to the combined OASI and DI trust fund as the OASDI trust fund and the combined OASI, DI, and HI trust funds as the OASDHI trust fund. It should be remembered that the Disability Insurance program, and therefore the DI trust fund, did not begin until 1957, and the Hospital Insurance program, and therefore the HI trust fund, did not begin until 1966. The trust fund for the entire social security program, therefore, includes only the OASI trust fund from 1937 to 1956, the OASDI trust fund from 1957 to 1965, and the OASDHI trust fund from 1966 to the present.

A trust is a legal title to property held by one party, the trustee, for the benefit of another, the beneficiary. A trust fund is held by the trustee to be used according to the orders of the creator of the trust for the benefit of the beneficiary, who may be the creator of the trust. A creator may, for example, set up a trust fund to pay a certain amount of benefits to a beneficiary for a certain number of years or for the rest of the beneficiary's life. The trustee will then invest the trust fund assets and use both the assets and the earnings on the fund to pay the stated benefits for the stated period. When a creator sets up a trust fund for this purpose, therefore, he must donate enough in assets to the fund so that these assets plus the amounts they can earn when invested will be sufficient to pay all the stated benefits for the stated period. If the trust fund is not this large, then the benefits promised the beneficiary are not held "in trust" for him, and unless his benefits are subsidized from some outside source, they will never be paid. When a creator sets up a sufficiently large trust fund, however, the future payments are virtually assured because the assets in the trust will naturally generate the income to pay them.

The use of the trust fund concept in reference to social security is meant to create the impression in the minds of taxpayers that the government as trustee is holding the tax payments for the benefit of the taxpayer. It is meant to create the impression that each taxpayer's tax payments are pooled in a special trust fund where they are accumulated and held to be returned in old age or upon the occurrence of disability, death, or hospitalization in retirement. It is meant to create the further impression that each program's trust fund is large enough to pay the benefits currently promised and that these future benefits are, therefore, virtually assured. These impressions have been created by the statements of politicians, government officials, and the Social Security Administration itself over the years. The truth is that the impressions are entirely false.

As table 19 shows, the OASI trust fund has increased steadily, with brief periods of decline, from $766 million in 1937 to $27.5 billion in 1978. Similarly, the OASDI trust fund increased from $23 billion in 1957 to $31.7 billion in 1978, and the OASDHI trust fund has increased from $23.3 billion in 1966 to $43.2 billion in 1978.

The table also shows, however, that benefit payments under all these programs have increased much, much faster. As a result, the ratio of benefits to trust fund assets has decreased steadily each year for all three trust funds. In 1978 the OASI trust fund held an amount equal to only 33% of one year's OASI benefit payments. The OASDI fund also held only 33% of one year's OASDI benefits, while the OASDHI fund held 38%. If a creator sets up a trust fund to pay an annual benefit to the beneficiary indefinitely, the trust fund must be large enough to pay the annual benefit out of the annual investment earnings of the trust fund assets. Thus, the trust fund must be at least ten to fifteen times the size of the annual payments it is supposed to support, depending on the rate of return the invested trust fund assets can earn.[23] This is a very rough estimate, and it could be higher or lower depending on the assumed rate of return, but for our purposes it is sufficient. This estimate indicates that for a trust fund paying an annual benefit indefinitely or in perpetuity, the ratio of trust fund assets to annual benefits must be 1000% to 1500% for the trust fund to have enough assets to guarantee the annual benefits.

Table 19 shows that in the early years, the social security trust funds held enough assets to truly be called trust funds. Even as late as 1950 the entire program's trust fund assets stood at 1343% of total expenditures for that year. But the very next year the ratio fell to 790%, and it has declined steadily to the present low level of about one-third of one year's payments.

---

[23]At after-tax rates of return of 10% to 6⅔%, a trust fund ten to fifteen times the annual payments it is supposed to support could support those payments indefinitely. These are feasible rates of return to expect a trust fund to be able to achieve, given the rates of return earned on typical investments such as common stocks of publicly held corporations, over the last fifty years (see chapter 4). These rates are especially feasible considering that many types of trusts are allowed various tax exemptions. Also, a government-held trust to finance social security would in all probability be tax exempt. If the rate of return earned on the trust fund assets was less than this, the trust would have to be larger, and if the rate was higher, then the fund could be smaller.

Nothing is expected to change in the near future. Table 20 shows that the trust funds may increase slightly relative to benefits over the next forty years, but not nearly enough to reach adequate levels for a secure trust fund. The existing trust funds are projected to be exhausted around 2030.

Although this analysis provides a valid general idea of the adequacy of the social security trust funds, it is technically an oversimplification. The system is analogous to a trust set up by a creator to pay a specific sum of benefits to a beneficiary for a certain number of years only, not forever. Such a trust requires trust fund assets large enough to pay these benefits over the years from the assets provided by the creator, plus the interest they would earn before dissipated. For social security, the trust funds would have to be large enough so that if the program were ended today and no future taxes were collected, and therefore no further benefit entitlements accumulated, the assets in the funds plus interest would be enough to pay all benefits to which existing workers and beneficiaries would be entitled. The social security trust funds would be able to make these payments if the government saved and invested each taxpayer's payments each year and returned them upon retirement.

The amount of these hypothetical payments is calculated each year by the Social Security Administration (see table 21). It is referred to as the unfunded liability. In 1978 the unfunded liability for the OASDI program was $3,971 billion, which is the size that the OASDI trust fund would have to be to be a secure trust fund. The actual OASDI trust fund held only $31.7 billion in 1978, however. The OASDI trust fund was thus less than 1% of the size necessary in 1978 to be secure. As table 21 shows, the trust fund was as high as 8.45% of the necessary size in 1969, but since 1967 it has not been anywhere near the full amount required.

The social security trust funds are trust funds in name only. There is nothing being accumulated, the funds cannot support future benefits, and at their current level they do not guarantee anything.

The way in which the program is actually operated can be determined by looking at total taxes and total expenditures. At the end of 1975 the total OASI trust fund stood at about $37 billion. Total OASI taxes in 1976 amount to $63.4 billion, and total OASI expenditures amount to $67.9 billion, leaving an OASI trust fund at the end of 1976 of $35.4 billion. In 1977 total OASI taxes were $69.6 billion, and total OASI expenditures were $75.3 billion, leaving a trust fund at the end of 1977 of $32.5 billion. In 1978 total OASI taxes were

$75.5 billion, and total OASI expenditures were $83.1 billion, leaving a trust fund at the end of 1978 of $27.5 billion. These figures show that it is not the trust fund that is guaranteeing current benefits but current taxes. Each year's taxes are approximately equal to each year's benefits, while the trust fund remains about the same. Rather than being accumulated in a trust fund, current taxes are being paid out immediately in current benefits on a pay-as-you-go basis. The so-called trust fund is really no more than a cash flow account where the money stops off just long enough for benefit checks to be written. (During their stay in the fund, the assets are invested in government bonds, and the small amount of earnings on these bonds is also used to finance current benefits.)

Social security is sometimes compared to a chain letter or Ponzi scheme. The benefits of those currently receiving funds are paid by those currently paying into the system, and those currently paying will receive their benefits in turn only if new participants are found to pay in. The benefits that will be received by those currently paying into the system are entirely dependent on future participants paying into the program. There are never any funds set aside to guarantee future benefits.

Pay-as-you-go financing can aptly be described as the fatal flaw of the social security program. It is the source of most of the worse defects and negative impacts of the current program, as we will see in later chapters. Yet, this method of financing is the essential, defining characteristic of the program. Once pay-as-you-go financing is dropped and the program becomes fully funded, as Professor Feldstein advocates, there is no reason to continue operating the program through the government. If the program is to be operated on a fully funded basis, there is no reason why it should not be privatized.

While all who have studied the program are aware that social security operates on a pay-as-you-go basis, despite government propaganda to the contrary, certain facts about this method of financing and its consequences are poorly understood. One of the most important of these facts is that a retirement program that operates on a pay-as-you-go basis goes through two phases, a start-up phase and a mature phase. During the start-up phase the first working generation begins to pay taxes, but there are no benefit entitlements to consume them. The first retired generation does not have any claim to benefits on the basis of past taxes, and therefore any benefits paid to this generation are unearned windfalls for which voters in that generation will be very grateful. These unearned benefits are simply well-disguised welfare payments. In the meantime taxes can be phased in slowly since there are no benefit obligations to be met. There is no problem or threat of bankruptcy because the program has not yet built up significant liabilities. During this period the program is likely to be very popular.

As the system matures and the first working generation retires, however, this picture changes dramatically. There are no longer any free benefits to pass out. Instead, the system has built up huge benefit obligations that the second working generation must meet. The focus now shifts from passing out free benefits to raising taxes to meet the enormous benefit demands of the second retired generation. This generation believes it has earned these benefits by past tax payments, and therefore its claims to benefits seem to have a particularly strong foundation in equity. The financial soundness of the program becomes a serious question for the first time because large, unfunded liabilities have accumulated and bankruptcy becomes a real threat. The popularity of the program in this stage is likely to be seriously eroded.

The 1970s marked the beginning of the transition of America's social security program from the start-up phase to the mature phase. Because the program itself was phased in slowly, this start-up phase has been dragged out considerably, but its inevitable end has come. The result is that the past experience of the program is a poor guide to the program's future. The windfall benefits and high returns on past tax dollars are over. Taxpayer willingness to continue to bear the program's heavy burdens will now become questionable. The financial soundness and possible bankruptcy of the program are now significant issues. The full implications of the maturity of the social security system will become apparent in more detail in later chapters.

The Two Goals of Social Security

This description of the development and operation of the social security system enables us to see more clearly how social security pursues two separate, distinct goals.

First, social security gathers funds from its participants to pay benefits when certain contingencies occur that result in a severe loss of income, such as retirement (old-age insurance), death (survivor's insurance), disability (disability insurance), or illness (hospital insurance). This is the insurance function of social security. Protection is paid for by the payroll tax, and benefits are based on the amounts one has paid into the system. Higher past taxes are the result of higher past earnings, which result in a higher AME and PIA. A higher PIA results in higher benefits; the more one pays for, the more one receives. Benefits are paid regardless of need because they are considered earned.

However, social security also gathers funds from taxpayers to pay benefits to some individuals solely because it is felt that they need these benefits, not because they have paid for them. This is the welfare function of the program, which is pursued through several elements in the current system.

The largest welfare element is represented by the start-up phase of the pay-as-you-go system. Congress began paying out benefits on a pay-as-you-go basis, initiating this start-up phase in 1939, because it felt that the recipients of these benefits were generally in need. The payment of benefits in this start-up phase was therefore justified on welfare grounds. In this start-up phase, taxes were collected from the first working generation, but there were little or no benefit entitlements belonging to the first retired generation because they had paid little or no taxes in the past. These initial taxes were nevertheless used to pay benefits to this first retired generation, and the members of this generation thus received high returns on any tax payments they may have made. To the extent that these returns were higher than market returns, they constituted a pure welfare subsidy. Over time, new retirees will have paid more in past taxes, and their returns relative to past taxes will fall. As the system matures, new retirees will have paid taxes over all of their lives and their returns in retirement benefits on these past tax payments will be less than market returns. At this point, the welfare subsidy will have been eliminated.

An example may clarify this analysis. If a person was sixty-two in 1937 when social security taxes began and he earned the maximum income until retirement at sixty-five, he would have paid $180 in taxes and would now be entitled to a pension for him and his wife for the rest of their lives. But this $180 with interest could not possibly finance their retirement and survivor benefits. Anything they receive above this, therefore, is a pure welfare subsidy from taxpayers. A person who was forty-nine in 1937 and earning the maximum income would have paid $1086 in taxes by the time he retired at sixty-five in 1953. He and his wife would then be entitled to an annual benefit of $1530 until one died and $1020 until the other died, not counting the benefit increases that Congress would vote over that period. It is clear that his tax payment, even if accumulated with interest, would not pay for these benefits, and anything he receives above this amount is again a pure welfare subsidy.

In an unpublished study, Douglas Munro of Ohio State University calculated the welfare component of social security retirement benefits from 1940 to 1971.[24] For males with median earnings retiring in 1940, 97.7% of benefits received constituted a welfare subsidy. This figure had fallen to 66.4% by 1971. The present discounted value of benefits was 43.3 times the value of taxes paid by the worker retiring in 1940. This benefit to tax ratio had fallen to 3.0 by 1971 (see table 22). Munro calculates that the value of all welfare benefits paid through social security in this manner to all retirees who retired through 1971 was equal to approximately $370 billion.

As the figures in table 22 show, the welfare component has declined steadily as the start-up phase has begun to pass into the mature phase. With workers paying the huge tax amounts of the 1970s and 1980s, the system will pass into the fully mature phase, and this welfare subsidy will be entirely eliminated.

The presence of this welfare subsidy in the benefits of the first retired generation has led most commentators to conclude that social security has represented a "good buy" for those workers because it paid them more than they could receive on their tax dollars in the private market. But this "good buy" essentially consisted of passing out free welfare benefits. There can be no conceivable justification for indiscriminately handing out welfare without requiring any showing of need. This handout has to be considered a terrible waste of hard-earned tax dollars or of assets available to help the poor because without a means test much of these welfare payments will go to individuals who are not truly needy or who could have saved on their own and thus avoided need if not promised welfare subsidies.

A second welfare element in the benefit structure is the progressive PIA formula. As was noted earlier, the PIA formula is heavily weighted so that those with low earning histories will receive relatively higher benefits for their past taxes than those with high earning histories. Those responsible for this aspect of the system felt that people with lower incomes would not have adequate old-age pensions if these pensions were based solely on past earnings or tax pay-

---

[24]Douglas Munro, "Welfare Component and Labor Supply Effects of OASDHI Retirement Benefits" (Ohio State University, Ph.D. diss., 1976).

ments. They are therefore given relatively higher benefits solely because they need them, not because they have paid for them. The result is that those at the higher end of the income scale must subsidize them by taking lower benefits than their payments would justify.

A third welfare element in social security is the provision for the minimum benefit, which is again based on a welfare rationale. It is felt that any retirement pension below the amount of the minimum benefit is inadequate, and the recipient needs more regardless of whether he has paid for it. These benefits are again subsidized by those at the higher end of the income scale, who end up with lower benefits than their payments would otherwise justify.

A fourth major welfare element in social security is the provision of benefits for spouses and dependents of beneficiaries who qualify for benefits themselves. As we have seen, a retired worker, for example, will receive higher benefits if he has a wife. He may have paid the same taxes as a co-worker without a wife, and yet upon retirement he will receive 50% more benefits. If he has dependent young children, he will receive still more. These benefits, therefore, are not earned by past tax payments. They are instead based on a welfare rationale. It is felt that a retired worker with a wife and children needs more than a single retiree, and consequently he is given greater benefits. These benefits must be subsidized by other workers in the system, who are therefore left with less than they paid for.

This system of allocating benefits applies to disability and survivor's insurance as well. Instead of receiving insurance sums based on past tax payments, beneficiaries receive more or less depending on whether they are married and are caring for dependent children. Two co-workers may have paid the same tax payments all their lives and both may die at the same age, yet if one leaves behind a wife with two grown children and the other a wife with two younger dependent children, the latter will receive much greater survivor's benefits. These benfits were not earned by past tax payments because both workers paid the same taxes. If they had paid the same taxes for term life insurance, both would have received the same amount upon their death. The greater survivor's benefits are granted to the second family because it is felt that they are in greater need, and therefore these benefits are justified on welfare grounds. These beneficiaries thus receive a subsidy from other taxpayers, who must then receive less than they have paid for.

Some of these taxpayers receive so much less than they pay for that they receive nothing. A single worker who dies before retirement receives no survivor's benefits for his heirs, even though he has paid taxes for them all his life. The same is true for a worker who leaves behind a childless wife who remarries. If these workers had paid the same amounts for term life insurance, upon their death they would have received large payments for their heirs.

Passing out welfare in this manner is extremely inefficient because the existence of spouses and dependents is a very poor surrogate for true need. A poor worker may die and leave behind a poor, childless wife who will receive no social security benefits. A wealthy professional may die and leave behind a large estate of investments for his wife and children as well as large life insurance policies, and yet his heirs will also receive large social security survivor's benefits. Passing out welfare in this indiscriminate manner without evaluating whether the recipients are in true need is a tremendous waste of both taxpayer's money and of assets available to help the poor.

The result of allowing these benefits for spouses and dependents is that the relation between actual benefits received and past taxes paid becomes extremely tenuous. Benefits are more closely related to the number of spouses and dependents one has than to the amounts one has paid into the system. Taxpayers are therefore unable to count on getting a fair return on their tax dollars and in many circumstances will get no return at all.

The welfare elements we have discussed thus far all grant benefits to recipients because it is felt they are in need rather than because they have earned these benefits with past tax payments. But there are also several welfare elements that limit benefits that may be justified on the basis of past taxes. These benefits are denied because it is felt that under certain circumstances the potential beneficiaries will not be in need.

The first of these elements is the earnings test. This provision reduces benefits one dollar for every two dollars that a beneficiary earns over a certain limit. It too is based on the welfare criterion of need: It is felt that one who is earning over a certain limit every year does not need the benefits, and therefore he is not allowed to receive them even though he may have earned them by past tax payments.

A second such element is the maximum family benefit, which limits the benefits that can be received on one individual's earnings record to a certain maximum amount each month. This provision is based on the judgment that at a certain level benefits are no longer needed by the recipient and therefore he should not receive them, regardless of whether he has paid for them.

The last of these welfare elements is the large number of qualifications on the receipt of benefits. These qualifications are based on the welfare rationale that under certain circumstances the recipient does not need the benefits, and they are therefore cancelled regardless of whether he or she has paid for them in past taxes. An example is the requirement that a widow under the age of sixty must remain single to receive survivor's benefits. Another example is the requirement that a wife must forgo her own retirement benefits to receive her wife's benefit on her husband's earnings record.

To the extent that these three elements limit unearned welfare benefits, they are merely an inefficient, *ad hoc* substitute for a means test because they do not precisely measure true need and thus do not often prevent the receipt of welfare benefits by those who are not in need and may prevent the receipt of benefits by those who are. But these elements in the social security benefit structure do not only serve to limit the payment of unearned welfare benefits within that structure. These provisions also often serve to limit benefits that have been earned and paid for by past tax payments. They therefore serve an additional, independent welfare function within the social security benefit structure, restricting earned benefits on the basis of need.

These are the most significant welfare elements in the program, but there are many others. Any element or provision in the program that distorts the payment of benefits so that it is not strictly related to the amount paid in past taxes may be considered a welfare element. These elements all serve either to pay increased benefits in circumstances where recipients are thought to be in greater need or to limit benefits in circumstances where they are thought to not be in need, regardless of the benefit amounts that may have been earned through the payment of past taxes. These elements, therefore, tend to cause benefit payments to be made on the basis of need rather than on what has been earned by past tax payments into the program.

It is thus clear that social security pursues both welfare and insurance objectives. As will be shown in detail in later chapters, these two objectives are inherently contradictory, and the result is to make the program bad welfare and bad insurance.

Supplemental Security Income (SSI)

The 1935 Social Security Act also provided for the establishment of the Old-Age Assistance program (OAA). Under OAA each state enacted a public assistance program for the aged with matching grants from the federal government. The entire program was financed by general revenues with recipients subject to a means test requiring that applicants actually be in need before they could receive benefits. The program also provided benefits to the blind and disabled under sixty-five.

In the early years OAA was much larger than OASI. In just the old-age portion of the program, OAA paid out $244 million in benefits in 1937 while OASI, then OAI, paid out $1 million. In 1940 OAA paid out $450 million while OASI paid out $35 million. As late as 1950 OAA was larger than OASI, paying out $1,454 million in that year as against $961 million for OASI. The OASI program, however, surpassed OAA the very next year and continued its phenomenal growth, while OAA remained virtually stable. By 1972 OASI was paying out $37.1 billion in benefits while OAA was paying only $1.9 billion (see table 10).

In 1972 Congress replaced all state-federal OAA programs with the Supplemental Security Income Program (SSI), a single, nationally uniform federal program. The new SSI program is financed entirely from general federal revenues, leaving the states with the option of supplementing federal benefit payments. It also includes a means test for eligibility. SSI went into effect on 1 January 1974.

The program covers all those age sixty-five and over as well as the blind and disabled. To be eligible, an individual must not have resources greater than $1,500, and a couple's resources must not be greater than $2,250. A recipient's home, car, personal effects, household goods and furnishings, if they are of reasonable value, are excluded from total resources for this evaluation. Recipients must also not have incomes above certain limits to receive benefits from the program. In July 1979 the income limits were $208.20 per month for a single person and $312.30 for a couple. Excluded from income are regular cash payments, based on need, from a state or local government and the first $20 of monthly income. Also excluded is earned income, such as wages or net earnings from self-employment, under $65 a month plus one-half of all earned income over $65 a month. In effect, therefore, an individual will be eligible for benefits if he receives less than $501.40 per month in earned income alone or less than $228.20 per month in unearned income alone. Unearned income over $20 a month reduces benefits dollar for dollar, while earned income over $65 a month, $85 if no unearned income, reduces benefits by $1 for every $2.

In July 1979 SSI provided an income of $208.20 a month for one recipient and $312.30 a month for a couple. Benefits under the new SSI program increased to $2.5 million in 1974, up from $1.8 million in 1972 under OAA.[25] Benefits payments to the elderly increased from $1.7 billion under OAA in 1973 to $2.4 billion under SSI in 1974 and remained at virtually the same level through 1978 (see table 10). Total benefit payments under the SSI program since its inception are shown in table 23. In 1978 just about 10% of the aged population were receiving SSI benefits, about the same percentage as those in poverty in the general population. This figure is down from 21.7% under OAA in 1950. About 70% of those receiving SSI benefits were also receiving benefits under OASDHI, which suggests that there is a considerable overlap between the two programs (see table 8).

Thus an alternative vehicle for the welfare element of the social security program has existed from the beginning. The fact that Congress enacted the OAA program at the same time as OASI indicates that it recognized that the welfare function served by OAA–SSI should be separate from the insurance function of OASI. Yet over the years Congress has polluted social security with elements that properly belonged in a separate program. Shifting the welfare function of social security to the SSI program need not necessarily mean a large increase in the size of SSI. It would mean simply that welfare would be paid only to those truly in need. It would mean also that the size and continuation of these welfare benefits would be properly weighed against the needs and rights of taxpayers instead of hidden in a putative insurance program as they are now.

The Incidence of the Social Security Tax

Another officially contrived public misconception about social security is that the employer pays half of the payroll tax. Most people believe that their total social security tax is the amount deducted from their paycheck designated in the box marked FICA. Many do not know that the employer is taxed for an amount equal to this deducted amount. Those who are aware of this tax are usually not aware of the economic process by which the tax is really imposed on them rather than the employer.

The Social Security Administration calls this tax the employer's

[25]Munnell, *The Future of Social Security*, p. 11.

share of the payroll tax, and those who are aware of its existence think of it as just that. The truth, however, is that both the employer's share of the payroll tax and the employee's share comes out of the employee's paycheck, as do employer payments for other fringe benefits such as pension plans, medical insurance, vacation benefits, etc. Over the long run, the employer merely passes the burden of the tax onto the employee by paying him lower wages than he would have without the tax. The employee really pays twice the amount deducted from his paycheck.

The imposition of the social security payroll tax on the employer raises the cost of labor. From the employer's point of view, this tax is simply part of the cost of hiring the employee. The imposition of the tax, T, raises the employee's wage, W, to $(W + T)$. Since this wage is higher than W, the employer will reduce his demand for labor. With a given capital supply, the more employees the employer hires, the less is the productivity of each one, or marginal productivity of labor (MPL). The employer will therefore hire workers until their productivity (MPL) has fallen to equal the wage. The number of workers hired at the higher wage $(W + T)$ will consequently be less than the number hired at wage W alone. This reduction in the number of workers hired will result in a certain number of unemployed workers, call it N. These unemployed workers will bid down the wage until the employer rehires them all. Since the tax component in the new wage $(W + T)$ cannot be reduced, this entire reduction will have to come in the after-tax wage component W. The employer will rehire all the workers N only when the before-tax wage he must pay $(W + T)$ is equal to the old wage W alone. This will occur when the after-tax wage component W has been reduced by the full amount of the tax T so that the wage is re-established at $(W - T) + T = W$. The cost to the employer is now the same as before, so he will hire as many workers as before, rehiring all the unemployed workers N. The amount each worker receives, however, is now the after-tax wage $W - T$. The worker's wage has therefore been reduced by the full amount of the tax. The employee thus bears the employer's share of the social security payroll tax.

However, as a result of the lower after-tax wage $(W - T)$ some workers may reduce their labor supply or leave the labor market completely because they feel that the lower wage does not provide adequate compensation for their former labor effort. This reduction is known as the substitution effect: Workers substitute more leisure for work because the lower wage no longer makes working worth forgoing available leisure. Using an overly simplified analysis, some economists contend that such a reduced labor supply, if it actually does occur in response to the tax, would cause the employer to bear part of the tax burden. We will first discuss the circumstances under which there will not be a reduction in the labor supply in response to the lower aftertax wage (W − T). In these circumstances, it is clear that the employee bears the full burden of the employer's share of the payroll tax as well as the employee's share. We will then demonstrate that even when such a reduced labor supply does occur, a precise analysis of the impacts of the tax on the employee and the employer shows that the employee will still bear the full burden of the tax.

To begin with, no reduction in the labor supply will occur if workers do not think of their compensation as reduced by the tax T, which would be the case if each individual worker saw the tax as a payment he was making for a service he needed or wanted, such as insurance protection. Under these circumstances each worker would see the tax as part of his wage, like a deduction for mortgage payments or for fringe benefits, and not as a tax that is reducing his compensation. The tax T would be like a payment in kind for insurance protection, and therefore it would be part of each worker's total compensation. Since each worker's compensation would be the same as before the tax, there would be no reduction in the labor supply.

As was noted briefly in chapter 1, however, workers are admittedly not likely to think of the tax in this way, but, because of the tenuous relation between taxes and benefits resulting from the welfare elements in social security, as a simple tax payment that is not part of their after-tax compensation. Since the program's benefits depend so little on past tax payments, the individual worker is not likely to think of his taxes as buying him any additional specific benefits on a direct personal basis. The worker is likely to expect to receive the program's benefits later, regardless of what he pays into the program now. The worker will, therefore, not view his tax payments as part of his compensation. The worker's perception of the social security payroll tax, and the resulting effect on his incentives, will be discussed in more detail in chapter 3. It is worth noting now, however, that to the extent that the employee *does* see the tax as part of his compensation, there will be no reduction in the labor supply in response to the lower after-tax wage (W − T), and the employee will bear the full burden of the tax.

Second, even if the worker does not view his social security tax payments as part of his compensation, the response to the lower after-tax wage (W − T) will not necessarily be a reduced labor supply. Even though the reduced compensation will lead to a substitution effect tending to reduce the labor supply, it will also lead to an income effect tending to increase the labor supply because the reduced compensation may no longer give some workers enough income at the same amount of work as before to buy all the goods and services these workers need or want. These workers will therefore tend to increase their labor supply so that each will earn at the lower wage a total amount closer to what each was earning before the tax. If this income effect is equal to or greater than the substitution effect, there will be no reduction in the labor supply and the employee will again bear the full burden of the social security tax.

Thus it is only if (a) workers do not view their social security tax payments as part of their compensation and (b) if the substitution effect outweighs the income effect that the total labor supply will fall in response to the lower after-tax wage (W − T). A common response among economists at this point is to argue that empirically the income effect is likely to be nearly as strong as the substitution effect, if not stronger, and consequently there will be no significant decrease in the labor supply and the employee will bear the primary burden of the tax. Yet instances in which the substitution effect substantially outweighs the income effect retain great interest for those who remain convinced that workers do respond to economic incentives. In such instances the labor supply will fall, and this fall will have some detrimental effects on the employer. But the employee will still bear the full monetary burden of the tax.

To see this, note that when the labor supply falls the marginal productivity of labor (MPL) increases. Consequently, the wage that employers pay, (W − T) + T, will also increase to equal the new higher MPL because the employers who lost workers because of the decreased labor supply will bid up the wage as they seek to hire replacement workers. The employers who are offering the most valuable and productive jobs will in fact bid the wage all the way up to the MPL so that those employers offering less valuable and productive jobs will be priced out of the market and unable to take workers away from the more productive employers.

It may at first appear that to the extent that the wage increases in response to the reduced labor supply, workers are passing along part of the tax burden and the employer therefore bears this part of the tax. If the amount by which the wage increases is E, so that the employer now pays $(W - T + E) + T$, it may appear that the employer bears E/T of the tax.

But the new, higher wage $(W - T + E) + T$ is still equal to the MPL or productivity of each worker. Thus the aftertax wage which the worker receives, $(W - T + E)$, is still less than the value of what the worker is producing—the before-tax wage $(W - T + E) + T$—by the full amount of the tax T. The entire tax, therefore, is still coming out of the worker's pocket. The share of national income actually produced by workers will be greater than what they receive by the total amount of the tax collected by the federal government. The employee, therefore, still bears the full monetary burden of the tax.

From the employer's point of view the key point is again that the wage is still equal to the MPL. Consequently, the full wage that the employer is paying is still equal to the productive value he is getting out of his workers, and he is not, therefore, losing anything to the tax. Although the wage is now higher than it was before the tax, the employer is merely paying the new, higher economic value of the workers he is hiring. The value of what the employer is receiving from these workers is sufficient to compensate him fully for the higher wage. This higher wage does not mean that the tax is merely being passed along because the wage increase occurs only to the extent that some workers reduce their labor supply. The idea that the tax is being passed along is also inconsistent with the conclusion that the employer receives full compensatory productive value in return for the higher wage. If the employer had to pay the higher wage and had to hire the same number of workers as before, then he would bear part of the tax because then he would be paying more than the MPL. But as long as the employer is free to vary the number of workers he will hire, as long as the wage equals the MPL, the employer will not bear any of the direct monetary burden of the payroll tax.

This discussion indicates that the basic reason that the employer will never bear any portion of the payroll tax is that he will never pay any wage greater than the MPL while an employee will accept a wage less than the MPL. The employer will never pay any wage greater than the MPL because when he does so, he simply loses money. He gains nothing from it; in fact he is made worse off. The employer would rather simply not hire the worker than pay a wage greater than the worker's MPL. The employer's demand for labor is therefore entirely determined by the MPL. However, an employee will accept an wage below the MPL because his labor supply has nothing to do with the MPL. His labor supply is entirely determined by his preference for income versus his preference for leisure. If an employer offers him a wage high enough to make working worth the forgone leisure, the employee will accept the job even if the wage is less than the MPL. Accepting the job is making the employee better off, even if his wage is less than his MPL. Thus the wedge created by the payroll tax is borne entirely by the employee.

The employer does, however, suffer some negative effects from the reduced labor supply and rising wages because there are additional costs of the payroll tax beyond the direct monetary cost. The additional costs are due to the economic inefficiency created by the tax. Unlike the direct monetary cost of the tax, part of these additional costs are borne by the employer.

Thus the employer responds to the reduced labor supply and rising wages by substituting capital for labor. This new mix of capital and labor is less efficient and more expensive than the old mix that the employer preferred when he had the choice of using it. The additional expense resulting from this inefficiency is not offset by any compensatory increase in value, as was the case of the increase in wages discussed above. This expense is therefore borne by the employer. In fact, if the payroll tax is raised high enough, the costs of the resulting inefficiency could be so high that the employer would be driven out of business.

Yet, even though the employer bears some of the costs of the economic inefficiency arising from the payroll tax, the employee still bears the full burden of the direct monetary costs of the tax. In considering who bears the burden of financing social security, the incidence of the direct monetary cost of the tax is the relevant question. We will, however, discuss in more detail in chapter 3 the economic inefficiency created by the payroll tax and the costs this inefficiency imposes on both employers and employees. The analysis of the incidence of the social security payroll tax presented here is shown in Appendix A in a graph format commonly used by economists.

An empirical study of the payroll tax by John A. Brittain also reached the conclusion that the employer's share of the payroll tax is borne entirely by the employee. Brittain examined data from numerous countries around the world and found that wages in countries with higher payroll taxes were lower than wages in countries with lower payroll taxes by roughly the full amount of additional tax. Brittain concludes, "The essence of the finding here is that given the level of productivity in a country, the presence of a payroll tax on employees tends to reduce the wage in dollars by roughly the amount of the tax."[26]

Finally, it should be noted that if the employer's share of the payroll tax was borne by the employer, it would cause unemployment because the tax borne by the employer would increase the cost of hiring the employee to W + T. At this higher cost the employer would reduce his demand for labor, but since the wage offered to the employee would still be the same as before, W, the labor supply would also still be the same. The drop in demand for labor with a steady labor supply means that some workers will no longer be able to find jobs and there will be unemployment, or at least reduced hours of work for those who remain employed. A payroll tax borne by the employer is a tax on the activity of offering employment, and, like a tax on any other activity, it discourages the continuation of that activity. A payroll tax borne completely by the employee, however, will not cause unemployment. In this case, the cost to the employer is the same as without the tax. He does not care if he pays the full wage to the employee or part to the employee and part to the government. He will therefore seek to hire as many workers as before the imposition of the tax, and there will be no unemployment.

Nevertheless, despite government propaganda to the contrary, both the employer and the employee share of the social security payroll tax are borne by the employee. The employer simply pays the employee less than he would if he did not have to pay an employer's share of the payroll tax to the government.

Politics and the Art of Lying

In a by now famous paragraph from a widely circulated booklet entitled *Your Social Security* put out by the Social Security Administration, the American people are told:

> The basic idea of Social Security is a simple one: during working years employees, their employers, and self-employed people pay Social Security contributions into special trust funds. When earnings stop or are reduced because the worker retires, dies or becomes disabled, monthly cash benefits are paid to replace part of the earnings his family has lost.[27]

[26]John A. Brittain, "The Incidence of Social Security Payroll Taxes," *American Economic Review* LXI (March 1971):110–25.

[27]*Your Social Security*, HEW Publication, N. (SSA) 76–10035, June, 1976.

As Milton Friedman has written, "It would be hard to pack a greater number of false and misleading statements into a single paragraph."[28] Employees, employers, and the self-employed do not pay social security contributions. Contributions are voluntary payments. Social security payments are involuntary taxes, and any attempt to evade payment of them is a felony subjecting the taxpayer to heavy legal sanctions, including fines and imprisonment. Furthermore, employers do not pay any share of these taxes, as we have just seen; the entire burden of the tax is shifted to the employees.

The paragraph states that these "contributions" are paid into special trust funds. One wonders what is special about them. Is it because they are the only trust funds in the world that hold less than 1% of the value of the benefits they are supposed to guarantee? Is it because they currently hold less than four months' benefits? Is it because at this level of funding the trust funds don't guarantee anything?

Furthermore, when one is told that his money is paid into a trust fund, one gets the impression that it stays there for a while and is accumulated. After all, what is a fund but an accumulation or pool of payments that are saved for a special event of purpose, such as Christmas funds, pension funds, vacation funds, investment funds, etc. Before there can be a trust there must be assets to be held in trust, but the money paid into social security is not saved or accumulated but immediately paid out to current beneficiaries on a pay-as-you-go basis. As a result, there is in fact no true trust fund, but merely a cash flow account where current taxes stop only long enough to pick up their marching orders.

Finally, when one is told in one sentence that his payments are paid into special trust funds and then told in the next sentence that in certain circumstances benefits will be paid to him, one gets the impression that these benefits will be paid from the trust funds and that these trust funds guarantee the future benefits. But as we have seen these future benefits will not be paid from the trust funds but out of the taxes to be collected from future taxpayers, some of whom are not yet born. The only guarantee for these future payments is the willingness of taxpayers to continue to pay social security taxes.

This paragraph is not a simple mistake emanating from a low-

---

[28]Institute for Contemporary Studies, *The Crisis in Social Security* (San Francisco; Institute for Contemporary Studies, 1977).

level scrivener at the Social Security Administration. Instead, it is a carefully contrived deception meant to mislead the public, as is shown by two changes that have been made in the paragraph in recent years to eliminate more obvious misstatements while not changing the overall impression the paragraph gives.

Before 1976, instead of saying that the contributions were "paid into special trust funds," the paragraph stated that they were "pooled into special trust funds," a phrase that strongly conveyed the impression that the tax money was saved and accumulated in these funds. When money is pooled, it is all kept together in the pool. If part of it is used for other purposes, such as paying current obligations, it cannot be said that the money has been pooled. In *Social Security: The Fraud in Your Future*, Warren Shore writes,

> A pool of money, dictionaries seem to agree, is a sum equal to the amount various contributors put there—an elementary, almost childish thought, but still one which the government tampers with for its own use.
> If I tell ten people that I have pooled their contributions of $10 each into a created account, those ten have the right to believe that the account now contains at least $100.
> If the ten people later look at the balance of the account and find that it contains, say, $75, they have the right to call me a liar and certainly the right to conclude that while something happened to their money, it was not pooled.[29]

Because this deception was so blatant, the Social Security Administration was forced by intense criticism to change the wording, although it did so in such a way as to retain the overall misleading impression conveyed by the paragraph.

Similarly, prior to 1965 the paragraph stated that benefits were paid "from the funds" instead of simply saying that benefits are paid, as it does today. By 1965 the trust funds had dwindled to such low amounts relative to benefits that this statement became embarrassing. The words "from the funds" were dropped, but the overall misleading impression conveyed by the paragraph remains.

These changes indicate that the Social Security Administration is well aware that this key paragraph in its booklet describing the system to Americans is deceptive. Yet, inexcusably, it continues to perpetrate this fraud. Employees of the Social Security Administration are public officials. They are paid by the public to serve the in-

---

[29]Warren Shore, *Social Security: The Fraud in Your Future* (New York: Macmillan, 1975), p. 21.

terest of the people, not to lie to them. If there were any shred of honesty in the government at all, this deception would stop.

Warren Shore reports that at least thirty-five times in the sixty-one current Social Security Administration booklets describing the system, the taxes are referred to as contributions or premiums.[30] However, the distinction between voluntary contributions and involuntary taxes was brought home with brutal effectiveness to an Amish farmer in Pennsylvania named Valentine Byler. Because of his Amish religion, Byler would not accept benefit checks from the government, so he asked to be exempted from social security taxes. The government responded by sending IRS agents to his farm, where they seized his work horses and sold them at public auction to collect the money for the tax.

Shore reports that in fifty-three separate references contained in social security pamphlets published during 1974, Americans are told that their tax money is being pooled and that contributions paid to the pool are available later to replace lost earnings.[31] But as we have seen there is no pool just as there are no trust funds.

The purpose of the deceptive public relations campaigns pursued by the Social Security Administration is to make the American people think that social security is just like private insurance. For example, in a government pamphlet describing the social security card, the American people are told, "Your card is the symbol of your insurance policy under the federal Social Security Law."[32]

The administration has told the public that payroll taxes "are strictly accounted for and kept separate from the general funds in the U.S. Treasury."[33] It has told the public that an individual account is kept for each taxpayer and "your wages are entered on your Social Security record throughout your working years."[34]

Former HEW Secretary Wilbur J. Cohen has told the American people to think of social security as "group insurance" granting "a legal right to benefits backed by a guarantee from the federal government and legal recourse to the courts for payment."[35]

---

[30]Ibid.
[31]Ibid., p. 19.
[32]Ibid.
[33]Ibid.
[34]Ibid., p. 23.
[35]Ibid., p. 22.

How do the courts describe the system when these statements are actually on the line? In a 1937 case upholding the constitutionality of the social security act, *Helvering* v. *Davis* 301 U.S. 619, the Supreme Court said, "The proceeds of both the employee and employer taxes are to be paid into the Treasury like other internal revenue generally, and are not earmarked in any way."[36]

In a 1960 case, *Flemming* v. *Nestor*, the U.S. Supreme Court considered whether social security benefits could be cut off to the wife of a deported Communist. Her husband had paid social security taxes, and she was now receiving retirement benefits. Her lawyer argued that the government had told workers that they had a legally enforceable property right to benefits because of the taxes they had paid. The Court cut off the benefits, saying, "To engraft upon the Social Security system a concept of 'accrued property rights' would deprive it of the flexibility and boldness in adjustment to everchanging conditions which it demands."[37] The Court also said, "It is apparent that the non-contractual interest of an employee covered by the Act cannot be soundly analogized to that of the holder of an annuity, whose right to benefits is bottomed on his contractual premium payments."[38]

Interestingly, in that case the Social Security Administration argued, "The OASI program is in no sense a federally-administered 'insurance program' under which each worker pays premiums over the years and acquires at retirement an indefeasible right to receive for life a fixed monthly benefit, irrespective of the conditions which Congress has chosen to impose from time to time."[39]

An outraged Justice Black described the meaning of the majority opinion in his dissent:

> The court consoles those whose insurance is taken away today, and others who may suffer the same fate in the future, by saying that a decision requiring the Social Security system to keep faith would 'deprive it of the flexibility and boldness in adjustment to everchanging conditions which it demands.' People who pay premiums for insurance usually think they are paying for insurance, not for flexibility and boldness. I cannot believe that any private insurance company

---

[36] *Helvering* v. *Davis*, 301 U.S. 609, at 619.
[37] *Flemming* v. *Nestor*, 363 U.S. 603, at 616.
[38] Ibid., at 610.
[39] Quoted by Roger Leroy Miller in "Social Security: The Cruelest Tax," *Harper's*, June 1974, p. 24.

in America would be permitted to repudiate its matured contracts with its policyholders who have regularly paid all their premiums in reliance upon the good faith of the company.[40]

Justice Black explained the majority opinion further, "These are nice words but they cannot conceal the fact that they simply tell the contributors to this insurance fund that despite their own and their employer's payments the Government, in paying the beneficiaries out of the fund, is merely giving them something for nothing and can stop doing so when it pleases."[41]

Milton Friedman sums up the current state of public discussion concerning social security:

> As I have gone through the literature, I have been shocked at the level of the arguments that have been used to sell Social Security, not only by politicians or special interest groups, but more especially by self-righteous academics. Men who would not lie to their children, their friends, or their colleagues, whom you and I would trust implicitly in personal dealings, have propagated a false view of Social Security —and their intelligence and exposure to contrary views make it hard to believe that they have done so unintentionally and innocently. The very name—old age and survivor's insurance—is a blatant attempt to mislead the public into identifying a compulsory tax and benefit system with private, voluntary and individual purchase of individually accrued benefits.[42]

What purpose does all this deception and misrepresentation serve? Why is the government so desperate to make the American people believe that social security is simply insurance?

The entire purpose of this deception is to hide the welfare elements in the social security system and attempt to create the impression that social security is simply insurance without any welfare elements. Hiding the welfare elements behind the insurance myth helps to serve several important purposes.

First, the insurance analogy leads the American people to believe that the system is more secure than it really is. It makes them think that their future benefits are guaranteed by funds currently accumulated and available to pay such benefits. It perpetuates the idea that they can count on their future benefits because they have already paid for them and have a contractual right to them that can-

---

[40]*Flemming v. Nestor*, at 624.

[41]Ibid., at 623.

[42]Wilbur J. Cohen and Milton Friedman, *Social Security: Universal or Selective?* (Washington, D.C.: American Enterprise Institute, 1972), pp. 26–27.

not be taken away. These beliefs are false, yet planting and cultivating these false beliefs helps to make the program more politically acceptable and popular.

Second, hiding the welfare elements leads people to believe that the social security benefits paid are earned entitlements rather than welfare handouts, which also helps to improve the program's political standing and allows the system to expand to a much greater size than it would otherwise. Taxpayers are more willing to pay taxes for earned benefits, which they will also be receiving in the future, than for benefits that are in large part welfare. Recipients feel more comfortable accepting benefits that they believe they have earned than substantial welfare subsidies. The public is probably more willing to support a system for the provision of insurance protection, which everyone needs to some degree and where everyone is paying his own way, than a massive welfare transfer payment scheme. But the major portion of social security benefits in the past has been simple welfare and while some of these welfare elements will decline in the future, most will remain.

A third purpose served by hiding the social security welfare elements behind the insurance analogy is that doing so tends to obscure the true costs of the program. Carl Patton, in his article "The Politics of Social Security," illustrates this point.[43] Patton notes that when social security benefits are increased, the impact is explicitly and immediately perceived through increased benefit checks. But if taxpayers are taught to think of social security as insurance, then increasing social security taxes does not lead to an immediate perception of increased costs because these taxes are seen as payments for insurance premiums rather than taxes. Taxpayers would not see the payment of these taxes as a reduction in wealth but as a change in the form of that wealth. They have substituted present wealth for entitlement to future wealth, as when buying an insurance policy. Taxpayers are therefore encouraged to think of social security spending as free because the payroll taxes are equivalent to insurance premiums. To make doubly sure that the true costs of the program remain concealed, half of them are hidden in the employer's share of the payroll tax. Employees do not see the employer's payroll taxes as a cost to them, even though they do bear these costs, and they remain unaware of the true cost of the program.

[43]Carl V. Patton, "The Politics of Social Security" in *The Crisis in Social Security*, (San Francisco: Institute for Contemporary Studies, 1977).

Obscuring costs in this way serves to increase the program's political acceptability and popularity and allows it to grow rapidly. Politicians continue to buy votes with substantial benefit increases, and there is very little taxpayer resistance. Patton writes:

> People will increase their payments far more willingly as "insurance premium" payers rather than as taxpayers. It is unlikely that people would tolerate the present payroll tax rates, especially the regressivity of the payroll tax, if they knew what the taxes were paying for. As long as people thought tax increases were going to benefit themselves directly, they were willing to support the increases, or at least not oppose them.[44]

Finally, as Patton notes, the insurance analogy provides the justification for financing social security by specially earmarked payroll taxes. Because taxpayers are supposed to be buying a service—insurance protection—they are charged a flat rate tax analogous to paycheck deductions for pension plans and other fringe benefits instead of being taxed through the progressive income tax. But because social security is financed by this special tax, it does not have to compete with other programs for funding. It has its own complete, independent revenue source, and the program can therefore grow to whatever level this source will support. The program has a privileged position within the government, much like a feudal barony with delegated powers from the crown. Earmarked financing serves not only to allow greater growth of the program but also to ensure the program's continuation because this method of financing automatically builds up benefit obligations over time. Any opposition to the program, therefore, will encounter resistance from those expecting future benefit payments that they perceive as earned by their past tax payments.

Patton quotes a Social Security Administration official in a frank moment recognizing the advantage derived from the perpetuation of the insurance myth. The official, John Carrol, wrote in 1966:

> It can scarcely be contested that the earmarking of payroll taxes for OASDI reduced resistance to the imposition of taxes on low-income earners, made viable tax increases at times when they might not otherwise have been made, and has given trust fund programs a privileged position semi-detached from the government. Institutionalists foresaw these advantages as means to graft the new program into the social fabric.[45]

44Ibid., p. 156.
45Ibid., p. 154.

Hiding social security's welfare elements behind the insurance analogy benefits the bureaucrats in the Social Security Administration the most. By improving the program's political acceptability and popularity, by clearing the way for more rapid growth of the program, and by reducing any taxpayer resistance, the insurance myth helps to provide these bureaucrats with more funding for their program, more power and prestige, and more jobs with greater security. It provides them with their own feudal barony complete with their own delegated independent revenue source, and they do not have to compete with any other power centers in the government for funding. It also provides them with a ready reserve of opposition to any cutbacks in the program. The Social Security Administration has an enormous vested interest in hiding the program's welfare elements and perpetuating the pure insurance myth.

3

Social Security and the Economy

The social security program has several important negative effects on the American economy. It causes severe losses in savings and capital investment, a reduction of national income and economic growth, and decreased employment. With the tremendous growth in the size of the program in recent years, these negative impacts have become too powerful and too serious to be ignored. Part of the problem, as we have seen, is that social security was tailored to the unique economic circumstances of the 1930s. Although these underlying economic circumstances have changed dramatically since then, the basic structure of the program has remained the same. The large and massive program that presently exists is inappropriate for the modern economy.

But this is not the entire problem. The social security program has several major negative economic effects that were never intended and are not widely understood. These negative effects are due to the faulty design of the program and have been present from the beginning. In fact, it may be argued that even the intended effects were based on fallacious economic theories and were also inappropriate from the beginning.

Martin Feldstein, professor of economics at Harvard University and chairman of the National Bureau of Economic Research, has summed up the problem of social security's negative economic impacts:

> Because of the vast size of the social security program and its central role in the American system of financing retirement, it has major effects on all the significant dimensions of our economy. These effects are currently unintended, generally unperceived and frequently undesirable. . . . Social security was the most important government innova-

75

tion of the Great Depression. Forty years later nearly every major aspect of our economic life has changed dramatically. Yet the basic structure of the social security program has not been reexamined and reshaped to fit the economic conditions of today. Instead the original program has simply continued to expand at an increasing rate.[1]

Social security has major economic effects in two areas: First is savings, capital investment, national income, and economic growth; second is labor, employment, and economic efficiency.

Savings, Investment, National Income, and Economic Growth

As we have seen, money currently paid into the social security system is not saved and invested for current taxpayers but instead is paid out immediately to current recipients. It is this flaw that is responsible for the most serious negative economic impacts of the program.

The operation of social security on a pay-as-you-go basis causes a massive decline in savings, which results in a decline in capital investment and, in turn, a decline in national income and economic growth. Feldstein has been the most forceful proponent of this criticism of the program. His econometric studies document the declines caused by social security in these areas and estimate the magnitude of these declines.

The way in which social security reduces savings can be seen by focusing on the individual taxpayer. Because the taxpayer thinks of his social security taxes as the equivalent of forced savings for retirement, he is likely to reduce the amount of savings for retirement that he would have accumulated in the absence of social security by the full amount of his social security taxes.

Feldstein uses the example of a person with an annual income of $10,000 who wants to save 10% of his total income for his retirement without social security.[2] With social security he need not do any saving at all for his retirement because the program already requires him to pay more than 10% of his income into the system. His savings will therefore be reduced by the full amount of his social

[1]Martin Feldstein, "Toward a Reform of Social Security," *The Public Interest*, Summer 1975, p. 75.
[2]Ibid., p. 82–83.

security taxes. Consider further an individual with an annual income of $20,000 who wants to save 10% of his income without social security. If social security requires him to pay $1,800 a year into the system for his retirement (because the maximum taxable income is less than $20,000), he needs to save only $200 a year on his own. The result is again a decline in savings by the full amount of social security taxes, or $1,800.

Because social security taxes are not saved by the government but immediately paid out to current recipients on a pay-as-you-go basis, there is no offsetting increase in savings through the program to counterbalance this decline. Thus the net impact on the economy is likely to be a decline in savings equal to the full amount of social security taxes.

In 1975 total social security taxes (OASDHI) were $75.9 billion and personal savings totaled $83.6 billion. If social security caused a reduction in personal savings equivalent to the full amount of taxes paid, personal savings would have been cut almost in half. Corporate savings in 1975 totaled $32.2 billion, making total private savings, personal and corporate, of $115.8 billion. If social security reduced private savings by $75.9 billion, total potential private savings of $191.7 billion would have been reduced by about 40%. In 1978 total social security taxes amounted to $106.2 billion. Personal savings in that year totaled $76.7 billion, with corporate savings at $53.5 billion to make total private savings of $130.2 billion. If social security reduced private savings in 1978 by $106.2 billion, then total potential private savings of $236.4 billion in that year would have been reduced by about 45%.

The reduction in savings caused by social security can be seen in another way. The individual taxpayer may focus on benefits instead of taxes and reason that with the promise of these benefits, he needs to save less for his retirement on his own. The taxpayer can think of his potential social security benefits as the equivalent of an annuity, giving him the right to annual benefit payments of a certain amount when he reaches sixty-five. The present value of this annuity can be considered by the taxpayer as part of his present personal wealth. He can therefore reduce the amount of personal wealth he would otherwise have wanted to accumulate, increasing his present consumption and reducing his savings while still attaining his previously desired level of retained wealth.

Again because social security operates on a pay-as-you-go basis, there would be no offsetting effect through the program to increase savings. The result is that total saved wealth will decrease by the full amount of the total present value of promised social security benefits. Feldstein defines this total present value as social security wealth. This "wealth" does not actually exist anywhere in the economy. It is not real wealth represented by any tangible assets. It is merely an implicit promise that the next generation will tax itself to pay currently promised benefits. But to the extent that this promise is reliable, it is perfectly rational for each individual household to regard this social security wealth as if it were part of the household's personal real wealth. The concept of social security wealth, however, does not refer to existing real wealth created by the program or depending on the program for its continued existence. Quite to the contrary, social security wealth represents the amount of additional real wealth households would have in the absence of the social security program. But since social security wealth is not real, the amount of social security wealth represents the amount of real wealth that is lost because of the program.

The value of this social security wealth can therefore be used as an estimate of the effect of social security on the total private stock of real wealth saved over time. Feldstein has estimated the 1971 value of this social security wealth at $2 trillion.[3] Total private wealth of households in 1971 was $3 trillion. This calculation suggests that social security may have reduced the private wealth saved or private savings accumulated over time from $5 trillion to $3 trillion, or 40%. This reduction in private savings is similar to the estimates derived by looking at social security taxes as an alternative to savings.

In a more recent and detailed study, Feldstein estimated social security wealth in 1972 at $1.85 trillion, using the most conservative assumptions.[4] This amount is almost twice the 1972 national income of $952 billion. Compared to the 1972 total financial net worth of the household sector, $2.4 trillion, it again implies a reduction in private savings of about 40%. Compared to total private wealth of households in 1972 of $4 trillion, it implies a reduction in private savings of 32%.

Assuming that social security wealth grew at the same rate as national income, Feldstein estimates that it had reached $3.4 trillion

[3]Martin Feldstein, "Social Security, Induced Retirement, and Aggregate Capital Accumulation," *Journal of Political Economy* 82, no. 5 (Sept.-Oct. 1974).

[4]Martin Feldstein and Anthony Pellechio, "Social Security Wealth: The Impact of Alternative Inflation Adjustments," Conference on Financing Social Security, American Enterprise Institute (Washington, D.C.: 1977).

by the end of the 1978 fiscal year.[5] Feldstein's calculations show that social security wealth has grown rapidly in importance in recent years, from 88% of GNP in 1950, to 133% in 1960, and over 200% in 1975.[6]

Feldstein bases his contention that social security reduces savings on these two arguments, focusing first on taxes, and then on benefits. These two arguments are perfectly consistent with the traditional life-cycle theory of individual consumption-saving behavior that forms a fundamental part of modern economic theory. According to the life-cycle theory, people attempt to even out their consumption over the course of their adult lives. Since the earnings capability of most individuals will increase as they grow older, individuals in their early working years will dissave by spending more than they earn and borrowing to make up the difference. Dissaving allows people to enjoy some of their future expected income earlier in life and thus partially even out their consumption over their working years. As people grow older and their incomes rise, they pay off their debts and begin to save for their retirement years, when their incomes from working will be much lower or nonexistent. This saving again allows individuals to partially even out their consumption over their lives by shifting some of their earnings from their prime earning years to their later retirement years. The life-cycle theory does not suggest that individuals will attempt to exactly even out consumption over their adult lives, but merely that they will shift some of the income from their high earnings years to years of low earnings earlier and later in life.

When a social security program is enacted that pays substantial retirement benefits, those attempting to even out their consumption in accordance with the life-cycle model need to save less during their high earnings years for their retirement years. In fact, if the theory holds, individuals will reduce their savings by the full amount of the present value of the retirement benefits they expect to receive from the program because they will no longer need to save for the portion of their planned retirement incomes provided by the program. In other words, after the program is enacted, people will be able to attain their planned level of retirement and preretirement consumption if, and only if, they view their social security taxes as a alternative to retirement saving and reduce such saving by the full amount

[5]Ibid., p. 11.
[6]Feldstein, "Toward a Reform of Social Security," p. 84.

of those taxes.[7] Since this is the only course of action under which people could attain their most preferred situation, as indicated by their prior choices, they are most likely to pursue this course. Thus the widely accepted life-cycle theory supports Feldstein's view that social security causes a substantial loss of private savings.

Many argue that there is a countervailing effect, fully consistent with life-cycle assumptions, under which social security tends to increase savings. According to this view, social security induces a higher rate of earlier retirement among older persons, and this increased retirement will increase savings. When a man decides to retire earlier than he would have without social security, he will want to make sure that he has sufficient savings to attain his desired consumption level for those additional retirement years. Since social security is likely to provide less than an individual will desire in those years, he is likely to increase his savings so that he can supplement his social security benefits in those years.

This countervailing effect on savings is called the retirement effect. Alicia H. Munnell, assistant vice-president of the Federal Reserve Bank of Boston, developed the theory. The effect tending to decrease savings emphasized by Feldstein is called the asset-substitution effect. Many argue that the impact of social security on savings is theoretically indeterminate because it depends on whether the retirement effect or the asset-substitution effect is stronger, which is an empirical question. The retirement effect theory, however, has two weaknesses that are likely to make it of much less empirical significance than the asset-substitution effect.

The first weakness is the degree to which social security induces earlier retirement. This inducement occurs because the program offers payments to retire at sixty-five, but because of the earnings test a person can receive all the benefits he has paid for only if he keeps his earnings below a certain amount. People who might have retired at a later age will retire at sixty-five to avoid losing the benefits they

[7]The contention that after the program is enacted people will be able to attain the levels of pre-retirement and retirement consumption they planned to attain before the program was enacted is based on the assumption that the implicit rate of return paid on social security taxes is the same as the market rate of return. But as will be discussed in more detail in chapter 4, this assumption appears to be false, and it is made only for the purposes of illustration. The social security rate of return appears to be below the market rate of return. As a result, after the program is imposed individuals will still not be able to attain their planned levels of retirement and pre-retirement consumption, even if they reduce their savings by the full amount of their social security taxes, because they will be poorer.

have paid for. It is the earnings test, not the social security program as a whole, that is the causative agent in this process. Without the earnings test, a person who wanted to retire later could continue to work at age sixty-five and collect his social security payments at the same time, using these funds for his later retirement. Without the earnings test, social security does not make earlier retirement any easier or more likely. If a worker wanted to retire at sixty-five without social security, he could simply save the money that he would otherwise have paid into the program. As long as the rate of return on payments into private alternatives is equal to or greater than the rate of return offered by social security, a social security program without an earnings test would not tend to induce earlier retirement.[8]

Even with the earnings test, however, if people would all have chosen on their own to retire at sixty-five without social security there would be no earlier induced retirement due to the program and therefore no countervailing effect tending to increase savings. The induced early retirement effect can therefore only operate on that portion of the population that would not have retired at sixty-five without social security.

In 1929, 45% of all individuals in the United States were already deciding to retire at sixty-five even without social security. By 1971 this number had risen to only 75%.[9] In 1940 the labor force participation rate for males age sixty-five was 66.9%. By 1970 this had fallen to only 47.1%.[10] In 1950 the labor force participation rate for all males over sixty-five was 45.8% and by 1975 this had fallen to only 21.7%.[11] Most of the induced early retirement effect from social security would have occurred after 1950. These statistics suggest that this effect could have operated on only 20% to 30% of the

---

[8]It is true that for the first generation of retirees in the start-up phase of the program, the rate of return offered by social security is greater than the rate of return from private alternatives. This might make earlier retirement easier, and therefore more likely, for the members of this generation. The effect of this increased wealth in inducing earlier retirement, however, is likely to be moderated by the option of individuals to use the increase instead to increase consumption before or after retirement, rather than choosing earlier retirement. Furthermore, any increase in wealth through this process is small compared to the increase in wealth due to economic growth over time, and therefore any induced retirement from this effect is likely to be relatively small.

[9]Feldstein, "Toward a Reform of Social Security," p. 85.

[10]Alicia Munnell, *The Future of Social Security* (Washington, D.C.: Brookings Institution, 1977), p. 62.

[11]Ibid, p. 70.

population because that is the degree to which retirement at sixty-five seems to have increased since the introduction of social security. It is probable that most of this increase in retirement at sixty-five has been due to increased income and affluence. Indeed, this moderate increase in percentage over the past twenty-five to fifty years would seem perfectly consistent with a gradual trend toward earlier and more frequent retirement as income and affluence increase. These figures do not suggest a big jump in earlier retirement due to the introduction of social security. It may be that the retirement age was politically set at sixty-five because most people would want to retire at that age even without social security. There would therefore be little induced retirement because of the program.

If we assume that at least half of the increased retirement at sixty-five over the last fifty years has occurred because of increasing affluence and other social factors, then induced early retirement due to social security applies to only 10% to 15% of the population. The retirement effect on savings therefore applies only to this portion of the population. The asset-substitution effect, however, applies to 100% of the population. Furthermore, the portion of the population subject to the retirement effect should decline to even lower levels in the future as the percentage of workers who would have retired at sixty-five without social security continues to increase. The retirement effect on savings should therefore decline even further in importance over time. The asset-substitution effect is not subject to any such process of decline in significance, however. In fact, as the social security program continues to expand, the asset-substitution effect will grow even more powerful. This, then, is one set of reasons why the retirement effect is likely to be empirically much less significant than the asset-substitution effect.

The second weakness of the induced retirement effect theory is that the increase in savings due to earlier induced retirement under social security is likely to be small. First, the additional saving that this retirement effect induces is only for the number of years of retirement that a worker would have spent working without social security. The asset-substitution effect applies to all years after the age at which the worker would have retired in the absence of social security, which is likely to be a longer period. Second, the savings induced by the retirement effect are only for the difference between the desired level of consumption in retirement and social security benefits during these extra retirement years. The asset-substitution effect is equal to the full amount of social security benefits for the years in which the worker would have been retired without social security. If the desired level of retirement income is less than twice the level of social security benefits, the asset-substitution effect would be stronger on this count also.

Furthermore, it is quite likely that a person induced to retire earlier under social security will reduce his desired consumption level in retirement because everyone is faced with a budget constraint over his entire life. To save for consumption in retirement, an individual must forgo consumption earlier in life. Without social security, a person would choose a particular retirement age, retirement consumption level and preretirement consumption and savings level based on preferences between consumption early in life and consumption later in life. When social security induces such a person to retire earlier, he has two extreme options. First, in order to maintain his planned retirement consumption at the same level, he may reduce his preretirement consumption level by the entire amount necessary to save enough to supplement social security in the extra retirement years so that his originally planned level of retirement consumption can be reached. This option would make the retirement effect strongest. But an alternative is for the individual to maintain his former preretirement consumption and savings at the same levels and reduce his planned retirement consumption level by spreading his available savings more thinly over the larger number of years. Given that his preferences before social security reflected an equilibrium between both his desire for preretirement consumption and his desire for retirement consumption, he is likely to choose neither of these two extremes but a course of action somewhere in the middle. He would reduce his planned retirement consumption somewhat, while enjoying retirement over a longer number of years, and reduce his preretirement consumption to provide the savings necessary to support the longer period of retirement, albeit at a slightly lower consumption level than previously planned.

In fact, given a person's prior choice of later retirement at a particular consumption level, it would be extremely unlikely for him to choose earlier retirement at the same level of retirement consumption in response to social security. Once the start-up phase of the program has passed, retirement at the earlier age at a given level of retirement consumption is at least as expensive after social security is enacted as before.[12] Yet, given his desired level of preretirement con-

[12]Before social security, a person would have to finance his retirement income by saving during his working years. Now he finances it by paying taxes. If the return on his

sumption, the person had decided that earlier retirement at his preferred retirement consumption level was too expensive. He did not want to give up the required amount of preretirement consumption to attain earlier retirement at his desired retirement income. Earlier retirement at his preferred retirement consumption level is the one option that he explicitly rejected when he made his original choice of later retirement at that consumption level. He decided that at his preferred retirement consumption level he would have to retire at the later age. After social security, that choice is no longer available because the program, particularly because of the earnings test, changes the costs and incentives that the person faces. Because the original choice is no longer available at its original cost, it is not inconsistent, and therefore theoretically possible, for the person to choose the formerly rejected option of earlier retirement at his originally preferred retirement consumption level. But his revealed preferences as suggested by his former choice makes the later choice of this option highly unlikely. If his preferences have not changed, he will still not want to give up the necessary amount of preretirement consumption to achieve this rejected option, even after social security induces earlier retirement. Rather, he is likely to reduce his desired level of retirement consumption a bit so he does not have to sacrifice so much preretirement consumption.

The reduction of his desired level of retirement consumption in response to the earlier induced retirement of social security will have two effects. First, it will lessen the difference between social security benefits and the desired amount of retirement consumption for the years of earlier retirement, and thus the savings induced to make up this difference will be less. Second, it will reduce the planned retirement consumption for the years after the original planned age of retirement, resulting in a decrease of savings for those years that will offset to a large extent the increase in savings for the earlier induced

---

savings is the same as on his taxes under social security, it will be just as expensive to finance a certain retirement level before social security as after it. In the start-up phase, returns on social security taxes will be higher than market returns, making retirement cheaper, because the program has just been recently enacted and the early beneficiaries have paid taxes for so few years. Over time, therefore, as the program matures, these returns will fall below market levels. Any induced savings effect from social security due to these high returns will thus last only a short time, but it is not clear exactly what impact on savings these higher-than-market returns will have. Because of these higher returns, the individual worker may simply not need much additional savings to supplement social security to reach his desired consumption level in retirement, and savings may therefore actually decrease.

retirement years. This decrease is not likely to more than offset the increase because in response to earlier induced retirement the individual will surely save at least as much as before during his preretirement years, at the most maintaining, and not increasing, his previous level of preretirement consumption.

Putting the two weak links together, we find that the retirement effect applies only to the percentage of the population which is induced to retire early, about 10–15% by crude estimates, while the asset-substitution effect applies to the whole population. We find that this percentage is likely to decline further in the future, leading to a decline in the significance of the retirement effect while the asset-substitution effect will continue to increase in significance. We find that even for this portion of the population the retirement effect applies only for the years of earlier induced retirement, while the asset-substitution effect applies to all years after the originally planned retirement age. Furthermore, even for the years of earlier retirement, the retirement effect applies only to the difference between the desired consumption level in retirement and social security benefits, while the asset-substitution effect applies to the amount of all social security benefits for all years after a worker's originally planned retirement age. We find also that this difference is likely to be reduced in response to the earlier induced retirement, largely offsetting any increase in savings. Savings for consumption in the later, originally planned retirement years are also likely to be reduced somewhat in response to the earlier induced retirement, further offsetting any increase in savings. As a result, even for the portion of the population induced to retire early, the asset-substitution effect is likely to dwarf the retirement effect.

Nevertheless, despite the improbability that the retirement effect is anywhere near as large as the asset-substitution effect, Feldstein accepts the proposition that the impact of social security on savings is theoretically indeterminate. However, he has completed several empirical studies that measure the relative magnitudes of these effects. Feldstein concludes from these studies that "It is clear that even if half of the increase in retirement were attributable to social security, the reduction in savings due to the replacement of private wealth by social security 'wealth' is almost certain to be much greater than the effect on savings of induced retirement."[13]

In an econometric study of savings behavior in the United States

13Feldstein, "Toward a Reform of Social Security," p. 81.

since 1929, Feldstein estimated the net impact of social security on the nation's private savings.[14] He concluded that social security reduced personal savings in 1971 by between $40 and $60 billion as compared to an actual level of personal savings in 1971 of $61 billion. This suggests that social security reduced personal savings by between 40% and 50% and total savings, including corporate savings, by between 32% and 42%. These estimates are close to the crude estimates obtained above by assuming that taxpayers reduce their savings by the full amount of social security taxes.

In another study, Feldstein examined international savings data and compared it to the differing social security programs in the different countries.[15] He concluded that countries with higher social security benefits and more complete coverage of the population by a social security program had lower rates of private savings.

Feldstein's empirical studies thus support the theoretical analysis presented here. The asset-substitution effect, tending to decrease savings, is much stronger than the retirement effect, tending to increase savings. The net result is that social security causes severe losses in private savings because of its pay-as-you-go method of financing. The immediate effect of reduced savings is a reduced stock of capital. It is savings alone that provides the resources for the nation's capital investment. Less savings and more consumption means less capital.

There has been much talk in recent years about a capital shortage. The heavy burdens of taxation and government regulation have slowed this country's investment in needed new capital equipment with the result that America today has one of the lowest rates of capital investment among the world's developed countries. Whether this phenomenon is referred to as a capital shortage or a capital crisis or by some other phrase, the truth is that new capital investment in the American economy is vitally needed. It is needed to modernize our factories to enable them to compete with foreign production and to improve the productivity of American workers. It is needed to finance the development and innovation of new technologies. It is needed to finance the discovery and development of new energy sources. It is needed to finance new pollution equipment that will

[14]Feldstein, "Social Security, Induced Retirement, and Aggregate Capital Accumulation."

[15]Martin Feldstein, "Social Security and Private Savings, International Evidence in an Extended Life Cycle Model," *Harvard Institute of Economic Research, Discussion Paper No. 361,* 1974.

enhance environmental quality and new medical equipment that will improve the quality of medical care. It is needed to finance the creation of new jobs and to upgrade existing ones. It is needed to build new homes and to finance construction to revitalize our urban centers. It is needed to finance the production of all the goods and services that Americans want to improve the quality of their lives. To the extent that social security discourages savings, it exacerbates the capital shortage and prevents the accumulation of needed capital for these critical and important uses.

The importance of the loss of this capital investment can be seen in the impact of this loss on national income and economic growth. With less capital, fewer of the nation's resources are devoted to production and to the materials necessary to increase that production. The result is less production and lower levels of national income and economic growth. By Feldstein's calculations, if social security reduces savings by 35%, then in the long run capital stock without social security would be 80% higher than it is today.[16] With this additional capital, Feldstein calculates that GNP would be 19% higher each year.[17] In 1975, then, in the absence of social security, GNP would have been increased by more than $285 billion. As Feldstein notes, in 1975 this was nearly 30% of total consumer spending, more than twice the total of individual income tax payments and substantially more than twice the level of national defense expenditures.[18] The total loss in GNP amounted to $1,300 per person and $3,500 per family.

In 1976 GNP totaled $1,700 billion. Without social security, GNP in that year would have been increased by $323 billion. In 1977 GNP totaled $1,887 billion. Without social security, GNP would have been increased in that year by $358.5 billion. In 1978 GNP was estimated at $2,017 billion. Without social security, GNP would have been increased in 1978 by $400.3 billion. Thus in a four-year period from 1975 to 1978 social security needlessly cost the American people $1,367 billion, or about $1 1/3 trillion in national income. This total loss amounted to $6,200 per person and $16,800 per family. This is what is meant when it is said that the negative impacts of social security have become too serious to be ignored. In

[16]Martin Feldstein, "Social Insurance," *Harvard Institute of Economic Research, Discussion Paper No. 477*, 1974, p. 31.
[17]Ibid.
[18]Ibid.

discussing this disastrous impact on national income Feldstein says, "Let me emphasize that this lower level of GNP reflects the pay-as-you-go nature of our social security system. It is because social security taxes are used to pay concurrent benefits that the capital stock is smaller and income is less than it would otherwise be."[19] This loss of national income, as well as savings and capital investment, is only likely to get much worse as the huge tax burdens in future years take their toll.

Feldstein's analysis is intuitively appealing, theoretically sound, and empirically well-supported, yet his empirical conclusion that social security substantially reduces private saving has become the focus of some controversy.

One of the staunchest critics of Feldstein's position is Robert Barro, professor of economics at the University of Rochester. In an article published in 1974, Barro argued that any negative impact on savings due to the asset-substitution effect of social security would be largely offset by savings induced by the program through a full bequest motive on the part of parents.[20] Barro argued that in the absence of social security, parents would plan to save a certain amount over their lives so that, after their death, they could leave an estate or bequest to their children. With social security, parents would realize that the program was imposing a forced transfer of income from their children to them and that this was undermining the parents' planned bequests to their children. Instead of receiving the full amount of their parents' planned bequests, the children would receive this amount minus the transfer imposed by social security. Barro argued that parents would try to offset this reduction in their bequests by increasing their savings over their lives so that they could leave a larger estate or bequest to their children. Parents would in fact attempt to increase their final estate by the full amount of the transfer imposed by social security so that they would effectively leave to their children the equivalent of what they originally intended to leave. Since the amount of this transfer is equal to the amount of taxes collected from children over the years, parents would increase their saving by the amount of these taxes to increase their final estate by the necessary amount. Thus even if children reduced their savings by the full amount of such taxes because of the asset-substitution effect, this reduction in savings

[19]Ibid., p. 32.

[20]Robert J. Barro, "Are Government Bonds Net Wealth?" *Journal of Political Economy* 82 (Nov./Dec. 1974) pp. 1095–1117.

would be completely offset by increased savings by parents due to the bequest motive.

In a later paper Barro suggested a second process by which any reduction in saving due to social security would be largely offset.[21] Barro argued that in the absence of social security, retired people would be supported by direct payments from their children rather than by their own accumulated savings. Their children would then expect to be supported in retirement by direct payments from *their* own children and would not save for their retirement. When social security is imposed, individuals would then simply reduce their direct payments to their retired parents and there would be no effect on savings. Social security would simply be replacing a private pay-as-you-go system with a public pay-as-you-go system.

In this later paper Barro presented an econometric analysis of consumption behavior in the United States from 1929 to 1974. This analysis was based on assumptions quite different from those used by Feldstein. On the basis of this analysis, Barro concluded that there was no evidence that social security significantly reduced private saving. Barro contended that this result was due to the two processes he had described — increased savings by parents as a result of the bequest motive and decreased direct payments from children to parents rather than decreased savings.

Another major critic of Feldstein is Alicia Munnell. Running her own econometric analyses, again on assumptions different from those used by Feldstein, Munnell concluded that social security reduced private saving by about 5% rather than the much greater reductions estimated by Feldstein.[22] Munnell believes that this small reduction is due to the power of the retirement effect in inducing substantial savings to offset the savings lost as a result of the asset-substitution effect. There are other critics of Feldstein, but these two are the most significant.[23]

The counterarguments advanced by Feldstein's critics remain un-

[21]Robert J. Barro, *The Impact of Social Security on Private Saving* (Washington, D.C.: American Enterprise Institute, 1977).

[22]Alicia H. Munnell, "The Impact of Social Security on Personal Savings," *National Tax Journal* 27 (December, 1974), pp. 553–67.

[23]A critic who emphasizes an entirely different effect of the program, one that he contends mitigates any loss of savings, is Michael E. Darby in *The Effects of Social Security on Income and the Capital Stock* (Washington, D.C.: American Enterprise Institute, 1979). Darby contends that because the implicit rate of return paid on social security taxes is less than market rates of return, the wealth value of a person's income over his life will be less after the program is imposed. To make up for this decrease in

convincing for several reasons. First, it is highly improbable that the various effects that these critics allege serve to offset or mitigate the asset-substitution effect really have any significant impact. We have already discussed the many reasons why it is quite unlikely that the retirement effect could induce enough additional savings to overcome the powerful impact of the asset-substitution effect. As noted earlier, the retirement effect is solely due to the earnings test. This seems like an awfully thin reed on which to base an effect that is supposed to induce several hundred billion dollars in increased savings, if not more. Furthermore, as also noted earlier, over time the number of people who would have retired at sixty-five even without social security has undoubtedly grown, consistent with historical trends and growth in wealth and income over the years, and this increase will simply continue. The retirement effect, therefore, should have an even more sharply diminished impact now and in the future as the number of people who could be induced by social security to retire earlier than otherwise has become much smaller than in the past. Actions taken by Congress in recent years to weaken the earnings test can only accelerate this trend. Indeed, Congress may

---

wealth, people will increase their savings and reduce their consumption. The meaning and significance of this effect is worth clarifying.

When the rate of return paid by social security is less than the market rate of return, the value of the benefits a person receives from the program is less than the value of the taxes he pays in (once the start-up phase is over). Darby's argument amounts to the correct proposition that in this case people are unlikely to reduce their savings on net by the full amount of their social security taxes. The asset-substitution effect will still induce them to initially reduce their savings by the full amount of these taxes. But because these taxes are not now providing them with as much retirement income as when the same amounts were saved at market rates of return, they will have to increase their savings to attain the same level of retirement income as they planned to attain before the program was imposed. To attain the same level, people will have to increase their savings by the full amount of the difference between the value of the program's taxes and the value of the program's benefits. On net, therefore, people will reduce their savings by at least as much as the present value of the program's benefits.

But since people are now poorer after the program is imposed, they will also probably reduce their planned level of retirement income, and therefore they will not need to increase their savings as much after the initial reduction. In fact, if people accommodate their new poorer status after the program is imposed by making all the necessary consumption cuts in their retirement consumption and none in their pre-retirement consumption, they will not need to increase their savings at all in response to their new poorer status, and the net result will be a reduction in savings by the full amount of social security taxes. It is more likely, however, that some of these cuts will be in retirement consumption and some in pre-retirement consumption so that the net reduction in savings will be somewhere between the value of the program's benefits and the value of the program's taxes.

We may note this same effect by focusing on benefits rather than taxes. Even when

eliminate the earnings test completely in the near future, completely eliminating the retirement effect as well.

Any significant impact on savings from Barro's full bequest theory is even more unlikely. His theory is in fact inconsistent with the very existence of the social security program. If people feel that they have to increase their savings over their lives to offset the main intended effect of social security in transferring income from their children to them, then why do we have the program in the first place? It is brutally obvious that there is no widespread feeling among the public that people must increase their savings to make a bequest to their children. On the contrary, most people believe that social security imposes a transfer from children to parents that ought to be made, and that is why we have the program.

Indeed, we may ask further just exactly when Barro's full bequest saving is to occur. When social security is first imposed, the program begins to transfer income immediately from the first generation of workers to their parents, the first generation of retirees. If Barro's theory holds, then this first generation of retirees would have to sharply increase their savings to offset this transfer. It is clear, however, that no such increase in savings occurred among the first gen-

---

the social security rate of return is less than market rate of return, people will still increase their savings by the present value of social security benefits because they no longer need to provide for this portion of their retirement income. In addition, because they are now poorer after the program is imposed, they are likely to reduce their planned retirement income levels somewhat and therefore will reduce their retirement savings even further. In fact, if they make all the necessary consumption cuts to accommodate their new poorer status in their retirement consumption, and none in their pre-retirement consumption, they will then reduce their savings by the full amount of their social security taxes. It is more likely, however, that they will make some cuts in their planned retirement consumption and some in their pre-retirement consumption and therefore that they will reduce savings somewhere between the value of the program's benefits and the value of the program's taxes.

Darby's argument does not represent a modification of Feldstein's analysis but merely an application of it to new circumstances. Even when the social security rate of return is less than the market rate of return, people will still reduce their savings by at least as much as the present value of social security benefits, as Feldstein contends. Although this value is no longer equal to the value of the taxes paid into the program, which is much greater, the actual amount of savings lost is most likely to be somewhere between these two values. Most important of all, the difference between these two values represents the minimum amount of wealth that people lose because of the program. Thus the amount of wealth lost will be even greater than the difference between the actual amount of savings lost and the value of social security taxes. Making people poorer is hardly a comforting way to mitigate any loss of savings caused by the program, if this difference indeed represents such a mitigation. This analysis merely suggests further negative impacts that demand the same solution. These negative impacts are discussed in more detail in chapter 4.

eration of retirees in the start-up phase of America's social security program. The members of this generation were considered relatively poor and in need of social security benefits to purchase basic necessities. The level of social security benefits they did receive was generally perceived as inadequate to provide for all their needs. It should be beyond contention that the members of the first retired generation consumed their social security benefits; they did not save them to leave them to their children, as Barro's theory suggests.

No such increased bequest saving would occur among the first generation of workers after the imposition of social security, either. The program imposes a transfer from this generation to their parents, the first retired generation. The individuals in the first working generation are not now going to feel compelled as well to save and leave a bequest to their children, the second working generation, in order to offset the transfer imposed by the program from this second working generation to them, the first working generation (or second retired generation). The members of the first working generation are simply going to feel that the transfer from the second generation to them is repayment for the initial transfer from the first working generation to the first retired generation.

At no point, therefore, after the imposition of the social security program is there any plausible possibility of increased savings in accordance with Barro's full bequest theory. A more detailed examination of the distribution of savings in the United States would further indicate the implausibility of Barro's theory. The great majority of savings and wealth in this country is held by a relatively small percentage of the population. This savings is not held for bequests or even for retirement but for the purpose of storing wealth and earning more wealth through investments. Even in the presence of social security, the great majority of the population has very little savings for bequests and very few significant bequests are actually passed along to children. We should note the irony that one of the popularly accepted rationales for the social security program is that people are too shortsighted to save on their own for retirement. Barro contends that, on the contrary, not only are individuals not too shortsighted to save for their retirement and for bequests to children, but that they are so farsighted that they will offset any transfer imposed by social security through increased bequest savings. There is little support in theory or in practice for Barro's notion that any such increased bequest saving is significant.

Although this analysis should dispose of Barro's full bequest theory, we should mention Feldstein's response to Barro.[24] Feldstein's counterargument is based on the fact that, because of technical progress and economic growth, children will tend to be wealthier than their parents were. Parents are therefore likely to feel that it is worth more to them to increase their consumption now than to forgo that consumption and save for bequests so that their children can increase their already greater consumption later. In economic terms, the marginal utility to the parent of additional consumption now is likely to be greater than the indirect marginal utility to the parent of additional consumption in later years by the child precisely because in those later years the child is likely to be richer than the parent is now. As a result, Feldstein argues, most parents are not likely to plan any significant bequests to their children. In fact, because children are likely to be richer than their parents were and because of sociological factors such as the support of children by their parents when the children were young, most parents are likely to believe that their children should transfer income to them in their old age. In other words, most parents are likely to prefer a negative bequest to themselves rather than a positive bequest to their children, as Barro suggests. A desire for significant, positive bequests is likely only among the very wealthy because without such bequests the children will in fact not be as rich as their parents were. This view is more consistent with actual savings and bequests behavior in America.

In the absence of social security, since parents cannot enforce their negative bequest preference, they will respond simply by choosing to make no positive bequest or any savings for such bequest. When social security is imposed, the parents' preference for a negative bequest is satisfied, and they will feel no obligation to increase savings and make a positive bequest to offset the social security transfer. There will therefore be no additional savings to offset the savings lost through the asset-substitution effect. Feldstein concludes, "It is clear that, for the vast majority of the population and therefore for most of the social security benefits, there are no significant bequests to children even in the presence of our current social security system. There is no evidence at all that the typical retired person wishes to offset social security's intergenerational transfer from the young to the old."[25]

---

[24]Barro, *The Impact of Social Security on Private Saving*, pp. 37–47.
[25]Ibid, p. 40.

The most plausible theory under which the loss of savings due to the asset-substitution effect might be mitigated is Barro's suggestion that social security merely replaces a private system of pay-as-you-go transfers, and therefore in response to the social security program people would merely reduce direct payments to their retired parents rather than any savings for their own retirement. Even this theory, however, is somewhat inconsistent with the existence of the program. If social security really does simply replace a private system of direct transfer payments, then, again, why do we have the program? We have the program precisely because most people believe that without it such transfers would not take place.

But the primary reason that a major impact from this effect remains unlikely is that without the social security program people are more likely to save and invest for their own retirement support rather than provide direct payments to their parents and then rely on their own children for retirement support in turn. Of course, if people would prefer this course, then social security would cause the substantial reduction in savings suggested by Feldstein rather than merely a reduction in direct transfers as suggested by Barro.

There are several reasons why people are indeed likely to prefer this course. Most Americans today have sufficient income to save enough over their working years to support themselves in retirement, especially if they did not have to pay social security taxes over those working years. Given this capability, most Americans are likely to prefer such savings for their retirement support, rather than relying on their children, simply because this alternative would give them more control over the level of their retirement incomes, make those incomes more certain and secure, and remove a burden from their children.

Even more important, however, is the fact that saving and investing for their own retirement would enable individuals to have higher retirement incomes at lower cost because the investments would earn a rate of return that could also be added to the amounts accumulated for retirement. If a person instead supported his retired parents with direct payments and in turn was directly supported in his retirement by his children, this rate of return on investments would be lost. Relying solely on their children, individuals could not even count on the rate of return implicit in social security, which, as we shall see in chapter 4, is much less than the return available through an invested system. As chapter 4 will show in detail, the loss of private investment returns for one's retirement provisions means the loss of enormously greater retirement benefits. Since most individuals now have sufficient incomes to save and invest for their own retirement and since the returns on such investments would be relatively high, it is unlikely that a large number of people would forgo this route to participate in a system of private, direct transfers from parents to children.

Another reason that a major impact from this effect remains unlikely is that the theory on which it is based relies on an outdated conception of the American family. We no longer live in an age of extended, closely-knit families. For better or for worse, people are today more independent of the family, taking more responsibility for their own support and less responsibility for the support of other family members. More and more children move away from their parents' home town. The great majority of the elderly now live apart from their children. Children from the same family follow diverse careers. Couples divorce and remarry more frequently. A system of private pay-as-you-go transfers is poorly suited to these modern American trends and is therefore unlikely as an alternative to social security. It seems far more in accordance with this modern setting for each individual or married couple to save for their own retirement. Indeed we may ask how Barro's system of private direct transfers is supposed to work at all for the growing number of people who are choosing to forgo marriage and children altogether or the growing number choosing to have very small families. It should be apparent, at any rate, that most Americans today do not think of their children as a major potential source of old-age support.

The direct empirical evidence available supports the belief that without social security people are quite unlikely to provide private, direct income transfer payments anywhere near as large as those imposed by the program. Thus, Feldstein writes,

> the survey evidence on gifts from children to retired parents shows that this second case is also of very limited importance. At no time have more than a small fraction of the retired received gifts from their children; moreover, the average gift received has been extremely small in comparison with concurrent income levels or to the corresponding rate of social security benefits to income today. It is beyond belief that the current working generation would, in the absence of social security, make gifts totaling $100 billion to retired parents in 1977.[26]

It appears, therefore, that without social security people are far

---

[26]Ibid, p. 41.

more likely to save for their own support in retirement rather than rely on their children for such support. The very large amounts invested in private pension systems, IRAs, and other retirement savings vehicles each year, compared with the small amount of direct support from children to retired parents each year, is further evidence favoring this view.

While the effects emphasized by Feldstein's critics appear implausible, the effect emphasized by Feldstein seems plausible. It seems reasonable to expect that without social security people would generally save something approaching the percentage of their income they are currently paying in social security taxes to provide for their retirement. With social security they are likely to reduce their private savings by this amount, feeling that they are saving for their retirement through the government program.

The effects emphasized by Feldstein's critics undoubtedly have some impact in mitigating the loss of savings caused by social security, but hardly enough to make an overwhelming difference. Even if social security reduced savings by half the amount suggested by Feldstein's studies, the resulting losses of capital investment, national income, and economic growth would still be enormous.

A second reason why Feldstein's critics remain unconvincing is that their counterarguments do not blunt the force of Feldstein's critique of the program, but rather merely change, or even add to, his indictment. For example, even if the retirement effect induced enough additional savings to fully offset the asset-substitution effect, this would not mean that the program had two mutually correcting effects but rather two negative effects, each obscuring the other. If social security did have a retirement effect this strong, then it would be forcing large numbers of people who did not want to save any more and retire earlier to do both, thereby depriving them of their preferred course of action. Yet, through the asset-substitution effect, the program would still be preventing those who did want to save and retire early from engaging in such saving. These are both negative effects on the economy, causing misallocation and inefficiency. The first effect prevents people from following a preferred course of action, making them worse off. The second effect decreases savings and consequently decreases capital investment, national income, and economic growth. In this event, the government would simply be forcing those to save who did not wish to save, but preventing those from saving who did wish to save. This is not sound public policy; this is nonsense. The retirement effect therefore does not correct for social security's negative effects on the economy but rather worsens them.

If, as Barro contends, individuals really did eliminate any decreased savings effect from the program by increasing bequest savings and decreasing direct transfer payments, then the program would simply be silly and irrelevant. In Barro's world the program would be forcing those who did not want to receive a transfer from their children to engage in extra saving to offset the program's transfer, and forcing those who did want to make such a transfer to make it through the program and eliminate their own direct payments. If this were indeed the case, social security could be eliminated immediately at this moment. Those who were seeking to offset the program through increased bequest saving could then use these savings for their retirement. Those who were reducing their own direct private transfers could then resume such transfers with the money they would have paid in social security taxes. The elimination of the program in this case would have important beneficial effects for everyone. Those who wanted to receive the higher market investment returns rather than participate in social security or a private pay-as-you-go system would be free to make this choice. Those who continued to make direct payments to their retired parents would have a better idea than the government of their parents' needs and could therefore better care for them.

A third reason why Feldstein's critics remain unconvincing is that they place far too much reliance on empirical, econometric studies of doubtful usefulness. Millions of factors influenced consumption and savings behavior in the United States from 1929 to 1974. Empirical studies that fail to find any loss of savings due to social security during this period remain open to two possible interpretations: (1) There was no such loss of savings over this period; or (2) The available econometric tools are incapable of finding it amid the mass of real-world data and complex web of real-world factors. When there are strong theoretical reasons for believing that such a savings loss does exist, when the proposed countereffects seem quite implausible, and when there is no reason to believe that if this loss did exist the empirical studies would necessarily be able to find it, then the latter interpretation appears to be the most appropriate.

What the critics of Feldstein claim to find in their studies is that there was no increase in consumption relative to income, and therefore no decline in savings, in response to social security. But social security could have caused a loss in savings without causing an increase in consumption relative to income. It could be that without the program, consumption would have declined relative to income while savings increased, and that the program aborted this change, thereby causing a loss of savings. This is the more likely chain of events because over time savings relative to income should have increased as people became richer, more and more chose to retire and to retire earlier, retired people began to live longer, and more people would have chosen without social security to rely on savings for their retirement rather than on their children. The studies of Feldstein's critics do not preclude the possibility that this is in fact what occurred.

The difficulties inherent in econometric analysis are clearly illustrated by the methodological disputes between Feldstein and his critics. Feldstein is able to isolate in his studies a substantial negative impact by social security on savings. His critics contend that he is able to do so because he leaves out of the consumption function in his studies variables for the unemployment rate and government surplus and that when these variables are included, as they are in their studies, one cannot find any such negative impact. Feldstein counters that these variables should be excluded, and he argues his case masterfully.[27]

Yet, this debate is really a debate over how to sort out the complex of real-world factors and data. Feldstein's critics have the easier side in the debate because, if the effect of social security cannot be precisely separated from the numerous other real-world effects on savings and therefore cannot be empirically demonstrated, they can always argue that there is thus "no evidence" to support the view that social security substantially reduces savings. These critics do leave one with the impression that they are resisting Feldstein's very skillful econometric work in isolating the impact of social security and that they are relying in rebuttal on the otherwise great difficulty in isolating the impact of the program, probably because of the public policy implications of Feldstein's work. At any rate, to the extent that this debate is ultimately unresolvable, it simply illustrates the inability of econometric analysis to precisely sort out real-world causes and effects and therefore to definitively resolve the question of the impact of social security on saving.

Since one cannot rely solely on econometric analysis to resolve this question, one must also rely on judgments based on theoretical

[27]Ibid., pp. 37–47.

analysis, the plausibility of the various positions taken, and sociological understanding of how people would behave without the program. As noted earlier, these factors all support Feldstein's position that social security substantially reduces private savings. This is not to say that the econometric work should be ignored, for there is a substantial, persuasive, and growing body of work in support of Feldstein's position. But in drawing conclusions from this work we must consider these other factors as well, and when these factors are considered Feldstein's critics remain unconvincing.

The fourth, and probably most important, reason why Feldstein's critics are unconvincing is that the real issue in the debate over social security is not what happened in the past but what is most likely to occur in the future. If the program were phased out today, would there be a sharp increase in savings approaching the magnitude suggested by Feldstein? There are several factors, in addition to those discussed above, that strongly suggest that the answer is yes.

Of course, much would depend on how the program was phased out or reformed. Under a proposal like that advanced in chapter 11, benefits currently promised to beneficiaries would continue to be paid out of general revenues, and working people would be able to save and invest the amounts they would have paid in social security taxes in special, tax-exempt retirement accounts.

In response to such a reform, people would almost certainly save and invest an amount equal to the present value of the social security benefits they would have been entitled to if the present program had continued, because they will have to replace this portion of their retirement incomes. Because the implicit rate of return paid by social security is less than market rates of return,[28] this present value of the benefits will be less than the value of the taxes that would have been paid into the program. It is likely that people will be richer after the reform than they are now because they will be receiving higher rates of return on the amounts they are now paying in social security taxes. Because they will be richer, they are likely to increase their planned retirement consumption somewhat and therefore to increase their current saving above the present value of the social security benefits that they would have been entitled to in order to provide for this portion of their retirement incomes. If people choose to devote all their increased wealth to retirement consumption, they will increase their savings to the full value of the taxes they would have paid into the program. In response to the

[28]This point will be demonstrated in detail in chapters 4 and 9.

reform, therefore, individuals will increase their savings by an amount somewhere between the present value of the benefits they would have been entitled to under social security and the full value of the taxes paid into the program.

Another factor tending to increase savings in response to the reform is that the retirement accounts, with their high, untaxed returns, would present a unique wealth-producing opportunity. These retirement accounts would, in fact, represent a large tax break for investment income, increasing the return to investments, and therefore they should induce additional amounts of saving and investment, apart from that for retirement. These additional savings would all flow into the retirement accounts in order to qualify for the tax advantages. This effect is more likely to be substantial if individuals are allowed to withdraw before retirement some or all of the amounts saved in these accounts or to use some of the funds in the accounts to make investments with current benefits, such as the purchase of a home or a private business. In any event, this effect tends to cause the additional savings induced by the reform to be closer to the full value of the social security taxes that would have been paid into the program.

It is highly unlikely that people would respond to the reform by using any of the amounts they would have paid in social security taxes to provide direct cash grants to their retired parents and relatives because these retired persons will still be receiving social security benefits. It is also highly unlikely that people will fail to save for their retirement and look to their children for retirement support. Because social security has largely replaced direct retirement support from children to parents, children today are not thought of as a major potential source of retirement support. After so many years with an institutional background largely preempting such direct support and leading to decay of the social ties necessary for such support, it is quite unlikely that such support would now be forthcoming when that institutional background is suddenly changed. Modern trends such as fewer closely-knit families, fewer and less stable marriages, and the declining birth rate make heavy reliance on such direct cash payments even less likely. Furthermore, after the reform current workers would have been relieved of the burden of supporting their parents directly, and thus they would hardly have a substantial moral claim for such support from their own children. Finally, as noted earlier, individuals relying on their own savings rather than on their children for retirement support would have higher retirement incomes, more control over those incomes, and more certainty concerning those incomes. Given the lucrative retirement account investment opportunity and the funds to take advantage of it (the amounts that would have been paid in social security taxes), people are far more likely to take the savings approach and obtain these advantages rather than rely on their children.

It is also highly unlikely that there would be a substantial increase in the number of people choosing to forgo retirement, and therefore retirement savings, in response to the reform. Consistent with historical trends toward earlier and more frequent retirement, social security would be inducing far less additional retirement now and in the future than in the past. Even more importantly, the reform would have a strong impact in actually making retirement more likely because it would be easier for people to attain attractive retirement income levels through the higher market returns paid on savings. People who had resigned themselves to retiring under social security would be strongly encouraged to maintain those plans by the higher retirement incomes available after the reform. Finally, even those who did not plan to retire or who planned to retire later than usual are quite likely to be induced by the lucrative retirement account opportunities to save in these accounts a substantial portion of the amounts they would have paid in social security taxes. They would earn increased wealth that could be used to increase consumption after sixty-five. There is therefore likely to be little net effect on savings because of changes in retirement plans after the reform.

Chapter 11 also discusses the possibility that the reform could include a requirement that individuals save for their retirement all or a portion of the amounts they would have paid in social security taxes. This requirement would make an increase in savings approaching or exceeding the magnitude suggested by Feldstein quite likely. Although people might decrease other savings if the retirement attempted to force them to save more than they wanted to, this would occur only if these other savings were not held for use in preretirement years. If these savings were held to increase wealth for consumption in later preretirement years, for example, then such savings could not be replaced by forced retirement savings. In addition, such a reduction could only occur to the extent that individuals had other savings to decrease, and a substantial portion of the population has very little such savings.

Thus, considering what is most likely to happen in the future rather than what has happened in the past, it seems even more likely that in the absence of social security there would be an increase in savings approaching the magnitude suggested by Feldstein. The countervailing effects advanced by Feldstein's critics have even less plausibility under future changed circumstances, and their empirical studies of past behavior also have less relevance. Since continuing social security in its present form would prevent this massive increase in savings from occurring, the program is causing a loss of savings of this magnitude.

Perhaps the best way to analyze the problem of social security's impact on savings is in terms of opportunity cost. No one disputes that social security taxes are not saved but immediately paid out on a pay-as-you-go basis. Feldstein's analysis shows that if this tax money were saved and invested, the GNP would be increased by at least the enormous amounts described above. Social security is, therefore, forcing Americans to provide for their retirement through an inefficient pay-as-you-go system rather than through a superior alternative where funds are invested. The program is forcing Americans to miss an opportunity to provide for their retirement in a more efficient manner that will result in increases in national income of several hundred billion dollars a year. Funding retirement through social security thus entails an opportunity cost of this magnitude.

Viewed in these terms, the issue is not whether Americans in the absence of social security would have saved as much as they pay into the program now, but whether it is worth saving and investing, through an alternative system, the huge sums that are now paid into social security, considering the large investment returns that would result. Whether this investment could be better accomplished through government or private institutions and whether it should be mandatory or voluntary are separate issues that will be discussed later. The large increases in capital, national income, and economic growth that would result from investing these funds suggests that such investments would be well worthwhile. There do not seem to be any advantages from the pay-as-you-go nature of social security that would justify forgoing these large investment returns. In fact, pay-as-you-go financing has several additional shortcomings that will be discussed in later chapters.

In one of his first studies on the impact of social security on savings, Feldstein dealt with the issue of whether the return from investing social security taxes was worth the investment. Feldstein noted that by focusing on this issue, "the problem is posed in such a way that the conclusions do not depend on the extent to which social security benefits are assumed to affect private savings."[29]

Feldstein concluded that investment of the money currently paid in social security taxes would increase national wealth by approximately $2 trillion and make everyone better off in monetary terms. Feldstein concluded further that, given the choices Americans make when faced with similar options in the marketplace, the investment of these funds for this return would be well worthwhile.

Ultimately, when viewed in opportunity cost terms, the issue is not even whether the investment of social security taxes would be worth the returns. The real issue is whether Americans should be forced to forgo these enormous returns and to bear this enormous opportunity cost. The real issue is whether Americans should be allowed the opportunity to provide for their retirement in a more efficient manner that will increase national income by several hundred billion dollars a year. As will become more apparent in succeeding chapters, there are no compensating, offsetting benefits from forcing all Americans to participate in social security's pay-as-you-go system and therefore in forcing Americans to bear this opportunity cost. Given this fact, it seems ludicrous to continue to impose the program in its current state, with this attendant opportunity cost, on the American people. (We should note that Feldstein's critics do not even address the savings issue in terms of opportunity cost.)

The negative economic effects of social security are all caused by the conflict between the welfare and insurance objectives of the program. The pay-as-you-go method of financing the program is the result of the pursuit of welfare objectives through social security. The program operates in this way because in the early years Congress felt that current retirees needed higher benefits than they had paid for in past taxes. As a result, taxes were not saved and invested but immediately paid out to these recipients. Because of this, there was no fund to finance future benefits, and all these benefits had to be paid out of current taxes on a pay-as-you-go basis as well. Thus the program operates on a pay-as-you-go basis because it pursued the welfare objective of paying benefits to those in the start-up phase who had paid little into the system themselves. The pursuit of this

[29]Martin Feldstein, "The Optimal Financing of Social Security," Panel of Actuaries and Economists, 1974 Advisory Council on Social Security.

welfare objective through social security meant that the insurance objectives of social security had to be pursued on a pay-as-you-go basis as well, resulting in all the negative economic impacts described above. If retirees in the start-up phase were truly needy, they could have been provided with welfare benefits directly from general revenues, and the negative effects would not have occurred.

National income losses of the magnitude suggested by Feldstein's work are plainly intolerable, especially because the loss is unnecessary. The only remaining question is what to do about these losses. Feldstein recommends that the government save and invest social security tax payments in a trust fund that can then be used to pay future benefits, but there are other possible solutions to this problem. Feldstein's reform proposals and others will be discussed later.

Labor, Employment, and Economic Efficiency

Social security has three separate effects that tend to distort the labor supply, discourage employment, and create economic inefficiencies. These effects have been emphasized by Arthur B. Laffer, professor of business economics at the University of Southern California and Dr. David Ranson, a Boston-based economist and consultant.[30] The first effect is caused by the payroll tax, which creates a wedge between what an employer pays and what an employee receives. The second effect is caused by the earnings test. The third effect is the result of the decreased capital supply, which is caused by the reduction in savings discussed above.

The Wedge Effect As noted in the discussion of the incidence of the payroll tax in chapter 2, the payroll tax creates a wedge between what the employer pays and what the employee receives. This wedge is equal to the full amount of the social security tax, including both the employer's and the employee's shares, and is borne entirely by the employee. As a result of this wedge, the employee will never receive full value for his work and the full amount paid by his em-

[30]The concept of the wedge has been emphasized by Professor Laffer in much of his writings. For the application of this concept to social security, as well as a discussion of the other problems noted in this section, see Arthur B. Laffer and R. David Ranson, "Some Economic Consequences of the U.S. Social Security System," National Tax Association/Tax Institute of America, Proceedings of the 66th Annual Conference (Toronto, 1973) and Arthur B. Laffer "Comments on the Social Security System," Conference on Ethics and the Aging Society, 1977.

ployer, but only this amount minus the wedge or tax. This wedge or tax thus reduces the compensation of workers and therefore discourages them from working, resulting in a reduced labor supply and reduced employment. The payroll tax is essentially a tax on employment and as always the result of taxing something is that there is less of it.

Workers who are likely to be able to vary their labor supply easily in response to the wage rate are especially affected by the payroll tax. Part-time workers and secondary workers who are not always in the labor market by necessity are likely to be very discouraged by reduced compensation. A college student who is working during the summer might take an extra four weeks off to travel if his wages are reduced and he no longer feels it is worth his time to work and miss a vacation. A housewife who works twenty-five hours a week may feel that at a reduced compensation rate she will work only fifteen hours and give the extra attention to her children because it is no longer worth sacrificing that much attention to her family. Full-time workers, however, are less likely to vary their work in response to the wage rate. Yet even here, many might stay in school longer, take more vacations, forgo overtime, etc., because of the reduced compensation.

An example will illustrate this point. In 1979 the OASDHI tax was 12.26%. If an employee is offered $100 a week in wages, it actually costs the firm, which ostensibly pays half the tax, $106.13 to hire the worker. This is what the employee's work is really worth and what the employer is willing to pay to hire him. Thus the employer is indifferent to the tax. He does not care if he pays $106.13 directly to the worker or $100.00 to the worker and $6.13 to the government. The worker, however, takes home $93.87 after paying his share of the tax, even though his work is worth $106.13. His compensation is therefore decreased by a full $12.26. This lower compensation means a decrease in the labor supply and in employment. Workers are discouraged from working because they cannot receive the full value of their labor.

As we noted in the discussion of the incidence of the payroll tax, this effect would not occur if the employee thought of the tax as a payment for a service he needs or wants, like insurance protection, rather than as a tax. The employee would in effect be paying the $12.26 for insurance protection, which is a service directly benefiting him and therefore part of his compensation. If social security were pure insurance with no welfare elements, then the taxpayer would be likely to think of his taxes in this way. If the tax-payer were receiving an actuarially fair return in benefits for his tax payments, if there were a direct link between taxes and benefits with every dollar paid in taxes resulting in a dollar with interest in later benefits, then paying the social security tax would be like putting money in the bank. The employee could expect to receive his $12.26 back later with interest, and therefore it would be part of his induce-ment to work. If this were the case, social security taxes would not significantly discourage employment.

But social security does not operate this way. All the welfare elements in the program weaken the link between taxes and benefits so that a dollar of taxes does not bring the worker a dollar of benefits plus interest. The level of benefits is determined much less by past tax payments than by the number of dependents at retirement, dis-ability, or death. Since the worker cannot count on increased tax payments bringing him increased benefits, he will not think of his taxes as part of his compensation.

In addition, the employee will not think of the full amount of the tax as part of his compensation to the extent that his taxes buy him more insurance protection than he wants or needs. In this case, part of his $12.26 will be wasted on something he does not need or want and it will not serve as an inducement for him to work. This effect stems from the compulsory nature of the program and would discourage employment even if there were no welfare elements in social security and the benefits were strictly related to taxes.

To the extent that these two effects lead the employee to think of his social security payments as taxes rather than as part of his com-pensation, employment will be discouraged. This discouragement will increase as the social security tax continues to grow. In 1984 the maximum tax will climb to over $4000 in constant 1980 dollars. A loss of compensation of this magnitude is likely to have a very discouraging effect on employment.

The result of this wedge effect is that there will be less employ-ment than both workers and employers desire. The wedge prevents an employer from hiring as many employees as he might like because it prevents him from paying employees what they are really worth and attracting as many workers as he is able and willing to hire at a given wage. It prevents employees from working as much as they would like at the full wage the employer is willing to pay because they can only receive the after-tax wage, for which they are not will-ing to work as much.

A further result of the wedge effect is economic inefficiency and misallocation of resources. Because labor does not receive its true worth, the labor supply is below the optimal amount. Workers who can produce $10.61 an hour but only receive $9.39 will not put forth the same labor supply that they would if they were paid their full value. Workers who could be producing and taking home $10.61 an hour will instead be consuming leisure time, which is only worth $9.40 to $10.60 to them. In the meantime, employers have to make up for the decreased labor supply with increased capital. The mix of capital and labor that results is a more expensive and less efficient way of producing the output than the mix of capital and labor that would exist without the tax.

With less employment, economic inefficiency, and misallocation of resources, the result is lower GNP. This loss of GNP is probably not anywhere near as great as the losses caused by the effect of social security on savings. But whatever GNP loss does occur because of these impacts on employment is in addition to the savings loss.

This loss is due to the conflict between the program's welfare and insurance objectives. If there were no welfare elements in social security, individuals would think of their taxes primarily as a charge for a service or good and there would be little or no loss of employment. It is because welfare elements are mixed with insurance elements that this loss occurs.

This analysis differs slightly from Laffer's and Ranson's because these authors believe that the burden of the social security tax is shared by the employee and the employer. In their analysis, the portion of the tax borne by the employee still discourages employment, resulting in the same effects discussed here. But the portion of the tax borne by the employer discourages him from offering employment, as explained in the discussion of the incidence of the payroll tax. This portion of the tax is like a tax on the activity of offering employment, discouraging the employer from continuing to do so. This leads again to less employment than both employers and employees desire, inefficiency and misallocation of resources, and lower GNP.

The Earnings Test Effect The earnings test reduces benefits for all beneficiaries under the age of seventy-two who have annual earnings above a certain limit. In 1978, for beneficiaries over age sixty-five this limit was $4,000, to be increased in annual steps to $6,000 in 1982. Benefits are decreased by $1 for every $2 earned above the limit.

The earnings test discourages employment by reducing the compensation for that employment. If social security benefits that the worker is already entitled to receive are reduced by $1 for every $2 above a certain limit, the worker is in effect receiving only $1 for every $2 worth of his work above that limit. The earnings test thus places a high marginal tax rate of 50% on all income earned over the earnings limit until social security benefits are eliminated.

The person who chooses to continue working after eligibility for social security benefits must also continue to pay social security payroll taxes. This requirement has a particularly harsh effect on elderly workers who can never receive any additional benefits for these taxes. The result is to reduce the compensation for working even further. In response, workers receiving social security benefits will reduce their labor supply and employment will decrease. The elderly in particular may choose to retire earlier, leaving the labor force entirely.

As we noted earlier, the earnings test may have induced early retirement for as much as 10% to 15% of the population. Although this percentage may not be significant in terms of inducing savings to overcome the asset-substitution effect, it represents a significantly negative effect on the labor supply, employment, and national income. If between 10% and 15% of the population will eventually lose several years of employment because of social security, national income will be substantially reduced. It should be noted that if the induced early retirement decision comes late in life there will be little or no induced savings under the retirement effect. Similarly, if the earnings test discourages a retired worker from engaging in part-time work that he did not plan to do before retirement, there will also be no induced savings for the retirement effect, and thus the earnings test can discourage employment without having any effect on savings. Furthermore, these responses to the earnings test are likely to be fairly typical, so employment discouraged in ways that will result in little if any induced savings probably represents a major portion of the total employment discouraged by the test. Finally it should be noted that those who contend that induced retirement plays a major role in mitigating the negative economic effects emphasized by Feldstein are suggesting that the negative economic effects described here that are due to the earnings test are much greater.

To the extent that the earnings test discourages employment among the elderly, it results in a loss to the nation of valuable skills, knowledge, and experience. The earnings test, however, does not apply only to the elderly, but to all who receive social security benefits, and discourages employment by younger workers as well. For example, a young widow with children who is receiving survivor's benefits may be discouraged by the earning's test from seeking employment to supplement the family income.

Discouraging employment through the earnings test results in the same negative impacts as discussed above for the payroll tax. It results in less employment than both workers and employers desire, making both worse off. It results in economic inefficiency and a misallocation of resources because it induces a suboptimal labor supply and suboptimal mix of capital and labor. Finally, it results in less GNP by causing less employment, economic inefficiency, and misallocation of resources.

These problems are again caused by the conflict in the program's objectives. The earnings test is one of the ways the program pursues a welfare objective. It seeks to prevent individuals who do not need them from receiving benefits. This would make sense if all social security benefits were welfare benefits because welfare should not be paid to those who are not in need. However, certain people cannot receive insurance benefits that they have paid for unless they meet the earnings test. The result is to discourage employment by everyone who eventually becomes entitled to receive these insurance benefits, thus making social security a bad insurance program with an unnecessary negative economic effect.

The Capital Effect As argued above, social security reduces savings and this reduction results in a reduction in capital investment. This loss of capital investment has several negative effects on the labor market.

Capital investment increases the demand for labor and thereby drives up wages. Because of investment in new and expanding businesses, employers seek employees to man this expansion, which translates into increased labor demand and, as a result, increased wages. Another way to see this effect is to note that capital investment leads to improved worker productivity. Workers with steam shovels are more productive than workers with manual ones; workers with copy machines are more productive than workers with carbon paper. Higher worker productivity results in higher wages. A reduction in capital investment like that caused by social security leads to a loss of potentially higher wages and lower worker productivity. These higher wages might also have induced a greater labor supply, so a loss of capital investment means less employment and less national income.

Capital investment also tends to upgrade jobs and thereby provide more of what are considered good jobs. It does this not only by increasing wages, but by improving the status of some jobs. For example, capital investment can make a steam shovel operator out of a ditch digger. And, in an economy with persistent involuntary unemployment, capital investment will decrease unemployment. As new businesses are created and old ones expanded, the increased demand for workers will reduce unemployment.

The loss in capital investment caused by social security therefore results in lower wages, lower worker productivity, less employment, lower GNP, fewer good jobs, and more unemployment. Once again all this is caused by the program's conflict in objectives. The loss of capital investment is caused by the pay-as-you-go system of financing, which in turn was caused by the pursuit of welfare objectives through social security.

The Income Effect Some authors have argued that social security causes a reduction in employment by inducing earlier retirement through an income effect.[31] This effect works by providing retirement benefits that allow people to retire and give up employment. Such an income effect does not reduce the employment of those who would have decided to retire at sixty-five without social security and would have saved to provide their retirement income anyway. For those who would have decided to retire later or not at all, the income effect does not work either. There is no reason why taxing such people early in life and returning these taxes to them at age sixty-five, whether they worked or not, would make them retire at sixty-five. If they retired because they would not get the benefits at sixty-five if they continued working, then that is an effect of the earnings test, not an income effect.

One way such an income effect would work is if social security provided a worker with greater returns in benefits than he could get through private alternatives. In such a case, social security would

[31]Munnell, *The Future of Social Security*, pp. 63–65.

provide him with income that he could not get otherwise and therefore provide him with the means to retire earlier. In the mature phase of a pay-as-you-go social security system, however, returns are not higher than in private alternatives. In fact, they are lower, as we shall see. But early in the start-up phase, returns to retirees are greater than in the private sector because these retirees have paid little or nothing in past taxes. In this case, these returns may induce early retirement apart from the effects of the earnings test. These benefits are, in effect, payments to people for not working like payments to farmers for not growing crops. They therefore reduce employment and lower national income, much as the other effects we have discussed, but this effect is rapidly reduced as the system matures and returns fall.

4

Social Security
and the Individual

"We can't ask support for a plan not at least as good as any American could buy from a private insurance company. The very least a citizen should expect is to get his money back upon retirement."[1] So stated the report of the House Subcommittee for Finance in 1935 when Congress was considering passage of the Social Security Act.

The truth is that young workers entering the social security system today will not do nearly as well in the program as they could do investing in private insurance and investment alternatives. If they were allowed to use the money they are expected to pay in social security taxes over the course of their lives to purchase these private alternatives, they would receive far more in return for their money than they would from social security. In fact, the difference is so great that in the future social security will be impoverishing the average American worker by preventing him from accumulating the wealth that would be available to him through private alternatives.

It is true that in the past the elderly have received much greater returns through social security than they could have received through private alternatives, but this was chiefly due to the effects of the start-up phase of the program. As the system matures, the returns paid by the program will fall far below market rates. As we shall see in chapter 5, there are other factors negatively affecting the returns future recipients can expect on their social security taxes.

In this chapter we will examine the benefits young people entering the program today could receive if they were allowed to invest the money they are expected to pay in social security taxes in

[1]Congressional Record, 12 June 1935; cited in Warren Shore, Social Security: The Fraud in Your Future (New York: Macmillan, 1975), p. 23.

available private insurance and investment alternatives. We will then compare these private returns with what social security promises to pay these young individuals in benefits. First we will examine some similar comparisons based on examples provided by the Social Security Administration.

More Politics and More Lying

In 1974 and 1975 the Research Institute of America and the California Taxpayers Lobby each requested information from the Social Security Administration concerning benefits promised to today's young workers. The Administration responded with the example of a hypothetical family headed by a young worker. Warren Shore analyzed this example in his recent book and brilliantly illustrated the numerous deceptions and falsehoods it contained.[2] He then compared the promised benefits to those available through private alternatives.

The Social Security Administration example focuses on a typical family in 1975 headed by thirty-five-year-old Richard Williams, a salesman who has paid the maximum tax since he started working in 1962. His wife Mary does not work at a salaried job, but instead cares for the couple's two children, aged four months and three years. This family, the government claims, is protected by a little more than $526,000 worth of benefits, even though Richard Williams has paid only about $3,000 in taxes in all his working years.

To arrive at this total, the Social Security Administration claims that if Mr. Williams died now his family would receive $213,762 in survivor's benefits, if he became disabled for life now the family would receive $205,394 in disability benefits, and if he worked until sixty-five and retired they would receive $107,172 in retirement benefits.

How Richard Williams could simultaneously die in 1975, become disabled in 1975 but live a normal life span unable to work, and work until sixty-five, retiring to collect retirement benefits until he dies a second time, is a mystery only the Social Security Administration can solve. It is a complete misrepresentation to say that Williams is protected by potential benefits of $526,000 because he could never receive this amount under any conceivable circumstances.

[2]Warren Shore, *Social Security: The Fraud in Your Future* (New York: Macmillan, 1975).

The most Williams could receive is the $213,762 in survivor's benefits that the government claims his family would receive if he died in 1975. This total is calculated by noting that if Williams died in that year his wife Mary and two children would receive $651.60 per month until the youngest child reached eighteen. The portion of these benefits paid for Mary would then stop, but the benefits paid for the two children would continue until the oldest reached twenty-two, assuming they both attended college. The family would consequently receive $558.40 per month during this period. After the oldest child reached twenty-two, the youngest child alone would receive benefits. These benefits, amounting to $279.20 per month, would last until this child reached twenty-two. At this point, all benefit payments would stop until Richard's widow Mary reached age sixty. She would then be entitled to another $266.20 per month for life. By adding together all these monthly benefit amounts, plus a lump sum death benefit for Richard of $255, the Social Security Administration arrives at the grand total of $213,762.20, all for just $3,000 in taxes.

But the value of the benefits paid in this example is grossly overstated, while the amount of taxes paid is grossly understated. First, if we include the employer's share of Williams's taxes which, as we have seen, Williams really paid, the actual total in past taxes is $6,000. In 1974 alone, Williams would have paid $772 in taxes deducted from his check and another $772 paid by his employer for a total of $1,544.

More importantly, however, none of the government benefit figures are discounted by the interest rate. As everyone except the Social Security Administration knows, a dollar today is not the same as a dollar one year from now. A dollar to be paid one year into the future is equal to $1 divided by one plus the interest rate. If that rate is 5%, a dollar a year from now is worth only about 95¢ today.

Thus the monthly benefits to be paid to the Williams family as described above must be discounted by the interest rate to determine their value at the time Richard died at age thirty-five. The present value of these benefits, discounted by a 5% interest rate, is only $107,143. This means that if Williams had purchased a term life insurance policy worth $107,143 with his social security taxes, he could have left his family the same amount in benefits as the Social Security Administration would pay them.

But a term life insurance policy of this amount is not worth $107,143. It is only worth this amount times the probability that

Williams would die at age thirty-five. This probability is less than three in a thousand. Multiplying $107,143 by this probability leaves $544.50, which is the real value of the benefits paid to the family of Richard Williams upon his death at age thirty-five, not $526,000 or $213,762. For this amount Williams could have purchased a term life insurance policy that would have paid his wife and family exactly what the Social Security Administration would pay. But the government charged him almost three times this amount in his last full year of work alone. If Mr. Williams had paid $544.50 per year for term life insurance and put the extra $1,000 he paid in taxes in his last year of work into a retirement fund, it would have accumulated with interest and he could have left this sizeable fund to his family at age thirty-five also.

This is not all. If Mrs. Williams had received the $107,143 from a life insurance policy, that money would be hers without condition, to spend or invest as she pleased. She would have complete control over the funds. The money she is "entitled" to through social security, however, is not hers. She has to accept it on terms and conditions laid down by the federal government.

The difference between owning your money with complete control over it and remaining subject to the terms and conditions of the government is enormous. First, despite the financial condition in which Mary Williams finds herself immediately after her husband's untimely death, she will receive her benefits only on the monthly schedule described above. If she needs a little extra money now to take care of unexpected expenses, she cannot accelerate her payments. She cannot use part of her future payments for a family emergency, to buy a home, or to make an investment. She must wait and receive her money slowly over time, as dictated by the federal government.

If she really owned her benefits, Mary Williams would be free to use them to pursue any of several different courses of action that would make her better off. If, for example, she owned these benefits in the form of $107,143 in cash as paid under a term life insurance policy, she could use part of this cash to pay off immediate and unusual expenses. She could consume more now and less later according to her needs and preferences. She would be free to use this cash to take advantage of lucrative business and investment opportunities. The money would be available to the family for immediate use in an emergency.

Take a single example of one possible alternative: If Mary Williams really owned her benefits in the form of a $107,143 cash fund, she could deposit it with a savings institution. This institution would pay her, at 7.5% interest, monthly interest payments of $670 forever, without touching the original principal. This compares with social security payments of $651 per month for seventeen years, eight months, $558.40 per month for one year, $279.20 per month for three years, nothing for three years, and then $226.20 per month for the rest of Mary's life.

Through the private alternatives of term life insurance and a long-term savings account, Mary Williams would have received $201,000 in monthly benefits by the time she reached sixty, and her fund of $107,143 would still be intact. This compares with $156,007 in monthly benefits through social security and no fund. Through the private system, where the money is really hers, Mary Williams could at this point make further changes to suit her needs and preferences. She could use the principal to buy an annuity that would pay her $761 per month for life, compared to $266.20 per month under social security. She could continue to draw the $670 per month interest for five years and then when she is sixty-five purchase an annuity of $846 per month for life. Under social security, she has the option of receiving nothing for five years and then $372.30 per month for life. Finally, under the private system, she could continue to draw the $670 per month interest for life and leave the principal of $107,143 to her children or other heirs. In any case, she makes out much better under the private alternatives than under social security.

But this is not all. Because the money social security promises the Williams family does not really belong to them as privately owned assets do, they will lose the various benefits they are promised if they do not comply with numerous rules and regulations governing the receipt of their social security benefits.

For example, if Mrs. Williams remarries before sixty, she will lose all the benefits to be paid to her as a widow, although her children will still receive benefits. Under the private alternatives, she can get married or divorced as often as she likes without any reduction in benefits. Since the money is hers, it cannot be taken away for failure to comply with rules and regulations.

Similarly, Mary Williams will lose her widow's benefits if the children do not remain in her care. They cannot, for example, be sent to live with their grandparents or at a school. The children also have to go to college between the ages of eighteen and twenty-two or they will lose their benefits. If the money promised under social security really belonged to Mary Williams, as in the private alternatives, she could care for her children as she deemed best, and they could decide for themselves whether and when they would attend college.

Probably most important of all, Mary Williams cannot go to work to supplement the family income. If she does, she will lose $1 in benefits for every $2 earned over $2,520 in 1975 under the earnings test. With the private alternatives, she could work and earn as much as she wanted and still keep her benefits intact.

The example provided by the Social Security Administration grossly overstates the value of social security benefits. Not only can private sector alternatives provide much higher benefits in monetary terms, but those benefits are worth much more to the recipient because the money he receives under the private system actually belongs to him as a private asset that he can use and control as he wishes. As a result, he can use this money according to his own needs and preferences to pursue courses of action that will make him better off. He also does not face the possibility of losing this money because of the rules, regulations, and conditions of social security.

This critique of the government example has already been advanced by Warren Shore, as noted above. This example is merely another shameful instance of the deliberately fraudulent campaign of deception and misrepresentation waged by the Social Security Administration against the public. The example indicates that comparisons between social security and private sector alternatives provided by the government cannot be trusted.

In the rest of this chapter we will undertake a more detailed and comprehensive comparison between social security and private sector alternatives.

Public vs. Private

For individuals there are several important reasons why the private system of insurance and retirement protection is superior to the public social security system. The most important of these is that the private system is not operated on a pay-as-you-go basis. The money paid into the private system is instead saved and invested and returned to each individual upon retirement. Under a private system each individual would pay the money he is now paying in social security taxes to an insurance company, pension plan, or other private institution that would invest that money in private productive assets. Alternatively, individuals could be allowed to use their money to make investments on their own if they desired. These capital investments would increase production and thereby earn investors an interest payment. These investments would actually produce the additional amounts necessary to pay this interest payment. Over time, this interest or return on investment could accumulate to significant amounts, providing individuals with money for their retirement years. The returns accumulated would allow individuals to receive far more in retirement benefits than they paid into the system over the years. These benefits are paid for by the increased production created or produced by the private system's investments. It is this increased production, therefore, that allows the private system to pay individuals more than they have paid into the program.

Because social security is operated on a pay-as-you-go basis, however, the money taxpayers pay into the system is not saved and invested but instead is immediately paid out to current recipients. Social security adds nothing to production, it just moves funds around from one part of the population to another. This means that individuals lose the full interest rate of return they would get on their money if it was invested in private productive assets. They lose the huge accumulation of assets and large estates they would have acquired through the private, invested system. In fact, since social security does nothing to increase production, each individual can get no more out of the program in benefits than he paid in taxes, unless the government increases the taxes it collects from other taxpayers to pay him increased benefits.

The essential difference between the private system and the public, pay-as-you-go system, then, is that the private system increases production while the public system does not. The private system provides individuals with more because the capital investment it generates increases production and this increased production can be used to pay individuals higher benefits. Since social security merely moves funds around from one part of the population to another, it does nothing to increase production. Individuals lose the higher returns and benefits available in a private invested system. Social security is inferior to private alternatives primarily because of its fatal flaw—its operation on a pay-as-you-go basis.

It should be noted that the argument we are making here concerning the superiority of the private system from the individual's viewpoint is merely the other side of the coin from the argument emphasized in Feldstein's critique of the program from the viewpoint of the economy as a whole, discussed in chapter 3. Feldstein argues that because social security operates on a pay-as-you-go basis, the econo-

my loses a large amount of capital investment that results in less production and a lower GNP. According to his estimates, this loss of
GNP is currently about $400 billion a year. We are merely noting
here where this $400 billion a year would go in a private system. It
would go each year as an interest payment into the retirement funds
that each individual would be accumulating by saving the money he
would have paid in social security taxes and investing this money in
private productive assets. The $400 billion represents the amount
each year that the private system would pay to individuals in additional returns above what social security would pay. Of course,
some of this $400 billion would go to the government in taxes, but
individuals would still be benefiting by this full amount. These taxes
would be providing individuals with government services chosen
through the political process, or they would be used to reduce other
taxes. Either way, individuals would still be benefiting by the full
$400 billion.

Another way of recognizing that the argument presented here is
merely the other side of the coin from Feldstein's argument is to
focus on Feldstein's conception of social security wealth. Feldstein
defines this as the present value of the future benefits social security
would pay to current taxpayers. Feldstein calculates that this social
security wealth was $2 trillion in 1971 and $3.4 trillion in 1978. This
is the amount that would have been in the individual retirement
funds of all social security taxpayers in those years under the private
system, assuming that they saved and invested just enough so that
they would receive in benefits exactly what social security would
have paid. Requiring individuals to pay their tax money into social
security instead of into a private system means that they lose this tremendous sum of wealth.

This theoretical discussion leads to the conclusion that the private
invested system is superior to the public pay-as-you-go system. Of
course, empirical comparisons between the private and public systems are tricky because the government can use the power of taxation to make the private system look bad and the public system look
good.

The government can, for example, raise the taxes on investments
in the private sector to such high levels that investors have very little
left after taxes. Reduced returns to private investments because of
high taxes would not make the private invested system any less superior to the public pay-as-you-go system, however. Rather, such
taxes would merely represent another government barrier prevent-

ing individuals from receiving the full benefits of the superior, private alternatives. The private investments, even with high taxes, still increase production. In this situation, the government rather than individuals would be receiving most of the benefits of this increased production. The government would be gaining greater tax revenues, which allow it to appropriate a larger share of the national output. Furthermore, these increased resources available to the government will either go to provide government services that voters have chosen through the political process, however mistakenly, or to reduce other taxes. Even when high taxes reduce the benefits available to individuals directly in the private system, individuals still receive these benefits indirectly in the long run.[3]

At the same time that the government reduces the returns to individuals in the private system by imposing high taxes, it can increase social security taxes to provide current recipients with high returns in benefits on the taxes they paid into the program. By means of this combination of taxes, the government can make the returns in the private system lower than the returns from social security. Even under these circumstances, however, the pay-as-you-go social secu-

---

[3]Inflation may also reduce the real returns that investors can receive on their investments, although, as we shall see later, in the long run investors should be able to count on a constant real rate of return over and above inflation. To the extent that inflation does reduce the real returns on investments further, this inflation is merely another form of government taxation. The government causes inflation by increasing the money supply. When the government first spends this new additional money, prices have not yet risen to reflect the increased money supply. It is only after this new money percolates throughout the entire economy, increasing demand, that the inflationary price increases result. By using this new money to purchase goods and services before these price increases occur, the government in effect appropriates a larger share of national output, as through taxation. For this reason inflation is often referred to as the cruelest tax.

But again reduced returns to private investments due to inflation would not make the private invested system inferior to the public, pay-as-you-go system. Rather, such inflation would merely represent still another government barrier preventing individuals from receiving the benefits of the superior private alternatives. Even with inflation the private investments still increase production. The inflation simply means that the government is again appropriating much if not most of the benefits of this increased production to itself. However, if this appropriated production is used to provide voters with government services or to reduce taxes, people would again still be receiving the full benefits of the private invested system indirectly. This is not to say that this inflation-taxation process is legitimate because individuals are later provided with government services or to say that individuals on net are not made worse off by all the negative effects of inflation. It is merely to note that reduced real returns to private investments resulting from inflation do not make the private system inferior to social security.

rity system is still not superior to the private, invested system. It is true that individuals in the pay-as-you-go system would seem to be richer because of the higher apparent returns in that system, but this increased wealth is an illusion. The individuals are actually poorer because the economy has lost the increased production available from the private system. Even if the tax system was such that individuals received a higher return from social security than from private investments, they would still be losing, through participation in the pay-as-you-go system, the $400 billion, or $1,800 per person, or $4,900 per family, that Feldstein calculates is available each year through an invested system. Thus the private invested system would still be superior to the public, pay-as-you-go system. By imposing high general taxes, the government would merely be preventing people from receiving the full benefits from the private, invested system and deluding the population about the real alternatives by continually increasing social security taxes. The pay-as-you-go system always makes people poorer even if the apparent returns from the pay-as-you-go system are higher than the after-tax returns in the private system.

There is a way in which the social security system automatically raises increased tax revenues over time without increasing tax rates. These naturally generated increased taxes can be used to pay higher benefits to individuals than they paid in taxes. These higher benefits are usually described as providing a social security rate of return.

This social security rate of return is the result of two economic circumstances that tend to increase total tax revenues collected over time without increases in tax rates. The first of these is the rate of growth in real wages. As wages (the tax base) increase over time, the total tax revenues collected from a fixed tax rate on those wages will increase by the rate of growth in those wages. The second circumstance is the rate of growth in the working population. As this population grows, the total tax collected from a fixed tax rate on the wages of these people will grow at the rate of growth of this population. Total taxes collected will increase by the rate of growth in real wages plus the rate of growth in the working population. The sum of these two rates is the social security rate of return.

In a pay-as-you-go system, where all collected in taxes is paid out in benefits each year, the benefits that can be paid are increased annually by this social security rate of return. A person who pays taxes into such a pay-as-you-go program all of his life, therefore, will receive back his tax money increased by this rate of return.

Under currently prevailing conditions, this social security rate of return is quite low. As we will see in chapter 5, the rate of growth in real wages over the past twenty-five years has been approximately 1.3%. Furthermore, as we will also see in more detail in chapter 5, if current trends continue the population will be decreasing. The effects from this declining population could conceivably overwhelm the effects from the increase in real wages, making the overall social security rate of return negative. Even if there were a reversal of this decline in population, however, given the strength of these trends and the strong social forces behind them it is unlikely that there would be much population growth in the forseeable future to add significantly to the social security rate of return.

In fact, because of recent demographic trends, social security is likely to experience the effects of a declining population in the near future even if such a decline does not actually occur. During the fifteen-year period immediately following World War II, known as the baby boom, fertility increased rapidly, resulting in a sharp increase in the population. Since then, however, fertility has experienced a dramatic decline, reaching the lowest levels in the nation's history. The result of this baby bust following so soon after the baby boom is to create the effects of a declining population. When the baby-boom generation begins to retire and the baby-bust generation is all working, the number of workers relative to the number of retirees will fall, as in a declining population. If fertility remains at current levels, the number of beneficiaries per one hundred workers will increase from thirty-one today to sixty-four in the year 2030. This decline in the working population relative to the retired population means that at fixed tax rates, taxes will be insufficient to meet escalating benefit obligations. In fact, if fertility remains at current low levels, tax rates will have to double to maintain benefits at current levels. This strongly suggests that the impact on social security from these demographic factors will be to make the social security rate of return negative.

It is quite unlikely that there will be further tax increases in future years to pay individuals more than the social security rate of return. One of the sources of increased taxes to pay increased benefits in the past has been the gradual extension of the program's coverage to include new groups of workers originally excluded. This increased the taxpaying population and therefore increased tax revenues available to pay current benefits, but expansion of the program along these lines is now virtually complete. Over 90% of the working population is now covered by social security, so this source of increased taxes is no longer available.

Another method of raising revenues has been to raise the tax rate. The tax rate has grown from 2% in the first thirteen years of the program to over 12% today. But primarily due to the demographic factors noted above and expected future economic performance, tax rates will already have to be increased dramatically in future years just to pay currently promised benefits. It is doubtful whether even these high rates will be politically acceptable, so raising tax rates further to pay high returns in benefits seems nearly impossible.[4]

A third way revenues have been increased is to increase the taxable wage base. This base has been increased from $3,000 in the early years of the program to $25,900 for 1980 and to $29,500 for 1981. This method, however, only provides additional revenues to increase benefits in the short run. In the long run, workers who have paid taxes on the higher wage base will be entitled to higher benefits calculated on that base, and these higher benefits will consume the additional taxes, if not more. The wage base has by now been increased to the point where additional increases would provide little additional revenues and these additional short-term revenues would probably not be worth the additional benefit obligations the tax base increase would create. This method of increasing revenues to increase benefits therefore has also been largely eliminated.

These revenue-raising devices were all merely devices for extending the start-up phase of the program, a phase that has now been extended as much as possible; we are now passing into the inevitable mature phase. Retirees in the near future, therefore, will be limited to the low social rate of return on their tax dollars that we have noted. Because of population trends, this return may well be negative.

But regardless of the level of this social security rate of return, or any higher returns paid from further tax increases, this return is entirely different from the returns generated by the private, invested system. The private returns come from increased production generated by the private system itself. These returns are, therefore, self-financing and do not constitute a burden to anyone. The social security rate of return, however, is generated by increased taxes. There is no increased production to pay for it, and it therefore con-

---

[4]As we will see in chapter 5, by the time young people now entering the work force retire social security tax rates will have to be raised to 25% to 33% of taxable payroll just to pay them currently legislated benefits. It is doubtful that taxpayers will be willing to accept these tax rates.

stitutes a burden on current workers. The belief that it makes individuals richer is an illusion. Production has not been increased, so individuals cannot be richer. In fact, these individuals would all be poorer because they would have lost the increased production available from the private invested system. Thus, even if the social security rate of return was equal to or greater than the return available to individuals directly in the private invested system, individuals would still be worse off in the pay-as-you-go social security program. The concept of a social security rate of return will be discussed in more detail in chapter 9.

It is important to remember these tricky empirical factors as we compare the private invested alternatives to social security in this chapter. Through high taxes on private investments and high social security returns paid merely by increased taxation, the government can make the public pay-as-you-go system look far better than it really is. Yet, while the deck is stacked against the private invested system, we will still compare the real, after-tax returns available to individuals in the private alternatives with the returns under social security generated not through increased production but through increased taxation. We will still find the private sector alternatives far superior to social security. But it should be remembered that the superiority of the private system is even much greater than this. A fair comparison would require us to compare the real before-tax returns under the private system with the returns under social security. These before-tax returns represent the full benefits available under the private system. These benefits are not any less because some of them are used to finance goods and services provided by the government. Even this comparison, furthermore, would not be entirely fair to the private system. We would still be comparing actual returns in the private system generated through increased production (and therefore actually making everyone better off and no one worse off) with illusionary returns in social security generated through increased taxation rather than production (and therefore making taxpayers worse off to the extent that they make beneficiaries better off).

We have shown that the chief reason for the superiority of the private system in monetary terms is that it increases total production while the public pay-as-you-go system does not, and this increased production can be used to pay higher benefits through the private system than the public system can pay. As we will see in the next section, this principle applies to a certain extent to all of the insurance programs under the social security umbrella, not just retirement insurance. There are several other important reasons why the private system is superior to a pay-as-you-go system from the individual viewpoint, and these will be discussed in the next section as well. The other chapters of this book provide additional reasons why the private system is superior to the public pay-as-you-go social security system.

In the next section we will undertake an empirical comparison between the public and private systems that will support the theoretical reasons provided here for the superiority of the private system, as well as offering several others.

The Comparison

In comparing social security to private alternatives, we will examine the returns and benefits available to three sets of young workers entering the work force today: low-income workers, average-income workers, and high-income workers. The low-income workers all start work at age eighteen in 1980, earning $5,742 in that year, about what a full-time worker earning the minimum wage would receive for a year's work.[5] After 1980 the wages of these workers increase each year at the average rate of growth in wages for all workers covered by social security, so these workers continue to earn about the minimum wage all of their lives. The average-income workers all start work at age twenty-two in 1980, earning $12,208 in that year,[6] the amount that the average worker covered by social security was expected to earn in 1980, according to projections of the Social Security Administration. After 1980 the wages of these workers are also assumed to increase each year at the average rate of growth in wages in covered employment, so these workers continue to earn the average wage for all workers covered by social security for all of their lives. This amount is probably somewhat below the average wage earned by a full-time worker responsible for the support of a family because this average includes the annual incomes of many part-time and secondary workers, such as students and

[5]This figure is for the Alternative II set of assumptions. Under Alternative I, low-income workers start earning $5,781 in 1980 and under Alternative III low-income workers start earning $5,731 in 1980.

[6]This figure is for Alternative II set of assumptions. Under Alternative I, average-income workers start earning $12,289 in 1980, and under Alternative III average-income workers start earning $12,105 in 1980.

housewives, who do not work regularly and who tend to have low wages. In 1977 families with one earner averaged $13,148 in annual income, but the average worker in covered employment earned only $9,779. The high-income workers in our comparison all start work at age twenty-four in 1980 earning the maximum taxable income in that year of $25,900.[7] After 1980 their income increases to equal the maximum taxable income each year, which, after 1981, will also increase at the rate of growth in wages in covered employment. These workers will continue to maintain about the same position in the overall income distribution that they hold today. This is a somewhat modest earnings history for professional workers.

We are assuming that each of these workers invests the money he would have paid in social security taxes over the course of his life in private investment and insurance purchases. The money each worker sets aside for his retirement is invested each year in a trust fund that is used to pay retirement benefits to the worker after age sixty-five. In our projections, we examine the amount of benefits each trust fund can pay out of the interest alone, leaving the principal intact to be left to the worker's heirs after death. We also examine the amount of benefits each trust fund can pay if it is used to purchase a life annuity, which will pay a certain promised amount each month for life. For single workers or workers with working spouses who can purchase their own life annuities, we assume that these annuities will pay benefits only for the life of the worker purchasing them. For workers with nonworking spouses, we assume that they purchase an annuity that will pay a certain amount of benefits while both spouses are alive, and 67% of this amount after the death of one of the spouses, as under social security. Our projections of the amount of benefits that can be paid under all these options have been adjusted so that there will be enough in the accumulated trust fund to increase the benefits to be paid after retirement at the rate of inflation. The benefits projected, in other words, can be paid in real terms throughout retirement.

We have deducted from the amounts paid into these trust funds each month sufficient amounts to pay premiums for term life insurance. The amount of term life insurance purchased each year was set high enough so that if the worker died he would receive benefits approximately equal to what social security would have paid in the event of death. Beginning two years after each worker starts work-

[7]High-income workers start earning $25,900 in 1980 under all three alternative sets of assumptions.

ing, the amount of term life insurance is set equal to an amount large enough to pay the maximum family benefit (MFB) for eighteen years and then to pay the benefits that social security would pay to the surviving spouse after age sixty-five. An amount of life insurance large enough to pay these benefits is in fact purchased for each of the next seven years. After that, the amount of life insurance purchased is reduced to pay the maximum family benefit for one less year for each additional year of work. Thus, in the first year after this seven-year period, the amount of term life insurance purchased is sufficient to pay the maximum family benefit for only seventeen years, in addition to paying full benefits to the surviving spouse after age sixty-five. In the second year, the amount of life insurance purchased is sufficient to pay the maximum family benefit for only sixteen years, etc. In every case enough term life insurance was purchased so that the benefits to be paid after death can be increased by the rate of inflation each year.

The amount of term life insurance purchased each year to pay these benefits is reduced by the amount accumulated in the retirement trust fund because if the worker dies before retirement, he will not need the fund to pay retirement benefits, and it can be used to pay survivor's benefits to his family. At every point in the worker's life, the amount in his personal retirement trust fund plus the amount of term life insurance he owns will equal the amount necessary to pay the benefits described above. This means that as the worker ages and his retirement fund grows, the amount of term life insurance needed will decline, as will the premiums to be paid. When the retirement fund alone reaches the amount necessary to pay the benefits described above, the amount of term life insurance and the monthly premiums to be paid fall to zero. As we shall see, this point is eventually reached by virtually all workers.

This system of life insurance protection was structured in this way to be as closely analogous as possible to the survivor's insurance protection of social security. A worker must work for six quarters before he is covered under social security, so no insurance protection is provided for the first two years and no deductions are made from the amounts paid into the retirement fund. Similarly, if a worker dies before retirement under social security, he loses all his retirement benefits, so the retirement fund in the private system is used to pay for survivor's benefits in event of the worker's death. In addition, the benefits under social security increase each year at the rate of inflation, as do the benefits in our private system.

Furthermore, as we saw in chapter 2, a worker receives survivor's benefits under social security only if he leaves behind children or a spouse over sixty. If a worker leaves behind two or more children along with his spouse, the family will receive the maximum family benefit. Survivor's benefits will continue to be paid until the youngest child reaches eighteen or as long as the surviving spouse is sixty-five or over, or elects to receive benefits at a reduced rate at age sixty.[8] Thus, as long as a worker has his last child within the seven-year period described above, he will receive at least as much in benefits if he dies as under social security. But, and this is the important point, if he does not have his children within this period, and instead postpones his child-bearing years until later in life, he can simply change his pattern of insurance purchases so this seven-year period will occur later in life. The worker can simply purchase much less life insurance, enough only to pay for his spouse's retirement benefits, until he has children, increasing his purchases at that time so he will have enough to pay what social security would pay. If the worker has all of his children within this later seven-year period, the cost should be no greater than in our example. Although life insurance rates will be higher for the worker later in life, his retirement fund will also be greater, and therefore he will need to purchase less life insurance. Given the small families that young people tend to have today, even if a worker does not have his children within a seven-year period, he can probably still rearrange his insurance purchases at no greater cost than in our example, so that at any point he will be covered for at least as much as social security would pay. Only for those who have relatively large families, at least more than three or four children, spread out over a relatively long period of time, at least more than ten years, will the cost be greater. For most workers, however, especially those who are single or married and childless, the cost will be much less than in our example if the worker seeks to match only what social security would pay in the event of death.

[8]Social security will pay survivor's benefits to a deceased worker's child between the ages of nineteen to twenty-two if the child attends college during those years. We did not include these benefits in our private alternative system primarily because not everyone attends college, and of those who do, not all attend for four years between the ages of nineteen and twenty-two. These benefits are therefore not available to everyone, and the proportion of the population to whom they are available is uncertain. The cost of purchasing additional term life insurance to pay these benefits would be minor, and the undercoverage of the private survivor's insurance system in this regard is far outweighed by the overcoverage in other areas. Furthermore, the Carter administration and many others have advocated phasing out these benefits, and it is therefore uncertain whether they will continue to be paid in the future.

Our pattern of life insurance protection covers all of the major contingencies that social security does through its survivor's insurance provisions. We will discuss later the many ways in which this private system of life insurance protection is both cheaper and better than social security's survivor's insurance.

We have also made deductions from the monthly contribution to the retirement fund for disability insurance. The pattern of disability insurance protection in our private system is similar to the life insurance protection described above. We assume that the definition of disability under the private system is the same as under social security and that individuals become disabled under the private system at the same rate at which they have become disabled under social security in recent years. The amount of disability insurance purchased each year was set high enough so that if the worker became disabled, he would receive benefits approximately equal to what social security would have paid in the event of disability. Thus, beginning two years after each worker starts working, the amount of disability insurance is set equal to an amount large enough to pay the maximum family benefit for eighteen years, 150% of the primary insurance amount (PIA) for the rest of the worker's life while his spouse is alive and 100% of the PIA after that, and 100% of the PIA for the rest of his spouse's life after age sixty-five if he should die first. If the worker recovers and starts to work again, his benefits stop, except that he remains entitled to the same old-age benefits after sixty-five that he would have received under social security if he had remained disabled. If the worker dies, his family continues to receive the maximum family benefit for the remainder of the eighteen-year period, and his spouse will also still receive the old-age benefits after sixty-five. An amount of disability insurance large enough to pay these benefits is purchased for each of the next seven years. After that, the disability insurance amount is reduced to pay the maximum family benefit for one less year for each additional year of work, as under the life insurance plan described above. Again, in every case enough disability insurance was purchased so that the benefits to be paid after disability can be increased by the rate of inflation each year.

The amount of disability insurance purchased each year to pay these benefits was also again reduced by the amount accumulated in each worker's retirement trust fund. If the worker becomes disabled, the amount of insurance plus the amount in his retirement fund will be enough to pay him the benefits described above, so if he remains disabled that is what he will receive. If the worker recovers before age sixty-five and goes back to work, he will still be entitled to retirement benefits equal to what social security would have paid him if he had remained disabled, but his retirement fund will have been used up to pay for these benefits. He will now, however, be able to begin contributing to a retirement fund all over again, and this fund will add more to his retirement benefits than contributing the same money to social security would have added. Thus he will have more in retirement benefits than under social security, but not as much as if he had never been disabled. Finally, if the worker dies after becoming disabled, there will be enough in the fund plus his insurance to pay the benefits described above for his survivors.

Because the amount in the retirement fund is subtracted from the amount of disability insurance to be purchased, this again means that as the worker ages and his retirement fund grows, the amount of disability insurance needed will decline, as will the premiums to be paid. When the retirement fund alone reaches the amount necessary to pay the benefits described above, the amount of disability life insurance and the monthly premiums to be paid fall to zero. As we shall see, this point is eventually reached by virtually all workers.

This pattern of disability insurance protection was again structured to match social security's disability protection. If a worker becomes disabled under social security he receives 100% of his PIA in monthly benefits plus an additional 50% if he has a spouse and another 50% for each child under age eighteen.[9] A disabled worker needs only one child and a spouse to receive the maximum family benefit. If the worker recovers, these benefits stop, and he will receive the usual retirement benefits after age sixty-five. If the worker dies after disability, the worker's family will receive the usual survivor's benefits. Insurance coverage does not begin until after six quarters of work, and benefits paid are increased annually by the rate of inflation.

Again, as long as the worker has his last child within the seven-year period described above, he will receive at least as much in the event of disability under the private plan as under social security. But even if he does not have his last child within this period, he can

---

[9]Social security will pay disability benefits to a disabled worker's child between the ages of nineteen and twenty-two if the child attends college during those years. We did not include these benefits in our private alternative system for the same reasons that we did not include the analogous benefits under the survivor's insurance program. See footnote 8, *supra*.

rearrange his pattern of insurance purchases so that he has higher coverage after he has children and less coverage before, as under the life insurance plan described above. Before he has children, the worker needs to purchase only enough insurance to pay himself 100% of the PIA in event of disability if he is single, and 150% of the PIA if he is married. When the worker has children, he needs to purchase only enough additional insurance to raise this benefit to the maximum family benefit (MFB), about 175% of the PIA, for the additional years until his last child reaches eighteen. Whether the worker purchases this additional insurance earlier or later in life, depending on when he has his children, the cost should be no greater than in our example. Although disability insurance rates increase for older workers, the fund will be greater so the amount of insurance it is necessary to purchase will be less. Only if the worker has a relatively large number of children, at least four, over a relatively long period of time, at least ten years, will the cost be greater than in our example. For most people, however, the cost will be far less if they seek to match only what social security would have paid them. This is especially true for single or childless people.

Our pattern of disability insurance protection covers all of the major contingencies that social security does through its disability insurance provisions. We will discuss later all of the many ways in which this private system of disability insurance protection is both cheaper and better than social security's disability insurance.

The private system of insurance protection that we have described also covers the contingencies covered by social security's hospital insurance (HI) program. Social security's system of HI benefits is simply the payment of retirement benefits in kind. The HI program pays for the major portion of expenses for a certain number of days of hospital care and certain amounts of other types of medical services. These benefits are available to all those over sixty-five who are receiving social security benefits. The private system can match these benefits by paying increased retirement benefits that can be used to purchase private hospital insurance or to pay for medical expenses directly. The workers in our private system can use part of their monthly retirement payments, which will be much higher than under social security, to pay for private hospital insurance premiums. Alternatively, they could use part of these monthly payments, or part of the large amounts accumulated in their retirement funds, to pay for medical expenses directly.

We can calculate the approximate value of the hospital insurance benefits provided under social security so that we can compare these benefits with those provided under the private system. The hospital insurance portion of social security is in the worst shape of all the OASDHI programs. It is the most unstable, the most poorly planned, and the most underfunded. Unlike the other OASDHI programs, the Social Security Administration makes no projections concerning the HI program past the year 2000. Even at that point, however, currently legislated taxes will be sufficient to pay only about 40% to 60% of the projected benefits.[10] Further projections made by others suggest that by the year 2025, about the time when the workers in our examples will be retiring, currently legislated taxes will be able to finance only about one-third of currently legislated benefits.[11] Since the HI program is so heavily underfunded, we will calculate only the value of the HI benefits that can be paid with currently legislated HI tax rates, rather than the value of HI benefits as promised. In fact, if only the amount of currently legislated HI taxes each year is added to the fund used to purchase our private alternatives, then such an adjustment in computing the value of HI benefits is necessary to make the comparison between the public and private systems fair.

All of the workers in our examples will be retired by the year 2030. In that year, the HI tax rate is legislated to be 2.9% of taxable payroll. This will yield approximately $68.2 billion to pay for hospital insurance benefits and the cost of administering the program.[12] If we assume that in 2030 the same proportion of those over age sixty-five and other eligible beneficiaries will be covered under the HI program as in 1978, there will be approximately 69.6 million HI

---

[10]*1979 Annual Report of the Board of Trustees of the Federal Hospital Insurance Trustees of the Federal Hospital Insurance Trust Fund.* Under the Alternative II set of projections, the Social Security Administration projects that taxes will be sufficient to cover only 60% of projected benefits. Under Alternative III, the SSA projects that taxes will be sufficient to cover only 40% of projected benefits.

[11]A. Haeworth Robertson, *The Financial Status of Social Security After the Social Security Amendments of 1977*, Social Security Administration, 1978. Robertson, a recent former chief actuary for the Social Security Administration, calculates that under Alternative II the HI program by 2025 will consume 7.61% of taxable payroll compared to an HI tax rate for that year of 2.90%. Given that the Social Security Administration's projections under Alternative III in the year 2000 were about two percentage points greater than Alternative II in 2000, we may assume that projections under Alternative III would indicate that the program will consume 9% of taxable payroll, or more than three times the scheduled HI tax rate.

[12]This figure is based on projections made by the Social Security Administration under the Alternative III set of assumptions.

beneficiaries in that year. This means that about $980 in benefits and administrative costs can be paid for each beneficiary. Our workers in 2030 can therefore receive the same benefits they would receive under the HI program by paying an annual hospital insurance premium of $980 to a private company. Those who have a spouse who has not worked and therefore not accumulated a retirement fund of his or her own will have to pay twice this amount each year to receive the same hospital insurance benefits they would have received under social security. To compare our private system of benefits to those provided under social security, therefore, we may merely subtract about $1,000 a year from the retirement benefits paid by the private system. For workers with spouses who have not worked, we should subtract about $2,000 a year.

Alternatively, we can devise a more imaginative private system of hospital insurance benefits to use in comparison to social security. Assuming an annual real rate of return of 6%, a life annuity purchased at age sixty-five which will pay $980 a year for life will cost $9,106 for a male and $10,507 for a female. A worker can accumulate these amounts by age sixty-five if he pays, starting at age twenty-four, $3.10 a month for a male and $4.15 a month for a female. A worker who has a nonworking spouse could pay $7.25 a month to accumulate enough to pay benefits to his spouse as well.[13]

In our private system, all workers could sign up for old-age hospital insurance at age twenty-four. This insurance would pay the same benefits that social security's hospital insurance would pay to all those after the age of sixty-five. To purchase this insurance these workers would have to pay only the monthly premiums described above.[14] The purchase of such private hospital insurance at age

[13]These monthly premium payments are lower than the actual amounts necessary to accumulate the stated totals by age sixty-five because some workers will die before reaching sixty-five. These workers will receive nothing for their premium payments, and these payments can then be used to pay benefits to the surviving workers. The monthly premium payments that all workers must pay can then be reduced by a factor to account for the fact that a certain percentage of workers will die before sixty-five.

[14]Social Security's hospital insurance also pays hospital insurance benefits to disabled workers under sixty-five. There was not sufficient available data, however, to calculate the year-by-year value of these benefits. The best possible estimate available suggests that for workers below the age of forty-five, monthly premium payments of less than $1.00 would be sufficient to cover these benefits. After that, workers could rely on their retirement trust funds, which would generally be large enough to self-insure each worker individually. Alternatively, if workers simply doubled the monthly premium payments for old-age hospital insurance, they would certainly be paying enough to provide for these disability hospital insurance benefits without ever having

twenty-four would avoid an important problem. If all workers waited until age sixty-five to purchase private health insurance, it might be apparent by then which are more likely to require the most in hospital and medical services in their retirement years. These workers would then have to pay significantly higher premiums to get the same coverage. Although the other workers would then have to pay less in premiums, the higher premiums for the more sickly workers might constitute a harsh burden on them. If all purchased the insurance at age twenty-four, however, all would present relatively equal risks and all could be charged relatively uniform rates, avoiding these problems.

In comparing our system of private insurance alternatives to social security, then, we need not reduce the annual benefits that the private system can pay by $1,000 to $2,000. Instead, we can merely keep in mind that to purchase old-age hospital insurance benefits equivalent to what social security would pay the workers in our private system must pay additional monthly premiums during their working years approximately equal to what it costs to pick up the *Wall Street Journal* at the newsstand every morning.

We have now described a plan of private investment and insurance alternatives that covers all of the major contingencies which social security covers—retirement, death, disability, and old-age illness. To purchase this plan of private alternatives, we assume that the workers in our private system use the full amounts that they would have paid in OASDHI taxes, as currently legislated, if they had remained in the social security system. That is, we make the deductions for life and disability insurance described above from the amounts that each of our workers would have paid in OASDHI taxes each year under social security, including both the employer and employee shares, and we assume that each of the workers saves and invests the rest in his own private trust fund to pay for his retirement benefits.

We add to this saved and invested amount an additional amount each year to make up for the deficits that the Social Security Administration projects for the OASDI program, excluding the HI program. As we will see in the next chapter, the Social Security Administration

---

to rely on their retirement trust funds. This still leaves these monthly premium payments at relatively insubstantial amounts. Furthermore, even if we do not provide for these disability hospital insurance benefits in our private system, the undercoverage of our private system in this area would again be more than outweighed by the overcoverage in other areas.

makes projections seventy-five years into the future concerning the amount of taxes to be collected and benefits to be paid each year under current law, and the resulting annual deficits to be expected. These projections include an average tax deficit for the entire seventy-five-year period under each alternative set of assumptions, indicating the amount by which taxes would have to be raised immediately for each of the next seventy-five years to finance the payment of currently promised benefits in each of those years. We have added these amounts to the amounts that each individual worker in our private system saves and invests each year in his retirement trust fund.

Since we are comparing the benefits paid under the private system with those promised under social security, we should make this comparison with the amount of private benefits that can be purchased with the amounts necessary to finance those promised social security benefits. However, we are adding the amounts necessary only to finance promised OASDI benefits, not promised HI benefits because we are making our comparison only with the amount of HI benefits that can be paid with currently legislated HI taxes, not currently promised HI benefits.

One of the most important assumptions in our projections concerns the assumed real rate of return that the investments in this private system can earn. We in fact make eleven separate projections of the amount of benefits that can be paid by the private system, assuming a different real rate of return for each. These assumptions range in steps of one-half of a percentage point from 3.0% to 8.0%. Since these are real rates of return, they represent the amounts that can be earned each year above the rate of inflation.

The real rate of return that can be earned on private investments depends on what one invests in. If we consider the historical returns on capital investments in the corporate sector and the historical performance of common stocks as well as the expected future performance of these investments, we can justify real rates of returns as high as 8%. This is especially true if we also consider an expanded and comprehensive system of tax exemptions for investments of private retirement and insurance accounts, which will be proposed later in this book.

According to Professor Feldstein, a real rate of return of 8% is entirely justifiable and a real rate of 5.5% is conservative. Feldstein writes, "Over the past twenty-five years, the real annual yield (after adjusting for inflation) was 8% for common stocks and 3% for corporate bonds. A conservative portfolio with half of each would have yielded 5.5%.[15] In fact, if half the annual payments into our system of private trust funds was invested each year in common stocks with an 8% real return and half was invested each year in corporate bonds with a real return of 3%, and the 8% return to common stocks was reinvested each year in common stocks and the 3% return on corporate bonds was reinvested each year in corporate bonds, the average real yield on the fund after forty-one years would be 6.3%, not 5.5%.

The record supports Feldstein's position. From 1945 to 1976 the average real rate of return earned on common stocks listed on the New York stock exchange was 7.5%. From 1945 to 1972 the real return earned on these stocks was 9.6%. From 1945 to 1965 the real return was 12%. If we change the basic date of reference, we find that from 1926 to 1976, a fifty-year period that included the Great Depression, the real rate of return on common stocks was 6.9%. From 1926 to 1972 this return was exactly 8.0%, and from 1926 to 1965 the return was 9.0%. The rate from 1933 to 1976 was 8.0%, from 1933 to 1972, 9.4%, and from 1933 to 1956, 10.9%.[16]

These performances are expected to continue. Under projections made by Roger G. Ibbotson of the University of Chicago Business School and Rex H. Sinquefeld of the American National Bank and Trust Company of Chicago, the real rate of return on common stocks from 1977 to 2000 is expected to be 6.78%.[17] With a portfolio of 80% common stocks, 10% long-term corporate bonds and 10% U.S. Treasury Bills, Ibbotson and Sinquefeld project a real rate of return of 6.24%. With a portfolio of 60% common stocks, 30% long-term corporate bonds and 10% U.S. Treasury Bills, the projected real return is 5.45%.

These returns represent after-tax returns in the sense that they are the returns left after the corporation that earned them has paid the corporate income tax. Although an individual in normal circumstances would still have to pay income tax on the dividends and capital gains tax on the appreciation, tax exemptions available today for Individual Retirement Accounts (IRAs), Keogh plans and similar

[15]Martin Feldstein, "Facing the Social Security Crisis," *Harvard Institute of Economic Research, Discussion Paper No. 492*, July 1976.

[16]Roger G. Ibbotson and Rex A. Sinquefeld; *Stocks, Bonds, Bills and Inflation: The Past (1926–1976) and the Future (1977–2000)*, (Chicago: Financial Analysts Research Foundation, 1977).

[17]Ibid.

types of tax-preferred pension plans would largely eliminate this taxation. We can therefore take these returns as the real, after-tax returns available on investments that can be made through a private retirement or insurance trust fund.

As we noted in the previous section, a truly fair comparison between social security and the private system would be based on the before-tax rate of return on private investments rather than on the after-tax return. Feldstein has estimated the real before-tax return on capital investments in several of his studies. In his most recent study he estimated that from 1946 to 1975 this return was 12.4%, based on data concerning the return on capital investments in the corporate sector over this period.[18] This average, however, includes two years at the end of this period, 1974 and 1975, during which the country experienced one of the worst recessions in U.S. history. Yet, the average excludes the higher returns during the recovery years since then. Feldstein's calculations also show that from 1946 to 1969, this return was approximately 13%. This is probably a better estimate of the actual long-term rate that would appear if the recovery years after the 1974–75 recession were included.

In other papers Feldstein's summaries of the results of economic studies on this subject indicate that the real, before-tax, rate of return on additional capital investment is 15%.[19] Studies conducted at the Brookings Institution have also concluded that the real, before-tax return on capital investment is within the range suggested by Feldstein.[20] It seems, therefore, that this return is somewhere between 12% and 15% and that 12% would be a conservative estimate. Although if social security were entirely replaced by a system of private investments this return might decline somewhat, Feldstein has calculated under pessimistic assumptions that this decline would not be substantial.[21] The possibility of such a decline will be discussed in more detail in chapter 11.

[18]Martin Feldstein, "National Saving in the United States," *Harvard Institute of Economic Research, Discussion Paper No. 506,* October 1976.

[19]Martin Feldstein, "Toward a Reform of Social Security," *The Public Interest,* Summer 1975, pp. 75–95; and Martin Feldstein, "The Optimal Financing of Social Security," *Harvard Institute of Economic Research, Discussion Paper No. 388,* 1974.

[20]Alicia H. Munnell, *The Future of Social Security* (Washington, D.C.: Brookings Institution, 1977), p. 128.

[21]Feldstein has calculated that if everyone saved and invested enough to replace his social security benefits, the real rate of return on capital investments would fall by two percentage points or less. See Martin Feldstein, "National Saving in the United States," *Harvard Institution of Economic Research,* Discussion Paper No. 506, October, 1976,

We will propose in chapter 11 a system of tax exemptions for investments made through individual retirement and insurance accounts as an alternative to social security. This system of tax exemptions would allow individuals to receive this full, real, before-tax rate of return on capital investments made through these accounts. In effect, this new system would simply allow individuals to receive the full amount of the increased production that they have created or produced with their capital investments.

We may conclude, therefore, that after-tax real rates of return of 6% to 8% on capital investments are certainly feasible. For long periods in our recent history we have experienced returns at least this high and for many of these periods much higher. We may therefore compare the benefits the private system can pay at these real rates of return with the benefits that social security can pay. A fair comparison between social security and the private system should be based on real, before-tax returns, rather than after-tax returns, and

pp. 31–32; Martin Feldstein, "The Optimal Financing of Social Security," *Harvard Institute of Economic Research*, Discussion Paper No. 388, 1974. However, this decline would not be complete until sufficient investments had been accumulated to replace social security, which would take decades.

Furthermore, Feldstein's calculation assumes that technology is constant, but new, improved technologies increase the productivity of capital. We are now in an era of particularly rapid technological advancement, and the new technologies that are now available and that will become available in the next few decades may completely offset any decline in the rate of return due to increased investment. This is particularly true in light of the energy crisis that is sweeping the world. For example, the solution to the energy crisis, whether through nuclear power, synthetic fuels, or more difficult recovery processes of conventional fuels, will require enormous capital outlays. The dissipation of easily obtainable fossil fuels means that the return on the capital intensive technologies that will replace these fuels has soared dramatically.

In addition, the low rate of saving in the United States in recent decades has meant little capital accumulation during this period and, more recently, actual capital disaccumulation that has been exacerbated by the combination in recent years of inflation and inadequate accounting and tax conventions for depreciation. These problems have meant delays in the introduction of available technologies and in the replacement of the housing stock and outmoded capital plants. Much of the additional capital investment from private retirement system, therefore, would go to replace the recently consumed capital and to embark on these delayed projects. If some changes such as social security reform are not made to reverse the trends in savings and capital accumulation, the return on capital investment will undoubtedly increase in future years. Much of the additional investment from a private retirement system is therefore likely merely to avert this increase in capital returns rather than lead to a decline in returns.

Additional factors tending to affect any decline in capital returns due to increased investment are the new opportunities for such investment in the developing third world countries and new government demands in this country for such investment to solve environmental and safety problems. These factors, as well as those noted above, will be discussed in more detail in chapter 11.

these before-tax returns have been much higher. A truly fair comparison between the private system and social security would therefore show the private system to be even more superior to social security than it appears assuming an 8% real rate of return. Given the new system of tax exemptions that we will propose in chapter 11, we may take the projections of the benefits that can be paid by the private system at an 8% real rate of return as quite conservative estimates of the least that the private system can pay under this new tax exemption system.[22]

The rest of the assumptions necessary to make our projections have been taken from the Social Security Administration. The administration uses three sets of assumptions in making its projections: an optimistic set, known as Alternative I, and intermediate set, known as Alternative II, and a pessimistic set, known as Alternative III. Each of these alternatives includes assumptions concerning inflation, unemployment, fertility rates, mortality rates, real wage growth, etc. We have made our projections separately under each of the three alternative sets of assumptions as presented in the 1978 Annual Report of the Board of Trustees for the OASDI program.[23] As we will see in chapter 5, however, Alternative III is by far the most realistic set of assumptions, despite its so-called pessimism. Alternative II, by contrast, is actually rather optimistic, and Alternative I is wildly optimistic. The most meaningful results, therefore, are those projected under Alternative III. But, as we shall see, the projections under all three alternatives ultimately lead to the same conclusion.

The projections of the amounts individuals would have in their retirement trust funds at age sixty-five, and the amounts these funds could pay each year in retirement benefits, are shown in tables 24–32. The retirement fund and benefit amounts are shown for each of the different assumed real rates of return. The projections for

[22]It is true that investors are not currently receiving very high real returns on their investments because of the recent tremendous increase in inflation, but this is merely a temporary phenomenon that will disappear as businesses adjust to the recent inflationary surge. Basic economics tells us that in the long run inflation has no effect on the real returns to capital investment. The best indication of this long-run real rate of return is the performance of this return over the last fifty years, through depressions, recessions, wars, and inflationary peaks. We should not take a network evening news approach to policy planning for a long-range program such as social security. The transitory nature of this current experience is indicated by the simple fact that if investors continue to receive little or no real return for very long, investment will virtually cease and the 1930s will be remembered as the good old days.

[23]*1978 Annual Report of the Board of Trustees of the Federal Old-Age and Survivor's Insurance and Disability Insurance Trust Funds.*

maximum-, average-, and low-income workers are shown three times, once for each of the three alternative sets of assumptions.

The "Perpetual Annuity" column shows the amounts that could be paid each year out of interest on the fund alone, leaving the fund intact to be passed on to heirs. The "Life Annuity, Single Worker" shows the amounts that could be paid each year for the life of the worker after age sixty-five, completely using up the fund. The "Life Annuity, Couple" shows the amounts that could be paid, completely using up the fund, while both spouses are alive and after one spouse dies. At the bottom of each table is shown the amount that social security would pay a single worker with the earnings noted and the amount that social security would pay such a worker with a spouse while both were alive and after one died.

In parentheses, next to each benefit amount, is the replacement ratio that this benefit amount represents. The replacement ratio is the annual benefit amount as a percent of the individual's income during his last year of work. A replacement ratio of 65% to 75% of before-tax income is sufficient to maintain an individual in retirement at the same standard of living as when he was working because of the reduced expenses of retirement.

All figures in these tables are in constant 1980 dollars, and thus the actual nominal amounts individuals would have in their retirement accounts and receive in benefits would be the amounts shown increased by an amount sufficient to fully compensate for inflation since 1980. As noted earlier, the benefit amounts shown will also increase each year at the rate of inflation once the worker starts receiving them. In other words, the benefit amounts shown can continue to be paid each year in real terms.

These projections represent the most detailed and comprehensive comparison between social security and private alternatives ever made. To examine these projections more closely, let us begin with a worker who starts working at age twenty-four in 1980 and earns the maximum taxable income all of his life. In 1980 this worker could be earning $25,900. He might be a young law or business school graduate or a graduate of some other professional school. It is not uncommon today for graduates of professional schools to start at salaries this high or even higher, and most should reach this level soon after graduation. At any rate, earning the maximum taxable income for an entire lifetime is a somewhat modest earnings history for a professional and does not necessarily mean that such a person is rich.

We will examine the Alternative III projections first since they are the most realistic. Social security would pay this maximum-income worker $12,125 per year in retirement benefits, or 27% of his pre-retirement salary, if he retired single. It would pay him $18,188 per year, or 40% of his preretirement income, if he retired with a spouse, paying $12,125 per year to the survivor. Social security leaves the worker with no fund that he could leave to his heirs.

If this maximum-income earner invested the amount he would have paid in OASDHI taxes over the course of his life in our private system of investment and insurance coverage, at a real rate of return of 6% he could retire at sixty-five with a retirement trust fund of $1,019,014 under the Alternative III set of assumptions. He could live off of the interest on this fund for life, receiving a perpetual annuity of $61,141 a year, or 132% of his salary the year before he retired. This amount is about five times what social security would pay a single or surviving retiree or three and one-half times what it would pay a worker with a spouse. At the same time, the worker in this private system could leave over $1 million to his heirs.

If the worker were single, he could purchase a life annuity that would pay him $114,932 a year, 248% of his preretirement salary and almost ten times what social security would pay him. If he had a spouse he could purchase an annuity that would pay him $98,895 a year while both were alive (214% of his preretirement salary), and $65,930 after one died (143% of preretirement salary). These amounts are about five and one-quarter times what social security would pay.

Assuming an 8% real rate of return, the private system would leave our maximum-income worker at age sixty-five with a trust fund of $1,726,449. This fund could pay him $138,116 a year for life in interest, about eleven times what social security would pay him without a spouse and more than seven times what it would pay him with a spouse. This figure is also about 300% of his preretirement income. Even with the receipt of these benefits the worker could still leave a fund of over $1.7 million to his heirs.

If the worker was single, he could purchase a life annuity of $221,521 per year for life, 478% of his preretirement income and almost eighteen times what social security would pay. If he had a spouse he could purchase an annuity that would pay him $193,884 per year while both spouses were alive, 418% of preretirement income, and $129,256 per year to the surviving spouse, 279% of preretirement income. These amounts are more than ten times what social security would pay.

These comparisons are based on the assumption that the wife does not work, but in fact, over half of all married women now work. If both spouses work they will both be accumulating retirement funds, and the superiority of the private system would be even greater. For example, let us assume that at age twenty-four the maximum-income worker marries an average-income worker age twenty-two who continues to work until she is sixty-five. She might be a secretary or a school teacher or anyone who has a job that would pay $12,105 in 1980. At retirement, social security would pay this couple $20,697 per year while both spouses were alive and $12,525 per year after one died.

If both husband and wife invested the amounts they would have paid in OASDHI taxes in the private system instead, at a 6% real rate of return they could retire on a combined fund of $1,503,411. This fund would pay them $90,205 per year in interest, about four and one-half times what social security would pay with both alive and seven and one-quarter times what it would pay with only one spouse alive. Even after receiving these enormous benefits they could still leave the $1.5 million fund to their heirs.

Alternatively, they could buy an annuity that would pay $114,932 per year for the life of the husband and $55,237 per year for the life of the wife, for a combined total while both are alive of $170,169 per year, eight and one-quarter times what social security would pay. They could also buy an annuity that would pay $146,425 while both were alive and $97,616 after one died, about seven to eight times what social security would pay.

At an 8% real rate of return, this couple could retire at sixty-five on a combined fund of $2,591,293. This fund could pay perpetual annual interest of $207,304, about ten times what social security would pay while both were alive and sixteen and one-half times what social security would pay while only one was alive, still leaving a fund of $2.6 million for the heirs.

Alternatively, the couple could buy an annuity that would pay $222,521 for the life of the husband and $110,968 for the life of the wife, for a combined total of $332,489 while both are alive, about sixteen times what social security would pay. The couple could also buy an annuity that would pay $291,008 while both were alive and $194,005 after one died, about fourteen to fifteen times what social security would pay.

It is increasingly common among young married couples today for both to have careers. The nation's law, business, and medical schools are graduating more and more women. It would therefore be useful to compare families with two young professionals under social security and our private system.

If a couple had both earned the maximum taxable income all their lives, social security would pay them $24,050 while both were alive, and $12,525 after one died. Under the private system, at a 6% real rate of return, the couple could retire on a combined trust fund of $2,030,806. This fund would pay $121,848 per year in interest, about five times what social security would pay with both alive and ten times what it would pay with one alive, all while leaving a fund of $2 million for the children. The couple could instead buy an annuity that would pay $229,864 per year while both were alive and $114,932 per year while one was alive, about nine times what social security would pay.

At an 8% real rate of return, the couple could retire on a combined trust fund of $3,452,898. This fund would pay them $276,232 per year in perpetual interest, about eleven times what social security would pay with both alive and twenty-two times what it would pay the survivor, leaving an enormous fund of about $3.5 million for the children. Alternatively, the couple could buy an annuity which would pay $443,042 per year while both were alive and $221,521 per year while one was alive, almost eighteen times what social security would pay.

Now let us examine our average-income worker who starts work at age twenty-two right out of college at the average income of $12,105 in 1980 and continues to earn an average income throughout his life. As we have noted, this average is based on a calculation that includes the salaries of younger and part-time workers, and thus the average income of the typical head of household responsible for the support of a family is actually larger. Most college graduates and union workers almost certainly earn more.

Social security would pay this average-income worker $8,172 per year, or 40% of his preretirement income, if he retired single at age sixty-five. It would pay him $12,258 per year, or 60% of his pre-retirement income, if he retired with a spouse, falling to $8,172 a year after one spouse died.

Under the private system assuming a 6% real rate of return, this worker could retire at age sixty-five with a private retirement fund of $488,008. This fund could pay him perpetual interest of $29,281 per year, 143% of his preretirement income. This would be about three and one-half times what social security would pay a single worker and about two and one-half times what it would pay a worker with a nonworking spouse, all while allowing the worker to leave about $0.5 million to his children.

Alternatively the worker could buy an annuity that would pay him $55,237 per year for the rest of his life, 270% of his preretirement income and almost seven times what social security would pay a single worker. If the worker was married, he could also buy an annuity that would pay $47,530 per year while both spouses were alive, 232% of preretirement income, and $31,686 after one died, 155% of preretirement income. This is almost four times what social security would pay.

Assuming an 8% real rate of return, this worker could retire at age sixty-five with a fund of $864,844. This fund would pay a perpetual annuity of $69,188 per year, 338% of his preretirement income. This is about eight and one-half times what social security would pay a single worker and about five and one-half times what it would pay a worker with a spouse; yet again he would be able to leave almost $900,000 to his children.

If the worker were single he could also buy an annuity that would pay him $110,968 per year for life, 541% of his preretirement income and about thirteen and one-half times what social security would pay. If he were married, he could buy an annuity that would pay him $97,124 per year, 474% of his preretirement income, while he and his wife were alive, and $64,749 per year, 316% of preretirement income, after one died. This is about eight times what social security would pay.

Now let us assume that at age twenty-two our average-income worker marries an eighteen-year-old low-income worker who earns $5,731 in 1980 and continues to work for the rest of her life with her wage increasing only at the rate of growth in real wages. This could be a worker who works full-time at about the minimum wage or a worker who works part-time at higher wages. This couple would have a modest earnings history. Social security would pay this couple at retirement $13,442 per year while both were alive and $8,172 per year after one died.

Under the private system, at a 6% real rate of return, this couple could retire at age sixty-five with a combined trust fund of $785,617. This fund would pay them a perpetual annuity of $47,138 per year, about three and one-half times what social security would pay with both alive and six times what it would pay with one alive, while leaving a fund of almost $800,000 for their children.

The couple could also buy an annuity that would pay $55,237 while the husband was alive and $33,686 while the wife was alive, for a combined total of $88,923 while both were alive, about six and one-half times what social security would pay. As another option, the couple could buy an annuity that would pay $76,516 while both were alive and $51,010 after one died, about six times what social security would pay.

At an 8% real rate of return this couple could retire with a combined trust fund of $1,426,231. This fund would pay them perpetual interest of $114,099 per year, about eight and one-half times what social security would pay with both alive and almost fourteen times what it would pay with one alive, still leaving a fund of almost $1.5 million for the children.

The couple could also buy an annuity that would pay $110,968 per year for the life of the husband and $72,032 for the life of the wife, for a combined total of $183,000 while both were alive, over thirteen and one-half times what social security would pay. Alternatively, the couple could buy an annuity that would pay $160,169 per year while both were alive and $106,779 per year after one died, twelve to thirteen times what social security would pay.

Assume now that our twenty-two-year-old average-income worker instead marries a worker of the same age who continues to work all of her life and also earns an average income. Social security would pay this couple $16,344 per year while both were alive and $8,172 after one died.

Under the private system, at a 6% real rate of return, this couple could retire at sixty-five on a fund of $976,016, paying perpetual interest of $58,562 per year. This is about three and one-half times what social security would pay with both spouses alive and seven times what it would pay with one spouse alive. Again, this would still leave a fund of about $1 million for the children. The couple could also buy an annuity which would pay $110,474 while both were alive and $55,237 while one was alive. This is almost seven times what social security would pay.

At an 8% real rate of return, this couple could retire on a combined fund of $1,729,688, which would pay $138,376 per year in interest. This is about eight and one-half times what social security would pay with both spouses alive and seventeen times what it would pay with one alive, all while still allowing these average-income workers to leave about $1.75 million to their children. Alternatively, the couple could buy an annuity that would pay them

$221,936 per year while both were alive and $110,968 while one was alive, about thirteen and one-half times what social security would pay.

Perhaps the most constructive comparisons of all are those using low-income workers. As we have noted, the social security system contains numerous welfare elements meant to provide additional benefits to those with low incomes. The deck is therefore stacked even more strongly against the private system with regard to low-income workers. However, the private system is still vastly superior to social security even for these workers. It should be strongly emphasized that this superiority is of greatest importance to these workers because it will provide them with the means to buy more of the essential necessities and basic comforts.

We will examine the example of a low-income worker who earned $5,731 in 1980, about what the minimum wage would pay a full-time worker. This worker's wage increases only at the rate of growth in real wages in employment covered by social security, so he will remain at or near the minimum wage all of his life. Social security would pay this worker $5,270 a year, or 53% of his preretirement income, if he was single. If he was married, he would receive $7,905 a year, or 79% of his preretirement income, while both spouses were alive, and $5,270 after one died.

At a 6% real rate of return, this worker could retire at age sixty-five on a trust fund of $297,609. This trust fund would pay him $17,857 a year in interest, or 177% of his preretirement income. This is about three and one-half times what social security would pay a single worker and more than twice what it would pay a couple. After all this, our low-income worker would still be able to leave a fund of about $300,000 to his children, a strong step toward breaking the cycle of poverty.

If this worker were single, he could buy a life annuity that would pay him $33,686 a year for life, 333% of his preretirement income and six and one-half times what social security would pay. If he were married, he could buy an annuity that would pay $28,986 per year or 287% of preretirement income, while both spouses were alive, and $19,324 per year, or 192% of preretirement income, after one died. This is more than three and one-half times what social security would pay.

At an 8% real rate of return this worker could retire on a fund of $561,387, which would pay him $44,911 per year in interest, 444% of his preretirement income. This would be about five and one-half times what social security would pay a couple and about eight and one-half times what it would pay a single worker, all while allowing this poor worker to leave well over $0.5 million to his children. If the worker were single, he could purchase a life annuity that would pay him $72,032 per year for life, 713% of preretirement income and over thirteen and one-half times what social security would pay. If the worker were married, he could purchase an annuity that would pay $63,045 per year, or 624% of preretirement income, while he and his wife were alive, and $42,030 per year, 416% of preretirement income, after one of them died. This is about eight times what social security would pay.

If we assume that this low-income worker has a spouse who is also a low-income worker, the private system does even better than social security. The social security program would pay this couple $10,540 per year while both spouses were alive and $5,270 per year after one died.

Under the private system, at a 6% real rate of return, this couple could retire at sixty-five with a trust fund of $595,218. This fund would pay $35,714 per year for life, about three and one-half times what social security would pay a couple and almost seven times what it would pay the survivor. Incredibly, this poor couple could then leave a fund of $600,000 to their children. The couple could alternatively purchase an annuity that would pay them $67,372 per year while both were alive and $33,686 per year after one died, about six and one-half times what social security would pay.

At an 8% real rate of return this couple could retire on a trust fund of $1,122,774, which would pay them $89,822 per year in interest, about eight and one-half times what social security would pay a couple and about seventeen times what it would pay the survivor. Yet, this formerly poor couple could still leave a fund of well over $1 million to their children. The couple could alternatively purchase an annuity that would pay them $144,064 per year while both were alive and $72,032 after one died, about thirteen and one-half times what social security would pay.

These additional benefits available to poor workers in the private system are probably the most important, even though the additional benefits available to average and maximum income workers are much greater. The higher private pension benefits will increase the retirement incomes of poor workers from modest levels up to levels that will enable these workers to enjoy fully the material benefits of modern American life. At the same time, these poor workers will have earned their higher living standards entirely through their own work, skill, and effort. The private system will enable low-income workers to enjoy these benefits while still leaving them with large trust funds that they can use to help their children and grandchildren attain higher standards of living. Reforming a program as large and fundamental to our lives as social security offers the potential for many substantial, beneficial side-effects. A sharp reduction in poverty just may be one of these side-effects. In fact, social security reform just may be the most successful government initiative to eliminate poverty to date.

It should be noted further that the private system overwhelms social security even at real rates of return below 6% to 8%. For real rates of return as low as 5%, 4.5%, and 4%, the private system provides much greater benefits than social security. Even at 3%, the benefits under the private system are substantially greater than under social security. For workers with nonworking spouses, the private system pays maximum-income workers about twice what social security would pay, it pays average-income workers about 50% more, and it pays low-income workers about the same. But if these workers have working spouses, then, assuming that both spouses earned the same incomes, maximum-income couples would get four times what social security would pay, average-income couples would get three times as much, and low-income workers would get twice as much. These figures suggest that for most workers, the real rate of return paid by social security is well below 3%.

The projections under Alternative I and Alternative II present the same basic picture as under Alternative III. The trust fund and benefit amounts of the private system are almost the same under all three sets of projections. The assumed superior economic performance under the more optimistic assumptions caused higher projections of annual wages and consequently higher annual taxes or contributions. This factor tended to increase the trust fund and benefit amounts more for the more optimistic assumptions. But the projected deficits for social security are higher for the more pessimistic assumptions, and we added an additional amount to the contributions each year to make up for these deficits. This factor tended to increase the trust fund and benefit amounts more for the more pessimistic assumptions. These two effects almost exactly offset each other, so that the projected trust fund and benefit amounts were almost exactly the same under all three sets of assumptions.

The major differences between the projections under the three alternatives occurred in the projected social security benefit amounts. Benefits for maximum-income single workers were $3,000 per year greater under Alternative II than Alternative III and $3,500 per year greater under Alternative I than Alternative II. Average-income single workers received $2,000 per year more under Alternative II than under Alternative III and an additional $2,500 per year more under Alternative I. Low-income single workers received $1,500 per year more under Alternative II and an additional $1,700 per year under Alternative I. For a worker with a nonworking spouse these differences would be 50% greater. Even with these additional social security benefits, however, the benefits available under the private system are still much greater. Under Alternative II, assuming a 5% real rate of return, workers at all income levels with nonworking spouses would receive at least twice as much under the private system as under social security, and in most cases they would receive much more. If these workers had working spouses, then they would need only a 3.5% real rate of return to achieve this same level of superiority under the private system. Chapter 5 will show in detail that Alternative III is easily the most realistic set of assumptions and that Alternative I is highly unrealistic.

It should be reiterated that all of the figures presented in this comparison between social security and private alternatives are in today's dollars (constant 1980 dollars) so the value of the amounts discussed will not be depreciated by inflation. A dollar of these retirement benefits will buy the same goods and services for the retired beneficiary that a dollar will buy today in 1980. It should also be reiterated that the amounts of the annual annuities discussed have also been adjusted so that there will be enough funds on hand to increase these annual benefits with the rate of inflation each year and thus hold them constant in real terms. The annual benefit amounts discussed were calculated on the assumption that the insurance company or other institution that promised to pay them had also promised to increase them each year to fully compensate for inflation.

This is especially important because government officials have heavily emphasized that social security benefits are indexed to rise with the rate of inflation and have claimed that this inflation-proof feature of the program cannot be matched by private alternatives, a claim that is simply not true. We have just seen the inflation-proof benefits that can be paid by the private system, and these benefits are far greater than those that can be paid by social security. The reason that a private, invested system can pay these inflation-proof benefits is that in general the returns to the investments in this system tend to increase when the rate of inflation increases so that the investment is still earning the same real rate of return after inflation. As prices increase with inflation, the value of the assets that individuals hold in their invested retirement accounts will, on average, increase at the same rate. The prices charged for the goods and services produced by these investments will also, on average, increase at the rate of inflation. The profit or rate of return on those investments will therefore remain the same in real terms. During periods of inflation the profits of businesses are not eliminated or sharply reduced by the rise in prices. On the contrary, it is businesses that are raising the prices on the goods and services that their investments are producing during the inflationary period. These price increases will not result in any long-term rise in profits for these businesses because the businesses are merely increasing their prices in response to excess demand, which will percolate throughout the economy and increase their costs. But the result will be to maintain long-term profit margins in real terms.

While an individual is working and accumulating his retirement fund, therefore, the future benefits that this fund will be able to pay will be increasing at the rate of inflation because of this automatic adjustment process. If an individual chooses to live off of the interest on this fund in retirement, his benefits will continue to increase at the rate of inflation because the interest rate or return on investment also generally increases with the rate of inflation. Thus the individual will be able to attain his same expected benefits in real terms. Similarly, if a person purchases an annuity, it will be possible for the seller of the annuity to agree to pay benefits in real terms, adjusted for inflation, because of this automatic adjustment process in the investments that support the annuity. The private system can match the inflation-proof benefits of social security.

The tremendous monetary superiority of our system of private alternatives is not limited to retirement benefits but includes other types of insurance coverage provided by social security.

For example, for life or survivor's insurance we deducted sufficient premiums from the worker's savings each year to buy enough term life insurance so that the insurance plus the retirement fund could pay survivor's benefits equivalent to what social security would pay. Well before retirement, however, virtually all workers reach a point at which the retirement fund alone can pay the necessary survivor's benefits without the purchase of any supplemental insurance. After that point, as the retirement fund continues to grow, the private system is able to pay more in survivor's benefits than social security.

Under Alternative III projections for maximum-income workers this point is reached by the age of forty-one, assuming a 6% real rate of return, and by the age of thirty-nine, assuming an 8% real rate of return. For average-income workers this point is reached by forty-two at a 6% real rate of return and by forty at an 8% real rate of return. For low-income workers, this point is reached at thirty-eight at a 6% real rate of return and at thirty-six at an 8% real rate of return.

After this point not only will the benefits paid under the private system continue to grow, but the benefits paid under the social security will actually decline because the children of most workers will be reaching adulthood in these years. If a worker dies after his children have grown up, social security will not pay any survivor's benefits until his surviving spouse reaches sixty-five, and thus as the children of workers in their forties and early fifties grow up, the survivor's benefits social security will pay will fall dramatically. Under a private system, however, if a worker dies after his children have grown up the worker will still leave behind his retirement fund. Since this fund will continue to grow larger after a worker's children have grown up, the survivor's benefits that can be paid by the private system will keep right on increasing.

We should also recognize that the chances of dying after forty are much greater than the chances of dying before, and the great majority of workers who die before retirement are over forty. A private system will pay more in survivor's benefits than social security during the period when the great majority of workers who will be needing such benefits because of preretirement death will actually die.

The substantial significance of the monetary superiority of the private system can be illustrated by a few examples. If our maximum-income worker who started work at twenty-four in 1980 died at age fifty, then under the private system, given an 8% real rate of return and Alternative III assumptions, the worker would leave behind a fund of $474,899. This fund could pay $37,992 per year out of the interest alone, about the same as this maximum-income worker would have been earning at the time he died. The surviving spouse could, therefore, live on this annual interest payment for the rest of his or her life and leave the fund of almost $0.5 million to the children or other heirs. Alternatively, the surviving spouse could live on the interest until age sixty-five, and then use the fund to purchase an annuity that would pay $60,934 per year for life. Social security, on the other hand, would pay this worker no benefits if his children had grown up, until his surviving spouse reached sixty-five. At that point the spouse would receive $10,428 a year for life, with no fund to be left to the children.

If our average-income worker who started work at twenty-two in 1980 died at fifty, then under the private system, given an 8% real rate of return and Alternative III assumptions, the worker would leave behind a fund of $241,983. This fund could pay $19,359 per year out of the interest alone, about $2,000 per year more than the worker was earning when he died. At age sixty-five the surviving spouse could use the fund to purchase an annuity that would pay $31,049 per year for life. Social security would pay nothing until the spouse reached sixty-five, assuming the children were grown, and it would then pay only $6,852 per year for life.

Finally, if our low-income worker who started work at eighteen in 1980 died at age fifty, then under the private system, with the same assumptions as above, the worker would leave behind a fund of $161,856. This fund would pay $12,948 per year in perpetual interest, about 50% more than the worker was earning when he died. The surviving spouse could also use this fund at age sixty-five to purchase an annuity paying $20,768 a year for life. Social security, by contrast, would again pay nothing until age sixty-five and then only $4,464 per year for life.

The monetary superiority of the private survivor's insurance system is even greater for those workers with working spouses. A man whose wife earns as much as he does will have his family covered by at least twice the amount of insurance coverage provided by social security because each spouse in the private system will be developing his or her own retirement fund and purchasing his or her own term life insurance, and each spouse's fund and insurance will be available to pay benefits without condition when the spouse dies.

Thus, if one of the two working spouses dies, under the private system the fund and the insurance for that spouse will be sufficient to pay the survivor's benefits described earlier. These benefits are analogous in every important respect to those that would be paid under social security except that under social security the benefits paid would be reduced because of the continued earnings of the surviving, working spouse. The earnings test would probably completely eliminate the benefits for the surviving spouse because of these continued earnings, especially if the surviving spouse is earning as much as the deceased spouse was, leaving only the benefits to be paid to the surviving children. Benefits under the private system, however, would not be reduced because of the continued earnings of the surviving spouse, and these benefits will continue to be equal to the MFB.

Similarly, when the surviving working spouse retires under social security, he or she will receive only the higher of his or her own retirement benefits or the survivor's benefits payable on the deceased spouse's earnings record. But under the private system the surviving, working spouse will receive both because the deceased spouse will have left behind enough in insurance and retirement funds to finance the post-age-sixty-five survivor's benefits, and the working spouse will have continued to accumulate his or her own retirement fund. Thus the private system will again pay more than social security.

If, however, after the first spouse dies the second working spouse also dies before retirement, and both spouses had the same earnings history, then the amount of benefits paid by the private system would double because the second worker's trust fund and life insurance would now be available to pay benefits as well. Yet, even after the second spouse died, the amount of survivor's benefits paid under social security would remain the same. Benefits would still be paid to the surviving children in the same amounts as before, with no benefits paid for a surviving spouse either before or after retirement.[24] The private system, however, would be paying the children twice the MFB, and they would also receive twice the post-age-sixty-five survivor's benefits that would have been paid to either spouse who had survived the other. Since the private system was paying more than social security before the death of the second spouse, and private benefits have doubled while social security's have remained the same, the private system would now be paying more than twice

---

[24]If the wages of the second spouse at death have grown larger than the wages of the first spouse at death, the PIA and hence the benefits for the children under social security would be slightly higher after the death of the second spouse than after the death of the first. But private benefits will also have grown because of the higher wages of the second spouse.

the benefits that social security would pay, assuming that both spouses have the same income level. With one spouse earning more or less than the other, the amount of benefits that could be paid by the private system would be commensurately more or less than double what social security would pay.

The private system of survivor's insurance can also be markedly superior to social security. Under the private system, the heirs of a single, childless worker, for example, could receive survivor's benefits, but under social security, the heirs of a childless worker would receive nothing at his death. Under a private system, the heirs of a married but childless worker would receive full benefits at his death, but under social security the only benefits paid would be to his surviving wife after she reached sixty-two and then only if she had not remarried or did not have her own benefits.

Even a married worker with one child would receive much more in benefits under the private system than under social security. In the private survivor's insurance plan we described earlier in this chapter we noted that every worker would have a seven-year period during his working years that he could start at any time and during which he would be covered with enough life insurance to pay the MFB to his survivors for eighteen years after his death. The period for which the MFB could be paid would then be reduced by one year for each year that passed after the end of this seven-year period. If the worker began this seven-year period in the year of his child's birth, the MFB could potentially be paid under the private system until the child reached twenty-five.[25] Social security would at most pay only 150% of the PIA until the child reached eighteen. If the worker had a second child in the third year of the seven-year period, the MFB could potentially be paid under the private system until this child reached twenty-three. Social security would at most pay the MFB until the child reached sixteen, paying 150% of the PIA after that. If the worker had a third child in the fifth year, the MFB could potentially be paid until this child reached twenty-one, while social security would again pay the MFB only until the child reached

[25]The MFB would be paid until the child reached twenty-five if the worker died at any time after the seven-year period passed. If the worker died before this seven-year period passed, the MFB would be paid for an additional number of years past the age of eighteen equal to the age of the child at the worker's death. The same would be true for the additional children described in this paragraph, except that the MFB could at most be paid until the ages noted.

sixteen, with 150% of the PIA for two years after that. Even if the worker had a fourth child in the seventh year of the seven-year period, the MFB could potentially be paid under the private system until this child reached nineteen, while social security would again only pay the MFB until the child reached sixteen and 150% of the PIA for two years after that. In short, even a worker with as many as four children could receive more in survivor's benefits under the private system. The amount of social security benefits in these examples is based on the assumption that the worker has a surviving, nonworking spouse who remains unmarried and cares for the surviving children.

It is true that those who have larger families over more extended periods of time will probably receive a little less insurance protection under the private system we have described than under social security, but at a little additional expense these workers could purchase enough additional term life insurance to make up for this difference. For example, assume a worker who has one child at age twenty-four, another at age twenty-six, another at age thirty-four and another at age thirty-six. If he starts the seven-year period at twenty-four, than at thirty-six he will be covered for only thirteen more years of the MFB in the case of death. Under social security he would be covered for sixteen years of the MFB and two more years of 150% of the PIA. The worker in the private system would therefore have to buy enough additional life insurance to pay for three more years of the MFB and two more years of 150% of the PIA, and he would have to continue to do this until his younger children reached fifteen and thirteen. After that these additional amounts would be reduced by one year for each year that passed. These additional term life insurance amounts are relatively small, however, and the additional premium payments necessary to purchase them would represent little additional expense.

There are three ways in which this additional expense would be largely offset by other factors in the private system. First, the two oldest children in this family would be protected for several years by more insurance coverage than is provided by social security. They could receive the MFB until they reached twenty-five and twenty-three, instead of eighteen. This amount of coverage could be reduced to match social security's protection more closely, and the savings here could be used to purchase additional insurance for the second set of children.

Second, before this second set of children grows up the retirement fund for most workers will grow large enough to pay the MFB out of the interest alone. At that point there will be no additional insurance expense because the fund alone will be sufficient to pay all of the worker's benefits, and he will not need to purchase any additional insurance. At an 8% real rate of return under Alternative III, this point will be reached by all workers sometime between the ages of forty-two and forty-five. At 6% this point will be reached sometime between the ages of forty-eight and fifty-three. The worker could thus probably stop buying the additional insurance amounts described above well before his children grew up.

After the worker attained these ages the private system would pay more than social security no matter how many children the worker had because the fund would continue to grow and become able to pay more than the MFB out of the interest alone, while under social security the worker could never get more than the MFB. In addition, once the children grew up the survivor's benefits social security would pay would fall dramatically, but the survivor's benefits under the private system would continue to grow. The private system of survivor's insurance would thus eventually become monetarily superior to social security even for workers with large families. This monetary superiority would again exist during the period of time when the worker's chances of dying before retirement are the greatest. The monetary advantages of the private system during these years would serve to offset further the monetary disadvantages of the private system during the earlier years.

Third, if these workers with large families had working spouses, then the monetary disadvantages of the private system in this area would be reduced further, if not entirely eliminated. With two working spouses, the amount of survivor's benefits that social security would pay would decrease substantially because it is likely that neither spouse would receive any survivor's benefits either before or after retirement, leaving only the benefits to be paid for the children. Workers under the private system would therefore not have to purchase as much additional term life insurance to match the benefits that social security would pay. Furthermore, if the second spouse died after the first spouse had died, social security would not pay any additional benefits to the surviving children. Under the private system, therefore, after one spouse died the second spouse could stop purchasing life insurance altogether and use these savings to supplement the family income. Each spouse in the private system would again not have to purchase as much additional life insurance during their working years to match the benefits paid under social security because of the availability of this additional income under the private system after the death of one spouse. These offsetting factors that arise when the second spouse works would probably be sufficient to eliminate completely any monetary disadvantage of the private system of survivor's insurance for families as large as most workers are likely to have.

Thus those workers who have reasonably sized families, perhaps with two or three children, but develop them over more extended periods of time than seven years, could probably attain the same level of survivor's insurance protection as provided under social security at no greater cost than provided by our examples by simply rearranging their private insurance purchases, purchasing more in the years their children are born and reducing the amounts purchased consistently after that, and by relying on the offsetting factors we have discussed. Similarly, workers with working spouses who have families as large and extended as most are likely to have can probably also attain the same level of survivor's insurance protection as provided by social security at no additional cost.

But for workers with nonworking spouses and larger and more extended families, the issue is more complicated. The private system of survivor's insurance will eventually become superior to social security for virtually all workers during the preretirement years when the worker is most likely to die. The superiority of the private system during this period will be substantial. But some families will be so large and developed over such extended periods of time that the private system of survivor's insurance we have described will be monetarily inferior to social security in the earlier years. While this inferiority may be said to be outweighed by the superiority of the private system in the later years, the family would still lack insurance coverage it probably needs in these earlier years. We may conclude, therefore, that for workers with nonworking spouses and with relatively large families, including at least more than three or four children, developed over relatively extended periods of time, at least more than seven to ten years, the private system of survivor's insurance we have described will be somewhat inferior in monetary terms to social security for some period of time. This inferiority occurs because under the current social security system workers with large and extended families are heavily subsidized by those with smaller families. Nevertheless, at little additional expense these workers could buy additional term life insurance to eliminate this inferiority. Deducting these additional amounts from each worker's annual contributions into his retirement fund would not significantly change the private system's retirement benefits for these workers. The private system as a whole, therefore, would still be vastly superior in monetary terms to social security as a whole, even for these workers.

For all other workers, however, the private system of survivor's or life insurance we have described is monetarily superior to social security's survivor's insurance. The number of workers for whom the private system is monetarily superior in this regard is probably far greater than the group for whom it is not and, given current social trends, this number is likely to increase. Americans today are choosing to have smaller families, and the trend toward having fewer children seems likely to continue and even intensify. The great majority of young people entering the work force today are probably not planning to have more than two or three children. Young women today also seem to be delaying their childbearing years until later in life, which will tend to reduce the number of years over which couples will be having children. More and more individuals are also choosing to remain single or to remain childless after marriage. More than half of all married women now work, and this proportion is likely to continue to rise. These social trends increase the number of workers for whom the private system's survivor's insurance protection is monetarily superior to social security.

There are thus three factors that tend to cause the benefits paid under the private system of survivor's insurance to be higher than the benefits paid under social security—reasonably sized families, working spouses, and the establishment of a large retirement trust fund by middle age. These three factors mean that for most young workers entering the work force today the private system of survivor's insurance will be substantially superior in monetary terms to social security's survivor's insurance.

The monetary superiority of the private system applies to disability insurance as well. We also deducted from the worker's savings each year sufficient premiums to buy enough disability insurance so that the insurance plus the retirement fund could pay disability benefits analogous to what social security would pay. And once again for all workers the fund alone becomes enough to pay all disability benefits long before retirement. After that point, as the retirement fund continues to grow, the private system is able to pay more in disability benefits than social security. Under Alternative

III projections, for maximum-income workers, this point is reached by the age of forty-three assuming a 6% real rate of return and by the age of thirty-nine assuming an 8% real rate of return. For average-income workers, this point is reached by the age of forty-five at a 6% real rate of return and by the age of forty-one at an 8% real rate of return. For low-income workers this point is reached at age forty-four at a 6% real rate of return and at age thirty-eight at an 8% real rate of return.

Again after this point the benefits paid by social security will actually fall, even as the benefits paid under the private system will continue to increase because the children of most workers will be reaching adulthood in these years. Social security's disability insurance will continue to pay benefits to the disabled worker and nonworking spouse after the children have grown, but all benefits paid for the children will stop. The decline in benefits will not be as great as under the survivor's insurance program, therefore, but it will still be substantial. Under the private system, of course, disability benefits will not decrease once the children grow up but will actually continue to increase as the retirement fund continues to grow.

Thus for most workers the private system of disability insurance will be able to pay more than social security's disability insurance as they near the age of forty-five, and this monetary superiority of the private system will continue to grow as the benefits that can be paid by the private system continue to increase and the benefits that can be paid by social security begin to decline. According to the Social Security Administration about 83% of all disability awards under the program are granted to workers over the age of forty-five.[26] Thus the private system will pay more in disability benefits than social security during the period of time when the great majority of workers will be needing such benefits.

Some examples will illustrate the substantial monetary superiority of the private system. If our maximum-income worker who started work at age twenty-four in 1980 became disabled at fifty, then under the private system, given an 8% real rate of return and Alternative III assumptions, the worker would have a fund of $474,899 that could pay $37,992 per year in interest, about the same as this maximum-income worker would have been earning when he became disabled. The worker and his spouse could live on the in-

26Social Security Administration, *Social Security Bulletin, Annual Statistical Supplement, 1975* (Washington, D.C.: U.S. Government Printing Office, 1977), p. 159.

terest from this fund for the rest of their lives and still leave the fund of almost $0.5 million to their heirs. Alternatively, the worker and his spouse could live on this interest until sixty-five and then purchase an annuity that would pay $53,332 per year while both spouses were alive and $35,555 per year after one died. Social security, on the other hand, would simply pay the worker, assuming his children had grown, $15,642 per year while both spouses were alive and $10,428 after one died, starting at the time of disability.

If our average-income worker who started work at age twenty-two in 1980 became disabled at fifty, then under the private system, given an 8% real rate of return and Alternative III assumptions, the worker would have a fund of $241,983. This fund would pay $19,359 per year out of the interest alone, about $2,000 per year more than the worker was earning when he became disabled. At age sixty-five the worker and his spouse could use the fund to purchase an annuity that would pay $27,175 per year while both were alive and $18,117 per year for the life of the survivor after one died. Assuming the children were grown, social security would pay $10,278 per year while both were alive and $6,852 per year after one died, starting at the time of disability.

Finally, if our low-income worker who started work at age eighteen in 1980 became disabled at fifty, then under the private system, given the same assumptions as above, the worker would have a fund of $161,856. This fund would pay $12,948 per year in perpetual interest, about 50% more than the worker was earning when he became disabled. The worker and his spouse could use this fund at age sixty-five to purchase an annuity that would pay $18,177 per year while both were alive and $12,118 per year after one died. Social security would pay, assuming again that the children had grown, $6,696 per year while both were alive and $4,464 after one died, starting at the time of disability. It should be noted that in all these examples if the disabled worker died before his spouse reached sixty-five, then all benefits under social security would stop until the spouse reached sixty-five, but under the private system benefits would continue to be paid at the same rate.

Under the private disability insurance plan we have described the worker's benefits begin immediately on the occurrence of a disability. Under social security, a disabled worker has to wait five months before his benefit payments begin, a waiting period that can result in substantial financial hardship. The private system completely avoids this problem.

Furthermore, social security deducts substantial amounts from its disability benefits if the beneficiary is also receiving workmen's compensation. Social security will reduce its disability benefit payments until the amount of these benefits plus workmen's compensation equals 80% of the worker's former salary. The private system we have described makes no reduction in benefits for the receipt of workmen's compensation benefits.

The monetary superiority of the private disability insurance system is even greater for those workers with working spouses, because each spouse will again have his or her own insurance and retirement fund, increasing the protection provided for the family under the private system at the same time that this protection is decreasing under social security.

If one of two working spouses becomes disabled under social security, benefits would be reduced because of the earnings test and the continued employment and earnings of the other spouse, probably eliminating entirely all benefits to be paid for the second spouse. The analogous benefits paid under the private system from the insurance and retirement fund of the disabled worker would not be reduced by the continued earnings of the other spouse. After the children have grown this factor will make a very substantial difference, with social security benefits decreasing by a third (from 150% of the PIA to 100% of the PIA) and private benefits remaining the same at 150% of the PIA.

Under social security, when the working spouse retires the family will receive only the higher of either the retirement benefits payable on the working spouse's earnings record or those payable on the disabled spouse's record. But under the private system the family will receive both because each spouse will have accumulated sufficient funds and insurance to pay these benefits. The benefits paid under the private system will therefore again be substantially higher.

Furthermore, if the second working spouse also becomes disabled, under the private system benefits paid would double, assuming that both spouses had the same earnings history. Benefits paid under social security, however, would not double. They would merely increase by 100% of the second worker's PIA.

The private disability insurance system is also monetarily superior to social security whether or not the worker has a family. A single, childless worker, for example, would receive the full disability benefits described earlier in the private system, but he could receive only 100% of the PIA for life under social security. A married childless worker would receive full benefits under the private system, but only 150% of the PIA for life with a nonworking spouse. The private system is also superior for most workers with children. Our private disability insurance plan also included a seven-year period like that under the survivor's insurance plan. The worker could start this period at any time, and during these years he would be covered with enough disability insurance to pay the MFB for eighteen years if he became disabled. After the end of this seven-year period the MFB could be paid for one less year for each year that passed. A married worker with one child in our private system would thus be potentially entitled upon disability to the MFB until the child reached twenty-five, assuming the worker started the seven-year period at the child's birth, but under social security the MFB would be available only until the child reached eighteen.[27] With two children, the worker could receive the MFB until the last child reached twenty-three assuming the second child was born in the third year of the seven-year period, while social security would again only pay the MFB until the child reached eighteen. With a third child born in the fifth year of the seven year period, the worker could potentially receive the MFB until the child reached twenty-one and with a fourth child born in the seventh year the worker could potentially receive the MFB until the child reached nineteen, so even a worker with as many as four children could receive more in disability benefits under the private system. The amount of social security benefits in these examples is based on the assumption that the worker has a nonworking spouse. Here again those who have larger families over more extended periods of time will probably receive a little less disability insurance protection under the private system than under social security. But again at a little additional expense these workers could purchase enough additional disability insurance to match social security.

These additional costs would be offset by the same factors that offset the additional life insurance costs. First, the insurance coverage provided for the first two children could be reduced, because

[27]The MFB would be paid until the child reached twenty-five if the worker became disabled at any time after the seven-year period had passed. If the worker became disabled before this seven-year period passed, the MFB would be paid an additional number of years past the age of eighteen equal to the age of the child at the time the worker became disabled. The same would be true for the additional children described in this paragraph, except that the MFB could at most be paid until the ages noted.

they otherwise could potentially receive the MFB until twenty-five and twenty-three, and these savings could be used to purchase the additional insurance for the second two children.

Second, once the fund reaches a point large enough to pay the MFB out of the interest alone, no supplemental insurance will need to be purchased, and the additional insurance expense will be eliminated. Once this point was reached, the private system would pay more in disability benefits than social security no matter how many children a worker had because the fund would continue to grow and be able to pay more than the MFB. Social security benefits would begin to fall as the children grew. The private system of disability insurance would also eventually become monetarily superior to social security even for workers with large families. This monetary superiority would again exist during the period when the worker's chances of becoming disabled are the greatest. The monetary advantages of the private disability insurance system during these years would further serve to offset the monetary disadvantages of the private system during the earlier years.

Finally, if these workers with large families had working spouses, the monetary disadvantages of the private system would be further reduced, if not entirely eliminated. Social security benefits would be decreased because of the working spouse because no benefits would be paid for this spouse on the other spouse's record either before or after retirement. In addition, after the first spouse became disabled the second spouse could reduce purchases of disability insurance because this worker would not receive as much in additional benefits as before under social security if he or she also became disabled. The savings from these reduced purchases could thus supplement the family income in the case of the disability of the first spouse. These two factors would further reduce the amounts of supplemental disability insurance workers with large families would have to purchase to match the benefits that social security would pay. These offsetting factors arising from the employment of the second spouse would probably be sufficient to completely eliminate any monetary disadvantages of the private system for the great majority of families.

Thus workers who have families with two or three children but who developed these families over more extended periods of time than seven years could probably attain the same level of disability insurance protection as provided by social security under no greater cost than in our examples by rearranging their insurance purchases and relying on the offsetting factors we have discussed. Workers with working wives and families as large and extended as most workers are likely to have can probably also attain the same level of disability insurance protection as provided by social security at no additional cost. For workers with nonworking wives and larger and more extended families the issue becomes more complicated, but even for these workers there will be a period of time during which the private system will be monetarily superior to social security. This will be the period of time during which workers are most likely to become disabled, and the superiority of the private system during this period will be substantial. Some families will still be so large and extended that the private system will be monetarily inferior in the earlier years. Although again the superiority of the later years could be said to outweigh the inferiority of the early years, the family will still probably lack insurance coverage it needs in those earlier years. Thus, we may conclude that for workers with nonworking spouses and relatively large families, including at least more than three or four children, developed over extended periods of time, at least more than seven to ten years, the private system of disability insurance we have described will be monetarily inferior to social security for some time because under the present social security system workers with large and extended families are heavily subsidized by those with smaller families. But it is nevertheless again true that at a little additional expense these workers could buy additional disability insurance to eliminate this inferiority. Deducting these additional amounts from each worker's annual contributions into his retirement fund would still not substantially change the retirement benefits the private system can pay. The private system as a whole, therefore, would still be sharply superior to social security as a whole, even for these workers.

For all other workers it would again be true that the private system of disability insurance we have described will be monetarily superior to social security's disability insurance. The number of workers for whom the private system is monetarily superior in this regard is again far greater than the group for whom it is not and, given the social trends described earlier, this number is likely to increase.

Five factors tend to cause the benefits paid under the private system of disability insurance to be higher than the benefits paid under social security—reasonably sized families, the elimination of the five-month waiting period, the elimination of the reduction for

workmen's compensation benefits, working spouses, and the establishment of a large retirement trust fund by middle age. These factors mean that for most workers entering the work force today the
private system of disability insurance will be substantially superior
in monetary terms to social security's disability insurance.

The monetary superiority of the private disability system is based
on the assumption that disability incidence rates, or the rates at
which workers become disabled, will be the same under both the
private and social security systems. It is quite likely, however, that
disability incidence rates under the private system will be lower
than under social security because the incentive structure under such
a system would be superior to the incentives prevailing under social
security. These superior incentives would apply to both beneficiaries
and administrators.

The administrators of social security have no incentive to keep
frauds off of the benefit roles or to encourage prompt termination of
benefits when a disabled beneficiary recovers. The Social Security
Administration will not lose money by failing to keep frauds and
malingerers from receiving benefits. It does not have to worry about
keeping costs and premiums low to make future sales of insurance
coverage. The administrators of the program lose nothing if they
allow the system to be ripped off. In fact, if they try to deny benefits
to a fraud or to remove a recovered beneficiary from the roles, they
may be faced with loud and vocal pressure from the individual
claimant. All the benefit from receiving unjustified payment accrues
to the individual claimant, and he will therefore be willing to ex-
pend considerable effort and exert considerable pressure to get those
payments. There is no representative of the taxpayers to exert
pressure on the other side of the ledger, however. The benefit to taxpayers from keeping one undeserving claimant from receiving unjustified benefits is diffuse, with a tiny part of the benefit accruing to
each taxpayer. No one taxpayer therefore has a sufficient incentive
to exert his interests. Unfortunately, the administrators of the program have no real incentive to represent taxpayer interests either. As
a result, the administrators are likely to be lenient with potential
fakes and malingerers because if they allow them to receive benefits
there is no one to complain, but if they seek to terminate these unjustified benefits they will have to contend with the heavily interested claimant.

A private insurance company, on the other hand, has a strong incentive to weed out fakes and malingerers. If the private company

pays unjustified benefits, its costs and premiums will rise, sales will fall, and the company will lose money, especially if competing companies do a better job of preventing the payment of undeserved benefits. The company will thus enact strong measures to deny benefits to the undeserving, which will tend to lower disability incidence rates and lower the costs of insurance coverage to the company's customers.

Similarly, there will be no problems of fraud or malingering if the worker is relying on his own trust fund to pay disability benefits. The worker will gain nothing by faking disability or delaying recovery if he is supporting himself during disability out of his own assets. There will thus again be fewer payments of unjustified benefits, lower disability incidence rates, and lower overall costs for disability coverage.

Thus disability incidence rates in the private system are likely to be lower than under social security. For the same price, therefore, the private system of disability insurance will be able to pay more in benefits than social security's disability insurance.

The monetary advantages derived from the private system's superior incentive structure apply to hospital insurance as well. The administrators of social security lack the incentive to represent the interests of taxpayers in keeping health care costs down. They lack the incentive to deny payments for unnecessary or overly expensive medical treatments. These unnecessary or overly expensive treatments will result both from doctors seeking business and from patients who are willing to abuse the system because they do not bear the direct costs. When the doctor knows that the patient is not paying the costs of the medical care, it is easy for the doctor to talk the patient into extensive and expensive treatments. When the patient knows he is not paying the costs directly, he will seek out extensive and expensive care even though he might feel that such care and treatment would not be worth it if he were paying the costs directly. The doctor and the patient are again heavily interested in receiving payment for these unjustified benefits, but the interests of taxpayers are again diffuse. The doctor and his patient will therefore be willing to exert considerable pressure to receive these individual benefits while individual taxpayers will not be. These problems exist to a certain extent in private health insurance systems as well, but there at least the private companies will have a strong incentive to exert effective pressure to discourage these practices. In a public program like social security, however, the administrators have no such incentive and these practices are likely to be rampant, increasing the costs of the program to taxpayers.

In a private system this problem would be alleviated to the extent that individuals relied on their own assets to pay for medical expenses. Doctors, realizing their patients' resources are limited, would be more careful about recommending expensive and extensive treatments. Patients would be more careful to seek medical care that is worth its actual cost. As a result, unnecessary or overly expensive medical treatment would be minimized.

We have now discussed the many ways in which the private system will be monetarily superior to social security in the areas of survivor's disability and hospital insurance protection, as well as in the provision of retirement benefits. We noted earlier that the primary reason for the superiority of the private system in the provision of retirement benefits is that the private system is run on an invested basis that results in increased production while the social security system is run on a pay-as-you-go basis that does nothing to increase production. This is also the chief reason for the monetary superiority of the private system in these other areas, although some of this superiority is due to the incentive effects we have discussed.

In the area of survivor's insurance, for example, the private system collects enough in premiums each year from all insured participants so that there will be a fund at the end of the year large enough to pay all future benefits that are to be paid on behalf of the insured participants who died during the year. This fund is then invested to earn enough to support these future benefit payments. The investments from this fund will increase production and thereby earn the beneficiaries an interest payment rate of return that can then be used to pay these beneficiaries increased benefits.

The private disability insurance program works in the same way. Enough is collected in premiums each year so that there will be a fund at the end of the year large enough to pay all expected future benefits to beneficiaries who became disabled during the year. The fund is then invested and the returns to these productive investments can then be used to pay higher benefits.

We should recall our analysis of the low monthly premiums necessary to finance the private hospital insurance system assuming that a worker signed up and began saving for such insurance at age twenty-four. The cost of this insurance is low because these premium payments would be saved and invested and forty years later they would have accumulated to a huge amount of interest. When the worker was sixty-five there would then be a fund large enough to pay all expected future hospital insurance benefits, and this fund would then continue to be invested. The returns on these investments would allow the private system to provide the same hospital insurance benefits as social security at lower cost.

Studies done by others, though less comprehensive and detailed than the present one, have also indicated that the private system is sharply superior in monetary terms to social security. In a recent paper, Feldstein calculated the net social security wealth for individual workers.[28] This net social security wealth was defined as the present discounted value of social security benefits that the worker can expect to receive minus the present discounted value of the taxes he has yet to pay over the course of his life. Assuming a real rate of return of 3%, Feldstein calculated that all workers at least age thirty-four and below with incomes over $6,000 a year have negative social security wealth. In other words, young people entering the program today will have to pay taxes into the program over the course of their lives, accumulated at a 3% real rate of return, that will be greater than the benefits they can expect to receive. In fact, if we take the taxes an individual will pay over the rest of his life starting at age thirty-four and accumulate them at a real rate of return of 3%, forgetting past taxes paid into the program, the total of accumulated taxes at retirement will still be greater than the value of the benefits the individual can expect to receive.

This fact indicates that the rate of return available through social security is much less than 3%. Given the much higher rates of return available under private alternatives, it also clearly suggests that the private system is vastly superior to social security in monetary terms. In fact, the private system will be monetarily superior to social security even for individuals who wait to enter the private system at least as late as thirty-four, assuming a modest real rate of return of 3%. At higher assumed real rates of return, this age would be higher.

Feldstein's figures also suggest that all future generations would be made better off by the elimination of the social security program because these future generations could do better outside the pro-

[28]Martin Feldstein and Anthony Pellechio, "Social Security Wealth: The Impact of Alternative Inflation Adjustments," Conference on Financing Social Security, American Enterprise Institute, 1977.

gram. If the present program continues, the actual value of the taxes all future generations will have to pay will be much greater than what they will ever receive in benefits. Even assuming a low real rate of return of 3%, this is true not only for all future generations but for at least all workers currently under the age of thirty-four. These workers would all be made better off if the current program was simply abolished.

In several other of his published studies, Feldstein estimates that the real rate of return for today's young workers under social security is about 2%.[29] This is far less than the returns available under the private system, and it further suggests that this system is vastly superior to social security in monetary terms.

In another recent study, Professor Robert S. Kaplan of Carnegie-Mellon University also calculated that the real rate of return one could expect under social security was 1% to 2%. Kaplan writes,

> While the real rate of return on social security taxes of 2 percent is reasonable relative to other default-free, fixed-income investments, it is much less than what individuals, their unions, or their employers could earn through investments in private projects. Even including the poor performance of the stock market in the past ten years, the long term rate of return on equity investments has averaged more than 6 or 7 percentage points above the rate of inflation. Thus, as individuals are forced to provide for more of their retirement income through social security, they are also being forced to invest in a program whose real rate of return is far below what could be earned through a private retirement program.[30]

In yet another study, June O'Neill, a member of the President's Council of Economic Advisers, estimated the real rate of return individuals could expect to receive on the taxes they would pay into the program over the course of their lives, assuming they started work in 1976.[31] She found that the real rate of return one could expect from social security was 1% to 2%, again suggesting the sharp superiority of the private system in monetary terms.

The private system thus appears to have enormous monetary advantages over social security. In addition, there are a number of im-

[29]See, for example, Martin Feldstein "Facing the Social Security Crisis," *Harvard Institute of Economic Research*, Discussion Paper No. 492, 1976.

[30]Robert S. Kaplan, "A Comparison of Rates of Return to Social Security Retirees Under Wage and Price Indexing," Conference on Financing Social Security, American Enterprise Institute, 1977.

[31]June O'Neill, "Return to Social Security," American Economic Association Meeting, 1976.

portant ways in which the private system is qualitatively superior to social security as well.

First, in the private system each individual can tailor his own package of insurance and investment purchases to suit his own needs and preferences. Each individual can purchase different amounts and types of insurance and make different investments in different amounts, depending on what he needs and wants. Social security, however, requires those who participate in it to accept one plan of insurance protection with one set of benefit provisions, even though no single plan can match the widely varying needs and preferences of everyone. With the diversity and adaptability of the private system, individuals will be able to get more for their money.

Perhaps the clearest example of the limitations of the government's program is provided by the provisions of social security's survivor's insurance program. Social security forces a single worker to pay for survivor's protection that he does not need and that will pay him nothing. If a worker dies leaving no spouse or children, social security will pay nothing in his name, despite his years of tax payments. A childless couple will receive only a pension in the distant future if the worker dies at a young age, and even this will not be paid if the surviving spouse remarries before age sixty. Social security is better suited to those with large families, especially those with nonworking wives, but for the large and increasing number of Americans who do not fit into this mold, social security's survivor's protection is not well suited to their needs.

Under the private system individuals would be free to buy life insurance depending on their family and financial situations and personal preferences. Single people could buy less insurance protection than married people and married, childless people could buy less insurance protection than those with many children. Individuals with large debts could purchase more insurance than individuals with large assets that they could leave to their survivors.

The same problems arise under social security's disability insurance program. Single workers are forced to purchase an insurance plan that provides greater benefits to those who are married and have children. They are thus forced to pay for benefits they can never receive. Married but childless workers are similarly forced to purchase insurance that is poorly suited to their needs.

Under a private system individuals could purchase insurance that matched their family and financial situations and their own preferences. Those in low-risk occupations would pay lower premiums than those in high-risk occupations. Individuals could also rely on alternative ways of providing this protection, such as developing large retirement funds during their working years.

Under a private system individuals could buy insurance to cover special risks that they have and others don't and avoid coverage for risks they don't have that others do. Individuals could also vary the types and amounts of retirement investments they make. Individuals who had special investment opportunities could take advantage of them, utilizing any special knowledge or expertise they might have, while others could rely on more traditional investments. A worker could also vary the amounts he saves and invests over the course of his life, perhaps saving more during the high earning years later in his career and saving less during the early years when he is trying to establish a new career.

The ways in which the private system of insurance and investment protection can be varied to suit individual needs and preferences are limited only by one's imagination. The important point is that with individually tailored protection, individual workers and their families will receive greater value for their money, a possibility social security completely precludes. It instead imposes one particular plan of insurance protection on everybody, and this inevitably leads to the imposition of a plan poorly suited to many individuals. What is needed is the adaptability and diversity of the private, market system. In chapter 6, we will examine further the many ways in which social security poorly serves the needs of the members of various minority groups in our society such as blacks, the poor, and women, especially single, working women.

A second reason that social security is qualitatively inferior to the private system is that the benefits promised under the program are subject to numerous conditions that might result in the nonpayment of benefits, conditions that would not be present in a private system.

For example, under social security a surviving wife with children must remain unmarried to receive her full survivor's benefits, but under the private system she can get married as many times as she likes. Under social security if she works and earns over a certain amount, her benefits will be cut, but under the private system her benefits would remain the same no matter how much she earned. Under social security the surviving mother would lose benefits if she put the children in the care of others, but under the private system she could make whatever arrangements for her children's care she thought best.

Similar restrictions are imposed on the family of a disabled worker. If the wife tries to work to supplement the family income, benefits may be reduced. If she gets divorced before ten years of marriage, benefits will be reduced. If she makes alternative arrangements for the care of her children, benefits will be reduced. Under the private system the benefits would remain the same no matter what the worker or any members of his family did.

The elderly will have their benefits reduced if they earn over a certain amount, a restriction that often prevents the elderly from receiving supplemental income that they may need badly and that may even force them to attempt to receive this supplemental income under a government welfare program such as SSI. If an elderly beneficiary gets divorced before ten years of marriage, benefits will be reduced. Many elderly people may actually be forced to marry to receive the additional benefits for spouses. If an elderly divorced wife gets remarried to a retired man on social security, her benefits may be reduced because the PIA of her new husband may be lower than the PIA of her former husband.

The result of these and numerous other provisions is that a beneficiary's personal life becomes subject to government control because he has to comply with numerous conditions and regulations to receive the money he has paid for under social security. Under the private system an individual can live his life as he pleases, and he will receive the benefits he has paid for regardless of what he does. In chapter 6, we will explore this particular problem further in its application to the elderly.

A third reason that social security is qualitatively inferior to the private system is that the money individuals are "entitled" to under the program does not really belong to them in the same sense that privately owned assets do. Individuals under social security do not really own their benefits or control their use, which means that they are foreclosed from pursuing various courses of action that could make them better off. Under the private system they would be free to pursue these courses of action as they pleased.

For example, under social security a beneficiary cannot accelerate his benefit payments. He must take his benefit payments as they come, under the schedule dictated by the government. He cannot dip into his future benefit payments for funds for an emergency, nor can he do so to make a lucrative investment that would give him higher benefits in the future. The beneficiary may want to use some of this future money to buy a home or make some other special purchase, but under social security he cannot. A beneficiary also cannot use some of these future payments to make a gift or provide other support to his children or grandchildren. He cannot live off the interest on his fund and leave the rest to his heirs.

Under the private system, a person would own his benefits and have complete control over them. He would be accumulating his own retirement fund with complete discretion over how to use the assets in the fund. If he died, his survivors would receive an additional fund from the term life insurance he carried. With these funds, individuals under the private system would be free to pursue any of the courses of action described above that are foreclosed under social security. People would then be able to use their benefits in ways that will most benefit them. We will also discuss this problem in more detail in chapter 6.

The comparison between social security and the private system that we have presented here should leave no doubt that the private system is vastly superior. In its new, mature stage, social security is impoverishing American workers, particularly young workers now entering the program. It is preventing these young workers from accumulating large retirement funds that would greatly exceed $0.5 million in real terms for the average worker and would be even greater than this amount for many others. It is preventing them from enjoying much higher benefits and higher standards of living in retirement. It is preventing them from being able to leave large estates to their children after enjoying these benefits. It is hurting most of all the poor who most need the higher benefits of the private system and who could help their children and grandchildren break out of poverty with the large amounts of assets they could leave to them. As the figures presented in this chapter indicate, this problem has now reached enormous, intolerable proportions, and it alone is sufficient reason for basic, wide-ranging, fundamental social security reform.

Welfare vs. Insurance

We should recognize that the problems we have discussed in this chapter are again a result of the conflict between the welfare and insurance goals of the program. As we have shown, the chief reason that social security is inferior to private alternatives is that the program is operated on a pay-as-you-go basis rather than on an invested basis, and the program is operated in this way solely because of the pursuit of welfare objectives along with insurance objectives. It was again the payment of unearned and unpaid for benefits to those who were thought to be in need in the early years of the program that led to its operation on a pay-as-you-go basis. However, the pursuit of welfare objectives through the program has led to the problems in the program's pursuit of insurance objectives that we have noted in this chapter.

The qualitative shortcomings of social security that we have noted are also due to the conflict between the welfare and insurance objectives of the program. Everyone is forced to accept one particular plan of insurance protection because of the welfare elements in the program. If people were allowed to choose whether to participate in social security those who did not benefit from the welfare elements of the program would opt out, leaving no one to pay for them.

The many conditions and qualifications in social security that could result in the nonpayment of putatively earned benefits are themselves welfare elements. They are provisions in the program meant to deny the payment of benefits to those who are not deemed to be in need, regardless of how much they may have earned by past taxes.

Finally, individuals do not own or control the benefits they are entitled to under social security because of the welfare elements in the program. Because the program is operated on a pay-as-you-go basis, people cannot be allowed to control or dispose of their future benefit payments currently because the money is not currently on hand. Because benefits are paid largely on a welfare basis rather than on a strict insurance basis, individuals have no ownership or control over the money they pay into the program. And because the welfare elements require that everyone be forced to participate in social security's social insurance program rather than a private, contractual insurance program, individuals lose the ownership and control rights they would have over their benefits in the private system.

The problems we have discussed in this chapter are thus again a result of the conflict between the welfare and insurance goals of the program.

5

Social Security
and Bankruptcy

In 1977, in order to save the social security system from bankruptcy, Congress enacted one of the largest tax increases in U.S. history. Under the new law, social security payroll tax rates will increase steadily through 1990, yet according to official projections of the Social Security Administration even this massive tax increase may not be sufficient to forestall threats of bankruptcy. Bankruptcy would occur if the program became unable to fulfill all the benefits promises it is currently making to future beneficiaries.

Public officials and ardent defenders of the program continue to insist that social security is financially safe, but the truth is that the threat of bankruptcy for the social security system remains quite real. This threat is again due to the pay-as-you-go nature of the program.

The financial soundness of social security is threatened in five ways. One of them has recently been solved, but it bears mentioning because it played a key role in arousing public awareness of the problem of potential bankruptcy. We will discuss each of them below. As we examine the financial status of social security, we will often refer to projections concerning the possible future performance of the program which are made by the Social Security Administration each year. These projections are published in the annual reports of the Board of Trustees for the social security trust funds. The projections are made under three alternative sets of assumptions: Alternative I, the optimistic set, Alternative II, the intermediate set, and Alternative III, the pessimistic set. We will discuss these assumptions in more detail later in this chapter and demonstrate that Alternative III is the most realistic set of assumptions.

175

The Maturity of the Program

The first threat to social security arises from the development of the program's maturity. In a pay-as-you-go system, the taxes of current workers are immediately paid out to current beneficiaries who became entitled to their benefits by paying taxes for the support of the generation before them. When such a program is started up, there are current taxpayers but no current beneficiaries entitled to benefits based on past tax payments. In the start-up phase, a pay-as-you-go system will be running up huge surpluses with nowhere to go. No one has to worry about meeting the obligations of the program because the program has no obligations.

In a fully-funded system, these initial funds would have to be saved and invested to finance the future benefits of current workers. But in a pay-as-you-go system the taxes of the next generation of workers will pay for the benefits of current workers, so the initial tax receipts are not invested.

In the initial start-up phase of a pay-as-you-go system, Congress can use whatever tax receipts are generated to pass out free benefits to those who have not paid for them. With the program generating huge unclaimed surpluses, the system appears to be financially sound. Current recipients are experiencing a windfall, current taxpayers are assured that their old age is secure, and current politicians are hailed as great humanitarians.

After the first generation of beneficiaries, however, the unclaimed surpluses of the program are gone. The program has now built up huge liabilities owed to the current generation of retirees. The problem becomes whether current taxes from current workers will be sufficient to pay the liabilities owed to current retirees. The task of Congress is to increase taxes on the current generation of workers until enough funds are raised to finance the program's obligations.

In the meantime, all workers in the program have been locked into a system that provides them with less than they could get in private investment alternatives and that places the entire economy on a permanently lower growth path with lower national income, a distorted labor supply, and gross economic inefficiency.

It is only after the start-up phase that the problem of financial soundness becomes apparent; it is only in the mature stage that potential bankruptcy becomes a threat. The program now has the financial obligation of support for a full generation of retirees, and this obligation will continue to grow as current taxes are paid and entitlements to future benefits continue to increase.

The development of a pay-as-you-go system into maturity does not mean that the system is about to go into bankruptcy, but it does mean that the *question* of financial soundness has now become a serious one. In the start-up phase there is a tremendous margin for error. Current tax receipts will surely outweigh current obligations by a vast margin. But once maturity has developed this margin for error has been eliminated. The program has now accrued an enormous number of liabilities but no assets to aid in paying them. Any social or economic developments that make payment of the program's obligations at this point more difficult could be disastrous. The question of whether taxpayers will balk at paying the huge obligations that have been built up now becomes critical.

The first thirty to forty years of operation of America's social security system have proved nothing about the stability and viability of a pay-as-you-go system because most of that time the program has been in the initial start-up phase. Only recently has the emphasis shifted from paying out surplus benefits to raising taxes to meet huge obligations, but already taxpayers are balking at paying their huge tax bills. Already there are social and economic developments that threaten the fragile balance of the pay-as-you-go system. These developments, such as the decline in fertility rates, are making it more difficult for the system to meet its obligations.

The Demographic Problem

For a pay-as-you-go system, population changes are critically important. Since current retirees are entirely dependent upon current workers for support, anything that increases the number of retirees or decreases the number of workers will make financing the system more difficult and require higher tax rates.

The United States has undergone a series of population changes in recent years that will tend to increase the number of retirees and decrease the number of workers and thus create difficult problems for the future financing of social security.

The population changes can be seen by noting the changes in the total fertility rate, which measures the average number of births each woman would have over the course of her life at the age-by-age birthrate for the year in question. Table 33 shows the total fertility rate in the United States since 1800. The table shows that fertility has exhibited a long-term trend of decline from 7.04 in 1800 to 1.757 in 1978. A fertility rate of 2.1 is required for zero population growth, that is, maintaining the population at a stable level. The most significant changes have occurred since the 1940s. The fertility rate in 1945 was 2.42. Starting in the next year, the rate began to increase sharply, reaching a high of 3.68 in 1957 and remaining relatively stable until 1960, when it was 3.61. These were the years of the baby boom, when the population was rapidly increasing. Since 1961, however, the fertility rate has resumed its downward trend. By 1972 the rate had fallen below that necessary for zero population growth to 2.00, and it has continued to fall, despite one year of increase in 1977, reaching 1.757 in 1978.

These changes in fertility create the worst possible population mix for a pay-as-you-go system—a baby boom followed by a baby bust. When the baby boom generation retires, the number of retirees will be greatly increased. At the same time, the working baby bust generation behind them will be relatively smaller.

In 1960 the population age sixty-five and over was 17.4% of the working-age population ages twenty through sixty-four. By 1975 this had increased to 19%. The Social Security Administration has projected this ratio into the future under the three alternative sets of assumptions presented in the 1979 Annual Report of the Board of Trustees (see table 34).

As we have noted, Alternative III, which assumes continued low fertility rates for the future, is the most realistic set of assumptions because it is consistent with birth data over the last two decades. Under Alternative III, by 2010, the first year of retirement for the baby boom generation, this ratio will have increased to 24.1%. After 2010, the ratio will begin to increase even more rapidly, reaching 39.4% in 2025 and 54.2% in 2050. Under Alternative II, the ratio will grow from 22.2% in 2010 to 32.6% in 2025 and 34.2% in 2050.

This increasing ratio of elderly to working people will cause benefits to outstrip taxes unless tax rates are sharply increased. As table 35 shows, in 1978 there were 31 beneficiaries for every 100 workers. Under Alternative III, by 2010 there will be 40 beneficiaries per 100 workers. This 30% increase in the relative number of beneficiaries to workers implies a necessary 30% increase in taxes to allow the program to continue to pay benefits at current levels. By 2025 the ratio of beneficiaries to workers under Alternative III will increase to 59%, implying a necessary tax increase of 90% to maintain current benefit levels. By 2050 this ratio will have increased to 75%, implying a necessary tax increase of 142% over current tax rates.

Although the fertility rate has been volatile since World War II, it appears that the low current rate is here to stay and may decline further in future years. The increase in the fertility rate from 1945 to 1960 was due to the cataclysmic experiences of World War II and the Great Depression and is unlikely to reoccur. The most recent decline in the fertility rate is a resumption of a long-term trend that social developments in recent years are likely to reinforce. Attitudes toward marriage and children have changed dramatically resulting in a declining marriage rate (see table 36) and a skyrocketing divorce rate (see table 37). Women are spending more time in the work force instead of at home raising children. As more and more women move into highly paid professional positions, the cost of taking time off to have and raise children is increasing sharply. People have also come to prefer the higher standards of living associated with smaller families. Birth control methods have become more available and effective. All of these trends would tend to keep the fertility rate low or depress it still further, while there seem to be few if any strong social trends that would tend to reverse the decline in fertility.

If the fertility rate stays at its current level or continues to fall, social security taxes will have to be increased sharply to compensate for it. To a large extent the problem is already unavoidable. The large baby-boom generation is now in the work force. It has been followed by twenty years of declining fertility, and it is the members of the small baby-bust generation who will be in the work force and primarily responsible for the support of the baby-boom generation when it retires. It is as if a time bomb had already been set for social security's pay-as-you-go system. Continued low fertility will only make the eventual problem worse. Only a startling reversal of recent trends could mitigate the problem substantially.

The Economic Effects Problem

The pay-as-you-go nature of social security makes its financial stability particularly vulnerable to three economic variables: the rate of growth in real wages, the rate of growth in employment, especially as it is affected by the unemployment rate, and inflation.

The faster real wages grow, the more tax revenues will be generated at fixed tax rates. If this rate of growth slows, however, tax revenues will not grow as fast, and they may become insufficient to meet growing benefit obligations. A slower rate of real wage growth can threaten the financial soundness of social security and require substantial tax increases.

Similarly, the faster total employment grows, the greater will be the total number of workers paying taxes into the system and the faster total taxes will grow. If this rate of growth slows significantly, however, taxes may not grow fast enough to keep pace with benefits. The most significant factor affecting total employment in the short run is the unemployment rate. As unemployment increases, total employment declines, at least from what it might have been, and consequently so do tax revenues. Unemployment may also induce older workers to retire earlier than they otherwise would have because of difficulty in finding new jobs. This would tend to increase benefits as well as decrease taxes. An increase in unemployment can therefore also threaten social security financing and require substantial tax increases.

Benefits after retirement are indexed to increase with the rate of inflation, and inflation directly increases the cost of the hospital insurance program by increasing the cost of hospital and medical care. If inflation accelerates rapidly, benefit payments will also increase rapidly. If wages do not keep pace with inflation, tax revenues will be insufficient to meet these increases, and further tax increases will be necessary to keep social security from falling into bankruptcy. Also, to the extent that inflation leads to further unemployment, it threatens social security in a second way.

Thus any sudden, unexpected changes in these volatile economic variables could endanger social security and threaten bankruptcy. In fact, this happened during the recession in the mid-1970s, just as social security was reaching the mature stage: Unemployment rose sharply while real wages fell, but inflation continued, increasing benefits. As a result, tax revenues fell sharply below benefit levels. The deficit between taxes and benefits for the OASDI program grew from $1.25 billion in 1973 to $1.7 billion in 1974, $4.9 billion in 1975, $6.6 billion in 1976, and $8.6 billion in 1977. Because real wages had not grown as fast during the recession as expected, wages were left on a permanently lower growth path, incapable of generating the tax revenues necessary to finance projected benefits. The result was steadily increasing deficits made worse by continued sluggish wage growth. The trust funds were projected to be exhausted by the end of the decade, leaving social security unable to meet its benefit promises. Only the massive tax increases in 1977 saved the system from bankruptcy.

A similar problem may develop for the program in the early 1980s. In the 1979 annual report of the Board of Trustees for the OASDI program, the Social Security Administration projected that if a general recession developed in late 1979 and lasted until early 1980, the OASI (Old-Age and Survivor's Insurance) portion of the program would experience cash-flow problems starting in 1983.[1] These cash-flow problems would make the system incapable of meeting its benefit payments on time. This recession was assumed under the assumptions for Alternative III. As table 49 shows, the projections under Alternative III indicate that by 1983 the OASI trust fund will hold only 8% of one year's benefits. If each month's benefits are to be paid on time, there must be at least 9% of one year's benefits in the trust fund because although benefit checks have to be sent out at the first of the month, that month's tax revenues come in slowly and evenly over the course of the month. The program will eventually have enough funds to pay its benefit obligation as long as the trust fund retains some assets, but if these assets are less than 9% of one year's benefits then the program will not be able to pay its benefits on time.

Table 49 also indicates that this cash flow problem will continue to be serious for some time, with the OASI trust fund assets falling to 5% of one year's benefits in 1984, 2% in 1985 to 1989, and 1% in 1990. The trust fund is projected to increase to 5% in 1991 and 10% in 1992, when the problem is expected to be eliminated. The problem will continue for this long because the assumed recession will dramatically slow the growth of wages and thus, after the recession is over and wage growth returns to normal rates, wages will still not attain the levels expected before the recession. Wages will have been permanently set back by slow or negative growth during the recession period. The result is that wages are placed on a permanently lower growth path, although they will eventually return to normal growth rates.

Even though the recession may end in 1980, it will continue to cause serious problems for social security until 1992. The impact of the recession can be seen most clearly by comparing these 1979 projections with the projections made in the 1978 annual report (see

[1] *1979 Annual Report of the Board of Trustees of the Federal Old Age and Survivor's Insurance and Disability Insurance Trust Funds*, 13 April 1979.

table 50).[2] Alternative III in the 1978 report predicted only a mild recession for 1979 and 1980. In that report the OASI trust fund was expected to be 13% of one year's benefits in 1983 under Alternative III as compared to 8% in the 1979 report. This difference of five percentage points between the two reports, instead of narrowing, continues to widen over the next decade, despite the fact that the recession ends in 1980. The difference climbs to seven percentage points in 1984, nine in 1985, eleven in 1986, fourteen in 1987, twenty in 1990, twenty-five in 1991, and twenty-eight in 1992. A large part of this widening difference occurs because the 1979 report assumes slightly lower wage growth through 1987 than the 1978 report and slightly higher unemployment through 1984. A large part also occurs because the 1979–1980 recession in the 1979 report places wages on a permanently lower growth path and thus prevents them from reaching the levels projected in the 1978 report. A recession will therefore have lasting effects on social security that will continue well past the recession's end.

The Alternative III assumptions in the 1979 report differ from those in the 1978 report in other ways besides the differences in economic performance noted here. The assumptions concerning fertility rates, for example, are quite different, but the assumptions about economic performance have the greatest impact on the projections for the first decade, the 1980s, while the other assumptions have a greater impact in later years.

The cash flow problem is projected to end eventually on its own only because Congress in the 1977 amendments sought to set tax rates high enough so that the trust fund would grow in the 1980s and 1990s to a level close to two year's benefits. Instead, in the event of a 1979–1980 recession along with sluggish wage growth in the 1980s, the tax rates intended to provide for this accumulation will serve to barely keep the program solvent, with all trust fund accumulation delayed until the 1990s. Even then, the trust fund will never reach the intended levels, growing to only 49% of one year's benefits by the year 2000. If this extra trust fund accumulation had not been provided for in the 1977 amendments, the economic performance projected here would have driven the program into bankruptcy in the 1980s.

By early 1980 the recession feared by the 1979 annual report's

---

[2] *1978 Annual Report of the Board of Trustees of the Federal Old Age and Survivor's Insurance and Disability Insurance Trust Funds,* 15 May 1978.

Alternative III assumptions had not developed in its entirety, but the economic circumstances that had developed were at least as bad for social security. Unemployment was a little lower than expected under these assumptions, but it was increasing and it certainly appeared capable of reaching the assumed average for 1980. Inflation, however, was much higher than anticipated, and it appeared capable of maintaining a level of about twice the assumed 1980 average. Even more important, wages did not appear to be rising nearly as fast as inflation, and this gap between wages and inflation appeared to be at least as large as assumed for 1979–1980, if not larger. This meant that benefits, which increase with inflation, would be rising much faster than taxes, which increase with wages. In fact, in mid-1980 the enormous inflation adjustments for 1979 went into effect, shooting up benefits at a time of rising unemployment and low or nonexistent wage growth.

Furthermore, most economists still expect a recession to occur. The recession, with its negative impact on employment and wage levels, would make the inflation adjustment benefit increases of mid-1980 even harder to finance. The combination of a recession as bad as that assumed under the 1979 report's Alternative III and the unexpectedly high inflation noted above could in fact drive the OASI program into bankruptcy in the mid-1980s unless further tax increases are enacted. Even without the dramatic and unexpected inflationary surge in 1979 and 1980 the assumed recession was already projected to cause the OASI trust fund assets to fall to only 2% of one year's benefits from 1985 to 1989 and to only 1% in 1990. This margin of safety is so tiny that the addition of the effects of the unexpectedly high inflation alone could tip the program into bankruptcy. If economic performance is otherwise only slightly worse than assumed, if the recession is only slightly more severe or prolonged, or if wage growth is only slightly slower or unemployment only slightly higher, then the likelihood will be further increased that the OASI trust fund assets will be entirely dissipated in the mid-1980s, leaving taxes insufficient to meet benefit obligations and driving the program into bankruptcy without further tax increases.

Continued high inflation or an otherwise worse economic performance than assumed could conceivably threaten the entire OASDI program as well as the OASI program alone. As table 49 shows, under Alternative III for 1979 the trust fund for the entire OASDI program will contain only 16% of one year's OASDI benefits in 1983 and only 15% in 1984 and 1985, not very far above the 9%

level at which cash flow problems begin. The differences noted above between the OASI trust fund projections in the 1978 and 1979 annual reports illustrate how great an impact the deeper recession and slower wage growth assumed in the 1979 report could make over the mild recession assumed in the 1978 report. These differences grew to 9 percentage points by 1985, 14 in 1987 and 20 in 1990. It is clear that with an impact of this magnitude a more severe and prolonged recession and a weaker recovery than assumed in the 1979 report could cause cash flow problems for the entire OASDI program and perhaps even throw it into bankruptcy without further tax increases. The recent, unexpectedly high inflation, if continued, could alone have this impact and therefore cause the same problems. This continued inflation would result in another enormous inflation adjustment in benefits in mid-1981, as social security was still reeling from the effects of the assumed 1980 recession on wages, employment and tax collections.

Looking further ahead, we might consider what would happen if another recession followed soon after the 1980 recession. It is quite possible that another recession will develop in the middle of the 1981–1985 presidential term or in the mid-1980s. A severe or prolonged recession in 1982 or 1983, for example, could quite easily tip the entire battered social security system into bankruptcy. And how willing will taxpayers be to bail out the system with yet another tax increase at the same time that they are trying to grapple with a recession? These developments would be disastrous for the social security system, yet they can hardly be considered unlikely.

The 1978 annual report said of the massive 1977 tax increases, "The Social Security amendments of 1977, enacted on December 10, 1977, restore the financial soundness of the cash benefit program throughout the remainder of this century and into the early years of the next one."[3] The 1979 annual report recommends using assets from the DI (disability insurance) trust fund, which was expected to grow through the 1980s, to solve the OASI cash flow problem. As we have seen, however, even this may not be enough to avoid the problem because continued poor economic performance could quite easily threaten the entire OASDI program. It is simply incredible that further tax increases may be necessary so soon after the 1977 increases.

It is possible, however, that the program could reach a point

[3]*1978 Annual Report, OASDI program*, p. 3.

where even further tax increases could not save it from bankruptcy because the additional tax increases themselves could create economic conditions that would lead to declines in tax revenues rather than increases, or at least to increases that were not as large as expected. As the wedge between what the employer pays and what the employee receives continues to grow with tax increases, employment will be discouraged more and more. As employment falls, so do tax revenues. This decline in employment could lead to declines in consumption demand which, under Keynesian assumptions, could cause further unemployment and declines in tax revenues. Higher taxes could also lead to further reductions in savings and capital investment, which could lead to even slower wage growth and lower total employment, depressing total tax revenues even further. We could thus reach a point at which the economy simply could not support the burden of social security benefit promises and their accompanying tax demands under the pay-as-you-go framework.

We should note that continued poor economic performance is devastating the HI (hospital insurance) portion of the program even more than the OASDI portion. With inflation hitting hospital and medical costs especially hard, the costs of the HI program are increasing far more rapidly than the growth in wages or employment. As a result, under Alternative III in the 1979 annual report of the Board of Trustees for the Hospital Insurance program, the HI trust funds are projected to be exhausted by the late 1980s.[4] The program will then be unable to meet its benefit obligations without further tax increases, despite the 1977 amendments. Under Alternative II the HI trust fund is expected to be exhausted in the late 1990s. Thus, under any assumptions, the Social Security Administration expects the HI program to soon go broke because of the harsh impact of inflation.

These examples all clearly illustrate that a mature pay-as-you-go system is extremely sensitive to trends in the growth of wages, the growth of employment, unemployment, and inflation. Once the system reaches maturity any sudden and unexpected changes in these unstable economic factors can disturb the delicate balance between taxes and benefits in a pay-as-you-go program, leaving the program in bankruptcy if taxpayers are unwilling to bear the heavy tax burdens to make up the difference. The social security system was born of the Great Depression, but if a similar depression were to oc-

---

[4]*1979 Annual Report of the Board of Trustees of the Federal Hospital Insurance Trust Fund*, 13 April 1979.

cur again the severe unemployment and stagnant or declining wages would almost certainly cause bankruptcy. Taxpayers are unlikely to be willing to bear devastating tax increases in such circumstances and benefit cuts would seem inevitable.

With a trust fund currently equal to less than four months' benefits there is precious little protection against the financial instability that could be caused by the adverse effects of even moderately poor economic performance. As a result, the pay-as-you-go system remains financially vulnerable to some of the most unstable factors in the economy.

The Decoupling Problem

The fourth element threatening the financial solvency of social security was due to an error in the benefit formula enacted in 1972. This error has been corrected by the 1977 amendments and therefore this particular problem has been eliminated, but it bears mentioning because the projected long-run deficits it caused first alerted the public to concern over the possible bankruptcy of social security.

In 1972 Congress enacted a benefit formula meant to adjust benefits automatically to compensate for inflation. Under the new method, the percentages in the PIA computation formula were multiplied by the rate of inflation each year so that each worker's PIA and therefore his benefits would be increased by the inflation rate.

However, because the wages of workers currently working also tend to increase with the rate of inflation, their average monthly earnings (AME) would also increase at this rate. When the AME was multiplied by the PIA formula to compute benefits, those benefits would be increased by twice the rate of inflation each year.

With future benefits increasing at twice the rate of inflation, the projected long-run deficits of social security exploded. In the year 2000 the OASDI program was expected to run a deficit of 3.5% of taxable payroll, with taxes covering less than three-fourths of expenditures. By 2020 this deficit would have increased to 9.4% of taxable payroll, with projected taxes covering just over half of projected expenditures. The OASDI tax rate would have had to be raised to 21.3% in that year, compared to about 10% today, to finance projected expenditures. By 2050 the deficit would have reached an incredible 16.7% of taxable payroll, with tax revenue covering just 42% of projected expenditures. To finance these expenditures, the tax rate would have had to be raised to 28.6% (see table 38). The prospect of most Americans having to pay well over one-fourth of their incomes in social security taxes alarmed the public and stirred concern over the future of social security.

In the 1977 amendments Congress corrected the benefit computation error by indexing the benefits to be paid to each worker to grow with the annual rate of growth of wages in covered employment while the worker is still working and to grow with the rate of increase in consumer prices (inflation) after the worker starts receiving benefits. This indexing method is usually referred to as wage-indexing. The chief alternative is simply to index benefits both before and after the worker stops working and starts receiving benefits to the rate of increase in prices. As we have noted, this alternative is known as price-indexing, and it would have been much cheaper than wage-indexing in the long run (see table 38). The relative merits˙ of wage-indexing and price-indexing will be discussed in chapter 10.

The years 1972 and 1977 will be noted in the future as turning points for social security. Congress had not realized in 1972 that social security was maturing and the years of free benefits were over. It continued to vote ever larger increases in social security benefits with little responsible concern for the future fiscal solvency of the program, as it had throughout the entire start-up phase. It was brought to a rude awakening when the enormous bankrupting deficits were uncovered and the press reported the shocking story with appropriate alarm. The press was severely criticized for headlines alleging that social security was going broke, but it was merely reporting the true state of affairs after the 1972 amendments and performed a vital public service in alerting voters.

While 1972 was the last year in which Congress tried to pass out free benefits as it had grown accustomed to in the start-up phase, 1977 was the first year in which the emphasis switched to raising taxes in the mature stage to finance the developed obligations of the program. Almost immediately the public attitude toward social security began to change from one of unquestioned popularity to skeptical disillusionment and growing protest. During the start-up phase, almost every amendment to social security was passed during an even-numbered year, an election year. The first set of amendments passed during the mature stage was in an odd-numbered year, 1977, right after an election. One can safely bet that all future major amendments will be in odd-numbered years.

The Trust Funds

The fifth and final factor threatening the financial solvency of social security is the absence of a true trust fund to ensure future benefit payments.

As we saw in chapter 2, the current social security trust funds contain less than 1% of the amount necessary to guarantee future benefits and therefore be called true trust funds. The assets in these trust funds could currently pay only about four months of benefits.

If there were a true trust fund, benefits would be assured and the other elements described here that threaten bankruptcy would be of no concern. The maturity of the program would not make financing any more difficult or precarious because future benefit payments would already be funded. Since the taxes that current retirees had paid would have been saved for their own retirement and the taxes of current workers would be for *their* own retirement, the decline in the fertility rate and changing demographics would not be a problem. With a trust fund assuring benefits, they would not be threatened by unemployment or sluggish wage growth. Since current benefits would no longer be dependent on current taxes, current beneficiaries would no longer be held hostage to the preferences and attitudes of current taxpayers, to the continued popularity of the program, and to changes in political fortune and shifts in political power. It should be clear that a true trust fund would make future benefit payments much more assured than they are now.

Since the current trust fund is wholly inadequate to guarantee future benefits, it can be argued that social security is already bankrupt by conventional accounting standards. The counterargument is that social security does not need a trust fund and is not bankrupt because, unlike a private insurance company, the government can compel future workers to enter into the program and pay sufficient taxes to meet all obligations. Social security cannot go into bankruptcy because future benefits are assured by the government's power to tax.

This counterargument is seriously deficient even though it is widely accepted. It assumes that the government's power to tax is automatic. It ignores the fact that because we live in a democracy and not a benevolent dictatorship, the taxpayers may have something to say about whether and how the tax power is to be used.

In fact, since in a democracy the taxing power is exercisable only through the will of the taxpayers, the situation of social security seems to be analogous to that of a private insurance company. Taxpayers will continue to pay and support the program only as long as they are convinced that it is a good deal, just as purchasers of private insurance will continue to purchase and pay premiums only as long as they are convinced that they are getting a good deal. If taxpayers no longer remain so convinced, they will elect representatives to vote the program out. The benefit payments of social security are really not any more secure than the benefit payments of a private insurance company without a trust fund. Future taxpayers can choose to end their participation in the program through their elected representatives, much as future purchasers of private insurance can choose to end their participation and payment of premiums. It makes no sense to say that the government can compel taxpayers to continue to make future payments unless it is assumed that if taxpayers should decide to refuse to pay, democracy will be suspended.

The real issue, therefore, over whether social security is bankrupt is whether taxpayers will continue to pay the tax burdens projected for the future. The real issue over whether a trust fund is necessary to ensure future benefits and prevent bankruptcy is whether the additional security provided by such a fund, above the taxing power, is prudently required for solvency. It is clear that a trust fund would make social security more secure because it would ensure future benefit payments independently of the desires of future taxpayers and insulate the program from the dangers described above. Whether this additional protection is necessary will also depend on one's evaluation of how reliable future taxpayers will be.

The question of future taxpayer acquiescence is not a simple one. Political support for social security has been taken for granted in past years because we were in the halcyon days of the start-up phase. Now that the program has entered the mature stage, political support is already eroding and taxpayers are already grumbling. Whether taxpayers can be counted on to continue to pay and whether counting on them to do so is a satisfactory basis on which to rest the financial solvency of the program will be examined later in this chapter. First we must examine the future financial picture of social security to discover just how heavy the tax burden will be. We will begin by examining the Social Security Administration's assumptions on which projections of the future financial stability of the program are based.

Social Security Administration Assumptions

As we have noted, every year the board of trustees for each of the social security trust funds is required to put out an annual report concerning the financial status of the program. These reports contain projections of the program's future financial status under three alternative sets of assumptions: Alternative I, the optimistic set, Alternative II, the intermediate set, and Alternative III, the pessimistic set. Each of these alternative sets makes assumptions about the future performance of a number of economic and demographic elements in American society. These assumptions need to be examined in detail to determine their reasonableness and to better understand the financial projections based on them. The assumptions for all three alternatives in the 1979 annual report are shown in table 39.[5]

The most important element in the future financial picture of social security is the fertility rate. A lower fertility rate will lower the number of workers relative to beneficiaries in the future, and, because social security operates on a pay-as-you-go basis, future financing will become more difficult. A higher fertility rate, however, will increase the number of workers relative to beneficiaries and make future financing of the program easier. Yet, despite the importance of future fertility rates, the Social Security Administration's assumptions concerning fertility are the most questionable of all.

As we have seen (see table 33), the total fertility rate in the United States has shown a long-term downward trend since 1800, with the exception of a brief upward trend from 1945 to 1960—the postwar baby boom. Fertility rates in the 1970s have declined to the lowest levels in our history, falling in 1972 below the rate of 2.1 required for a constant population. In that year the fertility rate declined to 2.00, down from 3.61 in 1960. The 1972 rate was the lowest in American history until that time. Since then the rate has continued to decline, falling to 1.87 in 1973, 1.83 in 1974, 1.77 in 1975, and 1.72 in 1976. Although the rate increased slightly to 1.78 in 1977, it resumed its downward trend in 1977, falling to 1.757. The slight increase in 1977 may have been due to the severe recession of 1974–75 when many people, for economic reasons, may have delayed their decision to have children until the recovery of 1976. The decline in 1978 would thus represent a continuation of the predominant down-

[5] *1979 Annual Report*, OASDI program.

ward trend. And, as we have noted, the social trends contributing to this sharp decline in fertility are also likely to continue to gain strength, while there seem to be few, if any, strong trends that would lead to their reversal.

The fertility projections for Alternative I in the 1979 annual report assume that the longstanding downward trend in fertility will immediately reverse itself, with the fertility rate increasing to 1.831 in 1979 and 1.952 in 1982.[6] The projected increase from 1978 to 1982 would be the largest four-year increase in fertility rates in American history except for the post-depression, post-World War II period of 1939 to 1955 and the roughly equivalent increases in the post-World War I period, 1919 to 1921, and the post-Civil War period, 1864 to 1869. This upward trend is assumed to continue throughout the rest of the century, with the fertility rate stabilizing at 2.5 in 2005. In other words, under Alternative I the fertility rate, for some unstated reason and in the face of all social trends, is expected to reverse a long-term downward trend that has accelerated for the past ten years and begin an unparalleled thirty-year increase, longer than the postwar baby-boom period, finally stabilizing just past the turn of the century at a rate more than 40% higher than the current rate.

Under Alternative II in the 1979 annual report, the long-term downward trend in fertility rates is also assumed to reverse itself immediately, with fertility rates again projected to increase steadily for the rest of the century, eventually stabilizing at 2.1 in the year 2000. Thus, even under the so-called intermediate assumptions, an immediate reversal is assumed in long-standing and accelerating fertility trends despite strong contrary indications. This sudden change is supposed to be followed by the most prolonged period of fertility-rate increase in the nation's history. These assumptions are advanced as the most realistic possibility for future fertility rates.

Under Alternative III in the 1979 annual report, fertility rates are assumed to continue their long-term downward trend for the rest of this century, eventually stabilizing at 1.5 in 2005. The rate of decline in this trend, however, is projected to slow considerably from the rate of decline over the past ten years. Fertility rates are expected to continue to fall, but not as quickly. Although Alternative III is supposed to be the pessimistic alternative, its assumptions about fertility rates seem to be by far the most realistic. Given the

[6]Ibid.

history of fertility rates and the current strong social trends involving women, families, and children, and with no good reason for expecting a reversal, the most reasonable assumption seems to be a continued decline in fertility rates, although at a slower rate of decline.

It will also be useful to examine the assumptions used in the 1978 annual report (see table 40).[7] Under Alternative I in 1978, the decline in fertility was also assumed to reverse immediately, with the fertility rate increasing for the remainder of the century, but the ultimate stabilizing rate was 2.3 rather than 2.5. Alternative II in 1978 was almost exactly the same as Alternative II in 1979, with the fertility rate increasing somewhat more slowly throughout the rest of the century but finally stabilizing at 2.1 in 2001. The most significant difference, however, is in Alternative III for 1978. Under this set of assumptions, fertility continues to decline slowly to a low of 1.682 in 1988 before increasing and eventually stabilizing at 1.7 in 2005.

Alternative III in 1978 thus assumes that fertility rates will remain at about their present low level and that the current declining trend in fertility will cease. Alternative III in 1979, by contrast, focuses on this current declining trend and assumes it will continue at a slightly slower rate of decline, resulting in a lower ultimate fertility rate of 1.5. Both are reasonable, realistic assumptions for an intermediate alternative, although the 1978 assumption is the more optimistic of the two. The 1979 assumption should probably be considered the more realistic because it assumes a continuation of current experience—a moderate declining trend in fertility—which, for the reasons stated above, seem to be the most likely possibility for the future.

This examination of the Social Security Administration's assumptions about fertility rates raises an important possibility: The assumptions for 1979 Alternative I are so unrealistic that they may have been included in the report for purely political reasons. The range of fertility assumptions was considerably widened in the 1979 annual report. The 1978 report based its alternatives on a range from 1.7 to 2.3, but the 1979 report widened the range to 1.5 to 2.5. It may be that the Social Security Administration, in the face of public criticism, felt that a more pessimistic assumption was necessary than appeared in the 1978 report, where the most pessimistic assumption it could imagine was fertility rates remaining at their cur-

---

[7] *1978 Annual Report*, OASDI program.

rent levels and falling no further after 175 years of decline. The 1979 Alternative III provided for a modest decline consistent with current trends. To compensate for the impact of this change on the financial projections of the program, the administration may have chosen to widen the range of assumptions by raising the Alternative I assumption to 2.5 from 2.3. This increase would serve to balance out and obscure the true significance of the more realistic Alternative III projections by presenting them alongside the unrealistically optimistic Alternative I projections as possibilities of equal plausibility, thereby confusing the public and hiding the real, long-term financial problems of social security.

An entirely unbiased series of assumptions would more likely have included 2.1 as the optimistic alternative, 1.7 as the intermediate alternative, and 1.3 as the pessimistic alternative. Fertility rates may well return to a level of 2.5 in the future. But the Social Security Administration would best serve the public by assuming each year intermediate fertility rates at about current levels, a pessimistic assumption below such levels by a given amount, and an optimistic assumption above by an equal amount, at least until the decline in fertility appears to have ended. Because these projections are made every year and the impact of a change in fertility on social security is not felt for several decades, there will be plenty of time to project the impact of higher fertility rates when recent trends give some clear indication of the possibility of such an increase. In the meantime, it would be naive for us to believe that the Social Security Administration is above playing politics with the assumptions underlying its projections.

The rate of growth in real wages also strongly affects social security projections. The faster real wages grow, the more taxes will be generated by the payroll tax, improving the financial status of social security. From 1953 to 1977 real wages for workers covered by social security grew at an annual rate of 1.37%.[8] From 1950 to 1975 real

---

[8]The growth of real wages in covered employment for 1955 and 1957 has been excluded from the calculation of this average because coverage was expanded in those years to include new groups of workers, and this expansion distorted the change in average wages in covered employment for those years. In 1955 farmers and self-employed professionals became covered for the first time. Since income for these groups is higher than for average workers, the growth in average wages in covered employment from 1955 to 1956 was higher than usual. In 1957 members of the armed forces became covered. Since the wages of these workers are lower than average, the growth in wages in covered employment from 1956 to 1957 was lower than average. To maintain consistency, therefore, data for the years 1955 and 1957 were excluded in

wages in the general economy grew at a rate of 1.30%.[9] With a decrease in capital investment in the economy, there has been a recent trend toward declining worker productivity and thus toward declining growth in real wages.

In the 1979 report, Alternative I assumes that real wages will grow at rates generally over 2%, reaching 2.5% in 1988 and remaining at that level for several years before beginning a decline that stabilizes at 2.25% in the year 2000. Under Alternative II real wages are expected to grow at rates between 1.5% and 2.0% in the 1980s, stabilizing at 2.0% in 1988, and declining eventually to a rate of 1.75% in 2000. Under Alternative III real wage growth is expected to slow considerably in 1979 and 1980 because of a general recession in the economy. The rate of growth then increases to between 1.0% and 1.5% in the 1980s, reaching 1.5% in 1988 and declining eventually to 1.25% in 2000.

Alternative III again seems to be the most realistic set of assumptions. It provides for a recession in 1979 and 1980, which already appears to have begun, and for wage growth at rates closest to recent historical experience. The Alternative III assumptions again project a continuation of current trends that seem unlikely to change. Alternative II again appears to be reasonable as an optimistic assumption but not as an intermediate assumption. Little or no provision is made for a recession in 1979 and 1980, and wage growth is projected to improve above current levels, despite a recent trend toward decline. Finally, Alternative I again appears to be unrealistic. Not only is no recession expected, but starting in 1980 wage growth improves dramatically over current levels, reaching a rate of 2.7% in 1982. By 1988 a long period begins during which wages grow at almost twice the average rate since 1950 before stabilizing at a rate of 2.25% in 2000, a rate almost 60% greater than average rates over recent years. All this occurs despite a trend toward decline in real wage growth reflecting a general decline in capital investment and worker productivity.

In the 1978 report, the real wage growth assumptions for all three alternatives are about the same as in the 1979 report, except that

---

computing the average annual rate of growth in real wages for 1953 to 1977 as presented. See Arthur B. Laffer and R. David Ranson, *The Social Security Problem*, unpublished manuscript, August 1978.

[9]Martin Feldstein, "Facing the Social Security Crisis," *Harvard Institute of Economic Research, Discussion Paper No. 492*, July 1976.

wages are projected to grow faster in the period 1979–1988 for each alternative as compared to its 1979 counterpart.

Inflation and unemployment are two other important factors affecting the financial projections of the social security system. Higher unemployment means lower tax revenues, and more rapid inflation means higher benefits. Consequently, the financial picture for social security is improved with lower unemployment and lower inflation.

Under Alternative I unemployment is expected to decline from its current level of about 6.0% to 4.0% in 1984 and thereafter. Inflation is projected to decline from its current rate of well over 10% to 3.1% by 1984 and 3.0% thereafter. Alternative II projects unemployment to decline from 6.0% to 5.0% in 1983 and thereafter, while inflation falls to 4.5% in 1983 and 4.0% thereafter. Finally, Alternative III expects unemployment to rise in 1979 and 1980, reflecting the general recession, and then to decline to 6.0% in 1984 and thereafter. Inflation is projected to decline to a stable rate of 6.0% starting in 1983.

Once again Alternative III seems to be the most realistic assumption. Its ultimate inflation rate of 6.0% is about one-half the current rate, and the decline to this level is projected to occur in just four years. This rate is the closest to the rates experienced in recent years and the most consistent with the recent general trend toward higher inflation. The assumed recession in 1979 and 1980 is already materializing, and the ultimate unemployment rate of 6.0% is equal to the average unemployment rate for the past ten years. Alternative II once again seems to be a good candidate for an optimistic rather than an intermediate set of assumptions. The low assumed levels of 5% unemployment and 4% inflation are below the rates experienced in recent years and contrary to the recent trend toward higher inflation and unemployment. Finally, Alternative I again seems to be wildly unrealistic. Assuming no recession, it projects the unlikely unemployment rate of 4% to be reached by 1984, a rate that has been experienced in the last twenty years only during the height of the Vietnam War. At the same time, inflation is supposed to drop precipitously to the implausible rate of 3.0%.

In the 1978 annual report, Alternative III projects unemployment to fall to 5.5% instead of 6.0%, with inflation falling to 5.0% rather than 6.0%. Alternative II is about the same as in the 1979 report except that both inflation and unemployment are projected to fall to their ultimate levels of 5.0% and 4.0% more slowly. Alternative I projects an ultimate unemployment rate of 4.5% rather than 4.0%, with inflation again falling to 3.0%.

The assumptions for disability incidence rates in the 1979 annual report turned out to have unusual significance. The disability incidence rate is the rate at which workers become disabled during the year and qualify for disability benefits. This rate dropped in 1978 by about 20% over 1977, contrary to a general trend toward increasing disability incidence throughout the 1970s. The Social Security Administration seized on this change to revise its projections on future disability incidence rates downward to such an extent that the ultimate cost of the OASDI program for Alternative II was reduced by almost one-half of one percent of total taxable payroll. This seems to be an incredibly large impact for a one-year change in one statistic, and this change may prove to be an insecure base for such a large cost reduction in the entire OASDI program. In analyzing future cost projections, we should remember that a reduction of almost 0.5% of taxable payroll was due to a change in this one assumption alone. If this change fails to materialize, costs will be increased by this amount.

Finally, putting the various economic assumptions together, we can gain further insight into the relative plausibility of the three sets of alternative assumptions. The unemployment, wage growth, and economic growth assumptions of Alternative I in 1979 make clear that this alternative assumes that there will not be another recession for the rest of the century, again a wildly unrealistic assumption. The averages in these economic variables assumed over this period are simply too high to be attained if any significant recession takes place. Under Alternative II only mild recessions are expected to occur over the rest of this century, a highly optimistic assumption. Only alternative III allows for the possibility of a future recession, and even here the leeway is not too great.

An examination of the assumptions for each alternative set used to make financial projections for the social security program leads to several important conclusions. It should be clear that, overall, Alternative III in the 1979 report is the most realistic set of assumptions despite the fact that it is supposed to be the pessimistic set. This Alternative, along with Alternative III in the 1978 report, should be considered the intermediate set of assumptions instead of Alternative II, which is merely a plausible set of assumptions for an optimistic alternative. Alternative I is wildly unrealistic on most key assumptions and hard to take seriously. For each of the major factors we have examined, Alternative III generally assumes the continuation of current trends and is the most consistent with recent experience.

Financial Projections

The tax increases passed by Congress in 1977 were intended to ward off bankruptcy and ensure that future taxes would be sufficient to meet future benefit obligations. An analysis of the financial data, however, shows that even these huge tax increases will not be enough to meet future benefit obligations and avoid bankruptcy.

The most common method of measuring the financial status of the social security system is to compare estimated expenditures as a percent of taxable payroll with the scheduled tax rate. These projections are made each year by the Social Security Administration and published in the annual reports of the Board of Trustees for the various social security trust funds.

Table 41 summarizes the projections made in the 1979 report for the OASDI program under the three alternative sets of assumptions discussed above. Expenditures projected as a percent of taxable payroll show what the tax rate would have to be in each year to cover expenditures. If the projected percentage is greater than the scheduled tax rate a deficit is projected for that year, and if it is less than the scheduled tax rate a surplus is projected.

Under Alternative III a deficit is projected for each year from 1979 through 1984. As we have already seen, this deficit is primarily due to the 1979–80 recession assumed under Alternative III and will result in severe cash flow problems for the OASI portion of the program in the 1980s. The program is nevertheless projected to be able to meet its benefit obligations during this period, although perhaps not on time. After 1984 the program is not expected to run a deficit again until the turn of the century. Beginning in 2010, however, deficits appear in every year projected, and these deficits eventually grow to astronomical proportions.

By 2015 the deficit is projected to be 2.5% of taxable payroll, which means that the scheduled tax rate in that year of 12.4% would have to be raised to 14.9% to meet total estimated expenditures. This would mean a tax increase over currently legislated tax rates in that year of 20%. By 2025, about when young people entering the work force today will be starting retirement, this deficit will be an enormous 7.24%, implying a necessary tax increase of 60% over currently legislated tax rates. If the benefits currently promised

to these workers are to be paid, the tax rate in that year will have to
be raised to about 20% of taxable payroll, consuming about one-
fifth of the income of most Americans. This is about twice today's
OASDI tax rate of about 10%. The deficits are projected to continue
to grow to 9.19% in 2030 and 10.53% in 2035, implying necessary
tax increases of 75% in 2030 and 85% in 2035. By 2050, currently
legislated tax rates will pay for less than half of projected benefits,
with a deficit of 12.77% implying a necessary tax increase of 103%.
To pay the benefits currently promised for that year, taxes would
have to be raised to 25.17% of taxable payroll, thus consuming
about a quarter of the incomes of most Americans.

  These enormous projected deficits are disastrous. Deficits of this
magnitude projected under a set of assumptions as realistic as Alternative III should be ample cause for serious alarm concerning the
future of social security. The spectre of social security taxes alone
consuming one-fifth of most paychecks in the United States by the
time today's young workers retire should be frightening. Yet this
may be necessary if the benefits promised young people entering the
work force today are to be paid.

  Under the 1979 Alternative II projections for the OASDI program, deficits begin to appear in the year 2015 and continue in every
year thereafter. By 2025, when today's young workers will be retiring, the deficit will be at 3.27 percentage points, implying a
necessary tax increase of 26%. To pay the benefits currently being
promised to these workers, the tax rate in 2025 would have to be
raised to almost 16%, more than one and one-half times current tax
rates. In 2035, the deficit increases to 4.18%, suggesting a necessary
tax increase of about 34% and a tax rate approaching 17%. Deficits
remain at this level or slightly lower through 2055, when the projections stop. It should be remembered that the assumptions underlying
Alternative II are in fact rather optimistic.

  The projections under Alternative I are interesting because they
show exactly what is needed to meet all the benefit obligations of
social security. Although the assumptions under this Alternative are
unrealistically optimistic, small deficits start to appear in the program in 2025 and continue until about 2040. These deficits would
require small tax increases in those years of 5% to 7.5%. The unrealistic assumptions necessary to attain this performance indicate the
tremendous financial instability of the current program. To meet its
eventual obligation under currently legislated tax rates, including
several future tax increases already legislated, social security will re-

quire the incredibly unlikely combination of occurrences assumed under Alternative I in the 1979 report.

Table 42 summarizes the projections for OASDI expenditures as a percent of taxable payroll as projected in the 1978 annual report under the 1978 assumptions. While no deficits are projected for the next twenty years under all three sets of 1978 assumptions, deficits appear in all three projections soon after the turn of the century. Under Alternative III, the program will be running a deficit by 2010, and under the other two alternatives the deficit appears by 2015. These deficits reach major proportions under all three sets of assumptions by 2020, with a deficit of 3.94% of taxable payroll under Alternative III, 2.34% under Alternative II, and 1.39% under Alternative I. By 2025, the projected deficit reaches 5.82% of taxable payroll under Alternative III, 3.66% of taxable payroll under Alternative II, and 2.45% of taxable payroll under Alternative I, implying necessary tax increases of 47% under Alternative III, 30% under Alternative II, and 20% under Alternative I. To finance these expenditures, tax rates will have to be increased to 18% under Alternative III, 16% under Alternative II, and 15% under Alternative I. By 2030, these tax rates will have to be increased to almost 20% for Alternative III, 17% for Alternative II, and 15% for Alternative I. By 2035 the deficit under Alternative III will have reached 7.82%, implying a necessary tax increase of 63%. The deficit under Alternative II in that year will have reached 4.40%, requiring a tax increase of 35%, and the Alternative I deficit will have reached 2.76%, implying a necessary tax increase of 23%. The deficit under Alternative III continues to increase, growing to 8.58% in 2055 with expenditures in that year requiring a tax rate of 21%. The deficits and percentages of taxable payroll under Alternatives I and II generally remain at their 2035 levels with only modest declines.

Even under Alternative III for 1978, which is more optimistic than Alternative III for 1979, the projected deficits are enormous, requiring tax rates of 18% to 20% if benefits promised to young workers entering the work force today are to be paid.

Another view of the financial status of the OASDI program can be seen by looking at the twenty-five year and seventy-five year averages at the bottom of tables 41 and 42. These are averages of the surpluses and deficits over the period in question expressed as a percent of taxable payroll. If the average is positive, then the program will have enough funds to meet its benefit obligations over that period. If it is negative, the program will not and will be faced with bankruptcy unless taxes are increased.

Table 41 shows that under all three 1979 projections the program will be able to meet its benefit obligations over the period 1979–2003, although the surplus under Alternative III is so small that poor performance by the economy during this period could easily throw the program into bankruptcy. Furthermore, without the more optimistic disability incidence assumptions in the 1979 report, the average under Alternative II falls to about the same level as projected for Alternative III. Since these more optimistic assumptions may have a weak basis in reality, the program may also be vulnerable under Alternative II.

For the period 2004–2028 the program shows a net deficit under both Alternative II and Alternative III and therefore will be unable to meet all its benefit obligations over this period. The deficit under Alternative III is 3.34% of taxable payroll, implying a necessary tax increase of 27% over the currently legislated tax rates in each year of the twenty-five-year period.

For the period 2029 to 2053, when young people entering the work force in the next few years will be retired, these deficits will be even greater. Taxes under Alternative III will be barely enough to cover half of projected expenditures. A deficit of 11.34% implies a necessary tax increase of 92% for each year of the entire twenty-five-year period. Under Alternative II the deficit of 3.90% implies a necessary tax increase over the entire period of 32%. These figures indicate that when young people entering the work force today are in retirement, there will not be enough funds to pay the benefits currently promised them unless taxes are raised sharply. These promised benefits are currently inducing young people to continue to pay their taxes and support the program, and many are currently making future plans in reliance on them. The potential withdrawal of these benefits therefore presents both moral and practical problems.

For the seventy-five-year period 1979–2053 there is an average deficit under both Alternative II and Alternative III, suggesting that the program will not be able to meet its obligations under either of these two sets of assumptions. The Alternative III deficit of 4.69% suggests that, on top of already scheduled tax increases, taxes would have to be raised immediately by almost 40% for every year of the projected seventy-five years to pay the benefits currently promised. This means that by 1990 tax rates for the OASDI portion of the program alone would have to be raised to 17% of taxable payroll, up from about 10% today.

The projections under Alternative I show a net surplus for the periods 1979–2003 and 2004–28, with a tiny deficit for 2029 to 2053. For the entire seventy-five-year period there is a surplus of 0.88% which would be cut in half without the more optimistic disability incidence assumptions. This suggests that the program under Alternative I will have just enough funds to meet its benefit obligations. Thus, the unlikely assumptions under Alternative I show just what is necessary for social security to fulfill all its benefit obligations without further tax increases.

Table 42 shows the average projections for these periods under the 1978 assumptions. While all three alternatives show surpluses for the period 1978–2002, all three also show deficits for the periods 2003–27 and 2028–52, suggesting that the program will be unable to meet its benefit obligations over these periods. The averages for the entire seventy-five-year period 1978 to 2052 also show deficits under all three sets of assumptions. Only under the assumptions in Alternative I in the 1979 report will social security be able to meet all its benefit obligations.

The seventy-five-year deficit of 3.22% under Alternative III in the 1978 report suggests that to meet all the program's benefit obligations taxes would have to be immediately raised 27% for each year over the next seventy-five years in addition to currently legislated tax increases. By 1990 tax rates would be close to 16% of taxable payroll for the OASDI program alone.

While these projections are dismal, they do not even include the projections for the HI program, which make the overall picture even more dismal. Projections of the estimated expenditure of the HI program as a percent of taxable payroll are shown in table 43. The projections under all three alternatives show deficits beginning in 1980. By 1990, Alternative III shows a deficit of 1.23% of taxable payroll, Alternative II shows a deficit of 0.61%, and Alternative I shows a deficit of 0.16%. Given the currently scheduled HI tax rate of 2.9% for 1990, this implies necessary tax increases for that year of 42% under Alternative III, 21% under Alternative II, and 6% under Alternative I for the HI program alone. This is the year in which currently legislated tax increases are to stop. By 2000, the deficits are 4.08% under Alternative III, 2.02% under Alternative II, and 0.68% under Alternative I, suggesting necessary tax increases of 141% under Alternative III, 70% under Alternative II, and 24%

under Alternative I. Under Alternative III currently legislated tax rates for 2000 will be sufficient to pay for only 42% of projected benefits in that year. The HI projections for 1978 presented in table 44 show a similarly dismal picture with projected deficits just slightly larger.

The Social Security Administration does not make projections for the HI program after the year 2000, but a former chief actuary of the administration has made such projections for assumptions equivalent to Alternative II (see tables 43 and 44).[10] Under these projections, by 2025 the Alternative II deficit will be 4.54% of taxable payroll, and by 2050 it will be 4.71%, suggesting necessary tax increases of 157% in 2025 over currently legislated levels and 162% in 2050. The average deficit of 3.58% for the twenty-five-year period 2002–26 suggests a necessary tax increase of 124% for each year of that period, and the average deficit of 4.63% for the period 2027–51 suggests a necessary tax increase of 160% for each year of that period. The seventy-five-year average deficit of 3.04 percentage points leads to a shocking conclusion: To ensure promised HI benefits over the next seventy-five years, the current HI tax rate would have to be increased immediately by 107% over currently legislated levels for each of the next seventy-five years, in addition to currently planned tax increases. It should be remembered that these are Alternative II projections.

Tables 45 and 46 provide a financial picture of the entire social security program (OASDHI). Putting both programs together basically pulls the financing problem into this century and makes the long-term problem of financing benefits for today's young workers even worse. As table 45 shows, under Alternative III for 1979 deficits begin to appear in 1990. By the year 2000 the deficit will be 3.12% of taxable payroll, implying a necessary tax increase of 20% over currently legislated tax rates for that year, just ten years after the tax increases mandated by the 1977 amendments will stop. The 1978 projections shown in table 46 indicate a slightly higher deficit and necessary tax increase for 2000 under Alternative III. Both the 1978 and 1979 projections suggest a necessary tax rate in 2000 of about 18.5% of taxable payroll. Under Alternative II for 1979 deficits begin to appear in 2000 and under Alternative II for 1978

[10]A. Haeworth Robertson, "The Financial Status of Social Security after the Social Security Amendments of 1977," 1978 Social Security and Health Care Costs Seminar, Bureau of National Affairs, Inc. and New York Chamber of Commerce and Industry.

these deficits begin to appear in 1995. Both projections suggest a tax rate in the year 2000 of about 16%.

By 2025, under Alternative II for 1979, the projected deficit for the entire program will be 7.81% of taxable payroll, and by 2050 this deficit will reach 8.46%, implying necessary tax increases of 51% in 2025 and 55% in 2050. These projections also show that if the program is continued on a pay-as-you-go basis, under 1979 Alternative II taxes for the entire program will consume 23.1% of taxable payroll in 2025 while under 1978 Alternative II social security taxes will consume 23.5% of taxable payroll in 2025. The major difference between 1978 Alternative II and 1979 Alternative II is that the 1979 assumptions include projections of disability incidence rates that, as we have noted, may be overoptimistic. Adding the projected increases from 2025 to 2030 for the OASDI portion of the program alone, the entire program will consume 23.88% of taxable payroll under 1979 Alternative II and 24.17% under 1978 Alternative II in 2030.

Furthermore, under Social Security Administration projections for 1979, by the year 2000 the HI program is projected to be consuming 2 additional percentage points under Alternative III than under Alternative II. If we assume that this difference between Alternative II and Alternative III remains this large until 2025, a conservative assumption, the HI program alone will be consuming almost 10% of taxable payroll by 2025. If we add this to the 1979 Alternative III projections for the OASDI program for 2025, the entire social security program will consume almost 30% of taxable payroll in that year under Alternative III assumptions. Adding the increases for the OASDI portion of the program alone, we find that under 1979 Alternative III by 2035 total expenditures for the entire social security program will have reached 33% of taxable payroll, and by 2050 these expenditures will have reached 35%. It should be remembered that these Alternative III projections are by far the most realistic.

What's more, the difference of 2 percentage points between the Alternative III and Alternative II projections for the HI program in the year 2000 is likely to widen considerably in succeeding years because the lower fertility assumptions of Alternative III have their greatest impact after 2000. The differences between Alternative III and Alternative II for the OASDI program grew five times between 2000 and 2025 and twelve times between 2000 and 2050. If the difference for the HI program grows at one-half this rate, by 2025 the entire OASDHI program under 1979 Alternative III will be consuming almost 33% of taxable payroll.

The projections under Alternative III for 1978 are slightly lower because the 1978 alternative assumes an ultimate 1.7 fertility rate while the 1979 alternative assumes an ultimate 1.5 fertility rate. Nevertheless, assuming an HI difference of only 2 percentage points between Alternative II and Alternative III, by 2025 the entire OASDHI program will be consuming 28% of taxable payroll under Alternative III for 1978, and by 2030 this will have increased to 30%. Assuming that the HI difference grows at half the rate of growth in the differences for the OASDI program between Alternatives II and III, the OASDHI program under 1978 Alternative III will grow to 31% of taxable payroll in 2025 and 33% in 2030.

We may safely conclude, therefore, that to finance expenditures for the entire OASDHI program in the years 2025 to 2035, taxes will have to be increased to 25% to 33% of taxable payroll. In other words, if the benefits currently being promised to people entering the work force today are to be paid, social security payroll tax rates will have to be raised to levels that will consume one-fourth to one-third of the incomes of most Americans. The real issue over whether social security is bankrupt, therefore, is whether taxpayers can be counted on to bear this enormous tax burden.

Another method of analyzing the fiscal soundness of social security is to look at the projected dollar amounts of expenditures against the projected dollar amounts of taxes. These figures in constant 1980 dollars are presented for 1979 Alternative II in table 47. Under these projections, by 2025 the OASDHI program will have benefit obligations of $770.2 billion, with OASDI expenditures alone at $522.2 billion. The deficit for the entire OASDHI program in that year is projected to be $260.3 billion, with the OASDI deficit alone at $108.9 billion. These projected expenditures and deficits continue to grow steadily after 2025, with OASDHI expenditures reaching almost $1.3 trillion in 2050 and the OASDHI deficit reaching $456.6 billion. Expenditures for OASDI in 2050 are expected to reach $871.6 billion with a deficit of $202.4 billion.

The same projections for 1979 Alternative III are presented in table 48. The totals for taxes and expenditures under this Alternative are smaller for two important reasons. First, the fertility rate is lower, so there are fewer beneficiaries as well as fewer workers. Second, the economy has grown at a slower rate, so the taxes and benefit obligations it has generated are smaller. But while total projected taxes and expenditures are smaller, the deficit totals are higher. By 2025 OASDHI expenditures are projected to reach $669.5 billion with a deficit of $317.2 billion. Expenditures for the OASDI program in that year were projected to total $452.2 billion with a deficit of $166.7 billion. By 2050 OASDHI expenditures under this Alternative will total almost $900 billion with a deficit of one-half trillion, about the size of the current federal budget. For the OASDI program in 2050, expenditures are projected to total $643.8 billion with a deficit of $326.6 billion.

A third method of measuring social security's financial solvency is to look at the projected ratio of the trust funds to benefits in each year. Table 49 shows that under all three sets of assumptions for 1979 this trust fund ratio is expected to decline for the next few years before starting a period of growth lasting past the turn of the century. Despite this period of growth, the trust funds will still not grow anywhere near levels necessary to guarantee future benefits, especially under Alternatives II and III. Soon after the turn of the century, these trust fund ratios begin to decline once again. Under Alternative III, the OASDI trust fund is expected to be exhausted in 2018, while under Alternative II this trust fund is projected to be exhausted in 2032. Thus, under currently legislated tax rates, the program will become unable to meet its benefit obligations starting in these years. Only under Alternative I is the program expected to be able to meet its benefit obligations.

Table 50 shows the same general pattern for the 1978 assumptions with the OASDI trust fund exhausted in 2019 under Alternative III and in 2028 under Alternative II. Even under Alternative I for 1978, the OASDI trust fund is projected to be exhausted by 2043. Again, only under Alternative I for 1979 is the program expected to be able to meet its foreseeable benefit obligations.

The projections for the HI program alone are even worse. Under Alternative III in both the 1979 and 1978 annual reports, the HI trust fund is projected to be exhausted in the late 1980s. Under Alternative II in both reports the fund is expected to be exhausted around 1990, and under Alternative I in both reports exhaustion is projected for around 2000.

Another method of measuring social security's soundness is to calculate the program's net worth and unfunded liability (see table 51). The net worth of the program is equal to the present value of estimated benefit payments over the next seventy-five years minus estimated tax receipts for those years. The net worth of the program therefore shows the present value of the deficits of the program over the next seventy-five years or the present value of additional taxes over currently legislated levels that will have to be raised to finance the program's obligations in the next seventy-five years. This figure is presented in the annual Saltonstall report of the U.S. Treasury calculated under assumptions equivalent to Alternative II. In 1978 the net worth of the OASDI program calculated in this way was a negative $929 billion. The 1978 net worth of the OASDHI program was a negative $1.189 trillion. These figures had decreased considerably from the year before because of the changes made by the 1977 amendments. In 1977 the net worth of the OASDHI program was a negative $5 trillion, and for the OASDI program it was a negative $4.8 trillion. While the 1978 totals are a substantial improvement, they still indicate significant difficulties ahead. The present value of future deficits under the entire OASDHI program in 1978 was still equal to more than half the entire GNP for that year.

The Saltonstall reports also calculate the unfunded net liability of the program under Alternative II assumptions. The unfunded net liability is equal to the present value of the benefits the government will have to pay over the next seventy-five years to current recipients and current workers paying into the program minus the present value of the taxes they have yet to pay. Because it is equal to the total amount of currently earned benefits, it represents the amount the government would have to pay to current social security participants to dismantle the system without taking away any currently earned rights to current or future benefits. It also represents the amount the government would have to pay a private insurance company to assume responsibility for the program.

The unfunded net liability is in reality a form of government debt. It represents the amount the government currently owes to the participants in the social security program, a financial obligation that the government is required to pay under current law to identified beneficiaries. It is as if each participant in social security held a government bond that would mature when his social security benefits became due. Nevertheless, social security's unfunded net liability is not included in official government figures on the national debt. It is easy to understand why. The unfunded net liability of social security is more than five times the national debt as presently calculated.

As table 51 indicates, in 1978 the unfunded net liability of the OASDI program alone was $3,971 billion or almost $4 trillion, about twice the size of 1978 GNP and equal to approximately $20,000 for every individual alive in the United States today. This figure was down considerably from $5.4 trillion in 1977, although it has grown considerably from $1.9 trillion in 1972 and $435 billion in 1971. This $4 trillion in national debt represents an enormous burden to leave to future generations. Excluding it from official figures on the national debt is another example of official disingenuousness.

Under any of the measures of financial stability that we have discussed, the social security program is presently bankrupt. Not only does it not have the funds on hand to meet the benefit totals it has promised, but at currently legislated tax rates future tax revenues will also fall far short of meeting benefit obligations. Under present law, social security will be unable to pay the benefits it is currently promising in the foreseeable future. In fact, under current law (and despite the 1977 amendments) social security will be unable to pay the benefits it is promising to young workers entering the system today, benefit promises that serve as the inducement to continued payment of taxes and support of the program.

Will Taxpayers Continue to Pay?

The real issue over whether social security is bankrupt is whether taxpayers can be counted on to pay the heavy tax burdens projected for the future, tax burdens that will consume 25% to 33% of taxable payroll.

It is hard to imagine taxpayers accepting social security taxes that will consume one-fourth to one-third of their paychecks. This would be two to two and one-half times current tax rates. Taxes at these rates are a far cry from the maximum $60 per year that prevailed over the first fifteen years of the program. Taxpayers are already objecting loudly to the tax increases of 1977, which set the current OASDHI tax rate at 12.26%. A Harris survey taken in April 1978 found that Americans opposed the 1977 tax increase by 45% to 39%.[11] A large plurality of 48% to 30% supported cutting back the increase by one-third. A sizeable majority (71% to 14%) felt that, "It is a prime example of irresponsibility by the federal government that social security was not funded properly in the first place."[12] An

---

[11]Louis Harris, "Americans Feel the Squeeze from Hike in Social Security Tax," *The Harris Survey*, 11 May 1978.
[12]Ibid.

earlier survey found that people eighteen to twenty-nine opposed
the 1977 tax increase by 53% to 33%.[13]

Furthermore, taxpayer protests and tax revolts have grown in recent years. California's Proposition 13, which cut that state's property
tax rate sharply, was opposed by virtually every establishment organ
in the state, yet the voters passed it by a wide margin. A small band
of libertarians at the National Taxpayers Union in Washington,
D.C., have almost single-handedly brought the nation to the brink
of a constitutional convention that would consider amendments to
limit taxes and require a balanced budget. The group's membership
rolls and contributions have skyrocketed, and some members of the
organization believe that a similar nationwide drive against social
security taxes could be mobilized. Those who take the taxpayer's
revolt lightly forget that this nation was born in a tax revolt.

The president of the National Taxpayers Union, James Davidson,
initiated a serious protest against social security taxes in the mid-
1970s. In 1972 Davidson refused to pay his social security taxes,
basing his refusal on the landmark Supreme Court decision of *Welsh
v. United States* (398 U.S. 408 1970), which held that conscientious
objection to the draft could not be restricted to religious grounds
alone. Davidson argued that the Social Security Administration recognizes the right of people to withdraw from social security on religious grounds and that on the basis of the *Welsh* precedent conscientious objection to paying social security taxes could not be limited to
religious grounds. He therefore refused to pay his social security
taxes as a nonreligious conscientious objector.

Initially, the IRS decided to drop the case against Davidson, undoubtedly for fear that it would lose, thus setting a precedent that
would allow individuals to voluntarily refuse to pay social security
taxes. Davidson then began advising other individuals to refuse to
pay their social security taxes on the same grounds and began raising
money for further legal battles. As Davidson's position began to
receive wider publicity, the IRS felt compelled to reopen the case.
At this point, faced with heavy legal fees, disillusioned with the
slowness of the legal process, and burdened with the other extensive
activities of his organization, Davidson decided to settle the case. A
similar legal challenge remains a possibility for the future, however.

Taxpayers have also shown an increased willingness to devise and
exploit tax loopholes to avoid social security taxes. Tax consultants

---

[13]Louis Harris, "Social Security," *The Harris Survey*, 1 December 1977.

have begun to advise employers to use an optional method of paying social security taxes that will result in a lower total tax bill. Under the optional method, the employer agrees to pay the worker's share of the social security tax and the worker agrees to take a salary cut for the full amount of the tax now paid by the employer. With a lower salary subject to the payroll tax rate, the total tax bill is lower, and the employer and employee can share the savings. With the new high tax rates, the savings from this scheme have become well worth the trouble for many employers and employees. On a nationwide scale this scheme could result in a large loss of tax revenues.

Taxpayer resentment over recent tax increases has also already spawned considerable talk of cutting back benefits. The Carter Administration proposed in its 1979 budget to cut back on disability benefits, students' benefits, parents' benefits and minimum benefit provisions. The *New York Times* supported these proposals in an editorial on February 1, 1979, which warned, "Social security costs more than $100 billion a year now; as the number of retired persons multiplies, the strain will become enormous. A backlash from over-taxed wage earners must be expected."[14] The Carter Administration has also circulated proposals to move the retirement age back to sixty-eight.

In addition, the tax burdens may increase in future years for reasons not provided for in the Social Security Adminstration projections discussed above. Anything that makes tax burdens heavier makes it less likely that taxpayers will pay the amounts necessary to save the system from bankruptcy.

For example, severe recessions are possible. The assumptions for the Social Security Administration projections do not make much provision for the possibility of additional severe recessions over the next seventy-five years, particularly recessions as severe as those in the mid-1970s. The assumptions for economic performance under Alternative III are low enough to be attained on average if moderate recessions are followed by strong recoveries, but even here the leeway is not too great. Besides, such projections do not indicate whether the program will get through the recession period, especially if the recession occurs at a crucial time for the program, such as the early 1980s. Even if the program struggles through such a recession, future projections will have been thrown way off, and even higher tax rates will be necessary to finance the program. And how

---

[14]"How to Save Social Security," *New York Times*, 1 February 1979, p. A 22.

long will it be after that until the next severe recession? How likely is it that there will not be several major recessions during the next seventy-five years?

The Social Security Administration projections also do not take into account the negative economic effects likely to be caused by the high social security tax rates themselves. A study by the staff of the Joint Economic Committee of Congress soon after the 1977 tax increases estimated that by 1982 those increases would cause a loss of $30 billion a year in GNP and an increase of 1.3 percentage points in the unemployment rate.[15] It seems likely that tax rates of 25% and more will discourage a major amount of employment and economic activity. If this happens, tax revenues will fall and tax rates will have to be raised further. As we have noted, a point could eventually be reached where higher tax rates will fail to yield higher tax revenues. These high tax rates will also cause a tremendous loss of savings and vitally needed capital investment, resulting in tremendous losses of national income and economic growth. The decline in capital investment will also result in fewer jobs and lower real wage growth, decreasing tax revenues once again. Considering all these effects, again we may well reach a point where the economy simply cannot support the high social security tax burdens.

If taxpayers do become unwilling to pay future taxes, they can vote to cut them by means of their elected representatives. As long as we live in a democracy, the power of taxation will rest with the voters, and the government cannot compel them to pay if they choose to vote otherwise. Future Congresses will not be bound by future taxes and benefits voted by current Congresses, and they can and will cut both benefits and taxes if the program is imposing unfair tax burdens on future working populations. The past popularity of the program in the start-up phase is no guide to voter sentiment in the mature stage. Furthermore, the political process is not the only way taxpayers can resist heavy tax burdens: They can drop out of heavily taxed employment and devise schemes to get around unfair taxes. Outright civil disobedience by a portion of the population could also ultimately bring the system down.

If the government does default on its social security promises, it will not be the first time that a government has reneged. Nor will it be the first time that a pension system has driven a government to bankruptcy. The recent cases of New York City, Chicago, and

---

[15]Brett Duval Fromson, Joint Economic Committee Staff, U.S. Congress, 1978.

Cleveland illustrate that the taxing power is no guarantee that a government entity will be able to meet all of its obligations.

It would seem, then, that complacency about the willingness of taxpayers to continue to bear future social security tax burdens is unreasonable and even irresponsible. What taxpayers will be willing to pay is a matter of judgment. Americans already feel squeezed by taxes and inflation, and demands on the average American's income are already great. The most reasonable judgment seems to be that taxpayers will not accept tax burdens in the range of 25% to 33% of taxable payroll. The social security program will therefore not be able to meet its future benefit obligations. Young workers entering the work force today cannot count on receiving the social security benefits currently being promised to them and they should not make their future plans assuming that those benefits will be paid. In short, if the willingness of taxpayers to continue to pay is the only thing standing between social security and bankruptcy, then social security is bankrupt.

Do We Need a Trust Fund?

A trust fund large enough to guarantee future social security benefits would clearly provide a great deal more financial security than the current pay-as-you-go system. Without a trust fund, current beneficiaries are literally at the mercy of current taxpayers. With a trust fund, the desires of current taxpayers are irrelevant. In a pay-as-you-go system, benefit payments are dependent on political fortune, fertility rates, total employment, unemployment, inflation, wage growth, and numerous other similarly unstable factors.

Is a trust fund, therefore, necessary to guarantee social security benefits and keep the program out of bankruptcy? Whether the additional margin of safety provided by a trust fund is necessary depends on one's judgment concerning the willingness of taxpayers to continue to pay the taxes necessary to support the program on a pay-as-you-go basis. The less one feels that taxpayers will continue to pay without objection, the more he will feel that the additional margin of safety provided by a trust fund is necessary. Simple prudence and good judgment would seem to dictate that a trust fund *is* necessary to secure and guarantee future benefit payments. As the Harris Poll cited above indicates, Americans agree with this judgment by a 71% to 14% margin.

An invested system is safer and more secure than a pay-as-you-go system, and this additional margin of safety is worth having. It can be attained by a private invested system as well as a government system. In fact, in many ways the private system may be even more secure. The appropriate reforms to remedy the problems noted here will be discussed later.

Why Worry?

The usual response by government officials and ardent supporters of the program to the concerns we have been discussing is, "Don't worry, there is plenty of time to solve the program's problems." But plenty of time to do what to solve them? There are three variations on this response corresponding to the three possible ways the bankruptcy problem can ultimately be resolved.

The first variation is "don't worry and it will go away." It is argued that the really serious financing problems for social security are not expected to occur for forty years and that in the meantime something may happen to prevent the occurrence of the problem. One or more of the negative projections of the program's financial status may turn out better than expected, for example. Besides, long-term projections are always tricky and we should not place too much faith in them.

But the most probable assumption is that the program will be unable to meet its future benefit commitments. It is true that given different assumptions, the program's problems will be small or nonexistent, but that does not mean that they should be ignored. If the program is suddenly unable to meet its benefit obligations, the social, economic, and political impacts will be disastrous. We are talking about the financial security of an entire generation of Americans. The potential seriousness of the problem is so great that even the possibility of significant financial difficulties should be cause for concern. Traditionally, in matters of basic financial security, the appropriate attitude has been one of conservatism and caution, yet the government encourages the people to be careless and even irresponsible about their future financial security.

Furthermore, social security's future benefit promises are being used to induce continued payment of taxes and continued support of the program. We therefore need an evaluation today of how reliable those future benefit promises are. If the best projections available suggest that those benefit promises are not very reliable, then those who are being asked to fork over their money now and sacrifice for the program have every right to object.

In addition, taxpayers, especially young taxpayers, have to plan today for their futures, and they must base their plans on what is most likely to happen, not on what defenders of the status quo can imagine. It is simply incredible that government officials are today trying to induce young people to base their future financial security on promises that seem at this point to be unreliable. Social security is usually perceived as a humanitarian institution, but there is nothing humanitarian about inducing an entire generation of Americans to rely on benefit promises that may never be paid. As Arthur Laffer and David Ranson have pointed out,[16] there is no conflict between humanitarian compassion on the one hand and financial responsibility and soundness on the other. On the contrary, financial solvency and responsibility are prerequisites to humanitarian compassionate action.

Finally, the social security financing problem is not remote or speculative, as supporters of the program seem to imply. The decline in fertility has already occurred, and social trends in America today reinforce this decline. American attitudes toward families and children are just not the same in the 1980s as they were in the 1930s or 1950s, and these changes have to be taken into account. Our economy is today wracked by inflation and substantial periodic recessions, along with slow or nonexistent growth in real wages, and these economic facts will cause financial problems for social security. The HI program is already expected to go into bankruptcy in the next decade, and a recession or two in the 1980s could easily bring the entire program to its knees.

The second variation is, "Don't worry, there's plenty of time to raise your taxes." It is argued that if the financing problem does develop as expected, the government can always raise taxes to finance the program's benefits. Since social security is supported by the government's power to tax, there is no need to worry about the potential bankruptcy of the program.

The prospect of payroll tax rates in the range of 25% to 33% is hardly a source of consolation. If this is the way we are going to solve the social security financing problem, then the solution constitutes a new problem in itself. As we have noted, this argument is seriously deficient because it assumes that the government's power to tax is absolutely within the discretion of government officials and

---

[16]Arthur B. Laffer and R. David Ranson, "A Proposal for Reforming the Social Security System," H.C. Wainwright and Co., May 19, 1977.

policy makers, especially those who support social security. As long as we live in a democracy, however, the government's power to tax can be exercised only with the political support of taxpayers. As we have demonstrated, taxpayers are not likely to support the enormous tax burdens projected for social security, and therefore the power to tax will not serve as a solution to the long-term financing problems of the program.

The third variation is the most incredible of all. It has been advanced by John A. Brittain, a Senior Fellow at the Brookings Institution, who writes, "In the event of demographic trends and productivity gains even more unfavorable than those currently projected, the social security system will still not collapse. Real benefits would simply be scaled down to allow for that situation."[17] In other words, "Don't worry, there is plenty of time to cut your benefits."

This is really not a counterargument to the problems noted here at all. It does not change our important conclusions that social security will be unable to pay the benefits it is currently promising for the future, that the program is therefore bankrupt, and that young people entering the work force today cannot count on receiving the benefits currently being promised to them.

The Conflict in Objectives

The financial problems of social security are all caused by the program's conflict in objectives. All the bankruptcy problems that we have discussed are due to the pay-as-you-go nature of the program. If the program was operated on a fully funded basis with current taxes saved and invested to pay the benefits of current taxpayers instead of immediately paid out to finance current benefits, then the program would be backed up by a trust fund large enough to guarantee future benefit payments. As we have noted, with such a trust fund the program would not be vulnerable to any of the economic hazards that are currently causing the program's financial difficulties and threatening bankruptcy. It is thus the pay-as-you-go nature of social security that is causing the program's financial problems, and this pay-as-you-go nature is itself the result of the pursuit of welfare objectives in the program's early years. The pursuit of these welfare objectives through the social security program has made it a financially unsound insurance program.

[17]John A. Brittain, "The Social Security System Is Not Perfect, But It's Not Bankrupt," *Challenge*, January-February 1975, p. 53.

6

Social Security and Minorities

Many believe that one of the chief purposes of social security is to help the weakest and most vulnerable groups in our society, especially the poor and the elderly. Indeed, this belief is one of the prime reasons for the strong public support of the program in the past.

In fact, however, social security has several major negative impacts on some minority groups, especially the poor, blacks, women, the elderly, and the young. The program hurts most the very people many of its supporters are trying to help. It is true that many aspects of social security are helpful to these groups, particularly the welfare benefits, but these same benefits can be provided through alternative programs or institutions without the negative effects of social security.

We will see in this chapter that many of the program's negative impacts on minorities are caused by one major, overriding factor: The social security program forces everyone in the program to participate in a single insurance program with one set of benefit provisions, provisions that are best suited to the circumstances and characteristics of the politically powerful majority. Members of minority groups may find that the uniform provisions are poorly suited to their particular needs and preferences. The result is that social security will invariably end up hurting members of minority groups by forcing them to participate in an insurance program that does not truly serve their needs.

In a nation as diverse and pluralistic as the United States there is no one set of benefit provisions that will suit the needs and preferences of everybody. A system of diverse, varied, and easily adaptable options is needed that will allow each American to choose the

215

program best suited to his or her individual circumstances. Such a system can be provided only by the private sector.

The Poor

Social security hurts the poor in numerous ways, all of which are easily avoidable and can be eliminated by a sensible restructuring of the program.

The first of these effects has been emphasized by Nobel laureate Milton Friedman.[1] According to Friedman's analysis, social security forces the poor to pay relatively more for their benefits while giving them less because the poor tend to start work earlier than other income groups in our society. The poor tend to start work right after high school or even before, whereas middle-class and upper-class individuals usually go to college. They may not begin serious, full-time work until sometime between the ages of twenty-five and thirty. The poor pay social security taxes for several more years than other groups in society, but paying taxes for these additional years does not earn them any additional benefits. In fact, years of work before the age of twenty-one are not even included in the benefit calculation.

The poor also pay more because there is a lower tax rate for self-employed than for employed workers. Tables 1 and 4 show that in general the tax rate on self-employed workers has been and will continue to be between two-thirds and three-fourths of the combined employer-employee tax rate. Since the employee bears the employer's share of the tax, the self-employed pay a lower rate of tax than the employed. But the self-employed tend to be wealthier than the employed and are generally members of the higher-paying professions.

It is also a fact of life that the poor tend to die earlier than those in the upper- or middle-income classes. The result is that the poor receive less in benefits because they are alive fewer years after retirement. Thus, the poor pay more for less.

In addition, a larger proportion of single, unattached individuals are poor than of married couples. Social security provides additional benefits for married couples that are not available to those who are single, even if they have paid as much as married persons. Once again, the poor pay more for less.

[1]Friedman has expressed similar views in numerous publications and forums. For one of his most comprehensive discussions of the problem see Wilbur J. Cohen and Milton Friedman, *Social Security: Universal or Selective?* (Washington, D.C.: American Enterprise Institute, 1972).

Finally, under the social security benefit computation provisions, the five years of lowest earnings are deleted before computing the AME (average monthly earnings). This benefits most those whose earnings will increase the most over the course of their lives. A wage or salary history with substantial and persistent increases is more characteristic of those with higher incomes than those with lower incomes.[2]

A recent study by Henry J. Aaron of the Brookings Institution concludes that the poor receive a lower return in retirement benefits on their past tax dollars than those with higher incomes, despite the substantial welfare elements in the program.[3] Aaron found that the tendency of the poor to die earlier is in itself enough to completely offset the welfare elements of the program. The other factors noted by Friedman mean that the poor receive less benefits per dollar paid into the program than those with higher incomes. These factors outweigh even the welfare elements of the program discussed in chapter 2. Even if they did not, it would still be true that these factors tend to make the poor worse off and mitigate the beneficial impact upon them of the welfare elements.

A second major negative effect of social security on the poor has been demonstrated with characteristic brilliance by Martin Feldstein.[4] According to Feldstein's analysis, social security tends to redistribute income and wealth away from the poor and toward the rich.

As noted in chapter 3, social security reduces savings and capital accumulation, which means that there is less capital per worker, and with less capital, workers are less productive. As a result, their wages are lower than they would be otherwise. On the other hand, with less capital the rate of return to capital, or the interest rate, may be higher. The poor are predominantly dependent on wage income, with little income from capital investments. Most of the return to capital, on the other hand, goes to the wealthier segments of society. Social security redistributes income from the poor to the rich by lowering wages and possibly increasing the return to capital.

---

[2] The argument in this paragraph was advanced by Henry J. Aaron in *Demographic Effects on the Equity of Social Security Benefits,* (Washington, D.C.: Brookings Institution, 1979).

[3] Ibid.

[4] Martin Feldstein, "Social Insurance," *Harvard Institute of Economic Research, Discussion Paper No. 477,* May 1976.

Social security also causes a heavier concentration of wealth as well as income because social security induces taxpayers to reduce their savings. Without social security, taxpayers would be able to save and invest the money they are currently paying into the program, and they would then hold real wealth approximately equal to the present discounted value of future promised social security benefits, which can be called social security wealth. As we saw in chapter 3, social security wealth is not real, presently existing wealth. It represents the amount of additional wealth households would probably hold in the absence of social security. As was also noted in chapter 2, Feldstein has calculated that social security wealth was equal to about $2 trillion in 1971, whereas real private wealth in that year was $3 trillion.

Social security wealth is distributed far more equally than real private wealth. If each household saved and invested a major portion of its income each year, individual households would begin to accumulate significant amounts of wealth. Each household would hold an additional amount of wealth approximately equal to the present discounted value of the household's expected future social security benefits. In other words, if social security wealth were held in the form of real assets, the distribution of wealth would be far more equal than it is today. In 1971 there would have been $5 trillion in real wealth distributed far more equally than the $3 trillion actually held in that year. The top 1% of households holds approximately 40% of the capital owned by all households. Feldstein calculates that if social security wealth were replaced with real wealth, the concentration of wealth in the top 1% would be cut in half from 40% to 20%.[5] This reduction in concentration would be achieved not by taking wealth away from the top 1% but by making it possible for the bottom 99% to accumulate more wealth.

In another recent study Feldstein calculated the distribution of real wealth, social security wealth, and total wealth, with real wealth plus social security wealth equal to total wealth.[6] The study was based on data for all households with a man between the ages of thirty-five and sixty-four. His results (see table 52) show that social security wealth is more equally distributed than private wealth, and therefore the distribution of wealth would be far more equal if in-

[5]Ibid., p. 33.

[6]Martin Feldstein, "Social Security and the Distribution of Wealth," *Journal of the American Statistical Association*, December 1976.

dividuals were able to save and invest the amounts they are currently paying in social security taxes.

Table 52 shows that while the top 1% of families own 28.4% of real wealth, they own only 1.2% of social security wealth and only 18.9% of total wealth. The reduction in concentration from real wealth to total wealth is about one-third. Similarly, while the top 4.1% of families own 44.6% of real wealth, they own only 5.2% of social security wealth and 30.8% of total wealth. This again suggests a reduction in concentration from real wealth to total wealth of about one-third.

On the other hand, the bottom 51.2% of families own only 8.7% of real wealth, while they own 40.4% of social security wealth and 19.8% of total wealth. The share of wealth held by the bottom half of families would be more than doubled if social security wealth were real wealth.

This discussion should not be taken to imply support for government policies of income redistribution away from the rich and toward the poor. If individuals earn their wealth and income through free and voluntary exchanges in a free market, then it is really not any of the government's business how much each citizen has. When the government actively intervenes in these exchanges to redistribute wealth and income towards the rich and away from the poor by placing artificial barriers in the way of the poor, then there is a basis for legitimate complaint. The complaint is not that this policy makes the wealth and income distributions more unequal; there is no reason why they should be equal. The complaint is that this policy harms the poor because it prevents them from earning and receiving as much as they might without this intervention. The poor and those with low incomes can least afford the losses due to barriers that prevent them from increasing their income, and any government policy that has this effect is subject to valid criticism.

A third way that social security hurts the poor is through the payroll tax. This tax is regressive, taking a higher percentage of the incomes of those at lower income levels than those at higher levels. Two features of the tax make it regressive. First the tax is applied only to income from wages. Income from all other sources, such as capital gains, interest, profits, or other types of investment income are not taxed. Because wages alone constitute a higher proportion of the incomes of the poor than those of other income classes, a flat rate tax on wage income will take a higher percentage of income from those with lower incomes than those with higher incomes.

Second, the tax is assessed on wages up to a certain limit. Those who have incomes above the limit pay a smaller percentage of their income in taxes than those who have incomes below the limit. For example, the OASDHI tax rate in 1979 was 12.26% assessed on wage income up to $22,900. A worker who earned $10,000 in that year paid $1,226 or 12.26%, and a worker who earned $20,000 paid $2,452 or 12.26%. But a worker who earned $30,000 paid $2,807.54 or 9.35%, and a worker who earned $40,000 paid $2,807.54 or 7.02%. The percentage of income paid in tax declines with increasing income.

As a result of the regressive payroll tax, those with low incomes may have to forgo necessities because such a large percentage of their income goes to social security. This is not to discount the hardship of the tax on all income levels, but merely to note that it will be harsher on the poor.

It makes little sense to finance the welfare element of social security with a regressive payroll tax. Such a program is plainly counterproductive, with the burden of the tax falling most harshly on the very income groups the program seeks to help. If the welfare portion of social security were made an entirely separate program, it could be financed by a nonregressive means that does not have this harsh effect. The poor could still receive the intended benefits of the program without the countervailing negative effects of the social security payroll tax.

In 1975 Congress passed an income tax credit for the poor to offset the harsh burden of social security taxes. This provision is known as the earned income credit, and it is available to low-income workers who have dependent children and maintain a household. The credit is equal to 10% of adjusted gross income in excess of $4,000. The taxpayer's income taxes are then reduced by the amount of the credit. While this credit may offset some of the harshness of the payroll tax, it does not solve the basic problem. The credit represents resources available to help the poor, resources that are consumed by the payroll tax. Without this regressive tax, these resources could be used to help the poor in other ways. There is no denying that the regressivity of the payroll tax hurts the poor, but when resources are used to mitigate this harshness they do not change this fact; it means only that the tax is now consuming resources that could have helped the poor in other ways.

Furthermore, even with the credit the tax remains regressive for most workers because only those with very low incomes and dependent children can qualify for the credit. And the earned income credit does not change the fact that a regressive tax is a foolish way to finance a welfare program.

Some argue that it is wrong to look at the payroll tax separately from the benefits.[7] They argue that the tax and benefit structures should be considered together, and since the benefits have a large redistributive welfare element, the net effect is to help the poor. But there is no reason why taxes and benefits must be analyzed together in this way. The benefits, especially the welfare portion, could be financed by means other than a regressive payroll tax. Since the regressive tax is not necessary for the benefits, we can make changes in one without changing the other. We should analyze taxes and benefits separately, therefore, so we can decide what modifications we want to make in each. Analyzing them together may hide offsetting defects in each that we could eliminate, thereby improving the whole package. As Milton Friedman has noted, social security is the only institution that could take a tax structure no one would support on its own and a benefit structure no one would support on its own, slap them together, and emerge with a combined tax-benefit structure that is supported by everybody.

A fourth set of negative impacts on the poor results from social security's harmful economic effects, which were discussed in chapter 3. These effects fall most heavily on the poor. For example, it is the poor who need most the additional GNP that social security is sacrificing through its effects on capital accumulation and employment. If a portion of the additional GNP were to go to the poor, it would raise their standard of living and provide them with more of the essentials of life.

There are many good reasons to believe that a major portion of this increased GNP would go to the poor. The additional capital investment that would occur in the absence of social security would reduce unemployment, the major cause of poverty. It would also provide more good jobs, raising wages and opening up new opportunities for both the working and nonworking poor. Some of the increased investment would go into mortgages, leading to an increase in the housing stock and thereby providing more good housing for the poor.

Similarly, it is the poor who need most the investment returns

---

[7]Alicia H. Munnell, *The Future of Social Security* (Washington, D.C.: Brookings Institution, 1977), pp. 90–93.

they could be getting on their social security taxes in the private sector. While it is true that social security contains a large welfare element in the benefit structure, these benefits could just as well be provided in a separate program apart from social security. This separate program would allow the poor to get the additional returns they could be getting in the private sector in addition to any necessary welfare supplement. Furthermore, as we saw in chapter 4, even with the welfare elements in social security, the poor can still get higher returns in the private sector than they can get through social security. This constitutes a fifth negative impact of the program on the poor.

Still another negative impact on the poor is caused by the financial problems of the program discussed in chapter 5. If the program is forced to default on its benefit promises, it is the poor who will be hurt the most because they are the least likely to have alternative means of support they can rely on. The least sophisticated and poorest members of society are also the least likely to foresee the problem in advance. Social security hurts the poor, therefore, by forcing or inducing them to depend on unreliable benefit promises and thereby expose themselves to unnecessary risks.

A final set of hardships imposed on the poor through social security results from the design of the program's benefit structure. Inequities in this structure waste a substantial amount of resources that were meant to be used to help the poor but are instead used to make payments to those who are not poor.[8] Social security benefits contain large portions of welfare, but these welfare benefits are not paid on the basis of need as measured by a means test. Instead, they are paid on the basis of other surrogates for need that are inadequate measures of true need. Many who are not in need are nevertheless able to qualify for these welfare subsidies, and the result is a waste of resources available to help the poor.

As we saw in chapter 2, the benefit computation formula is skewed so that those with relatively lower past incomes will receive higher benefits in relation to their past taxes than those with higher past incomes. The minimum benefit provision also provides a minimum retirement benefit regardless of the amount paid in past taxes. Benefits paid under these provisions are simply welfare payments, and many individuals are able to qualify for them under these provisions even though they are neither poor nor in need.

<hr />

[8] See generally Munnell, *The Future of Social Security*, chapters 1 and 2.

The most widespread abuse of these provisions occurs among government employees, who do not participate in social security through their government jobs. They are instead covered by the civil service retirement system, and about three-fourths of state and local government employees are insured under special pension plans administered by their state and local governments. These employees will often work the minimum number of years required to qualify for social security in a secondary part-time job while they are working for the government. Because these jobs tend be low paying and only part-time, annual earnings are low and consequently the earnings history for social security is low. These workers will then receive under the minimum benefit and progressive benefit formula provisions substantial benefits that were meant for needy workers. In addition, these workers also receive substantial pensions from their government jobs. Thus, even though they will have relatively high incomes in retirement, they will still be receiving welfare benefits through social security.

Another way that government workers take advantage of these provisions is to quit their government jobs after they have worked enough years to qualify for civil service pensions and work in a private sector job full time for the minimum number of years required to qualify for social security benefits. This is easy to do because the minimum number of years necessary to qualify under the civil service system is five, and the minimum number of years necessary to qualify for full social security benefits is ten. Because these workers will receive no credit toward social security for their earnings in the years they were employed in their government jobs, they will have an average earnings history that will appear quite low. As a result, these workers will qualify for benefits under the minimum benefit provision and progressive benefit formula. At the same time, these workers will be receiving pensions from their government jobs.

This abuse of the social security welfare provisions has developed into a significant problem. It has been estimated that 40% of all those receiving benefits under a civil service pension are also receiving social security benefits.[9] Government employees are not the only people who are able to take advantage of these welfare provisions. Individuals with substantial savings or a retirement income but a relatively low earnings history may also receive these welfare provi-

9Ibid., p. 15.

sions even though they are not in need. For example, persons who experienced financial success late in life, particularly of an entrepreneurial or investment nature, might qualify for benefits. So might persons who received property or other assets through inheritances, even if those inheritances were relatively modest. A woman who inherited, for example, a home with the mortgage completely paid off by her parents, or who inherited a small farm or a small apartment house, would not be as needy as her past earning history might suggest, yet she might be receiving substantial welfare subsidies through social security. A particularly frugal low-income person or a wealthy person who spent his life engaged in low paying pursuits such as charitable or volunteer work might also find himself eligible for substantial welfare subsidies through social security even though he was not in need.

Problems also arise from the payment of benefits for dependents of retired workers. As we saw in chapter 2, a retired worker will receive additional benefits if he has a spouse, young children, or other dependents, even though he may not have paid any more in taxes than a worker without such dependents. These provisions are based on the welfare rationale that an individual with dependents is more likely to be needy than an individual without. Benefits for dependents under these provisions are simply welfare benefits.

Yet wealthy individuals have wives and children too. In fact, families with both a husband and a wife tend to be poor far less often than families with a single parent, and these families tend to be poor less often than families including just single, unrelated individuals. In 1977 the median income for single, unrelated individuals was $5,907, with 23% below the poverty level, while families including both husband and wife and single parent families had a median income of $16,009, with just 9% below the poverty level.[10] The existence of a spouse and other dependents is a poor surrogate for true need, and paying out welfare benefits for them will result in a waste of assets meant to help the poor. A highly paid business executive with a wife and several young children may retire with a substantial estate accumulated through the availability of lucrative stock options, yet he could receive welfare benefits for his wife and children through social security. At the same time, his housekeeper, who was single all of her life, will retire without the

10President's Council of Economic Advisers 1979 *Economic Report of the President* (Washington, D.C.: U.S. Government Printing Office, 1977).

benefit of these provisions. She and others like her will receive less in benefits than they have paid for because some of their tax money will be used to pay benefits to individuals like her wealthy employer.

The benefit provisions to the dependents of a deceased worker are also primarily based on a welfare rationale. The benefits are not paid on the basis of what one has paid into the program in the past, as under term life insurance, for example, where upon the death of the insured the survivors are paid a certain sum based on the amount of insurance that was purchased. The payments are instead primarily dependent on the number of spouses, children, and other qualifying dependents one leaves behind. These benefits are primarily welfare benefits meant to help those in need, yet, as we have noted, the mere existence of a spouse and dependents does not mean that one is in need. On the contrary, husband and wife families tend to be wealthier than single parent or single individual families. These provisions again result in the payment of welfare benefits to those who are not in need. When our wealthy business executive dies, his surviving wife and young children will receive welfare subsidies even if he also leaves them a substantial investment portfolio and large life insurance policies. The housekeeper's heirs will receive nothing.

Finally, as we also saw in chapter 2, large welfare subsidies were passed out to all beneficiaries, rich or poor, in the start-up phase of the program. The result again was an inconceivable waste of taxpayer's dollars or resources available to help the poor.

The social security program's waste of resources meant to help the poor has led Alicia Munnell of the Brookings Institution to conclude that

> SSI is a more efficient vehicle for meeting this welfare criterion than social security, because a means test ensures that funds actually go to those with a demonstrable need. Progressive social security benefits distort the contributions-to-benefits ratio in the interest of social adequacy but actually augment the income of many elderly people who are relatively well off because of unearned income in a second pension. In effect, many who should be ineligible receive welfare through a social security program. . . .
>
> Using social security funds in such an inefficient way increases tax rates and lowers benefits for other recipients, most of whom have paid payroll taxes for many years and have no other pension.[11]

These negative impacts on the poor occur because the program

---

[11] Munnell, *The Future of Social Security*, pp. 11 and 15.

pursues inherently contradictory objectives. Social security benefits are paid without a means test because they contain large insurance elements that are considered earned. But because welfare benefits are passed out along with these insurance benefits, the welfare portion of the program is not subject to a means test either. Instead, the program attempts to adopt other surrogates for need in the payment of these welfare benefits. These surrogates are not adequate substitutes for a test that measures need itself, and the result is the problems discussed above.

The problems caused by the regressive payroll tax are also the result of the conflict in objectives. The program is financed by a regressive payroll tax because it is supposed to be an insurance program. This is an appropriate way to finance insurance because all should be charged the same price for a good or service, just as all are charged the same price for a loaf of bread. It is only fair that people should pay for the goods or services that they consume and the amount of this payment should depend on the value of these goods or services. But this value exists independently of whether the purchaser in any particular instance is rich or poor. It is the same regardless of the identity and circumstances of each individual purchaser and therefore all should pay the same price based on this value, whether they are rich or poor. But because a large welfare element is mixed with these insurance elements, the result is welfare benefits financed by a counterproductive regressive tax.

The perverse redistribution of wealth and income, as demonstrated by Feldstein, is due to the pay-as-you-go nature of the program, which, as we have demonstrated, is also the result of the conflict in objectives. The pursuit of welfare objectives through the pay-as-you-go structure of social security thus results in an insurance program with unnecessary perverse effects on the distribution of wealth and income.

Finally, the poor are generally required to pay more for less under the insurance provisions of social security because these provisions are poorly adapted to the circumstances and characteristics of the poor. It is easy to see why this is the natural result of a social security program such as we have today. Social security forces everyone to participate in one big insurance program with one particular set of benefit provisions. Since this set of benefit provisions is democratically chosen, it will be best adapted to the circumstances and characteristics of the typical, average, ordinary member of society, because it is these individuals that will comprise the politically powerful majority. Individuals with needs and preferences that deviate from this norm will therefore be poorly served by the uniform benefit provisions of the government program. Minority groups such as the poor who have circumstances and characteristics substantially different from the average member of society and who are relatively powerless politically, will find that the provisions of the social security program will be very poorly suited to their particular needs and preferences. Thus, a social security program, by imposing one insurance program with one particular set of benefit provisions on everyone, will invariably fail to serve the poor adequately.

Without social security, individuals could choose an insurance package from a more diverse and varied range of options offered in the marketplace. They could then each choose the insurance plan with benefit provisions best suited to their widely varying needs and preferences. Individuals with circumstances and characteristics which deviate from the norm would then be free to pursue options which are more finely tailored to these circumstances and characteristics. Poorer individuals, for example, could choose insurance programs suited to those who start work earlier in life than most and also have lower life expectancies. Social security, however, forecloses this opportunity to adapt insurance protection to the varying needs of different groups and individuals.

But why must everyone be forced to accept the one particular set of benefit provisions offered by social security? Because social security pursues welfare objectives in addition to insurance ones, it must be universal and compulsory. If it was voluntary, those who were not benefiting from the welfare elements would drop out, leaving no one to pay for them.

Would it be possible to change social security so that it did not offer just one set of benefit provisions but a wide array of alternative options? The answer is no. As long as the program must be run by the government, the terms and conditions of the program must be set politically through the political process, and there are no mechanisms in this process for varying the terms of the program to meet the needs and preferences of different groups and individuals. Congress cannot vote a different plan for each individual or group, nor can the public keep track of these individualized plans to make wise democratic decisions. Individual bureaucrats do not have the market incentive to develop different and diverse insurance options, and there is no market process through which consumers can express their desires and tell the government administrators whether the plans they do come up with are really what the public wants or prefers. The political process is just too cumbersome to allow for diverse individualized insurance plans. It cannot possibly match the diversity and adaptability of the market process. But, once again, the program must be operated by the government only because it contains welfare elements as well as insurance ones. It is again the conflict in objectives that is preventing the program from allowing a diverse, varied, more individually suited system of insurance protection.

Another reason that there must be only one set of benefit provisions that everyone must be forced to accept is that the program is operated on a pay-as-you-go basis. Everyone must therefore be forced to participate in the program because their taxes are needed to finance current benefits. Yet the pay-as-you-go system cannot be adapted to differing needs and preferences because people are not paying for their own benefits. There is no guarantee that current inflows will be able to finance the benefit options actually chosen, and people would tend to choose the most expensive options available because they do not bear the costs. Once again it is the welfare elements of the program that are making the insurance elements inadequate.

Thus it is the conflict between the welfare and insurance objectives of social security that causes the program's provisions to be poorly suited to the circumstances and characteristics of the poor and ends up making them pay more for less and it is this conflict that is responsible for the other negative impacts on the poor which we have discussed. All of these negative impacts of the program can be avoided by splitting the separate objectives of social security into two separate programs. The welfare benefits of social security can then be provided by a separate program or set of institutions. Resources meant for the poor would then be more likely to reach them and their impact would not be offset by the other negative impacts discussed here.

Blacks

Two of the negative effects of social security fall with special harshness on the black population.

First, unemployment is more widespread among blacks, especially teenage blacks, than among other social groups. Social security, by discouraging saving and capital investment, keeps unemployment higher than it would otherwise be. Thus social security works a particular hardship on blacks by exacerbating a problem of special severity for them.

Second, the mortality tables show that life expectancy among blacks is the lowest of any social group, even lower than among the poor in general. A white male at the age of twenty can expect to live another 51.6 years, but a nonwhite male at this same age can expect to live only 46.8 years.[12] He can therefore expect to receive benefits for approximately five fewer years than his white counterpart, although he must pay the same taxes. The young white male worker has a 27% greater chance of being alive at age sixty-five than the young nonwhite male worker, a 30% greater chance of being alive at seventy, and a 37% greater chance of being alive at seventy-five.[13] The retirement benefits that young blacks can anticipate are therefore much less than what young whites can anticipate. These benefits represent a much lower return on the taxes paid by blacks than on the taxes paid by whites.

It is true that the higher mortality rates for blacks mean that they have a higher chance of dying before the age of sixty-five and therefore their survivors have a higher chance of receiving survivor's benefits than whites. But the great majority of OASI taxes go for the old-age portion of the program rather than the survivor's portion. In 1978 only about 20% of OASI benefits went to pay for survivor's benefits, so any advantage in the survivor's portion of the program for blacks would be more than outweighed by a disadvantage in the old-age portion.

But more fundamentally, those who die before sixty-five and receive survivor's benefits in their name receive a worse deal from social security than those who live to receive retirement benefits. An individual who dies before age sixty-five could have used a small fraction of his OASI taxes to buy term life insurance that would have paid him at least as much as social security upon death and without all the restrictive terms and obligations of the program. Yet this individual receives nothing for all the taxes he paid for old-age benefits. In fact, if he were single or if he were married and his widow remarries, he will receive no survivor's benefits either. Therefore, individuals who die before sixty-five receive the lowest

---

[12]Life Tables, *Vital Statistics of the United States*, Volume II, Sec. 5, National Center for Health Statistics.

[13]Ibid.

return of all on their social security taxes. Even with the survivor's insurance program, the longer one lives the better he will do with social security, and the sooner he dies the worse he will do. The fact that blacks have a higher likelihood of dying before the age of sixty-five, therefore, means that they have lower expected benefits and a lower expected return on their social security taxes than whites.

Blacks pay the same taxes as whites, yet receive less in expected benefits because they are more likely to die at a younger age. This and the other negative impacts on the black population are again caused by the conflict in objectives of the program in the same way that this conflict causes the negative impacts on the poor.

Women

Since its inception the social security system has included numerous provisions that blatantly discriminate against women, particularly women who work, women who are childless and single women, although some of these provisions have been recently struck down by the U.S. Supreme Court. The benefit provisions of social security are based on a traditional view of the family, with the husband as wage earner, the wife as homemaker and mother of numerous children. This underlying model has been the primary source of the program's pervasive and systematic discrimination against women.

Social security works less well for those whose families differ from the traditional model. Those who follow the traditional path receive more in benefits and a greater return on their tax dollar than those who do not. Those who do not are penalized and forced to subsidize those who do.

Although social security's benefit provisions have not changed since the program's enactment in the 1930s, the American family has undergone dramatic changes. Since 1939 American women have greatly increased their participation in the labor force. In 1940 only 14.7% of married women worked, but by 1979 this number had increased to 50.0%. Labor force participation by single women has increased from 48.1% in 1940 to 57.0% in 1979 (see table 53). According to the U.S. Labor Dept., over half of all women—51.3% as of October 1979—now work. At the same time, marriage rates have declined and more women have chosen to remain single. Many more women are choosing careers rather than traditional homemaking responsibilities. Divorce rates have increased rapidly since the 1930s. Fertility rates, as we have seen, have been declining at an accelerating pace, resulting in smaller families and more childless families. As a result, the current structure of social security benefits is inappropriate for large numbers of American families.

As we saw in chapter 2, the social security benefit structure provides benefits to the wife of a retired worker if she is sixty-five, or at a reduced rate if she is at least sixty-two. This benefit is equal to half of her husband's PIA, which is the amount of her husband's retirement benefit. If the wife has worked and earned retirement benefits of her own, she must forgo these benefits if she chooses to accept the benefits for a spouse on her husband's record. The wife of a retired worker under sixty-two may still qualify for additional benefits if she is caring for a child or grandchild of the retired worker. The benefit in this case is again 50% of the husband's PIA. A divorced wife is entitled to the same benefits on the same terms if she was married to the worker at least ten years. Children and grandchildren of the retired worker may also qualify for a benefit equal to 50% of the retired worker's PIA. Wives, children, and grandchildren of disabled workers can qualify for the same benefits under the disability insurance provisions.

Survivor's benefits are available to widows of deceased workers at age sixty-five or at a reduced rate at sixty. This benefit is equal to 100% of the deceased worker's PIA, which is the same as his retirement benefit would have been. A widow under the age of sixty can qualify for a survivor's benefit equal to 75% of the deceased worker's PIA if she is caring for a child or grandchild of the deceased. Surviving divorced wives can qualify for these same benefits if they were married to the deceased for at least ten years. Children or grandchildren of the deceased worker can also qualify for a benefit equal to 75% of his PIA.

Thus, while a single working person will pay the same taxes as a married co-worker with ten children, he will receive nothing from these benefit provisions, while his co-worker can cash in. This single worker must pay for a wife's benefits, although he has no wife, and he must pay for children's benefits, although he has no children. He must pay for survivor's benefits that are totally useless to him. The money he pays into the system is used to subsidize his co-worker who has ten children.

Women should be particularly concerned over these inequities because they are part of a system that discriminates against women who work, women who are childless, and women who are single. A single working woman, for example, must pay for all benefit provisions that she does not receive, but a married woman with several children who does not work and pays no taxes may receive benefits on her husband's record for herself and her children when he retires, dies, or becomes disabled. The taxes of the single, working woman are used to subsidize the married, nonworking woman with children. The single, working woman is punished for choosing a career instead of marriage and forced to subsidize those who fit into the traditional mold.

Even if a working woman decides to marry, she is penalized if she remains childless. If she decides to get married and have children, a penalty may still be exacted if she chooses to work rather than stay home with the children because a wife must forgo the benefit she earns on her own earnings record if she chooses to receive the wife's benefit on her husband's earnings record. If the wife's PIA is equal to or less than one-half of the husband's PIA, she will receive nothing for all her own social security taxes because she will receive no additional benefits beyond what she is already entitled to on her husband's earnings record. If her PIA is greater than one-half of her husband's PIA, then she will choose her own benefits and forgo her wife's benefits. For all her years of tax payments, she will gain only the difference between her own benefit and one-half of her husband's benefit.

Some examples will illustrate this pervasive discrimination in the social security benefit structure.[14] Assume that both Mr. Swift and Mr. Sap are sixty-five in 1980 and ready to retire. Both have earned the maximum annual income all their lives, averaging over $9,400 a year in taxable income since 1959. Both will have a PIA equal to $571.25. Now assume that Mrs. Swift never worked but that Mrs. Sap worked every year with average taxable earnings of $3,095 since 1959 and total taxable earnings in 1979 of $5,321. She will therefore have a PIA of $279.25. Assume also that both Mrs. Swift and Mrs. Sap are sixty-five in 1980. For their retirement the Swifts will receive benefits equal to one and one-half times Mr. Swift's PIA, or $856.88 per month. But the Saps are faced with a dilemma. Mrs. Sap is entitled to benefits on her own account of $279.25 a month, and her husband is entitled to benefits of $571.25 a month for a total of $850.50 per month. If the Saps choose this alternative, they will

14The benefit amounts in these examples are projections based on the Alternative II assumptions used in the 1979 Annual Report of the Board of Trustees of the Federal Old-Age and Survivor's Insurance and Disability Insurance Trust Funds.

actually receive less than the Swifts, even though Mrs. Sap worked and paid social security taxes all of her life while Mrs. Swift stayed home and paid nothing. If Mrs. Sap elects to forgo her own retirement benefit and take the wife's benefit which she is entitled to on her husband's record, the Saps will receive the same as the Swifts. But Mrs. Sap will receive nothing for her years of working and paying social security taxes.

Now assume that Mrs. Sap, like her husband, earned the maximum taxable income all her life and therefore also had a PIA of $571.25. In this case, Mrs. Sap will forgo the benefit to which she is entitled on her husband's earnings record and take her own. The Saps will receive benefits of $1,142.50 per month, while the Swifts will receive only $856.88. The Saps will have paid twice what the Swifts paid in taxes, yet they will receive only 33% more in benefits. The taxes paid by Mrs. Swift all her life will entitle her to only an additional $285.62, while the identical taxes paid by Mr. Swift entitle him to $856.88.

Now assume that Mr. Sap and Mrs. Sap each earned exactly half the maximum taxable income all of their lives. This would have totaled $11,450 in 1979 and averaged $4,702 since 1959. Each of the Saps would therefore have a PIA of $350.33, while Mr. Swift would still have a PIA of $571.25. Upon retirement the Swifts will again receive a monthly benefit of $856.88. But the Saps, who paid the exact amount in taxes, will receive only $700.66.

The same inequities arise in the payment of survivor's benefits. Assume now that both Saps and both Swifts are thirty-five in 1980. Mr. Sap and Mr. Swift both have earned the maximum taxable income all their working years. Mrs. Sap has also worked all of her adult years and has earned the average wage in covered employment in each year, but Mrs. Swift stays home and does not work. The Saps have no children, but the Swifts have two, ages five and seven. If both Mr. Sap and Mr. Swift die in 1980, Mrs. Swift will receive $914.97 per month for eleven years and $784.23 per month for two years after that. But Mrs. Sap will receive nothing, even though she worked and paid taxes while Mrs. Swift stayed home and paid nothing. In fact, Mrs. Sap will continue to work and pay taxes while Mrs. Swift stays home, pays nothing, and collects benefits.

Assume now that Mrs. Sap continues to work and earns the average wage in covered employment in every year, retiring at age sixty-five. She will be entitled to a survivor's benefit on her deceased husband's earnings record of $522.82 per month in 1980 dollars and a retirement benefit on her own earnings record of $696.63 per month in 1980 dollars. Since she can only choose one, she will choose her own retirement benefit. Mrs. Swift, however, will be entitled to the same survivor's benefit on her deceased husband's earnings record that Mrs. Sap was. For all her years of work and tax payments, Mrs. Sap will receive only an additional $173.81 per month. Even though Mrs. Swift stayed at home and paid nothing while Mrs. Sap worked and paid taxes all her life, Mrs. Swift will receive old-age benefits not greatly smaller than those that Mrs. Sap will receive. The Saps will pay more in taxes than the Swifts over the course of their lives but receive less in benefits.

Now assume that the Saps also have two children, ages five and seven. Mr. Swift and Mr. Sap again die. Mrs. Swift is entitled to the same benefit of $914.97 per month, but Mrs. Sap receives only $784.23 per month. Since she is working, her benefit in 1980 is reduced $1 for every $2 above $3,730 until only the benefits for her children are left. At the average wage in covered employment in 1980, Mrs. Sap will earn $12,208 for the year, and her own survivor's benefit as a mother will therefore be completely eliminated. Even though the Saps have paid almost twice as much in taxes as the Swifts, they will receive less in benefits. Not only does Mrs. Sap in effect receive nothing for her past taxes, she will continue to pay taxes on her annual earnings, while Mrs. Swift receives higher benefits staying home and paying nothing. When both Mrs. Sap and Mrs. Swift reach sixty-five, Mrs. Swift will again receive almost as much in old-age benefits even though the Saps will have paid more in taxes than the Swifts.

If Mrs. Sap in these examples were Miss Sap and childless, she would be in even worse shape. Assume that Miss Sap and Mr. Swift were thirty-five in 1980 and both earned the maximum taxable income all their working years. Mrs. Swift, age thirty-five, stays home and takes care of her children, ages five and seven. If Mr. Swift and Miss Sap both die in 1980, Miss Sap will receive nothing paid in her name, while Mr. Swift's beneficiary will receive $914.97 per month for eleven years, $784.23 per month for two more years, and $522.82 per month for all of Mrs. Swift's life after sixty-five. This is true despite the fact that both Mr. Swift and Miss Sap paid the same amount in taxes all their lives. If Mr. Swift dies but Miss Sap does not, she will continue to work and pay taxes, and Mrs. Swift will receive the amounts described above. When both Miss Sap and Mrs. Swift reach sixty-five, Miss Sap will receive $1,068.82 per month and Mrs. Swift will receive $552.82 per month, even though Miss Sap made a lifetime of tax payments at the maximum taxable amount and Mrs. Swift paid absolutely nothing. If neither Mr. Swift nor Miss Sap die before sixty-five, the Swifts will receive $1,603.23 per month in retirement benefits, but Miss Sap will receive only $1,068.82 per month, even though she paid the same amount in taxes all of her life as Mr. Swift.

It is clear that the message from the Social Security Administration to women is get married, stay home, and have children. The effect of the program is to hamper the freedom of women, as well as men, to lead nontraditional lives by imposing its underlying traditional model on everyone. The result is discrimination against unmarried, childless women who work, against married childless women who work, and even against married women who have children and work. Though the program also discriminates against men in some of these circumstances, the discrimination against women should be of particular concern to those who have an interest in women's issues. The women's movement has been especially concerned with the freedom of women to work and to remain single and childless. Women have therefore sought to tear down barriers that impinge on these freedoms and to prevent the imposition of the traditional family model on those who do not wish to play the traditional family roles. The social security program is yet another barrier to the exercise of these freedoms, yet another institution that seeks to impose the traditional family model on unwilling women. This barrier or imposition operates through a system of financial penalties on women who attempt to exercise these freedoms and the forced subsidization or reward of those who do not.

The systematic discrimination through our country's largest social welfare program against those who choose nontraditional lives, men as well as women, is a gross inequity. Those who do not choose to get married and have children should not have to support those who do. People should be responsible for their own decisions and actions. If they wish to get married or have children or forgo working, they should have to pay the costs of doing so. They should not be allowed to impose these costs on others.

In addition to discriminating against working women, social security also discriminates against women in general. Several of the program's generally discriminatory provisions have recently been struck down by the U.S. Supreme Court as unconstitutional.

One such provision was struck down by the Court in 1975 in the

case of *Weinberger* v. *Wiesenfeld* (95 S.Ct. 1225, 420 U.S. 636). In
that case, the Court considered the provision granting survivor's
benefits to a deceased worker's widow who was under age sixty and
caring for the worker's children. The benefits provided were known
as mother's benefits, but there was no similar provision for father's
benefits. Widowers under age sixty who were caring for the children
of their deceased wives could not receive survivor's benefits. Men
paying into social security could earn mother's benefits to be paid to
their surviving wives, but women paying into social security could
not earn father's benefits to be paid to their surviving husbands. The
Court noted that this discrimination was based on the "archaic and
overbroad generalization. . . that male worker's earnings are vital to
the support of their families, while the earnings of female wage
earners do not sufficiently contribute to their family's support."[15]
The Court said further, "Obviously, the notion that men are more
likely than women to be the primary supporters of their spouses and
children is not entirely without empirical support. . . . But such a
gender-based generalization cannot suffice to justify the denigration
of the efforts of women who do work and whose earnings contribute
significantly to their family's support."[16]

A mere showing of discrimination is not enough for a finding of
unconstitutionality. In sex discrimination cases it must also be
shown that this discrimination is not rationally related to any legitimate government goal or purpose, although the Court has been willing to apply a stricter test of rationality in these cases than in cases
concerning many other types of discrimination.

In the landmark case of *Frontiero* v. *Richardson* (411 U.S. 677, 93
S.Ct. 1764 (1973)), the Court had struck down a similar provision
based on the same rationale in the compensation structure for mili-
tary personnel. Increased compensation was automatically provided
for male servicemen who had a spouse, but female service personnel
had to prove that their spouse was dependent on them before they
could receive the increased compensation. This presumption of
dependency was made for administrative convenience. Since wom-
en are usually dependent on their husbands for support, the government felt that it was not worth the resources to investigate in each
instance whether the wife was actually dependent on her service-

---

[15] *Weinberger* v. *Wiesenfeld*, 95 S. Ct. 1225 at 1231.
[16] *Weinberger* v. *Wiesenfeld*, 95 S. Ct. 1225 at 1232.

man husband. Since men are much less often financially dependent on their wives, however, requiring women to prove that their husbands were dependent before receiving the increased compensation would save far more in compensation than it would cost to administer the rule. But the Court held that such administrative convenience could not justify their discrimination against women. Too many men are dependent upon women and too many women are not dependent upon men to allow this discrimination to stand. The presumption of dependency does not have a sufficiently rational relation to the goal of administrative convenience for the discrimination inherent in such a presumption to pass the constitutional test. The Court therefore held that this provision violated the equal protection rights of women under the due process clause of the Fifth Amendment and was consequently unconstitutional.

Similarly, the presumption underlying the social security provision considered in *Wiesenfeld* was based on the rationale that women are usually financially dependent on their husbands and therefore the wife of a deceased husband caring for his children needs survivor's benefits, but since men are usually not financially dependent on their wives, a husband is not in need of survivor's benefits when she dies, even if he must also care for her children. The Court again held that too many men are financially dependent on their wives and too many women are not financially dependent on their husbands to allow this provision to stand under the equal protection requirements of the due process clause. The fact that a husband could not even receive the benefits by proving dependency in *Wiesenfeld* only made the provision even worse than the one considered in *Frontiero*. The Court concluded, "Since the Constitution forbids the gender-based differentiation premised upon assumptions as to dependency made in the statutes before us in Frontiero, the Constitution also forbids the gender-based differentiation that results in the efforts of female workers required to pay social security taxes producing less protection for their families than is produced by the efforts of men."[17]

The Court therefore held that these social security provisions unconstitutionally discriminated against women and ordered the Social Security Administration to pay benefits to surviving fathers on the same basis as surviving mothers.

The Court struck down another discriminatory provision in *Cali-*

[17]Ibid.

fano v. *Goldfarb* (97 S.Ct. 1021 (1977)). Before this case, a widower of sixty could not receive survivor's benefits on the record of his wife unless he could prove he was dependent on his wife for half of his support before she died. A widow could receive survivor's benefits without proving such dependency. This provision was again considered discriminatory against women. Taxes paid by a male into social security earned survivor's benefits for his wife regardless of whether she was dependent on him or not, but similar taxes paid by a woman earned survivor's benefits for her husband only if he was dependent. The provision is based, of course, on the assumption underlying *Frontiero* and *Wiesenfeld*, that a wife is usually dependent on her husband but a husband is rarely dependent on his wife. As the Court held in those cases, such an assumption of dependency constitutes a constitutionally impermissible discrimination against women, and the court ordered the Social Security Administration to pay benefits to surviving aged widowers without proof of dependency.

Califano led to the elimination of a similarly discriminatory provision that required the husband of a retired wife to prove dependency before he could receive spouse's benefits on his wife's record. The government now pays spouse's benefits to all retired husbands on the same terms and conditions as they are paid to retired wives. Retired husbands are now eligible to receive a benefit equal to half of their retired wife's PIA without proving dependency, but to receive this benefit they must forgo any benefits they may have earned on their own earnings records.

Despite these decisions by the Court, other provisions discriminating against women remain in the social security benefit structure. For example, a surviving divorced wife is entitled to benefits on her former deceased husband's record if she is caring for a child of the deceased worker or if she is over the age of sixty. A divorced wife of a retired worker is also entitled to benefits on her former husband's record if she is caring for his child or if she is over the age of sixty-two. But there are no provisions for benefits for surviving divorced husbands, whether they are caring for children or not, or for retired divorced husbands. Given the precedents discussed above, these provisions are probably also unconstitutional because they are based on the same underlying presumption of dependency that the Court has found insufficient in the prior cases.

Women have also complained that one of the major discriminatory elements in social security is the provision requiring that before a beneficiary accepts a benefit to which he or she may be entitled on someone else's earnings record, the beneficiary must forgo the benefits to which he or she may be entitled on his or her own earnings record. Women tend to earn on the average, only about sixty percent of what men earn. Women also tend to take more years off from work, particularly to have and raise children. As a result, a woman's PIA is often less than half of her husband's PIA, in which case she will take her wife's benefits on her husband's earnings record rather than her benefits on her own record. Many women receive no benefits for the taxes they paid for all of their working years. In general, therefore, women again tend to receive less in social security benefits for their taxes than men.

It is unlikely that this provision will be considered unconstitutionally discriminatory against women because the provision is discriminatory in impact only. The discrimination is not written into the terms of the law; the statutory provisions do not deny any benefits to women that are given to men. The rule requiring a potential beneficiary to choose only the one highest benefit available to him applies to men as well as women. Its impact is harsher on women because they tend to have lower earnings.

Almost every law has harsher impacts on some groups than others, even apart from the intended impacts that are part of the policy the law is meant to pursue. For a law or statute to be found unconstitutional on equal protection grounds, there must be a finding of discriminatory intent, which may or may not be expressed by explicitly discriminatory statutory language, in addition to a discriminatory impact. This discrimination must then be found unconstitutional under the tests the Court has devised to enforce the equal protection doctrine.

For this reason, the Court is also unlikely to find unconstitutional the other forms of discrimination we have discussed. The provisions that discriminate against single and childless people in general apply to men as well as women. It may be true that these impacts are currently of greater concern to women than men, but this fact alone is insufficient to support a finding on unconstitutionality. The program's discrimination against single and childless people is unlikely to be found unconstitutional under traditional equal protection analysis because the Court is likely to find that this discrimination is rationally connected to the program's welfare objectives.

The many ways that social security discriminates against women illustrate several important points about the program. First, one insurance program for everybody will invariably fail to serve the interests of minorities and those who do not play traditional social roles. Social security was structured to fit the needs of the average American family, especially as it was constituted in the 1930s, and consequently it was based on a traditional family model. As long as the structure of the program is politically chosen, one cannot expect anything else. The average Americans who constitute the politically powerful majority will vote to structure the program to fit their needs. Those whose needs differ, such as single, working women, will find that the program is poorly structured to fit their circumstances. Single, working women will be forced to pay for spouse's benefits though they have no spouse, for children's benefits though they have no children, and for survivor's benefits though their survivors cannot collect the benefits. Married women who are childless and work and even married mothers who work, as well as single or childless men, will also find that the system does not suit their circumstances. Yet these individuals will be unable to change the system to serve their needs because the politically powerful majority will use their power to keep the system best suited to them.

Second, it should be clear that one insurance plan with one particular set of benefit provisions cannot possibly match the widely varying needs and preferences of individuals in a nation as diverse as ours. A single person has different needs than a married, childless couple, who, in turn, have different needs than a married couple with several children. Working women, single or married, have different needs than nonworking homemakers and mothers. Because of these important differences, it is necessary to have a system that can be individually adapted to varying needs.

Only a private insurance system than enables individuals and families to choose the plan best suited to them can fill this need. The diversity and adaptability of such a system cannot be provided through one big government plan for everybody like social security. A pay-as-you-go system cannot be individually adapted to differing needs because people are not paying for their own benefits. Even if a pay-as-you-go system could be individually adapted, the political system is too unwieldy and too cumbersome for individuals to assert their particular needs and preferences.

A third point is that more flexibility and adaptability is needed so that changing needs can be served by changing insurance plans and benefit provisions. When social security was first enacted, the kind of family on which it was based was extremely widespread, but times have changed and this family is now far less typical. Although the program fails to serve the needs of larger and larger numbers of Americans, changes to take this fact into account have been slow or nonexistent. After long and costly legal battles, some of the old provisions have been struck down as unconstitutional, but this process has not even begun to eliminate all of the program's provisions that discriminate against those who do not fit into the traditional mold, and it is unlikely that it ever will. Congress has also done little or nothing to change the program to meet newly emerging needs or preferences.

The changes have been slow because the current social security system is rigid and inflexible. It is a political institution and all changes in it have to be made through the unwieldy and cumbersome political process. If one wants to make a change to meet emerging needs under the current system, how can it be done? One way is to finance a long and costly legal battle to take one's complaint to the Supreme Court. Another is to start a political movement that will convince the country and Congress to change the provisions. Needless to say, this is also a long, expensive, and arduous route.

A more flexible system that will respond more quickly to changing social trends would serve the consumer of insurance protection far better. Such a system can be provided only by private alternatives. As needs and preferences changed, private companies would be quick to offer different plans and forms of insurance protection to fit those needs. These private companies would be driven by the incentive to win new customers and keep existing ones, and if current companies failed to meet new needs, new companies would not be slow to take advantage of this business opportunity. The flexibility and adaptability of the private market is in large part due to the improved incentive structure that a market provides, but it is also due in part to the fact that changes in the goods or services provided in the private market do not have to be made through the political process. Necessary changes can be made immediately and spontaneously by buyers and sellers. One does not need to start a national social movement to get the change made.

A fourth important point is that the discrimination against women described in this section shows how an apparently benign social welfare program can seriously restrict individual liberty. The system of financial penalties that social security imposes on women who work and pursue careers, choosing to not get married and choosing to not have children, tends to impair their freedom to do so. The program currently takes one-eighth of the wage income of most Americans and in future years will take one-fourth or more. To have such a large portion of one's income go toward a good or service that does not adequately match one's needs or preferences may be a greater financial penalty than many women are able to afford. When the government takes such a large portion of one's income and agrees to return it only if one pursues certain courses of action, one's freedom to choose *not* to take those courses of action is significantly impaired. This, coupled with the forced subsidies and substantial rewards for women who choose the traditional path, may make forgoing this traditional path simply too expensive. This system of penalties and rewards, therefore, may help to induce many women to acquiesce in the acceptance of a traditional role and forgo a preferred alternative. While the program is probably unlikely to have a decisive impact in itself, it is one more factor among many in our society whose cumulative effect is to impose a traditional role model on many unwilling women. Furthermore, the program's system of financial penalties does result in a significant reduction in the compensation for employment and may thus serve to keep many women out of the labor market. A deceptively benign social welfare program like social security, therefore, can seriously restrict individual liberty and personal freedom in ways that have not been widely recognized. This problem will be discussed in more detail in chapter 8.

A final point is that all this discrimination against women is again due to the conflict in objectives pursued by social security. All the provisions in the program that discriminate against women are based on welfare rationales. Benefits for spouses, children, and grandchildren are provided because it is felt that they are needed, not because they are paid for. These benefits, as we have seen, are provided largely without regard to the amounts one has paid into the program. They are justified on a welfare rationale. These provisions, however, result in a significant discrimination against single and childless people, and they therefore make social security a bad insurance program. As we have seen, the program is also a poor way of satisfying need because it is not even certain that the recipients of these benefits will be truly needy. Wealthy people and middle-class people have wives, children, and grandchildren too. The mixing of insurance and welfare objectives in the same program once again results in a program that is both bad welfare and bad insurance.

Similarly, women are forced to choose between either the spouse's benefit on their husband's earnings record or their own benefit because it is felt that they do not need both, regardless of how much has been paid in taxes. This is again a welfare rationale, seeking to regulate the amount of benefit payments on the basis of need rather than past tax payments. The result is that the program discriminates against working women, who will receive little or nothing more for their past tax payments than women who stay at home and pay no taxes. These working women will also generally receive less in benefits than working men, who will receive their full benefits plus additional benefits for their wives and other dependents, even though these working men pay no more in taxes than working women. Again, the welfare elements in social security make it a bad, discriminatory insurance program.

Women are also denied many benefits that can be obtained on the records of men because it is felt that the woman's benefits will not be needed. The old provisions requiring a surviving widower over age sixty and a retired husband over age sixty-two to prove dependency before they could receive benefits on the earnings records of their wives were based on the welfare rationale that without such dependency these individuals would not be in need. Similarly, the lack of a provision for survivor's benefits for a surviving father caring for his deceased wife's children was based on the welfare rationale that such a father would not be in need. These provisions for many years made social security a bad insurance program because it discriminated against women by not paying them the same benefits as men for the taxes they paid.

The Elderly

Even though the main purpose of social security is to help the elderly, the truth is that in several significant ways the program actually hurts them and makes them worse off.

The most obvious detrimental effects of social security upon the elderly stem from the earnings test. As discussed in chapter 2, the earnings test reduces social security benefits $1 for every $2 earned above a certain limit. In 1978, this limit for those over age sixty-five was $4,000, scheduled to increase by $500 a year to $6,000 in 1982 and increase at the rate of growth in wages in covered employment after that. The earnings test does not apply to those over age seventy-two, and this age limit will fall to seventy in 1982. As was noted in chapter 3, the most notable economic effect of this provision was to discourage employment and thereby lower GNP. Here we are focusing on the impact of the test upon the elderly.

The first negative impact of the test is its harsh unfairness. In-dividuals who have worked all their lives and paid for retirement benefits are denied those benefits merely because they desire to con-tinue to be working, productive members of society. The govern-ment simply denies elderly persons benefits they have paid for all of their lives on the arbitrary grounds that they have enough as it is. This is just as if a bank denied a customer a withdrawal of his own funds because in the bank's opinion the customer did not need them, and instead granted those funds to someone else. The inequity of the earnings test has been widely recognized.

Second, the earnings test makes it difficult for the elderly to sup-plement their incomes by working and supporting themselves. They are allowed to keep only half of what they earn above the limit, and they still have to pay federal, state, and local taxes on their full in-comes besides. Many of the elderly need this supplemental income badly, but the earnings test forces them to work twice as hard to get it. In many cases the result is that the elderly are discouraged from working and instead receive the needed supplemental income through the SSI program. The government prevents people from working and supporting themselves, instead forcing them onto the welfare roles as a burden to the general public.

The earnings test applies only to income from wages and salaries. It does not apply to various kinds of returns to capital investment such as dividends on stocks and bonds, interest income, capital gains, or rentals from real estate. But once again the poorer seg-ments of society rely primarily on wage income, while capital in-come is concentrated among the wealthier groups. The wealthy retired can supplement their income through a multitude of invest-ment alternatives without losing social security benefits, but the poor who may need such supplemental income to purchase basic necessities cannot work for it without being subject to serious penalties.

Many of the elderly have special knowledge acquired through their long years of experience. Discouraging these elderly persons from continuing to work results in a loss of their special skills and ex-perience. Many could pass on their knowledge and skills to others through occasional periods of work after retirement. Teachers, doc-tors, lawyers, engineers, and other professionals could teach and consult during retirement, putting their acquired skills to productive use. Blue collar workers also have special skills and experiences that could be used productively after retirement and taught to others.

But the earnings test, by discouraging employment of the elderly, results in a loss of their unique resources.

In addition, the elderly lose the extra assets and income they could have in old age if their social security taxes had been used to take advantage of private alternatives. This problem has not been of much significance in the past because most recipients up until now have been enjoying the benefits of the start-up phase of the program, but this problem is now growing into one of major significance as the program matures.

As we saw in chapter 4, the loss of assets and income in old age because of social security will grow to enormous proportions. The social security program forces the elderly to use their incomes earlier in life in an inefficient way. The result is the loss of large amounts of wealth that could be accumulated if the government allowed individuals to take advantage of the available alternatives. This money could greatly improve the living standards of elderly, retired people. Another set of negative impacts on the elderly stems from the fact that the money promised to them under social security does not belong to them in the sense that private assets do. The elderly are not able to use the money in a way that will most benefit them individually according to their needs and desires. This point was discussed in chapter 4 in relation to the young, but it applies here as well.

If at age sixty-five the elderly owned their social security benefits in the form of a presently discounted trust fund, their range of options and alternatives for the future would be greatly expanded. Many of the elderly may have exceptional investment or business opportunities for some or all of the funds or other special uses. They may want to buy a home where they can live during their retirement or make some other purchase they can use in retirement. With the fund, they could vary their consumption over the years as they desired, increasing it in some years and decreasing it in others. They could use some of the funds to make immediate gifts to their children and others. They could help others in emergencies or draw on the fund for their own emergencies. They could live off of the interest on the fund and leave it as an estate to their children. With their money tied up in the government's pay-as-you-go system, however, the elderly lose all these options.

Furthermore, because the benefits promised under social security are not owned by the elderly recipients, they must live their lives according to government regulations and requirements just to get their own money back and acquire the benefits they have paid for. One of the most widely publicized examples of this was changed by the 1977 amendments. Before these amendments were passed, widows and surviving divorced wives over sixty who were receiving old-age benefits had to remain single to collect their full benefits on the records of their deceased former husbands. If they married, their benefits would be eliminated or reduced. As a result, many elderly persons were forced to live together unmarried rather than marry and lose social security benefits they needed to purchase necessities. Widespread news accounts of elderly persons living together for these reasons led to the changes in 1977. Widows and surviving divorced wives receiving old-age benefits can now marry without a reduction in benefits. Widowers, however, must still remain single.

On the other side of the ledger, if an elderly couple prefers to live together and not get married, one of the partners will not qualify for spouse's benefits. They may be forced to get married to maintain their standard of living. A divorced wife of a retired worker still must remain unmarried to receive her benefits. If an elderly couple wants to get divorced before ten years of marriage, they will have to wait until their tenth anniversary or lose benefits. A retired worker's dependent child or grandchild aged eighteen to twenty-one must remain a student or lose benefits. A wife of a retired worker under sixty-two must continue to care for her child or grandchild or lose benefits. Probably most important of all, an elderly person cannot earn wage income above the earnings test limit without receiving reduced benefits.

If elderly individuals actually owned their social security benefits in the form of an IRA account or trust fund, they would not have their lives restricted by these regulations. They would be free to get married, to get divorced, or to live together as they chose and to divide up their funds according to their preferences. If a parent wanted to continue to support a child or grandchild regardless of whether the child remained in school, he could do so. If a husband wanted to continue to support his younger wife regardless of whether she cared for his child or grandchild, he could do so.

Because the money would be theirs to do with as they pleased, the freedom of elderly persons to live their own lives as they preferred would be greatly expanded. The result would be a significant improvement in individual welfare. The elderly would be free to choose the courses of action that best suited their own needs and situations and would not be restricted by government regulations concerning their personal lives.

But there is more. Because the money is not really theirs and the government can change the rules at any time, the elderly face a great deal of insecurity. Any of the program's regulations and qualifications could be changed at any time to the detriment of current beneficiaries. There is also the constant possibility that the government will renege on benefit promises. The power to do this was expressly upheld by the Supreme Court in *Flemming* v. *Nestor* (363 U.S. 603 (1960)), discussed in chapter 2. An example of this possibility is the currently advanced proposal to delay the retirement age to sixty-eight. While it is unlikely that the retirement age would be pushed back immediately for current retirees, this problem applies to current workers who are future retirees. The retirement age becomes a matter of political controversy in the hands of the government, rather than in the control of each individual. Finally, contributing to the insecurity of the elderly is the problem of bankruptcy which, as we saw in chapter 5, remains a real threat. A sudden sharp rise in unemployment or fall in wages or a severe recession or depression could threaten the continued payment of benefits. In a serious crunch, the elderly may not be able to count on the government to pay all the benefits promised, especially if the government feels that the benefits for particular beneficiaries are not needed.

These shortcomings are again all due to the conflict in objectives. It is this conflict that has produced the inequities of the earnings test. The rationale for this test is based on the welfare goal. It is argued that social security benefits should not be paid to those who do not need them and those who are earning incomes above the earnings test limit do not need them. But this makes social security an inequitable insurance program because individuals cannot receive the insurance benefits they have paid for if they continue working after age sixty-five. The insurance benefits of the program as well as the welfare benefits become subject to the test even though they should not be. The earnings test means that those who have relied on promises of benefits and worked to earn them will see these promises broken and their earned rights taken away from them. Thus the pursuit of the welfare goal through the earnings test makes social security a bad, inequitable insurance program.

Indeed, the corruption of the social security insurance program by the welfare objective pursued through the earnings test puts the average citizen in a very difficult position. With the high tax rates projected for the future, it is doubtful whether the average person can afford to supplement his promised social security benefits through alternative savings programs, at least to any significant degree. Social security forces the average person to purchase virtually all of his retirement protection subject to an earnings test. If he desires to put money aside for his old age that will not be lost if he continues working, as most would undoubtedly prefer, he cannot do so. He is forced to purchase all of his retirement protection with an undesirable provision that he cannot avoid.

Furthermore, the earnings test hardly fulfills its welfare objective efficiently either. It is meant to prevent the payment of benefits to those who do not need them, but it allows unreduced benefits to continue to be paid to those who do not need them because they are receiving substantial pensions from other sources or have substantial investment income or other sources of support. Yet those who do not have these other sources of income and feel that they must work to supplement social security so they can purchase basic necessities are penalized. One can only expect such anomalous results from building welfare elements into an insurance structure.

The loss of the extra assets and income that the elderly could have through private alternatives is due to the pay-as-you-go nature of social security. It is this method of financing that causes the low returns in the program and the loss of the high returns available from an invested program. This financing method is again the result of the pursuit of welfare objectives.

Similarly, the qualifications upon the receipt of many benefits are based on the welfare rationale that if the qualifications are not met, the recipient will not need the benefits. If the divorced wife of a retired worker marries, for example, it is felt that she can look to her husband for support and no longer needs her social security benefits. This welfare rationale means that people must subject their lives to government control if they want to receive insurance benefits that they have paid for.

Finally, under social security individuals do not have any ownership rights or discretion over the benefits promised to them because they are forced to participate in a government program where they can receive these benefits only under the terms and conditions set by the government. This forced participation is necessary because of the welfare elements of the program.

The Young

The social security program's negative impacts on the various minority groups discussed above are certainly serious, but the program's negative impacts on the young go beyond any of these. For young workers today the social security program is quite simply a wholesale disaster.

The program's most important negative impacts upon the young were discussed in chapter 4. Social security forces today's young workers to pay extremely high taxes into a low-yielding insurance program, making them forgo private alternatives that would pay them much higher returns on their tax dollars. The loss of these higher returns adds up to a massive loss of wealth by retirement. Many young couples today will lose over a million dollars in real terms through this process by the time they retire. As we saw in chapter 4, the losses imposed on young people through this process are so great that this problem alone requires that the social security program be overhauled.

Furthermore, as we saw in chapter 5, the benefits promised to young people today are not only far below those available in private alternatives, they are also highly uncertain. Unless future taxpayers are willing to pay one-fourth or more of their wage incomes in social security taxes alone, these benefits will never be paid. Yet young people today are being induced to make their future plans in reliance on these dubious benefit promises. If these promises are not fulfilled these young people could be left in calamitous circumstances in the future.

In addition, as we saw in chapter 3, the program is seriously damaging the economy. The loss in capital investment caused by the program means lower wages and fewer jobs, especially good jobs. It means less money for new homes, new energy sources, new factories, new innovations, and the production of the many goods and services young people need and desire. It means a loss of over $400 billion a year in national income and slower economic growth. It probably means the difference between a sluggish economy and a vigorous, prosperous one. It therefore also means the loss of opportunities for careers and advancement for young workers.

The lives of the young are seriously restricted by substantial monetary penalties exacted through the program on those who do not fit into the traditional molds. Young people who do not get married or have children are forced to pay large amounts in taxes for benefits they can never receive. Women are especially penalized for working. The result is that young people are monetarily penalized for not living as the government expects, and they are taxed to subsidize those who live more traditional lives. The freedom of young people, therefore, to live their personal lives as they wish is seriously impaired.

Furthermore, once they start receiving benefits their lives are subject to government control, for if they don't comply with the qualifications placed upon the receipt of those benefits, they will lose them. If a widow with children, for example, gets married or gets a decent job, she will lose her benefits.

Finally, the program forces young people to pay large amounts in taxes while they are trying to start families and careers and struggling to hold down new mortgages and to generally make ends meet. Over the next decade, many young people will be forced to pay $4,000 a year and more in real terms. Much of this money is being used to pay large welfare subsidies to those who are not poor or in need. These taxes are also being used to purchase retirement incomes that may be in excess of what most of these young people want or need. By the time young people entering the work force today are in retirement, many will be eligible for annual pensions of between $17,000 and $20,000 in 1980 dollars, and average workers will be eligible for annual pensions of between $11,000 and $15,000 in 1980 dollars. It is quite likely that many young people would prefer to forgo some portion of these large pensions later so that they could keep now some of the money they are currently paying in social security taxes and use these funds to meet some of their current vital needs. It should also be apparent that it makes little sense to force young people to finance such large pensions through the low-yielding social security program and forgo the much higher returns available in private alternatives. Through these private alternatives, young people could sharply reduce the amounts they are currently paying and still receive the same annual retirement pensions they are promised now or they could reduce their payments by moderate amounts and still receive higher pensions. In the private system, young people could also delay their payments for several years until they became more established and still receive the same retirement pensions social security now promises.

These problems are again all caused by the conflict in objectives, as we have discussed in this and earlier chapters.

7

Social Security
and Politics

Social security is run by the government rather than private market institutions, a fact that has significant implications for the program. It means that the entire program becomes a political institution operating in the political realm. Every question concerning the program becomes a political issue to be decided by political forces. Extraneous, noneconomic, and perhaps irrational political considerations will enter into the determination of how the program will be run. It means that the program will be run on a political basis rather than on an economic basis.

It is reasonable to ask whether an insurance program can be run this way. It may be that the government cannot provide a stable, efficient, and fair insurance system. Such an insurance program is likely to become a political football subject to the skills of demagogues and opportunists, the ambitions of politicians and power brokers, and the influences of special interest groups seeking special advantages. In addition, difficulties arise because the desires and needs of the participants can be asserted only through political channels. The combined impact of these political influences and difficulties can make a public insurance program like social security an undesirable way for the program's participants to receive insurance protection.

The operation of social security on a political basis results in two major sets of problems. The first is that the program becomes subject to political influences, and consequently there are numerous opportunities for individuals and groups to use the program to achieve their own ends at the expense of the goals of the program's participants. The second is that the nature of the political process makes it difficult for the program's participants to effectively express their desires, needs, and preferences concerning the program's insurance goals. We will discuss the problems arising under each of these sets of difficulties below.

Politicians vs. the People

The goals of the program's participants are to gain insurance protection against retirement, disability, sickness, and death. However, there are two groups who may try to achieve their own personal goals and ambitions by using the social security system. The first group consists of politicians and elected officials. Their goals are to advance their political careers and get or remain elected. They may try to achieve these goals through the social security system by operating it in a way that is politically popular in the short run but will redound to the detriment of the participants in the long run, making the achievement of their goals more expensive and difficult. Examples include offering benefits that the program cannot afford, delaying a necessary tax increase, or offering special benefits to politically powerful groups.

A second group that may seek to advance their own ambitions at the expense of the goals of the program's participants are politically powerful special interest groups. These groups may use their political power to gain special advantages for themselves at the expense of other participants in the program. Or they may use their power to advance social goals through the program that will make it more difficult and expensive to achieve the program's insurance goals. These social goals may include the elimination of poverty, the redistribution of income, or the preservation of the family.

There are numerous important examples of politicians using social security to advance their political interests at the expense of the interests of taxpayers and beneficiaries. Perhaps the most important of these is the way the program was handled during its start-up phase.

As we saw in chapter 2, social security was initially sold to the public on the premise that it would be operated as a private insurance program. The tax payments of current taxpayers were to be saved and invested in a trust fund and later used to pay for the benefits of these taxpayers. The trust fund was expected to grow large enough to support and guarantee future benefit payments, as in a private insurance program. When the program was originally enacted, benefit payments were to be delayed for several years and tax rates were set high enough and benefit rates low enough to allow the accumulation of a fund that would support the program. Taxpayers were originally convinced to accept the program, therefore, under assurances that it would be operated on a fully funded basis, rather than on a pay-as-you-go basis.

As table 19 shows, the social security program originally accumulated enough assets in its trust funds to support benefit payments until 1950. (Congress had already begun to seriously undermine the principle of full funding in 1939 by voting to increase benefits and accelerate their payment and delay tax increases.) But 1950 was an election year, and Congress took the opportunity to sharply increase benefits in relation to taxes. As a result, the trust fund ratio, or the ratio of trust fund assets to one year's benefits, fell from 1343% in 1950 to 790% in 1951. These benefits, it should be noted, constituted pure welfare. They had not been earned or paid for by their recipients.

Congress followed this pattern in every election year for the next several years. Benefits were again increased in 1952 while taxes remained stable, and the trust fund ratio fell to 605% in 1953. The 1954 amendments increased benefits relative to taxes again, and by 1955 the trust fund ratio had fallen to 427%. The year 1956 was a presidential election year, and the result was a major increase in benefits with only moderate increases in taxes. This led in 1957 to a further decline in the trust fund ratio to 305%. The 1958 amendments continued this pattern of increasing benefits relative to taxes, and the result was a decline in the trust fund ratio by 1959 to 204%. Finally, in 1960 Congress raised benefits relative to taxes again, and in 1961 the trust fund ratio fell to 166%.

This pattern was changed in the 1960s. The next major increase in benefits was in 1965 with the introduction of Medicare. The provisions offered by Medicare were widely controversial, and politicans may have felt more comfortable voting for them immediately after an election rather than immediately before. By 1965 the trust fund had fallen to 103% of one year's benefits, and therefore the potential for increasing benefits relative to taxes had greatly decreased.

What does this pattern prove? It shows that Congress simply raided the trust funds in the 1950s to buy votes. Congress used the money that taxpayers thought was being saved to ensure their retirement to provide payments of unearned benefits in every election year during the decade. The purpose of these payments was clearly to advance the political careers of the politicians in power by inducing the recipients of these gratuitous payments to vote to keep their benefactors in office. But as we saw in chapters 3, 4, and 5, the loss of the trust funds and the establishment of a pay-as-you-go system was a serious detriment to the program's participants. The result was that politicians used the program to advance their own goals to the detriment of the goals of stable and efficient insurance protection.

It would seem, then, that if a funded insurance system is necessary for a stable, profitable, and efficient program, it is doubtful that the government can be trusted to run such a program. Politicians will always face the short-term temptation of raiding the trust funds to hand out free benefits and buy votes.

A second example of politicians pursuing their own ends through the program at the expense of taxpayers and beneficiaries is the deception surrounding the program. As was shown in chapter 2, the government has sponsored a massive public relations effort over the years to convince taxpayers that social security is different from what it really is. This effort has attempted to hide all the welfare elements in the program and make taxpayers think it is just like private insurance. It has attempted to hide the pay-as-you-go method of financing the program. It has attempted to mislead tax-payers into believing that they are getting much more out of the program than they really are.

This deceptive campaign serves the goals of politicians in several ways. For one thing, it helps to hide the raiding of the trust funds that occurred in the 1950s. It also serves to deceive voters into believing that the program is something it is not. It deceives them into believing that the program is safer and more secure than it really is and that it pays more than it really does. This helps to advance the careers of the politicians responsible for the program because it leads the public to believe that they are getting a better deal from these politicians than they really are.

By deceiving the public, this false public relations campaign is detrimental to the goals of the program's participants. They are led to believe that they have achieved a certain level of protection when in reality they have not. Thus they may not take the steps necessary to attain that level or make the reforms necessary to improve the defects of the program. Their interests will have in effect been sacrificed to the goals of self-serving politicians.

Past experience indicates that the public cannot count on the government to tell the truth concerning the operation of a detailed and complex insurance program. Politicians and elected officials will simply attempt to cover up their past mistakes and the defects in the program. Frauds in the private sector are deterred by enforcement of antifraud statutes, and the victims of fraud can look to the courts for restitution and punishment of the malefactors. But who will prosecute a similar fraud by the government? Who is there to investigate and stop such frauds and prevent future ones? Where can the victims of such a fraud look for restitution?

A third example of abuse of the social security program by politicians is the short planning horizon of politicians, who are likely to take a short-term view on all questions pertaining to the program. That is, they will look only at what is necessary to get them past the next election, which will provide a planning horizon of from two to four years. They will take into account events beyond that time only to the extent that they are currently anticipated and a cause of concern to voters. It is true that the Social Security Administration provides seventy-five year projections of the program's financial future, but the question is what the Congress actually acts upon. These actions will be based on a short-term view even though the interests of taxpayers and beneficiaries require otherwise.

In the 1950s Congress raided the trust funds to buy votes, even though doing so made the program less secure and made all of the drawbacks of pay-as-you-go financing highly apparent. In 1972 Congress voted huge increases in benefits, promising that the system would be able to support its new obligations. With characteristic carelessness, it enacted a flawed benefit formula that would surely have bankrupted the program if it had not been repealed. Congress also failed to provide for the possibility of a severe recession, which later developed, again threatening the program with bankruptcy. Soon after the 1972 elections Congress discovered that under the new benefit formula the trust funds would be exhausted by the end of the decade. Despite this fact, Congress delayed the bitter medicine of the 1977 amendments until after the 1976 elections. Under currently legislated tax and benefit schedules the HI program will be unable to meet its benefit obligations sometime around 1990, and the rest of the program will be unable to meet its benefit promises at about the time that today's young workers will be retiring. But these matters are of no concern to currently elected officials, who will not be around to suffer the wrath of future beneficiaries.

Others who will seek to use the social security program to advance their goals at the expense of the public are politically powerful special interest groups. These groups are of two types — those seeking nominal gain and those seeking ideological gain.

The first type may seek a special benefit provision that will provide extra benefits to its members. For example, blue-collar labor unions might support increased benefits for spouses and children. Most of the members of such unions are more likely to have families, who will benefit from these provisions. Groups can also seek special benefit provisions that will result in indirect gains, such as an increase in customers for their particular business. For example, the provision giving benefits to a child of a deceased or retired worker while that child is a student over eighteen has long had the heavy lobbying support of the education industry.

The entire social security benefit structure has been shaped by political forces, and it should therefore come as no surprise that this structure most benefits politically powerful groups. As we saw in chapter 6, the structure benefits most those who get married, have children, and rely on the husband to be the primary money earner. The structure treats unfairly those who follow nontraditional paths, such as single working women. How much political power do single working women have today, let alone in 1939 when these provisions were passed? One can only expect that in a politically operated program those who follow traditional routes will benefit most at the expense of those who pursue the uncommon, the nontraditional, and the experimental. Similarly, we saw in chapter 6 that the benefit provisions of the program are not well suited to minorities such as the poor and blacks, groups that had even less political influence in the past than today.

Another form of personally interested political influences will emanate from those in charge of administering the program — the Social Security Administration (SSA). The SSA possesses a substantial degree of political power as a result of its knowledge of the program. Its employees are experts on every facet of social security. It possesses all the data and statistics on every detail of the system, and it is taken as the authoritative source for all information concerning the program.

This superior knowledge and authority can be used in politically influential ways. It can, for example, be used to present the program in its best light and mislead the public. The SSA can publicize information that is favorable to the program and bury unfavorable information. It can use its superior knowledge and access to information to develop sophisticated defenses of the program and to undermine critics.

It is in the interest of the SSA employees to expand the program to advance their own personal careers. A larger program means more responsibility, higher salaries, increased prestige, and more room for advancement. The SSA will use whatever political power it has to advance its self-interest by expanding the program. This is again contrary to the interest of the public because it will tend to cause the program to expand beyond the point preferred by the program's participants.

It is also in the interest of the SSA to hide the drawbacks of the program and make it seem better than it really is. This will aid in increasing the size of the program and gaining public approval of the performance of the SSA. It will help to avoid taxpayer opposition that could lead to a reduction in the size of the program. This again operates to the detriment of the participants in the program. They are prevented from making plans and taking corrective actions based on fact.

Past experience indicates that the SSA has acted precisely as its self-interest would dictate. As we saw in chapter 2, the SSA has long engaged in a public relations campaign that has deceived the public concerning the actual nature and method of the program's operations. It has attempted to hide the welfare elements of the program and make people think that it is just like private insurance. The SSA, with its superior knowledge and authority, is well equipped to carry out this campaign, which operates to the detriment of the taxpayers and beneficiaries.

A second category of special interest groups that may seek to use the program are those trying to advance some social goal or principle even though it may be irrelevant to the interests of the program's participants and may detract from the achievement of their insurance goals.

For example, those in favor of increased welfare subsidies to various groups have used their power to pursue this goal through the social security system. They encouraged Congress to raid the trust funds and use the saved assets for welfare. They have worked for the addition and expansion of each of the welfare elements in the program, arguing that social security is a good program because it allows them to use their influence to increase welfare benefits. We have already seen in detail, however, that mixing the welfare elements of social security with the insurance elements has ruined the insurance portion of the program for taxpayers and beneficiaries.

Similarly, those who advocate certain income redistribution goals have sought to use the program to attain their ends. They have supported the addition of welfare elements to the program (even though the payments under these elements would not necessarily go to those who are poor) on the grounds that they would *in general* go to those who have low incomes. Yet the program does not actually serve this end because of many countervailing effects and, even if it did, would be an inefficient means of doing so because the insurance elements of the program would prevent it from paying benefits only to those who are poor.

Politics vs. the People

The second set of difficulties arises because the political operation of the program makes it difficult for the program's participants to express their desires, needs, and preferences about the program's insurance goals.

To express their wishes, taxpayers and beneficiaries must act through political channels. To make these wishes effective, the participant must start a national political movement. He must convince others of the validity and desirability of his preferences and exert enough political pressure to bring about the desired changes. If single people want to change the provisions for survivor's protection, which presently give them nothing, if young people want to push the retirement age forward or backward, or if the elderly want to change the earnings test, their only recourse is to build a national political movement, at great expense in time and money, to exert the necessary political pressure.

This task is made even more difficult by the fact that many of the issues surrounding social security are extremely complicated and detailed. How can voters democratically express their preferences over whether children should be allowed survivor's benefits until eighteen or twenty-one, or how many years a divorced wife has to have been married to her former husband to qualify for survivor's benefits? Voters usually have a choice between candidates who don't state their views on issues and would lie about them if they did. And how can one be expected to get enough public attention on detailed and minor issues to exert effective political pressures?

Another factor increasing the difficulty of this task is the enormous amount of information necessary to perform it effectively. One must first become an expert in all the intricate details of the program, as well as an expert in economics and demography. One must then gather all the information necessary to carry on a successful political campaign. He must become a political scientist, a communications and media expert, and an organizational wizard. The cost of obtaining the necessary information and expertise to change the program is likely to be prohibitive.

Another factor increasing the difficulty of changing the program is that there is one set of benefit provisions for everyone. There are no mechanisms to allow for individualized insurance plans, and individuals have no vehicle through which to assert their individual needs and preferences other than political channels. The result is that one particular plan is imposed on all participants. A second reason is that the program is operated on a pay-as-you-go basis and individuals are not paying for their own benefits. There is no mechanism by which individuals can pay only for the benefits they want and not for others. What they must pay is determined by current benefit obligations. Since individuals have not paid for their own benefits, they have no basis on which to claim individualized benefits. Finally, as long as the program contains welfare elements, there cannot be individualized protection. Otherwise, those who do not benefit from the welfare elements would not choose them as part of their individual plan and there would be nobody left to pay for them.

But there isn't any one plan of insurance protection that is right for everyone. Married people will need and want different benefits than the unmarried, childless couples will want different benefits than those with several children, the poor will want different benefits than the rich. The result of having one plan for everyone therefore is that there will be inherent conflicts between the desires of individual taxpayers and beneficiaries. If one group of individuals has a provision better suited to them, this will result in less suited provisions for others with different needs and preferences. Thus, with one insurance plan for everyone, not everyone can have the plan best suited to his individual needs and preferences.

The result is that some, the politically powerless, will naturally be stuck with a plan of insurance provisions that is poorly suited to their individual needs so that others, the politically powerful, can have the provisions best suited to them. We saw in chapter 6 how the current set of provisions is poorly suited to minority groups with relatively little political power. Furthermore, due to compromises in the political process, it is quite possible that no one or only a small minority, will have the provisions that are best suited to their individual needs and preferences.

The conflicts inherent in a political insurance program make it difficult, if not impossible, for individuals to change the program to fit their needs. The advocates of any change will have to convince others not only that the change is good and desirable for them, but that there is some special justice to their claim that justifies the sacrifices necessary on the part of others to satisfy it. This may make most changes politically impossible.

In addition, because social security is a bureaucratic institution operating through the political process rather than a private institution operating through a market process, those who administer the program have little or no incentive to make changes in it that will better serve the needs of taxpayers and beneficiaries. The SSA does not have to worry about selling additional social security "policies" to stay in business. No particular benefit will redound to the SSA from making changes in the program to suit the needs of the public better. No one stands to gain a profit or other financial reward from revamping social security to improve it.

Even if the SSA did come up with a change to improve the program, it could not just make the improvement and test it out in the marketplace as a private market institution could. It would have to take its case to Congress just like everyone else. It would have to start a national political movement or perhaps a major political controversy to make the change, but doing so would probably work to the detriment of the bureaucrats at the SSA who started the controversy because they might earn themselves reputations as troublemakers. Since bureaucratic institutions cannot profit from innovations, they do not encourage innovation.

The lack of incentive and the poor service it results in have been correctly identified by economist Murray N. Rothbard as a problem common to all institutions that provide goods and services to the public but rely on the taxing power of the government for their revenues. There is a split between the provision of the service and the payment for it: Because the institution does not have to depend on the acceptability of the product for its continued revenue, it will not be concerned about the quality or acceptability of that product. Product quality will therefore invariably decline to minimal levels. Rothbard writes,

> Inherent in all government operation is a grave and fatal split between service and payment, between the providing of a service and the payment for receiving it. The government bureau does not get its income as does the private firm, from serving the consumer well or from consumer purchases of its products exceeding its costs of operation. No, the

government bureau acquires its income from mulcting the long-suffering taxpayer. Its operations therefore become inefficient, and costs zoom, since government bureaus need not worry about losses or bankruptcy; they can make up their losses by additional extractions from the public till. Furthermore, the consumer, instead of being courted and wooed for his favor, becomes a mere annoyance to the government, someone who is "wasting" the government's scarce resources. In government operations, the consumer is treated like an unwelcome intruder, an interference in the quiet enjoyment by the bureaucrat of his steady income.[1]

The situation that Rothbard describes contrasts sharply with the kinds of insurance protection provided by private market institutions. In a private market system, instead of launching a national political movement to get the provisions best suited to him, an individual need only purchase, from a wide variety of available options, the investment and insurance plan that will best suit his own needs and preferences. He may develop this protection merely by rearranging his own personal and financial affairs. If an individual wants to change his plan, he need only change his purchase or rearrange his affairs. He need not call a press conference or hold a congressional hearing. He does not need to convince others that his plan is right or that he has come special claim to justice. He need only know his own affairs and desires and what is available in the marketplace, which private companies will not keep a secret. There will be no conflict between individuals because what one buys or does to provide himself with insurance protection does not depend on what others buy or do. Each individual is free to maximize his individual welfare by purchasing a plan of insurance protection that is best suited to him.

Private market institutions have an incentive to restructure their products to make sure that they are well suited to the needs and desires of customers. They stay abreast of social trends so that they can remodel their insurance products and keep up in the competitive battle to sell new policies. The company's continued receipt of income is solely dependent on the degree to which the firm's products match the needs and preferences of consumers. Well-designed products will result in financial reward for the company and the people who work for it. Insurance protection that serves the diverse and changing needs of consumers is far more likely to be provided by market institutions than political, bureaucratic ones.

[1] Murray N. Rothbard, *For a New Liberty* (New York: Macmillan, 1973), p. 197.

Why Social Security Is Too Large in a Democracy

The seriousness of some of the problems we have been discussing is analyzed in some recent work by Professor Edgar K. Browning of the University of Virginia. In two articles, Browning demonstrates why some of the political difficulties discussed above are likely to cause social security to be larger than people really desire.[2]

Browning examines the different political preferences that arise with respect to age in a pay-as-you-go system and shows how the expression of these preferences through the political process will naturally lead to an overexpansion of the program. Assume a social security program operating on a pay-as-you-go basis and providing a social insurance rate of return of 3% because of growth in real wages. The population is assumed to be constant, and everyone between the ages of twenty and sixty-five works and is forced to participate. At this potential rate of return, each individual taxpayer will prefer a certain tax rate based on the amount of taxes he would like to invest in the program over the course of his life to get this return. Assume for simplicity that all taxpayers prefer a rate of 10%. Browning demonstrates that because of the dynamics of the political process the ultimate level of taxation will always be higher than the level that people prefer.

When tax rates are increased in a pay-as-you-go system, older taxpayers near to retirement and current retirees receive substantial benefits from a start-up phase effect. Assume that there is a proposal before Congress to raise the tax rate, but there is a considerable debate over exactly how much. Since the program is operated on a pay-as-you-go basis, all of the additional taxes generated by this increase will be immediately paid out in current benefits to current retirees. All voters over the age of sixty-five, therefore, will support a tax increase to any level because they will get increased benefits from these taxes but will not have to pay any additional taxes themselves.

Those age sixty will prefer sharp tax increases because they will have to pay the increased taxes for only five more years, but they will receive benefits as if they had paid these higher tax rates all of

---

[2] Edgar K. Browning, "Why the Social Insurance Budget Is Too Large in a Democracy," *Economic Inquiry*, 13 (1975): 373–387; Edgar K. Browning, "The Politics of Social Security Reform," Conference on Financing Social Security, American Enterprise Institute for Public Policy Research, Washington, D.C., October 27–28, 1977.

their lives because the benefits paid when they retire will be divided out of the total tax revenues generated by the higher tax rates. These individuals will in fact receive a 27% rate of return on the amount of additional taxes they will pay over the original tax rate of 10%. If taxes are raised now, these individuals will thus have a higher return than 3% on the total amount of taxes they pay into the system for their last five years of work and will therefore be willing to pay more than the 10% in taxes that they preferred when they were receiving a 3% return. They will not prefer every tax increase, however, as those over sixty-five do, because at some point the increase in taxes, which still must be paid for five years, will outweigh the value of the increase in benefits.

Those aged fifty-five will prefer lower tax increases than those aged sixty because they have to pay the higher taxes for more years and therefore their rate of return will be lower than for those aged sixty. It will still be higher than 3%, however, because they do not have to pay the increased taxes all of their lives, and so they will prefer a higher tax rate than 10%. The same is true to a lesser degree for those aged forty-five. In fact, all those past the age of entering the work force will now prefer a higher tax rate than 10% because they will not have to pay the higher rate all of their lives, yet they will receive benefits as if they had. If tax rates are increased, the rate of return will thus be higher than 3% for all those past the age of entering the work force, although it will decline steadily from a very high rate for those at ages near retirement until it reaches exactly 3% for those just starting to work. At these higher returns all will prefer higher tax rates than 10%, although the actual rate preferred by different individuals will decline from very high rates for those near retirement to exactly 10% for those just starting to work. Congress will therefore choose to increase the tax rate to a compromise level between the rates preferred by those near to and after retirement and those who are younger. The equilibrium tax rate will therefore be above the rate all would prefer if they had to pay it all of their lives.

All young workers entering the system will prefer the 10% tax rate because they are all still receiving the 3% return. But they will have to pay the higher tax rate supported by those who are older and who received the start-up benefits of the tax increase. As these young workers get older, however, it is no longer in their interest to lower the tax rate to 10%. They will take their place in the balance of political forces that is maintaining tax rates at the new, higher levels. Once the worker reaches thirty, for example, he will have the same preference in regard to paying the difference between the higher tax rate and the old rate of 10% that the original thirty-year-olds did when they voted in the tax increase. This thirty-year-old will have to pay the higher tax rate for only thirty-five more years but will receive benefits as if he had paid the higher rates all of his life, just as the original thirty-year-old did. Considering just the taxes he has yet to pay, he will receive a higher return than 3% and therefore will prefer a higher tax rate than 10%, just as the original thirty-year-old does. It is true that since he has had to pay the higher tax rates all of his life, unlike the original thirty-year-old, he will not do as well as the original thirty-year-old and will still only receive a 3% return on his taxes. But a proposal to lower tax rates now at the age of thirty will not change that. Those taxes are gone, and lower tax rates now will not bring them back. In fact, a tax cut now back to 10% will create a start-up effect in reverse because the individual will receive benefits as if he had paid the lower tax rates all of his life, even though he paid higher tax payments for many years. He will then receive a lower return than 3% on his tax payments. The individual will therefore look to the future and will prefer tax rates above 10% by the same margin as the original thirty-year-olds because he will have to pay these tax rates for as many more years as they did to receive the same benefits as they did. This preferred tax rate will probably be less than the actual tax rate, which is likely to have been set higher in compromise with older workers who preferred higher rates. But the new thirty-year-old worker will now be taking exactly the same place in the balance of political forces that led to the current compromise level of tax rates as the original thirty-year-olds who voted in the tax increase.

As this individual gets older, he will stop preferring tax cuts and prefer tax increases. When he reaches age sixty, for example, he will prefer increasing taxes to the same level that the original sixty-year-olds did because he will have to pay these higher tax rates for only five more years to receive benefits as if he had paid these taxes all of his life, just as the original sixty-year-olds did. This will be higher than the current compromise level of taxation brought down by the younger voters. But this sixty-year-old will have taken the same place in the balance of political forces determining the tax rates as the sixty-year-olds who voted in the tax increase.

The result is that tax rates will remain at this permanently higher level even though all would prefer to pay a lower level over the course of their lives. The generation that follows the first one to vote in the tax increase will receive a 3% return on their tax dollars but pay a higher tax rate than the 10% that all would prefer to pay at this rate of return. This will be true for all future generations, but it won't pay any one generation to lower taxes to the preferred rate once its members have paid taxes for a number of years. This is true even though all future generations would be made better off by doing so, and even the current generation would have been made better off if this had been done earlier. Thus, the program will be larger and taxes higher than individuals prefer, making everyone worse off.

Browning notes other factors that are likely to lead to an overexpansion of the program, all stemming from public misconceptions concerning the way the program operates. These misconceptions lead people to believe that social security is a better deal than it really is and thus to support a greater expansion of the program than they would if they knew its true worth.

The first misunderstanding is that young people entering the program today may base their expectations on what they will receive from social security on the experience of elderly retired individuals in the early years of the program. The returns from social security for this elderly group were quite high, as we have noted, because of the effects of the start-up phase. These returns will not continue as the program matures, and young people today will receive far lower returns from the program than retirees in the early stages. If young people base their expectations of what they will receive on the returns to these early retirees, they will support a much larger program than they would if they knew the truth.

A second misconception is that taxpayers probably underestimate the tax burdens they bear because they are probably not aware that they bear the employer's share of the payroll tax as well as the employee's share. They believe that social security costs less than it really does and again are likely to support a larger program than they would if they knew the true costs.

A third misunderstanding is that the public probably does not realize the significance and the magnitude of the negative economic effects (discussed in chapter 3) that result from the program. This lack of awareness will again lead the public to underestimate the true costs of the program, which include these negative economic effects. This cost underestimation is again likely to lead voters to support a larger program than they would if they knew all of its real costs.

Because of difficulties inherent in the political process, the true preferences of taxpayers and beneficiaries are likely to be frustrated and the program will probably be bigger than they prefer. Politicians, looking only at their own interest in reelection, will vote for an expansion of the program, even though this will make everyone worse off in the long run. Politically powerful groups, such as the elderly, will use their political power to vote for tax increases that will benefit them in the short run, even though the increases will lock young people and all future generations into an overexpanded system. To change the program to suit their true preferences, individual taxpayers will have to start a national political movement. They will have to convince a majority of the validity of their claims and desires and will have to demonstrate that there is some special justice to these claims and desires to justify the sacrifices which their accommodation would require from others.

8

Social Security
and Morality

Liberty is a question of morality. Whether individuals should be free from government coercion in certain circumstances depends on fundamental moral principles concerning how human beings, including those who work for the government, should treat one another. Whether it is right or wrong to allow individuals the freedom to take certain actions can be answered only by reference to the moral principles that define human rights. Liberty is not a question of economic efficiency or political expediency. Whether it is right to allow individuals the freedom to control their lives in certain situations does not depend on whether doing so will increase or lower the GNP or on what a majority is willing to vote to allow. Neither increased prosperity nor the ballot box can define what is right or wrong.

A law or government program that unjustifiably restricts individual liberty, therefore, is immoral and unjust. In this chapter we will examine whether and how social security, the largest of all government programs, restricts individual liberty. We will evaluate the significance of any such restriction and examine whether it can be tolerated in a free, liberal, and civilized society. We will finally discuss whether social security can really be considered a moral and just government program. Ultimately, however, the answer to this question will depend on the possible justifications for the current program, to be discussed in chapter 9.

The chief concern of any true liberal will be individual liberty. This has been the main focus of the great liberal tradition of western civilization, stemming from John Locke, Thomas Jefferson, and John Stuart Mill in the past and from Milton Friedman, Friedrich A. Hayek, Robert Nozick, and Murray N. Rothbard in our own day. This liberal tradition has also been characterized by a fundamental opposition to the growth of governmental power. This is not the phony liberalism of modern welfare state advocates such as George McGovern, Edward Kennedy, the late Hubert Humphrey, Paul Samuelson, and Arthur Schlesinger, Jr. Some of these men and their sympathizers are social democrats and some are socialists. They are not liberals. Nevertheless, because of the confusion surrounding the term liberal, the tradition in political philosophy we are discussing here is often referred to as classical liberalism or libertarianism. We will analyze the impact of social security on individual liberty and the morality of the program from this liberal or libertarian perspective.

Social Security and Coercion

A key characteristic of social security is that it is compulsory. If a person feels that he has better uses for his own money, he cannot voluntarily drop out of the program and forgo both taxes and benefits. Anyone who attempts to do so will face heavy legal penalties, including fines and imprisonment. Social Security is not based on the voluntary consent of the individual participants but on naked coercion. The entire coercive apparatus of the state is employed in the effort to compel participation in the program by over 90 % of working Americans.

Considering that social security currently consumes over 12 % of taxable payroll and that this may increase to 25 % or more over the next forty years, this coercion and compulsion must be considered a serious restriction on the freedom of American citizens to run their own lives and enjoy the fruits of their own labor. The program mandates that one-eighth to one-fourth of the incomes of most Americans will be used for one purpose and that this purpose will be pursued by one means — participation in social security. Americans are denied the freedom to control a major portion of their incomes. They are also denied the freedom to choose other means of pursuing the insurance goals of social security.

It is hard to understand why most writers do not seriously consider the major loss of freedom that this entails. The loss of control over a major portion of one's income means that all the options and goals that one may have pursued with those assets are now foreclosed. When the government deprives an individual of the means of action, it deprives him of the freedom of action altogether and restricts individual liberty.

For example, a young married couple struggling to establish a family and one or two careers may not feel that this is the best time to devote from 12% to 25% of their income for their old age. They may wish to devote their resources to the critical needs of family and career now and provide for their old age in later years, but social security forecloses this option. A middle-aged father may have had a lifelong dream of putting his son or daughter through law school or medical school, but if he has to pay prohibitive social security taxes, he may lack the resources to do so. Social security has seriously restricted his liberty.

Another individual may have an opportunity to start a lucrative business, but the loss of control over a portion of his income may prevent him from acquiring the necessary capital to take advantage of this opportunity. This will be especially true if he is relatively poor and has little capital of his own in the first place. Establishing his new business or career might have led to a much more secure old age, but social security eliminates this alternative by consuming the needed funds.

These are just hypothetical examples, and one can imagine many more. The important point is that a loss of control over a major portion of his income results in a serious loss of freedom for the individual to run his own life, to arrange his own affairs as will best suit him, and to engage in the pursuit of happiness.

The freedom to provide for one's old age by alternative means is equally important. We saw in chapter 4 the superiority of many alternatives to social security. The loss of the option to pursue these alternatives results not only in a major loss of material prosperity but also in a major loss of the freedom to control one's own life.

For some unknown, unstated reason, in recent years economic liberty has not been accorded the same respect as civil liberty. Today we hear more about the rights of individuals to smoke dope and read pornography than about the rights of individuals to earn a living, engage in free trade, and control their own property. In fact we seem to have reached a point where the only freedoms cherished in our society are those that are important to the authors and academics who write about them. Freedom of speech and freedom of the press, as well as academic freedom, are the only freedoms in our society considered almost absolute and protected rigorously against all forms of government encroachment. Authors and academics have spent a great deal of time expounding the crucial significance of these freedoms, but they have accorded little respect to similar freedoms in the economic realm. Apparently they, like most other individuals, can see only the importance of freedom for themselves. To journalists, the most important freedom in a free society is freedom of the press, or free speech, because this freedom is supposed to serve as the guardian of all the other rights and freedoms of the people. To academics this role is served by academic freedom, or freedom of inquiry. Both groups are clearly wrong, however, for while we have gone to great lengths to safeguard these freedoms, precious little has been done to protect most of our other freedoms. A nation may have absolute freedom of the press and yet be virtually enslaved because of other restrictions on the lives of its citizens, particularly economic ones. Yet the American press has intellectually deteriorated to the point where it judges the degree of freedom in other nations as well as our own primarily on the degree to which these other nations enjoy freedom of the press. It seems that the result of leaving the task of defining the proper scope for individual liberty to authors and academics is that only authors and academics will have individual liberty.

Despite the lack of respect for economic freedom in recent years, these freedoms are at least as important to the great majority of Americans as most of the highly publicized civil freedoms. To most Americans, it is probably at least as important to be able to earn a living, engage in free trade, and own property as it is to be able to smoke dope and read pornography. The subject matter of these freedoms is simply far more important to the average, working person than those that have been given so much significance in recent years.

Economic freedoms guarantee that a person will be free to earn a living and acquire the necessities and amenities of life. To most Americans it is at least as meaningful to be able to own and dispose of their own homes as they see fit as it is to read the uncensored columns of Art Buchwald. Yet any attempt to build, buy, and sell a home is burdened with tangled webs of government regulation. Most Americans are at least as concerned with the freedom to pursue their careers as with the right to see x-rated movies. Yet many careers in America, from medicine to law to taxicab driver, are blocked by occupational licensure requirements. The exercise of other careers is burdened with the heavy regulation of economic transactions between individuals. To most Americans, the freedom to enjoy the fruits of their own labor is at least as significant as the freedom to enjoy getting stoned, yet Americans are today burdened with excessive and oppressive taxation that denies them the full enjoyment of what they have produced. Few Americans will ever make speeches, write columns, or engage in academic pursuits, yet all will engage in economic transactions daily, and the freedom to do so is of direct and fundamental importance in their lives.

Economic freedom is crucially important because it is necessary as a safeguard to all our other freedoms. Before we can enjoy any of our civil liberties, we must be free to acquire the means necessary to exercise them. A newspaper publisher, for example, must acquire newsprint, printing presses, and labor to exercise the right to freedom of the press. If the government can place restrictions on the freedom to acquire the necessary means, the government may threaten freedom of the press by undermining the publisher's ability to exercise it. If the government has nationalized the paper industry and prohibits competition, it can undercut freedom of the press by refusing to sell to hostile publishers. Under the guise of labor regulation, the government can put such heavy economic burdens on a publisher that he will be forced out of business. But if the publisher's economic freedoms are assured, he will be able to acquire all the means necessary to exercise his freedom of the press.

Because people are material beings who exist by material means, the acquisition of these means is crucial to the exercise of all our rights and liberties. Economic liberty assures individuals that they will have the freedom to acquire these means, and it therefore protects all our other rights.

This is by no means to deny the great importance of our rights and liberties in the civil sphere or even to suggest that they have less meaning on a moral or intellectual basis. It is merely to point out that to emphasize civil freedoms to the exclusion of economic freedoms is an unjustifiable error.

The restriction of individual liberty entailed by the social security program, even though it may be considered a restriction of economic rights and liberties, should therefore be judged by a standard as strong as that which we use to judge any other restriction of liberty. The freedom to control 12% of one's income is at least as important to the average American as freedom of speech and freedom of the press. The options foreclosed to individuals by the loss of this freedom are at least as valuable as the options foreclosed by other restrictions of liberty.

Another way to see the great loss of liberty entailed by the social security program is to focus on some of the highly cherished rights in the liberal tradition that the program violates. The liberal tradition has long recognized the importance of economic rights as well as civil rights. These economic rights include the right to freedom of contract, freedom of exchange, freedom of choice, and freedom of association. Other concepts in the liberal tradition that apply here may be designated as the right to enjoy the fruits of one's own labor and the right to control one's own life.

The right to freedom of contract means that individuals should be free to enter into binding contracts and also free to refuse to enter into such contracts. Freedom of contract has long been a fundamental right in the Anglo-Saxon legal framework. It is a right that the U.S. Supreme Court has recognized as having constitutional protection, although admittedly at varying degrees, throughout our history.

It is well that this important right has received such recognition. The right to freedom of contract ensures that we will be able to procure the means necessary to exercise all our other rights. As long as a newspaper publisher is free to contract for labor, newsprint, printing presses, and customers, freedom of the press will not be suppressed by a lack of access to the necessary means. The right to freedom of contract also protects one's ability to procure one's own livelihood through economic transactions. It thus prevents others, especially the government, from gaining power over individuals by cutting off their source of livelihood. Freedom of contract also protects the right of individuals to engage in transactions to arrange their other financial affairs and to acquire the goods and services they desire. These are all subjects of direct, immediate, and fundamental importance to individual happiness and prosperity. The freedom of contract is one of the most crucial and cherished freedoms in a truly liberal society.

The right to freedom of exchange is a right of similar stature and importance. This right entails the freedom of individuals to exchange or trade the property they own for the property of others or to refrain from such exchanges. This right serves the same function as freedom of contract does in safeguarding all our other rights and in ensuring access to our means of livelihood and the goods and services we desire.

Another important and fundamental right in the liberal tradition is freedom of association. This right provides individuals with the freedom to associate, or to withdraw from associating, with whomever they please. People are thus guaranteed the freedom to build organizations for religious, civic, educational, economic, or political purposes. It also means that people will not have to associate with or support those of which they disapprove. It would seem that the fundamentally personal nature of this right would make it a right of great importance to individuals.

The right to freedom of choice means that individuals should be free to decide for themselves between alternative courses of action as long as none of these courses violates the rights of others. This right is widely recognized in the sphere of civil liberties and is often asserted in opposition to victimless crime laws. For example, in opposition to laws against pornography, many would agree that individuals should be free to choose for themselves whether they wish to purchase and read pornographic literature. In opposition to laws against marijuana use, many would argue that individuals should be free to choose whether they want to smoke the forbidden weed.

Unfortunately, the economic application of this principle is not as widely recognized, but it is just as important as its civil application, if not more so. The freedom to choose between alternative courses of economic actions is at least as important to most Americans as the exercise of civil liberties. Harvard professor of philosophy Robert Nozick has recognized this key insight by expressing support for the freedom of individuals to engage in "capitalist acts between consenting adults."[1]

The right to enjoy the fruits of one's own labor was perhaps the prime inspiration of the founding of this nation. The American Revolution was stimulated in large part by opposition to oppressive taxation denying this fundamental right. Another way of stating this principle is to say that every individual has the right to what he creates or produces.

This right has been recognized not only by true liberals but implicitly even by Marxists. Milton Friedman in *Capitalism and Freedom* endorses the principle that each man has the right "to what he or the instruments he owns produces."[2] Friedman goes on to note that Marx also recognized this principle in his theory of surplus value. Marx argued that labor was unfairly exploited because it produced all value yet received only part of it in wages with the rest going to the capitalists in profits, which can be considered unfair only if the workers have the right to what they create or produce. Thus, Marx implicitly accepted the principle that they do. His error was to ignore the productive role played by capital and entrepreneurship in the production process.

[1] Robert Nozick, *Anarchy, State and Utopia* (New York: Basic Books, 1974).
[2] Milton Friedman, *Capitalism and Freedom* (Chicago: University of Chicago Press, 1962).

This right is surely as important to individuals as any other. What can be more important than to be guaranteed that one has a secure right to what he has labored so painfully to produce? To be assured that one's successful productive effort will receive its just reward? To know that one is free to work and produce and better his condition as his talents allow? Because we do not live in the Garden of Eden, men must work and produce to sustain their lives and acquire what they have. The right to what one creates or produces is essential to secure one's rights to life, liberty, and property. No issues are more basic and fundamental to individual freedom and happiness than these and therefore this right is as crucial to a truly free society as any political liberty.

The most basic right of all, from which all others stem, is the right to control one's own life. This right is based on the principle that your life belongs to you. Murray N. Rothbard has labeled this the axiom of self-ownership — each individual owns his own life.[3] To own something means to have the exclusive right to use, control, and dispose of it. The doctrine of self-ownership holds that each person has the right to use, control, and dispose of his own life, and more significantly, that no one else does. This means that other individuals do not have the right to initiate the use of force against you to force you to take actions against your will. If other individuals did have the right to use such force, then they would have the right to use and control your life. They would in effect own your life, which would be tantamount to the immoral institution of slavery. The right to control or own your own life, therefore, implies that interaction between individuals should be based on voluntary consent.

To accept the doctrine of self-ownership one need go no farther than to reject the alternative, slavery, as immoral. If all men have equal rights, then some cannot have the right to dominate, use, control, and dispose of others. The right to control your own life is nothing more than the right to life itself, for if others can dispose of your life, then you have no right to live without their permission.

From this most basic of all rights flow all other rights. It is because your life belongs to you that you have the right to engage in contracts, exchanges, associations, and personal choices without interference from others. If others can interfere in these activities, then they are controlling your life as if they owned it. Similarly,

[3]Murray N. Rothbard, *For a New Liberty* (New York: MacMillan, 1972), pp. 26-28.

because your life belongs to you, you own what you create or produce with that life.

These are just some of the important rights of the liberal tradition. Others include the whole spectrum of property rights, but these are the most relevant to the public policy under discussion — the social security program.

These rights belong next to the other widely respected rights in our society that also stem from the liberal tradition, such as freedom of speech, freedom of the press, freedom of religion, and freedom of assembly. Why they have received less attention in recent years than this latter set of rights is an important question that deserves further treatment elsewhere. These economic rights are at least as important to the freedom and well-being of individuals as the civil rights that have received more attention in recent years. A truly free society will recognize the rights of people to act in the economic realm as well as in the civil and political realms. It should be clear that America would be a far freer country than it is today if we gave the same attention and respect to these economic rights and liberties as we do to civil rights and liberties.

It is true that these economic rights have never been recognized as absolute in the United States or anywhere else, and they are all abridged in numerous ways in American life, but that does not mean that they should be forgotten or ignored. They should continue to carry strong weight and serious respect in issues of public policy. Furthermore, the fact that they have never been treated as absolute does not mean that this treatment is correct.

The origin of these rights is a difficult question requiring too extensive an answer to be dealt with here. It has been widely discussed by a number of libertarian writers. For example, Robert Nozick argues that such rights are essential to the meaning of human life. Murray N. Rothbard and Ayn Rand argue that such rights are required by the inherent nature of man. Others have offered other justifications. The important point is that these rights have been recognized by our society as important, and they retain appeal today as essential guarantees of the freedom and dignity of individuals.

It should be apparent that the coercive character of social security violates all of these rights. It forces individuals to enter into contracts, exchanges, and associations with the government that they should have the right to refuse. It prohibits individuals from entering into alternative contracts, exchanges, and associations with others concerning the portion of their incomes that social security consumes. It prevents individuals from choosing courses of action other than participation in social security, although these courses of action will hurt no one. It prevents individuals from enjoying the fruits of their own labor by taking control of a major portion of each individual's income. The program prevents individuals from arranging their own affairs and controlling their own lives. It operates by the use of force and coercion against individuals rather than through voluntary consent. The social security program thus restricts individual liberty in major and significant ways, violating rights that are worthy of great respect.

If all men are indeed created equal then some men should not be allowed to initiate the use of force and coercion to compel other men to take involuntary actions. This is the fundamental libertarian principle. On libertarian grounds, the use of such force and coercion is immoral except when used in self-defense to protect individual rights, and the legal right to use such force or coercion is tantamount to the immoral institution of slavery. Yet social security uses simple force and coercion to compel individuals to participate in a program that seizes control of a portion of their incomes. Allowing these individuals the freedom to pursue alternatives to social security would hurt no one, and therefore this force or coercion is not employed in self-defense or to protect individual rights. On libertarian grounds the coercion involved in the social security program is immoral.

In a free, liberal, and civilized society relationships between people should be based on voluntary consent, not the use of force. The freedom and rights of individuals should be deeply respected. The type of coercion involved in social security should be avoided whenever possible. The private alternatives to social security are based on principles of voluntary exchange and consent. When a program the magnitude of social security, reflecting a large portion of the social interaction in our society, replaces these alternatives, our society begins to change from one based on voluntary consent to one based on force and coercion. The result is to make our society less liberal, less free, and less civilized.

It might be argued that social security is not the only government program that is guilty of these shortcomings. In fact virtually all the programs, restrictions, and regulations in our welfare state are guilty of restricting individual liberty, violating basic rights, and employing force and coercion against individual citizens.

That this is true hardly justifies it. Even if we accept restrictions on individual liberty and violations of certain rights under certain circumstances, that does not mean that we should be willing to do so under all circumstances, forgetting the fundamental importance of individual rights and personal freedom and the fundamental morality of consent. Even in the face of the overwhelming welfare state apparatus, in evaluating a public policy we should still be willing to grant significant weight to the fact that it restricts individual liberty, abridges important human rights, and employs force and coercion.

Just because the Supreme Court has allowed certain laws prohibiting pornography does not mean that we should forget about free speech. The Court will still scrutinize violations of free speech to determine whether they are justified, and the protection of such speech still carries a heavy weight in this evaluation. Similarly, just because restrictions on economic freedom and violations of economic rights are allowed under some circumstances does not mean that these rights and freedoms should no longer have any importance in public policy discussions.

An Analytical Framework

We can break down the various elements of coercion in the insurance portion of social security into an analytical framework similar to one advanced by Milton Friedman.[4] These elements are as follows:

1. The requirement that individuals must make some provision for their old age and other contingencies
2. The requirement that this provision be made by buying one type of insurance — social security
3. The requirement that this one type of insurance be purchased from one "seller" — the federal government

If any one of these elements were to be eliminated, freedom and individual liberty would be increased, even though the other elements remain. Even if individuals are required by the government to accept the first element and make some provision for their old age and other contingencies, freedom will still be increased if individuals are allowed to drop out of social security and pursue this goal by alternative means of their own choice, which would eliminate the remaining two elements. In essence, individuals would be

[4]Friedman, *Capitalism and Freedom*, p. 183.

freer if the old-age insurance business were denationalized and they were free to choose their own insurance plans. This is analogous to the voucher proposal for public education. The voucher proposal would still require individuals to use certain amounts of their income to educate their children, but it would allow them to choose the school and type of education for their children that they desire, thereby increasing individual liberty.

This analytical framework will be useful in considering justifications for social security in the next chapter. It will help make clear exactly what elements of the program each argument justifies and what remains unjustified. It will also be useful in considering possible reforms in succeeding chapters.

9

The Rationales
for Social Security

We have seen that the social security program has numerous serious shortcomings. If the program is so bad, why do we have it? Is there any convincing rationale or justification for it? Does the program have positive attributes that outweigh its negative ones?

These questions and related issues will be discussed in this chapter. We will examine the possible rationales for social security and ask what functions or purposes the program might serve. We will also discuss whether these rationales provide public policy goals worthy of support, and, if so, whether they justify all the elements of the present program. Finally we will question whether worthy rationales can be better served by alternative means, and, if not, whether their pursuit is really worth all the negative elements inherent in the program.

Public opinion on these questions is heavily divided. Some feel that social security serves an important role in a democratic society. Others, such as Milton Friedman, conclude that "social security involves a large scale invasion into the personal lives of a large fraction of the nation, without, so far as I can see, any justification that is at all persuasive, not only on liberal principles, but on almost any other."[1] These issues remain far from settled at the present time.

We will consider below each of the major justifications for the program that have been advanced in the literature.

Forced Saving

Perhaps the major popular argument advanced to justify social security is that without the program people simply will not provide

[1]Milton Friedman, *Capitalism and Freedom* (Chicago: University of Chicago Press, 1962), p. 182.

for their old age on their own. It is argued that individuals tend to be myopic, giving too much weight to current consumption and not enough thought to the future, and once they reach old age they will regret that they had not saved more. We must therefore force people to provide for their old age through social security so they will not starve, or live in poverty, misery, and regret in old age. This justification offers a paternalistic rationale for the program, arguing that we must force people to participate in social security for their own good.

This argument is highly questionable on several grounds. On the most fundamental level, many valid objections can be raised against government paternalism. Any such policy by its nature seriously restricts the freedom of individuals to control their own lives. It forces people to live by government standards rather than their own. It prevents people from pursuing their own goals and objectives merely because others think they are mistaken. Individuals should be free to run their own lives according to their own tastes and desires. If some believe that others are living their lives in error, then they have the right to try to persuade them that a mistake is being made. But what right do they have to use force to compel them to change their ways? As Friedman writes:

> Those of us who believe in freedom must believe also in the freedom of individuals to make their own mistakes. If a man knowingly prefers to live for today, to use his resources for current enjoyment, deliberately choosing a penurious old age, by what right do we prevent him from doing so? We may argue with him, seek to persuade him that he is wrong, but are we entitled to use coercion to prevent him from doing what he chooses to do? Is there not always the possibility that he is right and that we are wrong? Humility is the distinguishing virtue of the believer in freedom, arrogance of the paternalist.[2]

Government paternalism again violates the basic liberal axiom that your life belongs to you. Paternalism implies that your life belongs to the government, and therefore it has the right to make sure that you care for it properly according to government standards. If your life truly belongs to you, then you have the right to live it in any way you please according to your own desires and tastes. No one has the right to compel you to live your life according to his desires.

Furthermore, if the government is going to pass into law the one right way to live, then we must ask whose views on this matter are

[2]Ibid., p. 188.

going to be granted the force of law? There is no objective basis for determining the one right way to live. How then are we to determine whose views are correct? In practice, the subjective views of a politically powerful group of individuals will be imposed on others, but why are their views on the matter any more valid than any others? And what right do they have to impose their values on everyone else? As Friedman writes of the paternalist, "Basically he believes in dictatorship, benevolent and maybe majoritarian, but dictatorship nonetheless."[3]

One must ask further that if the government has the right to force us to take action which it deems to be in our own good, where will it stop? Might not the government justify equally well on paternalistic grounds laws requiring everyone to take vitamins, eat yogurt, jog, read Shakespeare, and go to the opera? The point is that once paternalism is accepted as a valid function of government, there is no limit to the actions that the government may take in controlling our lives and restricting individual liberty. Every politically powerful pressure group would then be justified in seeking to impose its conception of the good life on everyone else. The ultimate result is a totalitarian cage for each individual in which his every action is prescribed for his own good. As Murray N. Rothbard has written:

> Sometimes it seems that the beau ideal of many conservatives, as well as of many liberals, is to put everyone into a cage and coerce him into doing what the conservatives or liberals believe to be the moral thing. They would, of course, be differently styled cages, but they would be cages just the same. The conservative would ban illicit sex, drugs, gambling, and impiety, and coerce everyone to act according to his version of moral and religious behavior. The liberal would ban films of violence, unesthetic advertising, football and racial discrimination, and, at the extreme, place everyone in a "Skinner box" to be run by a supposedly benevolent liberal dictator. But the effect would be the same: to reduce everyone to a subhuman level and to deprive everyone of the most precious part of his or her humanity — the freedom to choose.[4]

A final flaw in the paternalistic argument is that it suffers from an inherent irony. Paternalists contend that individuals are too stupid to take care of themselves, and therefore the government must take care of them. But none suggest that the government should not be run on a democratic basis. The paternalistic policies the government

[3]Ibid., p. 187.
[4]Murray N. Rothbard, *For a New Liberty* (New York: Macmillan, 1973), p. 118.

pursues are presumably to be chosen by the voters, the very same
people who are supposed to be too stupid to run their own lives. The
paternalist position, therefore, is simply that individuals are too
stupid to run their own lives but not too stupid to run everyone
else's. The very same people who are supposed to be incapable of
making intelligent choices on relatively simple issues in their own
personal lives are supposed to be perfectly capable of making complex public policy choices on how to resolve issues in the personal
lives of everyone in the entire society. Democratic theory assumes
that these very same stupid voters are supposed to be perfectly
capable of making even more complex public policy choices about
how to run the economy, stop inflation and unemployment, solve
the energy crisis, and conduct foreign affairs. Somehow it seems
hard to accept the proposition that the very same people who are expected to make intelligent choices on these issues are incapable of
making a simple choice concerning how much of their current income they want to save for their old age.

There are other flaws in the forced saving argument besides these
objections to its underlying paternalism. Though this argument is
often cited as a justification for social security, no one has every provided any empirical support for it. No one has ever shown what
percentage of people would fail to make adequate provision for their
old age in the absence of social security. It is hard to believe that the
same people who go to colleges and graduate schools, who engage in
sophisticated business enterprises, who have built the most im-
pressive technological economy in the world, cannot understand the
value of deferring current consumption for greater enjoyment in the
future and are therefore incapable of providing for their old age on
their own.

Another problem with the forced saving argument is illustrated
by the shortcomings of the program discussed in previous chapters.
The basis of the argument is that the government is supposed to
force people to participate in social security for their own good. As
we saw in chapter 4, however, young people entering the program
today could do far better in private alternatives outside the program. Forced participation in social security is hardly a way to help
people, especially considering the negative impacts of the program.
Even assuming that some unknown number of people would not
provide for their old age without social security and that paternalism is a valid function of government, it seems that social security
is a poor way of helping them. The program forces everyone to pro-

vide for their old age through a means that, along with several other negative impacts, will leave them less well off in old age than private alternatives, forces them simply because a few might not otherwise make any provision for their old age at all.

Finally, even if we accept the forced saving argument fully it does not justify the entire social security program. The purposes underlying the argument could be achieved by a simple requirement that all individuals save some portion of their income for their old age and other contingencies, but not necessarily through social security. Individuals could instead be allowed to take advantage of private alternatives for the provision of these services. The entire social security apparatus is therefore unnecessary to achieve the goal of forced saving. Replacing social security with such a simple requirement would eliminate most of the negative effects that we have discussed, except some of those described in chapter 8. Though this requirement would not be perfect, it would clearly be a vast improvement over what we have now.

The forced saving argument is thus wholly inadequate to justify the current social security program.

A variant of the forced saving argument emphasizes the potential harm to others from the failure of a person to provide for his old age. This argument contends that those who fail to save for their old age will impose costs on others because these others will not allow the improvident to starve or live in misery. They will feel compelled to provide the improvident with costly welfare payments. Furthermore, the improvident may tend to rely on the prospect of these welfare payments and become even more likely to fail to provide for themselves. Thus, it is argued, the public has the right to force people to provide for their old age to prevent some from imposing unnecessary costs on the public.

This argument may seem plausible on the surface, but it is based on some questionable assumptions. It suggests that because some individuals, out of compassion, offer benefits to those in need, these individuals have the right to use force to compel the recipients of their charity to behave in ways that will reduce its costs. But this just does not seem to follow. One who offers charity to another may make his payments contingent on certain behavior. He is free to offer charity or not. But if he chooses to do so, he must bear the costs of his decision. He cannot impose some of these costs on the recipient by using force to restrict the latter's liberty. It is his decision to provide charity that results in the costs, not the actions of the beneficiary, and if he does not desire to bear these costs, he can reduce or eliminate his charity. He cannot — or should not — use it as an excuse to seize control over the life of the beneficiary. This argument goes even farther by suggesting not only that the provider of charity has the right to use force against the recipient, but against everyone else in society to ensure that they don't become eventual recipients. It suggests that if A gives charity to B, A has the right to restrict the liberty of C lest C to anything to evoke A's reflexive pangs of compassionate conscience. A's conscience is A's own problem, however, and providing charity does not give A the right to restrict the liberty of others. A's justification is that by failing to provide for their old age the improvident will impose costs on others, namely A, who will feel compelled to provide them with welfare. The imposition of costs on others is the classic justification for restricting liberty, but the actions of the improvident are not imposing costs on others. The givers remain free to give or withhold charity regardless of the actions of the improvident. It is thus the giver's decision to give that results in the costs, and if he is unhappy with these costs then he should reduce his giving. The decision to give is certainly no justification for restricting the liberty of others.

Another curious difficulty with this argument is the strange kind of compassion it implies. If one who could have provided for his retirement fails to do so, then he should simply have no retirement. At age sixty-five he will have to continue working until he dies or becomes disabled, just as a person who is not wealthy enough to retire at forty must continue working. Someone who cannot retire at age sixty-five because he failed to make provisions that he could have made is hardly a particularly sympathetic object of compassion. If individuals still feel driven to provide charity for this person so that he can retire, then they can hardly complain about the costs, and their peculiar sort of compassion hardly justifies restricting the liberty of others.

The usual argument against this variant of the forced saving justification is that it has no empirical basis. Without social security, what percentage of people would not save and become public charges in old age? No one has ever provided any data on this question, and again it seems that the number would be small. Surveys indicate that at most 15% of the elderly give disability as a reason for not working.[5] If welfare payments are limited to those in this group

[5]Edgar K. Browning, "The Politics of Social Security Reform," *Conference on Financing Social Security*, American Enterprise Institute (Washington, D.C.: 1977), p. 4.

who failed to provide for their old age, then the magnitude of the problem would appear to be rather small. If people realize that if they don't save for retirement they will not be able to retire unless they become disabled, there will be no incentive to ignore retirement needs in the expectation that these needs will be provided for through welfare. If on this basis we assume that only 10% of the public will fail to provide for their retirement and that they are as likely to become disabled as the rest of the population, only 1.5% of the elderly would become public charges in the absence of social security. It seems to make little sense to force the entire population to participate in social security to avoid the additional welfare costs which will result from the improvidence of 1.5%.

Again the inescapable flaw in this variant of the forced saving argument is the same as in the first variant. The argument doesn't justify the entire social security program but merely a requirement that all individuals make some provision for their old age and other contingencies. There is no reason why this provision has to be made through social security. In fact, given all the negative impacts of the program, we would be better off if it was made outside of the program through private alternatives.

The forced saving rationale in all its forms seems seriously inadequate and even if accepted does not justify the entire program as presently constituted.

Market Failure

Some argue that social security is necessary because of imperfections in the marketplace that make private market alternatives unavailable or unattractive.

The first of these alleged imperfections is that actuarially fair annuities, which guarantee an individual monthly payments for life, cannot be made available in a private market. These annuities would be one of the chief private alternatives to the old-age insurance benefits of social security. The alleged unfairness results because of a supposed adverse selection problem in the private market. Those who anticipate a long life or have characteristics that make the collection of benefits more likely will tend to purchase annuities heavily. The rates charged for these annuities will have to be increased to reflect the fact that the purchasers have nontypical characteristics that impose greater risks for the company than the average person. If an average person wants to buy such an annuity, he will then have to pay the higher rates for the greater risks that most purchasers of these annuities impose, but which he does not. Thus the average person cannot purchase private annuities at actuarially fair rates to protect himself from the same contingencies that social security does.

But actuarially fair rates should be based on the characteristics of the group of purchasers, not on the actuarial characteristics of the population as a whole. In any insurance system some purchasers of insurance will impose greater risks than the average purchaser and some will impose less. As long as the rates are based on the actuarial characteristics of the average purchaser, a potential purchaser does not face actuarially unfair rates. A seller of annuities cannot and does not attempt to charge each purchaser a price equal to the risks imposed by that particular purchaser. The seller has to charge purchasers a rate sufficient to cover the measurable risks imposed by an identifiable group to which those purchasers belong, and there is nothing unfair about rates determined in this way.

Furthermore, if more and more average and even below average risks purchase annuities, rates will decline to reflect the lower overall risks. This decline would occur in the absence of social security because people would then turn to private alternatives. As the group of purchasers grew in number, its actuarial characteristics move closer to those of the whole population, and the average person would then begin to pay lower rates more closely reflecting the actual risks imposed by him. If social security were replaced by a simple rule requiring all to make some provision for old age and other contingencies through private alternatives, then the group of purchasers would be even more likely to resemble the general population, although there would still be some deviance because individuals could choose other private alternatives besides annuities.

If life insurance or auto insurance can be offered at actuarially fair rates, then so can retirement annuities. Insurance companies respond to widely varying risks by trying to focus on the different characteristics that make individuals high risks, such as bad health or bad driving records, and charging those individuals higher rates. There is no reason why the same could not be done for retirement annuities.

Furthermore, any higher costs are surely quite small when one considers the massive advantages that private sector alternatives have over social security. Because these private alternatives are run on an invested, fully funded basis, most individuals could receive several times what they would receive under social security. Any higher costs would be even further outweighed by the negative impacts of social security that we have discussed.

Finally, this argument does not justify making social security compulsory. It only justifies offering it on a voluntary basis to make sure that there would be competition for private insurers who might not offer annuities on an actuarially fair basis. If these private alternatives can be shown to be superior, then there is no justification for preventing individuals from taking advantage of them.

A second market failure argument contends that the cost to each person of obtaining the necessary information to make individual decisions in the private market would be too high. Like many arguments about social security, this one conveniently forgets that we are supposed to live in a democracy, not a benevolent dictatorship. Presumably government action is based on informed, democratic choice, which also has high information and decision-making costs. In fact, the information and decision-making costs of the political process are much greater than those of market processes.

The information necessary to make an informed choice concerning social security policy is much greater and infinitely more complex than the information necessary to make a choice concerning one's personal financial affairs. Each individual is already intimately informed about his own financial needs and abilities, and he has only to learn about alternatives to social security available in the marketplace. People engage in millions of economic and business transactions every day, and there is no suggestion that the cost of learning about market alternatives is prohibitive. Because of their business and financial dealings, many will already be familiar with the information necessary to make a choice on different types of insurance and investment alternatives. Also, to the extent that social security exists only to provide a floor of old-age income, many people will already have made decisions about ways to supplement it. The additional cost of learning how to replace social security entirely by private alternatives is likely to be minimal. The information necessary to make an informed choice concerning social security policy, on the other hand, is limitless. One needs to know about demographic, economic, and social trends, the needs and desires of everyone in society, available resources, the economic and social impacts of the program, and numerous other factors. The information necessary to make an informed, private financial decision is much more manageable than the information necessary to make an informed, democratic, public policy choice for everyone through social security.

In fact, the very process of socializing the old-age, survivor's, disability, and health insurance industries infinitely increases the information necessary to run these programs. One of the great insights of Nobel Prize–winning economist Friedrich A. Hayek was that the market serves as a great information-gathering mechanism that reduces the amount of information it is necessary to collect explicitly. For example, for the government to determine the appropriate retirement age for social security as desired by its participants, it would have to poll members of the public and decide what each desired. In the market, however, this would not be necessary. Each individual already knows his own preferences and can act on them without needing to know the preferences of others. If sixty-five were the preferred age of retirement, pensions and policies that featured this age would be in greater demand than others, and companies would adjust their policies to satisfy the demand. No surveys or intricate information gathering would be necessary. The same is true for all the other provisions of the program. The information necessary to provide these insurance services in the marketplace would be much less than the information necessary to provide them through nonmarket political processes.

Also, it can hardly be assumed that everyone will make the same decision concerning retirement benefits and that the government can therefore anticipate it. Individual preferences and needs vary widely. A single worker does not require the same insurance protection as a married person with several children. As we saw in chapters 4 and 6, the widely varying individual needs and preferences in American society cannot possibly be satisfied by a single program with a single set of benefit provisions. Yet this is the price of avoiding individual information and decision-making costs — a program poorly suited to individual needs and tastes. Individuals should be allowed to decide for themselves how much it is worth to them to tailor a retirement program to their individual tastes and desires and how much in information and decision-making costs they are willing to undergo to attain that goal.

Furthermore, these information and decision-making costs are once again sure to be far outweighed by the financial superiority of private alternatives to social security that we examined in chapter 4 as well as by negative impacts of the program that we have noted throughout this book.

Finally, this rationale again fails to justify much of the current social security program. There is no reason on this basis to make the program compulsory. It could be made voluntary, and—even with a requirement that some provision for old age and other contingencies be made—if individuals found the private alternatives worth the information and decision-making costs, they could be free to pursue these alternatives, as they should be. The market failure argument fails to justify the current program.

Welfare Benefits

Another rationale for social security is that it is needed to provide benefits to the poor and needy. It may be argued that the elderly, the disabled, and surviving dependents include a high proportion of poor persons and therefore social security serves an important welfare function in providing income to the needy.

We have already discussed all of the substantial ways in which social security is a bad method of providing welfare benefits to the needy. These basically fall into two categories. The first includes the many ways that social security wastes assets meant to help the poor by paying welfare benefits to those who are not poor. Social security is fundamentally an inefficient method of channeling welfare benefits to the poor because, as a result of the insurance elements in the program, many of those benefits go to individuals who are not poor. The second category includes the large number of negative impacts on the poor that result from the current program. These impacts are all unnecessary because the welfare benefits currently provided to the poor through social security could be provided through alternative programs that would not have these negative impacts. It would therefore be far better to fulfill any necessary welfare goals with other programs or institutions than social security.

Another problem with this welfare rationale is that it again fails to justify most of the elements of the program. If we wish to give the poor financial assistance, that does not mean that we have to force others into a social security program that pays benefits with little regard to actual need. The goals of this rationale can be satisfied with a simple means-tested welfare program that directs all its assets to the truly needy. The welfare rationale does not justify all the insurance elements of the program. It justifies a simple welfare program, not social security.

It is sometimes argued that social security is an ideal way to pursue welfare goals because it allows the government to pay welfare benefits without a means test. A means test, some people contend, is degrading to welfare recipients. This argument is advanced even though without a means test much of the money intended for the poor will be wasted because it will go to those who are not poor. However, this argument hardly justifies social security because if a welfare program without a means test is truly desirable, we could have one without social security. We must also ask if a means test is in fact degrading and, if it is, does that mean it should be avoided.

The means test is often considered degrading because it requires the poor to divulge intimate details of their lives to welfare officials to prove that they are truly needy. It also means that they have to be subject to investigations by welfare officials to make sure that they have not lied about these details. A means test thus invades the privacy of the poor.

Is it really too much, though, to ask of a person who wants to receive payments intended for the poor and needy that he prove that he *is* really poor and in need? Why should a person be entitled to such benefits without proof? How can anyone conceivably be so arrogant as to demand that the taxpayer pay out his hard-earned money indiscriminately to whoever has the audacity to ask for it?

Economic value does not appear like manna from heaven. All economic value must be created or produced. One who asks for welfare benefits is asking that he be given value produced by others, though he has produced nothing himself. He is asking that he be allowed to enjoy the fruits of someone else's labor, that he be allowed to live at the expense of others. Anyone who asks for such a privilege should have to prove some unusual circumstances making this privilege absolutely necessary. It would be unfair to those who have earned and produced what they have to demand that they hand it over to others without a good reason for doing so.

Many who oppose a means test because it is degrading are living in a dream world. Without a means test many who are not truly poor or needy will try to take advantage of the program and get funds intended for the poor. If such a test is imposed but not strictly monitored, many will simply lie to get the handouts.

The real cause of opposition to the means test is not a blindness to reality but an attempt to cover it up. A means test requires the welfare recipient to justify his receipt of welfare. By implying that there is a need for justification, the means test suggests that the recipient hasn't earned his benefits but instead is receiving them at the expense of others who have the right to demand this justification. It suggests that the welfare recipient is different from others because he has to supply a special justification for his income and open up his personal life to detailed probing. This view was summed up by a panelist at a Brookings Institution discussion of the issue when he said he opposed the means test because it implied to the welfare recipient that "you can't make it on your own."[6]

The welfare recipient can't make it on his own; that is why he is on welfare. And he does need to justify his receipt of welfare because he is living at the expense of others and consuming the assets that they have earned through their work and productive effort. He is different from other members of society because they must work to earn their own living without being a burden to others, while he receives his living for free without working and thus imposes a burden on others.

These facts remain true regardless of whether there is a means test, and these facts constitute the real reason why welfare is degrading. Welfare is degrading not because of the means test but because the recipient is living at the expense of others, because he is a burden to those around him, because he is different from the other members of society who are working to support themselves and earning their own way, because the recipient in fact cannot make it on his own.

It is hoped that by removing the means test these facts will remain hidden. It is hoped that by removing the requirement for a justification the reason that such a justification is necessary will be forgotten. It is hoped that welfare will no longer be degrading.

But the facts cannot be covered up. They remain true regardless of whether there is a means test, and welfare remains degrading with or without the test. Furthermore, there is no reason why these facts should be covered up; they are true and there is no justification for deception. Furthermore, the recipient should feel remorseful at accepting welfare because he is living at the expense of others and imposing a burden on his neighbors.

There is no valid reason for opposition to a means test in a welfare program. Such opposition is totally unreasonable and should receive far less serious consideration than it does today.

A final argument based on the welfare rationale is that social security is a good way to provide welfare because it allows the gov-

[6]Alicia H. Munnell, *The Future of Social Security* (Washington, D.C.: Brookings Institution, 1977), p. 140.

ernment to grant welfare benefits under the false guise of social security, even though the public would not explicitly vote for such welfare payments in a separate program.[7] Even if true, this is an argument based on the deception of voters and is therefore unacceptable and even immoral. It basically holds that voters can be fooled into paying for welfare benefits if these benefits are smuggled into social security even though they would not vote for these benefits if the issue were presented to them directly. Deceiving the voters can hardly serve as a valid justification for any government program.

We see, then, that the welfare rationale is an inadequate justification for social security. The program is a poor way of providing welfare, and any necessary welfare benefits can be provided in a superior fashion through a simple welfare program. Furthermore, this rationale does not justify all of the insurance elements of the program and the compulsory requirement that a high percentage of Americans participate in these insurance elements.

Income Redistribution

Another possible justification for social security is that it may aid in income redistribution. An income redistribution goal is different from a welfare goal. Welfare seeks to provide a minimum income to those who are poor and in need, whereas income redistribution policies seek to equalize incomes by taxing those with higher incomes and granting benefits to those with lower and moderate incomes, even though they may not be poor or in need. Such a policy could conceivably be pursued through social security by a progressive benefit structure that gave a lower return on tax dollars paid by those with higher incomes and a higher return to those with lower incomes.

It is a mistake to use income redistribution to justify the present social security program because it is quite likely that the program redistributes wealth and income from those with lower incomes to those with higher incomes. We have already recounted in earlier chapters the various ways the program hurts those with lower incomes and tends to concentrate wealth and income. It is doubtful that countervailing factors in the benefit structure offset these effects. The present program does not serve any income redistribution goal.

[7]Friedman, *Capitalism and Freedom*, pp. 184–85.

Furthermore, the social security program would be an inefficient means of redistributing income. Not only do many of the program's effects work contrary to such a goal, but because of the insurance elements in the benefit structure many of the program's benefits would not go to those with low incomes. A program entirely separate from social security could achieve income redistribution by taxing those with higher incomes and providing benefits to those with lower incomes. Such a program would not entail the counterproductive and wasteful effects of social security, nor would it have the other negative impacts of social security that we have discussed.

Still another problem with this rationale is that it too fails to justify all the elements of the program. There is no reason why we should pursue income redistribution goals through an insurance program. If we want to redistribute income, we can have an income redistribution program, but that does not mean that we should force the entire population into a social security program that attempts to provide people with insurance services. This rationale does not justify any of the insurance elements of the program. It justifies an income redistribution program, not social security.

Finally, it is time that the worth of income redistribution as a goal of government policy was challenged. Why should the government equalize and redistribute incomes? If those with high incomes have earned them through productive effort and free exchanges in the marketplace, they are entitled to keep them. A man is entitled to what he creates or produces, to enjoy the fruits of his own labor. If one man produces more than another, he is entitled to his higher income, and there is nothing unfair about it.

Pay-As-You-Go Financing

A fifth possible justification for social security is based on the argument that a pay-as-you-go system may be superior to a private, invested system and such a system can be provided only through a government program like social security.

One can imagine certain circumstances under which a pay-as-you-go system would at least appear to be superior to a private system. These circumstances were explored originally by Nobel laureate Paul Samuelson in an article in 1958.[8] Assume that the rate of

---

[8]Paul A. Samuelson, "An Exact Consumption-Loan Model of Interest with or without the Social Contrivance of Money," *Journal of Political Economy* LXVI (December 1958): 467–82.

population growth is zero and that the rate of growth of real wages in employment covered by the program is greater than the rate of return on capital investments (the interest rate). A constant tax rate, say 10 %, is imposed on all taxpayers, and the total amount collected each year is distributed in benefits to current retirees. If an individual enters such a system when he begins working and continues to participate through retirement, he will receive in retirement benefits a rate of return on his tax payments equal to the rate of growth in real wages covered by the program. This will happen because with a constant tax rate applied to payrolls, total taxes collected and therefore total benefits paid would increase by the rate of growth in these payrolls. If the individual had saved these same tax payments on his own, his rate of return on them would be equal to the interest rate. If this interest rate is less than the rate of growth in real wages, as we have assumed, the individual would seem to do better in the pay-as-you-go system than in the private system.

Now assume a zero rate of growth in real wages but a rate of growth in population that is greater than the rate of return to capital. This increase in population will cause a similar increase in workers, and, because there is a fixed tax rate on payrolls, total taxes collected and therefore total benefits paid will also increase at this rate of growth in population. If this rate is greater than the interest rate, as we have assumed, then the individual would again appear to be better off in the pay-as-you-go system than in the private system.

The pay-as-you-go system, then, would appear to be superior to the private system when the rate of growth in real wages plus the rate of population growth is greater than the interest rate. This is known as the social insurance paradox.[9] Somehow, all individuals appear to receive more from such a program under these circumstances, even though the program does nothing to increase productivity or national income.

This argument also fails to justify the current social security program. First the conditions that would make it valid do not exist, and it is unlikely that they ever will. According to studies by Martin Feldstein, the real rate of return, net of inflation, on invested capital in the United States is approximately 12 % or more before taxes.[10]

[9]A precise mathematical representation of this paradox was provided by Henry J. Aaron of the Brookings Institution in 1966. See Henry J. Aaron, "The Social Insurance Paradox," *Canadian Journal of Economics* 13 (1966): 371–74.

[10]In a recent study, Feldstein estimated that from 1946 to 1975 the pretax real rate of

Although individuals receive only the after-tax rate of return directly, the before-tax rate is the correct one to consider because it represents the full amount gained through the private system. The tax money could be returned to taxpayers, in which case they would receive the full 12 % or more, or it could be used by the government to provide services for taxpayers if they prefer this alternative to receiving the money directly. Which alternative taxpayers would prefer is a separate issue. The important point is that the full return on the invested system is 12 % or more.

The rate of growth in real wages, by contrast, has historically been about 2 % and in the past twenty-five years has been approximately 1.3 %. Population factors have also been adverse. Fertility rates have already fallen well below the rate for zero population growth, and if this continues, as appears likely, the population will soon begin to decline rather than grow. A declining population could easily make the social insurance rate of return negative. Furthermore, the baby boom followed by the baby bust is already creating the effects of a falling population because, when the baby-boom generation begins to retire, the percentage of aged population relative to the working population will increase, rather than decline, as in periods of population growth. This increased ratio of aged to working population will subtract from the social insurance rate of return and could even make it negative.

Neither population growth nor the rate of growth in real wages is anywhere near the levels necessary to overcome the interest rate of return in an invested system. This fact was brought out in chapter 4 when we saw that greater returns are available to individuals in the private sector than in social security. The private returns were greater even despite the tremendous tax increases that must occur in future years to support current benefit promises. These tax increases mean that the future benefits promised current workers represent

return on invested capital was 12.4 %, but this includes two years—1974 and 1975—of the worst recession in American history since the Great Depression and does not include the recovery years of higher returns since then. Feldstein's calculations also show that from 1946 to 1969 this rate of return averaged 13 %. It is therefore quite probable that after the recovery from the sharp recession of the mid-1970s the rate will return to 13 %. See Martin Feldstein, "National Saving in the United States," *Harvard Institute of Economic Research, Discussion Paper No. 506*, October 1976. In other papers Feldstein estimated the real rate of return as 15 %. See Martin Feldstein, "Toward a Reform of Social Security," *The Public Interest*, Summer 1975, pp. 75–95, and Martin Feldstein, "The Optimal Financing of Social Security," *Harvard Institute of Economic Research, Discussion Paper No. 388*, 1974.

returns greater than the social security rate of return. Yet the returns from the private investments were still greater, which suggests that the social security rate of return is actually negative, probably because of the effects of population trends.

These factors are not likely to change in the foreseeable future. The interest rate or return to capital has always been much higher than the rate of growth in real wages, and there are no economic trends suggesting that this will change. The baby-boom generation is already aging, and it has already been followed by a baby bust, which means that a sharp increase in the aged population relative to the working population is inevitable. The recent decline in fertility rates has not even stopped, let alone shown signs of rebounding, and it is already in a range that will result in a declining population. Even in the best circumstances, we can expect to sustain a rate of population growth of only about 2 % for a long time. If real wage growth also returned to historical levels of around 2 %, the highest social security rate of return we could possibly expect, under the most ideal conditions, would be about 4 %. This is still less than one-third the return available on capital investments. On empirical grounds, therefore, the social insurance paradox argument does not justify social security.

There are other objections to the argument. An additional disadvantage of the pay-as-you-go system as compared with a private system is that pay-as-you-go has a restrictive, lock-in effect. A pay-as-you-go system develops tremendous liabilities as it matures, liabilities that must be met. The retired generation in a mature system has been induced to rely on the promises of the system and may have made no other provisions for its old age. If these promises are not kept, the retired generation may live in extreme hardship. Thus, the working generation in a mature system has important options foreclosed to it. This generation cannot decide to stop paying into the system for any reason; it has been burdened with a heavy debt obligation that it must pay off.

It is true that the working generation is promised future benefits to be paid by the next generation, but the working generation cannot decide that these future benefits are not worth what they are currently paying and use these funds instead for other purposes. It must meet the benefit obligations to the current retired generation, which would otherwise live in poverty. In a private system, the working generation could decide to stop paying into its retirement fund if it had more urgent and important uses for its savings, but once locked into a restrictive, pay-as-you-go system it cannot make this choice.

Suppose, for example, that the nation was at war, perhaps a world war. It might urgently need funds to defend itself against conquest, defeat, or domination by the enemy. If the current working generation was paying into a private system for its old age, it could suspend payments into the system for a few years and use these funds for the war effort. The only result would be a decreased retirement income that could be made up after the war. If the current generation was locked into a pay-as-you-go system, the consequences of suspending payments into the system for a few years would be extreme misery for the current retired generation. The resources could not be used to aid the war effort even for a few years.

Suppose the nation was met by an energy crisis that required a massive investment of funds to find and develop new energy sources to avert disaster. With an invested program, funds currently set aside for retirement protection could be diverted to this use. In fact, investments toward this end could conceivably be made within the program, with the returns going into the retirement fund. With a pay-as-you-go system, such a diversion of funds could not be made unless society was willing to impose unexpected and undeserved hardships on current retirees.

Or imagine an important new invention that required great amounts of funds for development. This invention might make everyone much better off if developed. If the current working generation was involved in an invested system, it could choose to divert its retirement funds for a while into taking advantage of this opportunity, thus making all much better off. Conceivably, it could divert funds for this development within the retirement system by changing investments, but with a pay-as-you-go system this opportunity may have to be delayed or missed entirely.

It may be simply that as a result of changes in population trends, wage growth, and interest rates, a pay-as-you-go system is simply no longer a sound investment in comparison with the private system, although it may have appeared to be so when it was started. Yet once locked in a mature, pay-as-you-go system, the current working generation will find it very difficult to switch over to an invested program. It still must meet its current obligations to today's retirees.

These considerations apply to individuals as well as groups. A particular individual may be struck by an emergency that requires urgent expenditures. If he were in an invested program, he could suspend payments into his retirement fund temporarily to take care of the emergency, even though he might have to live with lower retirement benefits or make up the difference later. With a pay-as-you-go program he could not use the funds he has to deal with such an emergency. He would instead be faced with a liability that had to be met, a debt to a current retiree that that retiree was counting on for his subsistence. Similarly, a lucrative opportunity may appear for an individual taxpayer, and he may be much better off if he is able to use the money he was paying into his retirement fund to take advantage of this opportunity, but if he is locked into a pay-as-you-go system, this opportunity may be delayed or missed altogether. The individual may simply want to vary his payments over time, paying more in some years and less in others. With an invested system his ability to do so would be unrestricted. With a pay-as-you-go system he could never reduce his payments below the amount of liabilities due to current retirees. He may wish to make less provision for his old age than required by the pay-as-you-go system. Under his particular preference scheme, he may be better off with less during his retirement years if he could consume more during his working years. Once locked into a pay-as-you-go scheme, however, he could not simply cut down on his payments into the program, as he could under a private system.

The pay-as-you-go system burdens the working generation with a heavy debt that must be met, preventing the entire generation individually or as a group from taking courses of action with its retirement funds that could make its members better off. By foreclosing options and opportunities that could be pursued in a private program, the pay-as-you-go program makes individuals worse off. This is to say no more than that a person would be better off if his parents had their own fund to finance their retirement than if they were relying on him to do so, even if, as a consequence of supporting them, he could rely on his children to support him.

There is a third flaw in the argument that a pay-as-you-go system is superior that is even more fundamental than the first two. The pay-as-you-go system, it should be remembered, adds nothing to production. It is simply a tax-and-transfer scheme that takes funds from current workers and gives them to current retirees. This transfer does nothing to increase total output. An invested system, however, increases total production because the funds paid into the system are invested in productive capital equipment that raises the output of the economy. This increased production plus the original amounts paid in are what pay the retirement benefits in an invested system, rather than taxes, as in a pay-as-you-go system.

The rate of return in an invested system is self-financing as a result of the increased productivity and output generated by the system itself. The rate of return in a pay-as-you-go system, on the other hand, comes from taxes collected from the current working generation. If current workers are taxed at higher amounts than current retirees were taxed, social security can use these higher taxes to pay more in benefits to current retirees than they paid in taxes, resulting in an implicit rate of return on taxes paid. These higher taxes may not come from higher tax rates, but they nevertheless constitute higher absolute amounts of taxes drawn from the population. Even though the tax rate is constant, the growth in wages and the growth in population will result in higher total tax collections, which will pay the social security rate of return. But neither of these factors will result in increased productivity and output. They merely make it easier to draw the higher absolute taxes from the population. They result in increased taxes collected without positive action, and hence the tax increases may not be noticed. Although they also make the higher tax payments easier to take, they do not change the fact that the social security rate of return is merely the result of increased taxes rather than increased production.

The "rate of return" in a pay-as-you-go system is therefore not a rate of return at all, and it is totally misleading to call it one. The use of this term incorrectly implies that the return to individuals in the pay-as-you-go system is the same as the return in the private system, which consequently implies that it is financed through increased production as well, but this is not so. The social security rate of return is derived from increased taxes rather than increased production. Since this return is not the result of increased production through the pay-as-you-go system, it can only be paid by appropriating a share of the productive effort of current workers. The social security rate of return is therefore a burden on current production. This is totally unlike the return paid in a private system, which is not a burden on current production. Instead, it is a self-financing benefit that is paid entirely out of the increased production resulting from the investments of the private system. The social security rate of return is in reality a government subsidy to current retirees from current taxpayers out of current tax revenues. At least when it is higher than market rates of return, it is nothing more than a form of welfare, a particularly unjustifiable form of welfare since it is paid to everyone, rich and poor alike.

Because the basis for these two types of returns is entirely different, comparing them is like comparing apples and oranges. Despite this fact, writers will often compare the rates of return from the two alternative types of programs as if they were referring to similar concepts. They will argue, for example, that with the invested system the economy gains productivity and output at a rate of 13%, reflecting the invested system's rate of return, as compared to 2% for the pay-as-you-go system, reflecting the social insurance rate of return. But this comparison is fallacious. Output in the economy under the pay-as-you-go system is not increased by 2% a year. It is not increased at all. The correct comparison is thirteen to zero, not thirteen to two. This is what the social insurance paradox is all about. Somehow, returns to individuals are supposed to be increased under the program while total output remains the same.

A particularly clear example of this error was provided by Edgar K. Browning in a paper presented at an American Enterprise Institute Conference in 1977.[11] In the paper, Browning assumes a 10% rate of return from invested capital, a 3% rate of growth in wages, and a 0% rate of growth in the population. He notes that under Feldstein's calculations, social security wealth stood at approximately $3 trillion, representing the amount that would have been invested in a fully funded program. He argues that this fully funded program would add to the national economy 10% × $3 trillion or $300 billion per year. He then contends that the pay-as-you-go system produces 3% × $3 trillion or $90 billion a year. He then argues that the result of having a pay-as-you-go system instead of an invested system is an annual loss to the economy of $300 − $90 = $210 billion per year. This calculation is erroneous. The pay-as-you-go system does not add $90 billion a year to the economy. It adds nothing to the economy. The correct comparison is not $300 billion to $90 billion but rather $300 billion to 0. The loss due to pay-as-you-go therefore is not equal to $210 billion, but $300 billion.

It should be said that Browning has written some of the most brilliant and insightful articles published about social security, yet he makes this simple error, as does almost every other writer on the subject.

With a pay-as-you-go system, society loses the increased production and output that would occur in an invested program. According

[11]Browning, "The Politics of Social Security Reform."

to Feldstein's calculations, this loss is approximately $400 billion a year at present, as we saw in chapter 3. There is no increase in production from the pay-as-you-go program to offset this loss.

Even if the social security rate of return were equal to or greater than the return available to individuals in the private, invested system, it seems that they would still be worse off under a pay-as-you-go system because society would still be losing the increased production available from the invested system. For example, if the real interest rate available were only 3% instead of 13%, and the rate of growth in real wages was 3% with a constant population, the nation would still be losing $90 billion a year under the pay-as-you-go system. People would therefore be worse off, despite the social security illusion, because they would all be poorer. Even if the investment return was below 3%, individuals would still be losing the increased productivity from the invested system. In fact, as long as the interest rate was above 0% and there was some increased production from capital investment, the population would all be poorer as a result of the loss of the increased production available through the invested system.

They would be worse off no matter how high the government subsidies paid through the social security rate of return may be. This return, no matter how high, is still an illusion. Everyone cannot be made better off by paying government subsidies to everyone else. Individuals in the pay-as-you-go system will still be poorer because of the loss of the increased production available through the invested system. The decision to pay everyone welfare payments through social security does not eliminate the loss. If people could be made better off by the universal granting of subsidies, it could be done independently of social security. We could offer everyone the opportunity to invest as much as they want in a government investment program and raise taxes high enough to pay returns on these investments, which are much greater than returns on private capital investments. Why should we compare what individuals receive from these subsidies with private returns on capital investments? There is simply no basis for comparison. What sense does it make to say that the government subsidy investment program is superior to private investments? In what sense could we say that individuals are made better off because of the government subsidy investment program? The government would merely be taxing everyone to make welfare subsidy payments to all.

Finally, the pay-as-you-go system suffers from the additional shortcomings noted in previous chapters. A pay-as-you-go system must be compulsory to be sure that benefits promised will be paid, and therefore it restricts individual liberty and personal freedom, as noted in chapter 8. Since a pay-as-you-go program must be run by the government, it is subject to all the political instabilities noted in chapter 7. The system also suffers from the vulnerability to bankruptcy noted in chapter 5. Given these drawbacks in addition to those mentioned above, the pay-as-you-go rationale hardly seems to justify social security.

The Compact Between Generations

We have examined all of the major rationales advanced for the social security program and have found that all fail to justify it. This leaves us with the question with which we began this chapter: If social security is so bad, why do we have it? Before we can answer this question and expose the perhaps surprisingly evil heart of social security, we must reexamine some important concepts.

As we have seen, the fatal flaw of social security is its operation on a pay-as-you-go basis, and it is this fatal flaw that leads to the social insurance paradox. Because the program is operated on a pay-as-you-go basis, the rate of return under the program is determined by the rate of growth in real wages and rate of growth in population. Somehow this rate of return can be paid, even though the pay-as-you-go system does nothing to increase total output. How can this be? The resolution of this paradox will uncover the real reason why we have the social security program.

As we saw, the rate of return from a pay-as-you-go system comes not from increased output but from increased taxes. At constant tax rates, as wages and population grow total tax collections in absolute terms increase and thus greater benefits can be paid out. These greater benefits embody an implicit return to current retirees on their tax dollars equal to the rate of increase in wages and the rate of increase in population. Why is the population willing to pay these continuing increases in absolute taxes?

When social insurance is first imposed, the current retired generation gets together with the current working generation, constituting all current voters, and they make a deal. The retired generation borrows from the working generation and puts the next working generation up as collateral. The funds for the benefits of the current retirees are borrowed from current workers, but the liability for this debt, the responsibility for paying it back, is imposed on the next working generation. The debt is not paid back by current retirees. The next working generation cannot vote on this issue because they are either too young or unborn. Yet they come into the world bearing the burden of a public debt that won't come due until the current retired generation is gone, the current working generation is retired, and the next working generation becomes the current working generation. When the program begins current voters borrow from themselves, but the debt does not become due until they are all gone or retired, and those who could not vote to incur the debt are left with it.

This public debt is tantamount to the taxation of future generations. The burden of this debt must be met out of the tax funds of these future generations. It is the agreement to vote to tax these future generations that leads the current working generation to agree to lend funds to the current retired generation for their benefits when the system is first imposed. The tax rates imposed on these future generations are determined by the amount of liabilities incurred by the first retired generation when they borrow their benefits from the first working generation. The amount of these liabilities and hence future tax rates are determined before these future generations can vote. When a pay-as-you-go program like social security is begun, current voting generations are in effect voting to tax future generations. This is not all just theory. The Social Security Administration is today making seventy-five-year projections of the tax rates necessary to finance the benefits promised to current workers. These taxes will, of course, be paid by those who cannot yet vote because only they will be working when these taxes must be paid.

The first generation gets free benefits, leaving future generations to foot the bill. When the next working generation becomes the current working generation, they face a huge debt owed to the current retired generation. If they continue to participate in the program, they will lose the returns to the economy from capital investment noted in chapter 3 and the returns to themselves noted in chapter 4. They will also suffer all the other shortcomings of the pay-as-you-go system noted throughout the text. Yet they must pay back the liabilities owed to the current generation, who might otherwise suffer. Since they have to pay back these liabilities regardless of whether they continue the program, they decide to keep the program and vote to tax the next generation even more to finance even greater benefits to themselves.

When this generation retires and the next generation starts to work, they face the same dilemma. They would have been better off if the program had never been started, but now that it has they must meet their liabilities to the current retired generation. If they had to pay these liabilities as well as provide for their own retirements themselves they would be even worse off, so they vote to continue the program and tax future generations to support their retirement. Generation after generation, the program continues to operate in this way. Since each generation is faced with the liabilities to the previous generation that must be paid, it doesn't pay any single generation to liquidate the program. All future generations are not only made worse off, but far more worse off than the first generation is made well off.

The social insurance paradox can now be explained. The social security rate of return is paid by increased taxes rather than increased production. These increased taxes and the rate of return are the result of the current generation's voting to tax future generations to pay benefits to itself, and thus the social security rate of return can be paid even though production is not increased. This return is in fact an illusion because individuals are all still worse off by the full amount of the lost, increased production and lost returns that would be available in an invested program. All individuals are not getting more; some are merely being taxed to pay benefits to others. It is true that these current taxpayers later become beneficiaries, but that does not mean that all have more. Money is just being moved around from one group to another. Only the politicians benefit because they now become crucially important to all those who are financially dependent on them. Instead of all having more they all actually have less because they have lost the increased production from the invested program. Because all individuals do not really have more in a pay-as-you-go system, and because the social insurance rate of return is really just paid through increased taxation rather than increased production, the paradox is resolved. The realization that social security is merely a means by which the current generation taxes future generations provides the clue to the paradox.[12]

The solution of the social insurance paradox is also social security's dirty little secret — the real reason the program exists. The program

---

[12]The credit for solving the social insurance paradox belongs to Paul Samuelson, who, in raising the paradox in his 1958 article, explained it and essentially solved it.

is a means for the current generation to tax future generations. The initial generation votes for the program because it allows them to tax future generations and thereby pay free benefits to themselves. The first retired generation and a large part of the first working generation are made better off because they get benefits while paying little or nothing themselves in taxes. The future generations, however, are all made worse off because they are burdened with the liabilities of these benefits and locked into a pay-as-you-go system with all of its drawbacks and negative effects. Unlike the first generation, they cannot get free benefits for themselves through the program. Future generations do not vote, and therefore they cannot object to the taxation being imposed on them. In the first generation there will be enough votes to enact the program, even though no one would vote for the program if they had to participate in it throughout their whole lives. Because the first generation in a pay-as-you-go program gets free benefits but does not have any liabilities to pay, they are glad to vote to impose the program. As the system matures the free benefits disappear, and future generations are left in a pay-as-you-go straitjacket.

The solution of the social insurance paradox explains why we have the program even though there is no rational justification for it, and all future generations are made worse off by it. The real reason for the program is that it allows the initial generation that adopts it to tax future generations to pay free benefits to itself. These free benefits are simply a function of the pay-as-you-go system. When such a system is begun, huge tax increases are generated with nowhere to go because there are no accrued benefit obligations built on the basis of past tax payments. These tax revenues, however, are not to be saved and invested to pay the future benefits of current taxpayers, as in an invested system. They are therefore paid out to the first generation of retirees as free benefits. The fatal flaw of social security, its operation on a pay-as-you-go basis, is the real reason for its creation in the first place, as well as the real reason why it must ultimately meet its downfall.

The actual reason for the program's existence is hardly an attractive one. There certainly seems to be something immoral about taxing future generations who do not yet have voices, let alone votes, to object. Doing so is nothing more than taxation without representation.[13] Revolutions have been known to occur for similar transgres-

---

13Ultimately the program is not quite the same as taxation without representation but

sions. This immorality is especially brazen since the benefits to the first generation are bought at the cost of locking all future generations into a program that makes them more worse off than the first generation is made better off. Seen in this light, the first generation politicians who imposed the program seem less like statesmen and more like demagogues. The program seems less like a benevolent method of helping the elderly and more like a giant con game.

It is not surprising that the decision to tax future generations to provide benefits to current generations could lead to the imposition of a program that makes all future generations worse off than it makes the current generation better off. When the government is allowed to operate in this way, there is an externality in the political realm perfectly analogous to externalities in the marketplace. This externality arises because while current voting generations are receiving benefits they are not paying the costs, and those who will bear these costs do not yet have voices or votes to object. The true costs of the program will not be taken into account, and it is likely that the program will be instituted and expanded even though costs exceed benefits. This externality is likely to lead to political failure just as externalities in the marketplace lead to market failure.

This explanation of how the social security program began again illustrates how the program is like a Ponzi scheme or chain letter. When such devices are used, those who get into the system first make money quickly. That is one of the reasons why these schemes are illegal. Those who enter first are made better off by getting much more from those behind them than they paid to get the scheme started. They get these increased payments by fraudulently inducing larger and larger numbers of individuals to pay in, thus increasing the amount available to the system to pay benefits to the initial recipients, but the later entrants are not told the true nature of the program; its method of operation is not adequately explained. When

---

instead taxation with delayed representation. As we saw in chapter 5, future taxpayers have the option, when they become current taxpayers, to vote to renege on their benefit obligations and leave future retirees with sharply reduced benefits or no benefits at all. But as long as this option is perceived as unthinkable and the program is continued, it will be no different than the current generation voting to tax future generations. The option of voting to renege on benefit promises does not make the program any the less a taxation of future generations by current generations. All taxpayers have the option of voting against a tax when it is first imposed and, unless it passes unanimously, many will have exercised this option. Once the tax passes, all taxpayers have the option of voting to repeal or decrease the tax. But the existence of these options does not mean that these taxpayers are any the less taxed.

the number of individuals participating in the program can no longer increase, the participants can no longer receive more than they paid in. In fact, if individuals are not somehow induced to continue to pay into the program even though they will receive no benefits, those who have not yet received all the money back that they have previously paid in will never do so, and they will lose as the entire system collapses. This ultimate limitation is what is not explained to later entrants. It is covered up, and their participation is fraudulently induced. The entire scheme is a fraud perpetrated by the initial participants to rob later participants. The social security system is analogous to these schemes in virtually all important respects.

Fortunately, this explanation of the real reason behind the program's existence also provides us with a way to get out of it. We have seen that when the system is imposed the first generation is made better off, but all future generations are made worse off because the program is a grossly inefficient way of providing these benefits to the first generation, entailing all sorts of unnecessary costs. Similarly, once the system matures, it doesn't pay any single generation to end the program, even though all would be better off without it. The benefits to all future generations of ending the program would outweigh the costs to the current generation of doing so, just as the benefits to all future generations of never starting the program would outweigh the costs to the first generation of forgoing the program. Therefore the way to get out of the pay-as-you-go, lock-in effect without simply reneging on benefit promises is to adopt a reform proposal that will phase out the current system by compensating the present generation for the costs of ending the program out of the benefits of ending the program to future generations. This means that future generations will not be as well off as they would be if social security had never been started, but they will be better off than if the system were not phased out. The difficult question is whether enough of the benefits to future generations are currently realizable to be used to offset the costs to the current generation of ending the program. In chapter 11 we will conclude that they are.

Social security is often highly touted as a compact between generations. The current working generation pays benefits to the current retired generation in return for the promises of the next generation to care for it in its old age. Our discussion of the true nature of social security and the real reason we have it allows us to see the true nature of this compact. A compact implies consent between all parties to the agreement, but one wonders how there can be consent or agreement from generations who do not yet have voices. In this compact the future generations are not around to bargain for their side of the compact. Only the current generation is present. The current generation is on both sides of the bargaining table, as it were, representing future generations in negotiations with itself. It is not surprising that in this type of bargaining process the absent party comes out holding the short end of the stick. In the law, when a party is on both sides of the bargaining table, representing someone in negotiations with itself, the courts will scrutinize the contract for self-dealing — any unfair advantage taken by the party over his absent adversary. For example, a corporation president who hires himself at an exorbitant salary is guilty of self-dealing. The courts will void contracts where self-dealing is found because such contracts are simple fraud. The self-dealing party has represented to the absent party that it will represent the absent party's interests fairly, but then it does not.

The social security compact between generations is itself a contract corrupted by self-dealing. The first generation has taken unfair advantage of the absent generations. Under traditional principles of equity, therefore, the social security compact between the generations is unfair, immoral, fraudulent, and voidable.

Part Two
The Major Reform Proposals

10

Social Security and Reform

Many of the shortcomings of the social security program that we have discussed have been recognized by others. The growing realization that social security has serious defects has resulted in an ever-increasing list of reform proposals designed to remedy those defects. These reform proposals will be discussed in this chapter.

Numerous reforms have been advocated to deal with some of the problems we have discussed by juggling the tax and benefit formulas. While some of these reforms may be useful in alleviating some of these problems, they fail to solve the more fundamental and serious flaws of the program. Imaginative and courageous reform is called for, not cosmetics, and therefore this discussion will be limited to the fundamental reforms that have the potential to solve the deeper, more serious shortcomings of the program.

Brookings Institution Proposals

The conflict in objectives in the social security program was recognized by Joseph Pechman, Henry Aaron, and Michael Taussig in a study published in 1968 by the Brookings Institution entitled *Social Security: Perspectives for Reform*. The authors wrote:

> The basic dilemma in considering reform of the social security system is that the United States has attempted to solve two problems with one instrument — how to prevent destitution among the aged poor and how to assure to people, having adequate incomes before retirement, benefits that are related to their previous standard of living.[1]

[1]Joseph Pechman, Henry Aaron, and Michael Taussig, *Social Security: Perspectives for Reform* (Washington, D.C.: Brookings Institution, 1968), p. 115.

The authors advocate separating the two functions into different programs. Social security would continue to perform the insurance function with a wage-related benefit system. Retirement benefits would be paid strictly on the basis of how much each individual earned in the past. Most of the welfare elements discussed in chapter 2 would be absent. The welfare function would be transferred to a negative income tax system or a comprehensively reformed public assistance program. The authors also advocate abolishing the payroll tax and financing both programs entirely from general revenues.

The negative income tax or public assistance allowance would make up the difference between the income of all households and a minimum guaranteed annual income. The aged would be allowed to choose the benefits offered under either the welfare program or the insurance program, but they could not choose both.

The authors also recognize that the current program cannot be correctly characterized as being just like private insurance and that any such contention is deceptive and misleading. They write, "(W)hen the terminology of social security is stripped away and the structure of the system is examined, it becomes clear that the insurance analogy is no longer applicable to the system as it has developed."[2]

Yet having stripped away the insurance crust on social security, the authors overemphasize the welfare elements of the program. Their unrestrained support for all forms of welfare begins to engulf all of their reform proposals. They advocate financing even the strictly wage-related insurance portion of the program with general revenues, making it more like welfare for everybody rather than insurance. They uncritically and carelessly endorse financing this insurance element on a pay-as-you-go basis, failing to perceive the serious shortcomings in this method of financing. Finally, they passively accept simplistic rationales for this structure of the insurance program without advancing a convincing reason why the government should be paying so-called insurance benefits for everyone out of general revenues, especially when there is already supposed to be a welfare program to take care of the needs of the poor.

An even more advanced study of the program was published by the Brookings Institution in 1977: *The Future of Social Security* by Alicia Munnell. Munnell also recognizes the conflict between the welfare and insurance objectives of the program, and she also advo-

2Ibid., p. 68.

cates separating the functions into two separate programs. The welfare function would be shifted to a separate program, such as the recently enacted SSI program, to be financed from general revenues.

The insurance function would remain with the social security program. Retirement benefits would be strictly related to past wages without regard to any other factors. Since the payroll tax would continue to finance the program, the amount of benefits paid would depend solely on how much each beneficiary had paid into the system in the past. Most of the welfare elements of the program would be eliminated. Munnell advocates eliminating the progressive PIA formula in the calculation of benefits and phasing out the spouse's and dependent's benefits and the minimum benefit. Consistent with the insurance approach, she suggests liberalizing or eliminating the earnings test, exempting the earnings of those aged sixty-five and over from the payroll tax, and giving increased benefits for delayed retirement past age sixty-five to compensate for the years of missed benefits.

To help ease the tax burden and encourage later retirement, Munnell also discusses delaying the retirement age past sixty-five. This can be justified by the increased health and life expectancy of the aged and the desire of many to continue working past age sixty-five. The 1975 Social Security Advisory Council recommended the gradual extension of the retirement age to sixty-eight. The council suggested increasing the age by one month every six months beginning in the year 2005 and ending in 2023. This proposal would reduce the tax rate by 1.5 percentage points per year in the period from 2025 to 2058.

Munnell does not overemphasize the welfare aspects of social security as do Pechman, Aaron, and Taussig, nor does she advocate a guaranteed annual income for everyone as does the former study. Furthermore, she would keep payroll tax financing for the insurance portion of the program as opposed to the welfare portion. (General revenue financing of the insurance portion of the program is a complex question that will be discussed in further detail later in this chapter.)

Munnell still uncritically accepts simple rationales for the program and the validity of pay-as-you-go financing. Furthermore, both studies fail to solve many of the shortcomings of social security discussed in earlier chapters. Since both sets of reforms leave pay-as-you-go financing intact, the negative effects from this form of financing would remain. While the separation of the functions of social security into two separate programs would alleviate many of the inequities discussed in chapters 4 and 6, many would remain. These would stem largely from the fact that one set of benefit provisions, even if strictly wage related, will not suit the diverse and varied needs of all Americans. The political instabilities discussed in chapter 7 and the moral issues discussed in chapter 8 would also still remain important problems. By retaining pay-as-you-go financing, these reforms would not completely separate the welfare function from the insurance function of the program because this form of financing is one of the chief welfare elements of the program. Although the payment of welfare benefits through this element will cease as the program matures, as long as this method of financing is continued the negative effects from having pursued welfare objectives alongside insurance objectives will also continue. Thus these reforms by themselves would not solve all of the major problems of the program.

Nevertheless, separating the welfare and insurance functions of the program, as these authors advocate, would be a substantial improvement. It is the essential first step after which further reform can follow.

Price Indexing (The Hsiao Proposal)

In 1972 Congress amended the Social Security Act to allow benefits to increase with the rate of inflation. Unfortunately the formula included a mistake that increased benefits at twice the rate of inflation. Projected benefit levels and deficits exploded, creating a financial crisis. As the mistake became apparent, there was agreement that the benefit formula had to be changed, but there was some controversy over just how to do it.

Two alternative methods were proposed. One was called wage indexing. This alternative would raise benefits to be paid to a worker at the rate of growth in real wages while he was working. The other alternative, price indexing, would raise benefits by the rate of increase in prices, or the rate of inflation, while the worker was still working. The chief advocate of this alternative was William Hsiao, professor of economics at Harvard University, and it came to be known as the Hsiao Proposal. In the 1977 amendments Congress corrected the flawed 1972 formula and chose wage indexing over price indexing.

Although the public did not realize it at the time, the difference between these two alternatives is enormous in both monetary and philosophical terms because wages usually rise much faster than prices. Wages typically rise at the rate of increase in prices, plus the rate of increase in the productivity of labor, and therefore indexing benefits to wages will cause them to rise much faster than indexing them to prices. This difference is so significant that price indexing retains considerable support as a policy option for the future.

Some of the differences between the two options are shown in table 54. With wage indexing, taxes will have to rise to pay out promised benefits under the OASDI program from 10.9 % of taxable payroll in 1979 to 19 % in 2030 and 17.8 % in 2050. This is under the equivalent of the Alternative II economic assumptions of the Social Security Administration. Any difference between these projections and those discussed earlier is due to the fact that these projections were made in 1977 and the earlier projections were made in 1978 and 1979. Under price indexing, taxes would not have to increase at all over the next seventy years. Benefits under price indexing would be financed with taxes at 10.9 % of taxable payroll in 1979, actually falling to 10.6 % in 2010 before rising to 12.8 % in 2030 and falling again to 10.9 % in 2050.

With wage indexing, deficits at currently legislated tax rates begin to show up in the year 2000, reaching a critical level in 2020 at 4.3 % of taxable payroll. These deficits continue to increase to 6.6 % in 2030 before falling to 6.0 % in 2040 and 5.4 % in 2050. Wage indexing will require percentage point increases in the tax rate equal to these percentage points of deficit, on top of the tax rates already scheduled for these years by the 1977 amendments, which substantially increased these rates. With wage indexing, by 2030 taxes will have to almost double over 1980 levels and increase by 53 % over the rates currently scheduled for that year.

With price indexing, large surpluses begin in 1990, falling to more moderate levels through 2050 with one brief period of deficit. Taxes would not have to be increased above present levels at all, and currently legislated tax increases for the future could be repealed. Taxes from 1990 through 2050, except for one brief period, could actually be reduced below their currently legislated levels.

As table 54 shows, price indexing would devote a rather constant percentage of GNP to social security benefits. Wage indexing, however, would devote a constantly increasing percentage of GNP to these benefits. Wage-indexed OASDI benefits would increase from 4.5 % of GNP in 1979 to 7.8 % in 2030 and 7.3 % in 2050. Price indexed benefits would grow from 4.5 % in 1979 to 5.3 % in 2030 and fall to 4.5 % once again in 2050.

These differences are shown in dollar terms in table 55. Under wage indexing, social security OASDI benefits in constant 1980 dollars will double from $119.3 billion in 1980 to $254.8 billion in 2000 and double again to $509.8 billion in 2020. By 2050, wage-indexed benefits will reach almost $1 trillion in constant 1980 dollars. Price-indexed benefits, by contrast, will grow to $214.1 billion in 2000, $366.3 billion in 2020, and $581.9 billion by 2050 in constant 1980 dollars. Wage-indexed benefits will be 39 % higher than price-indexed benefits by 2020 and 63 % higher by 2050.

Deficits under the wage-indexed OASDI system in 1980 terms will total $35.8 billion in 2010, $131.3 billion in 2020, $239.9 billion in 2030, and $288.2 billion in 2050. Price indexing shows surpluses of $22.4 billion in 1990, $45.9 billion in 2010, and $80.1 billion in 2050.

An alternative way to look at the contrast between the two systems is to look at replacement ratios. A replacement ratio is the amount of retirement benefits expressed as a percentage of the recipient's wages in the year before retirement. Table 56 shows replacement ratios of before-tax incomes for workers with low incomes, average incomes, and high incomes under both systems. Workers are assumed to be single at age sixty-five. Under wage indexing, these replacement ratios remain at constant levels over time, stabilizing at 55 % for low-income workers, 42 % for average-income workers, and 28 % for high-income workers. Under price indexing, these replacement ratios decline steadily. For low-income workers, they fall from 63 % in 1979 to 33 % in 2055, for average-income workers they fall from 48 % to 22 % over the same period, and for high-income workers they fall from 35 % to 17 %.

Table 57 shows replacement ratios of after-tax income. Considering single workers under wage indexing, replacement ratios of after-tax income stabilize at 69 % for low-income workers, 57 % for average-income workers, and 47 % for high-income workers. Under price indexing, these same replacement ratios fall to 39 %, 34 %, and 32 % for the same workers. For a worker with a spouse, replacement ratios of after-tax income under wage indexing stabilize at 101 %, 85 %, and 67 % for these three types of workers. Under price indexing these numbers fall to 58 %, 50 %, and 46 %.

Thus, price indexing keeps benefits at a stable level of taxable payroll and GNP, eliminates all projected deficits, and requires no tax increases. Benefits will still increase over time, but at a rate parallel to GNP and taxable payroll. Replacement ratios will, however, decline over time.

Wage indexing, on the other hand, will sharply increase benefits relative to taxable payroll and GNP. Huge deficits will appear in the future amounting to $200 to $300 billion in constant 1980 dollars. Wage indexing will, therefore, require huge tax increases. Under wage indexing, however, replacement ratios will remain constant over time.

To understand more clearly the difference between wage indexing and price indexing we must focus on the nature of replacement ratios and why they fall under price indexing. These ratios fall under price indexing not because benefits are falling but because wage incomes are rising even faster than benefits. Wages are increasing at the rate of increase in prices plus the rate of real increase in the productivity of labor, whereas benefits are increasing only at the rate of increase in prices. Thus under price indexing benefits are still increasing in nominal terms and are constant in real terms.

Focusing solely on replacement ratios as the correct measure of the adequacy of each of the two alternative methods of financing can lead one to erroneously view price indexing as a cut in benefits when it is really a maintenance of benefits at current levels in real terms. It can also lead one to erroneously view wage indexing as a maintenance of current benefit levels when it is in reality a sharp increase in benefits in both nominal and real terms. This is shown by the fact that wage indexing sharply increases benefits relative to GNP and taxable payroll, while price indexing will take a constant share of these two economic benchmarks. The choice between price indexing and wage indexing is therefore not a choice between cutting and maintaining benefits but between maintaining benefits and increasing benefits enormously.

It should also be recognized that with the significantly higher incomes of the next century, high replacement ratios will not be necessary to provide an adequate floor of income protection for retired workers. Those who will retire in 2025 are entering the work force today. Under present law, which provides for wage indexing, a worker who has earned the maximum taxable income all his life and who retires in 2025 will receive an annual pension under social security of $100,252 in nominal terms. This pension will increase annually with the rate of inflation. An average-income worker who retires in that same year will receive a pension of $63,987 in nominal terms. If these workers have spouses, their pensions will increase to $150,378 for the maximum-income worker and $95,980 for the average-income worker. In constant 1980 dollars the single maximum-income worker will receive $16,818 and the average-income worker will receive $10,735. If they have spouses, the maximum-income worker will receive $25,227 and the average-income worker will receive $16,103.

Furthermore, the average worker in these examples provided by the Social Security Administration is actually at an income level below that of the average-income worker in the economy.[3] The average-income level used in these projections is for the average worker in employment covered by social security, which includes part-time and secondary workers such as high school students and others who are not the primary earners in their families and whose wages tend to be low. In 1977 the average wage in social security covered employment was $9,779, while the average income for families with one earner was $13,148. The second figure more closely approximates the average income of a full-time worker who is a regular participant in the economy and who is responsible for the support of a family. Extrapolations based on this figure indicate that the average-income worker retiring in 2025 will receive social security retirement benefits of $73,354 in nominal terms and $12,306 in constant 1980 dollars. If he has a spouse these figures will be $110,031 in nominal terms and $18,459 in 1980 terms. It should also be remembered that a worker earning the maximum income, though he may be relatively well-off, is hardly rich. In 1980 the maximum taxable income will be $25,900.

Although benefits under price indexing will be lower they will clearly be far from inadequate as a floor for old-age protection. A single maximum-income worker retiring in 2025 will receive $71,608 in nominal terms under price indexing. The average worker will receive $42,657 and heads of one-earner families will receive $50,135. With spouses these workers would receive $107,412, $63,986, and $72,503 respectively. In constant 1980 dollars, single workers with maximum incomes will receive $12,013, those with average incomes will receive $7,157, and the average head of a one-earner family will receive $8,411. For the same workers with spouses, these figures will be $18,020, $10,736, and $12,617.

We should also consider the replacement ratio necessary to main-

[3]Steven F. McKay, Social Security Administration, August 10, 1978.

tain preretirement standards of living during retirement. A retiree needs less income to maintain the same standard of living as younger working people. Because he is not working, he has fewer expenses for clothing, transportation, food away from home and other work-related items. The children of most retirees have now grown up and are self-supporting. Elderly people have already acquired most of the necessary household appliances and other personal items for everyday living. Social security and many other types of pension incomes are not taxed. The elderly also receive many in-kind benefits through government programs. Finally, they can consume their savings slowly over time, rather than accumulate funds as they must during their working years. Because of these and other reduced expenses, retired elderly people need only 60–65 % of their preretirement, before-tax incomes or 70–75 % of their preretirement, after-tax incomes to maintain the same standard of living as they had when they were working. All retirement needs, therefore, can be met with replacement ratios in this range.

Table 57 indicates that under wage indexing for workers with spouses, low-income workers will be receiving 101 % of their preretirement, after-tax incomes, average-income workers will be receiving 85 %, and maximum-income workers will be receiving 67 %. These benefits will therefore fulfill just about all retirement needs and allow workers to maintain the same standard of living as during their working years. Under price indexing, replacement ratios for workers entering the labor force today and retiring in 2020 will be 72 % for low-income workers, 58 % for average-income workers, and 51 % for maximum-income workers, assuming they all have spouses. Even these benefit levels will not require much supplementation to maintain former living standards. By 2050, these replacement ratios will have fallen to 58 % for low-income workers, 50 % for average-income workers, and 46 % for high-income workers, all with spouses. Given the much higher incomes of 2050, these replacement ratios will provide retirement incomes that will buy much, much more than the basic necessities of life. The annual benefits in dollar terms under these replacement ratios will be even higher than the benefits described above for the year 2025. These 2050 replacement ratios for price indexing will still be high for a program that is supposed to provide a basic floor of old-age income.

It is clear that benefits under both wage indexing and price indexing will be more than adequate as a floor of income protection for the aged. In fact, wage indexing will provide workers with virtually all the retirement income necessary to maintain the same living standards as they had when they were working. The real issue in choosing between wage indexing and price indexing, therefore, is whether social security should provide all old-age income or a basic floor of protection.

Viewed in this manner, wage indexing is clearly a sharp departure from the original intent of the program, which, as we saw in chapter 2, was to provide a basic floor of income protection in old age, allowing individuals to build additional protection through alternative means to the extent they desired. The original purpose was to ensure that individuals would have a basic floor of income in old age that would keep them from destitution, misery, and want. The program was never intended to provide all old-age income.

This original purpose would clearly be served by price indexing, which would provide annual retirement incomes for most young workers today of between $11,000 and $18,000 in 1980 dollars, assuming they retire with spouses. The replacement ratios even under price indexing, ranging from 51% to 72% for workers with spouses, would leave little room for supplementation through private alternatives before preretirement living standards were attained. Wage indexing, with retirement incomes between $16,000 and $25,000 for most of today's young workers who will retire with spouses, goes far beyond this purpose and seeks to provide all retirement income through social security. Its replacement ratios, ranging from 65% to 101% for workers with spouses, would provide many if not most workers with retirement living standards even greater than they enjoyed while working, all without a penny of supplementation through private alternatives.

It should be noted that if social security consistently follows the original intent of providing only a basic floor of old-age income, replacement ratios will fall over time because the basic necessities of life can be acquired with a certain amount of real income. As real incomes in the economy continue to grow, the ratio of this certain amount to these growing incomes will fall. If social security benefits in general aim to provide this minimum amount, replacement ratios will also fall, but if the program is only supposed to provide a basic floor of old-age income there is nothing wrong with this decline in replacement ratios.

Even if a change in the original intent of the program were desirable, it should be made only after public scrutiny and debate and careful consideration of the full implications of the change. It should not be made by a technical adjustment in the benefit formula when the general public is not aware of the full implications of the issue and poorly understands the quirks of the benefit computation. The decision in 1977 in favor of wage indexing was made by lobbyists and a few self-chosen experts, many with vested interests in the matter. In fact, it is doubtful that many of the lobbyists or congressmen really understood the issue. A change in the fundamental and original intent of the massive social security program should be made in the full light of day after complete and thorough public consideration.

Furthermore, it should be clear that such a change is not desirable. In chapters 3 and 4 we saw that high returns and productivity gains are available to the individual taxpayer and to society by using social security taxes to purchase private alternatives to social security that would invest these funds in productive assets in the private economy. Such investments would bring returns of 13%–15% in real terms, financed by increased production and output. If social security taxes had been invested through private alternatives in the past, we would have a GNP today over $400 billion higher. Although individuals would not receive the full 13%–15% return because of taxation, the returns left after taxation would still be much greater than social security offers. Furthermore, individuals would still benefit from the full 13%–15% because the remainder would go to defray their tax bills and provide them with the government goods and services that the political process has chosen. If they decide they do not want these goods and services, they can receive the full 13%–15%. Our projections in chapter 4 showed that with the higher returns in private alternatives to social security, young individuals entering the work force today could retire with retirement funds of over one-half million for most families and over one million for many, in constant 1980 terms. Investments in social security bring no increase in production and output for the economy and in the future will provide individuals with no more than an illusory 1%–2% return, if not less.

Now what sense can it possibly make to force individuals and society to forgo these much higher returns to finance huge pensions through the much lower yielding social security system, as wage indexing does? Why should young workers starting their careers be forced to finance pensions as high as $25,000 per year and more in real terms through the inefficient social security program, losing the much greater returns available in private, productive assets? With these greater returns, individuals could either receive vastly greater benefits in retirement or they could sharply reduce their current tax payments and still enjoy the same retirement incomes they are currently promised under social security. One can understand, perhaps, a desire to require individuals to invest enough in social security to ensure that they will avoid poverty and misery in old age, but once this is achieved, what conceivable reason could there be for requiring them to finance all of their retirement incomes through the inferior social security system? It should be clear that the wage indexing alternative is unreasonable and its enactment in the 1977 amendments as the method for indexing social security benefits was as big a mistake as the original indexing error in the 1972 amendments.

This conclusion is reinforced when one focuses again on the crushing taxes required to finance wage indexing. In 2025 the maximum social security tax will be close to $10,000 per year in 1980 constant dollars (see table 5), and this will not be enough to cover the currently promised wage-indexed benefits. The actual payment of these benefits will require tax rates well over 20% of taxable payroll and, including the HI program taxes, will have to be 25% to 33% of taxable payroll. Why should young people struggling to start families be crushed with these taxes to provide pensions of $25,000 per year and more to elderly couples? Can the country really afford to finance all retirement income through the grossly inefficient social security system?

Those who support wage indexing argue that it is necessary because replacement ratios must be maintained at constant levels. Otherwise, individuals who retire further in the future will receive lower replacement ratios even though they paid social security taxes all of their lives just as those who retired before them. They argue that individuals who pay into social security all of their lives should receive the same replacement ratios no matter when they retire. Why? Because it is relative incomes that are important to people, not absolute ones. Therefore, people are more concerned that they have the same relative incomes, or replacement ratios, as someone in the past, than that they have the same absolute incomes. This concern is met by wage indexing, which keeps replacement ratios and therefore relative incomes constant, rather than price indexing.

This is the chief argument for wage indexing, but it is so confused that it is embarrassing. Individuals who pay into social security all of their lives should receive what they have paid for — no more, no less. If they have paid enough to have a pension that gives them a replacement ratio as high as someone received in the past, then they have earned it and are entitled to it. If they have only paid enough to finance a pension that supplies a lower replacement ratio, then they are not entitled to the higher replacement ratio and have no valid claim to it, and it does not matter what is most important to them or what they are most concerned with. Everyone in the nation cannot be given more than they have paid for. The question then is how much should we force them to pay for, assuming that we should force them to pay for anything at all. Should we force them to pay for a minimum floor of income and allow them to supplement this through higher yielding alternatives? Or should we force them to pay more so that they can have the same replacement ratio as in the past? Given the inefficient low yields of social security, it is clear that there is no excuse for forcing everyone to pay so much into social security that replacement ratios will never decline and real benefit levels will continue to increase with economic growth.

Another argument for wage indexing is that price indexing constitutes a radical deliberalization of benefits because under price indexing replacement ratios fall. This argument is at least as confused as the first one. As we have noted, declining replacement ratios under price indexing do not mean that benefits are falling or becoming deliberalized. Instead, they are being held constant in real terms and actually increasing in nominal terms. Those who advance this argument are falling prey to the potential confusion, noted earlier, that may arise from focusing solely on replacement ratios. Such an exclusive focus can lead to the erroneous belief that price indexing constitutes a cut in benefits, and wage indexing is a maintenance of benefits at current levels. This is the implicit view of those who suggest that price indexing is a deliberalization of benefits, but as we have seen, this is totally fallacious. In reality, price indexing is a maintenance of benefits at current levels, and wage indexing is a massive increase in benefits requiring massive future tax increases.

It seems that even if no further reform steps were taken, replacing the current wage-indexed system with a price-indexed system would be extremely beneficial in and of itself. It would remove some of the cost pressures on the program and allow future tax increases to be avoided. It would reaffirm the original intent of the program. It would allow individuals to take advantage of higher yielding private investment alternatives to the benefit of themselves and the economy. Finally, it would allow individuals a tiny bit of liberty in controlling their own lives and their own hard-earned incomes.

In addition, this reform would be a useful step on the road to further reform. It would make future moves to privatize or fund the pay-as-you-go insurance system easier because there would be fewer current liabilities to pay off before the shift could be made. It would be a way of winding down the huge outstanding unfunded liability of the program, a liability that stands in the way of serious, fundamental, and much-needed reform.

General-Revenue Financing

Because of the extreme financing difficulties faced by the social security program in recent years and those predicted for the future and because of the regressivity of the payroll tax, many have proposed funding all or part of the program with funds from general revenues rather than the payroll tax. This would shift the social security tax burden onto the more progressive elements of the federal tax structure such as the individual income tax and the corporate income tax.

One of the foremost advocates of this reform is Democratic congressman James Burke of Massachusetts, chairman of the Social Security Subcommittee of the House Ways and Means Committee. He advocates funding social security one-third from general revenues, one-third from the employer share of the payroll tax, and one-third from the employee share. He contends that the original drafters of the bill expected that the program would eventually be financed in this way.

A method of funding the entire program from general revenues was advanced by Pechman, Aaron, and Taussig in 1968.[4] Under this proposal, amounts deducted for the payroll tax would be considered amounts withheld for the income tax. The amount by which the payroll tax plus the regular withholding tax exceeded income tax liability at the end of the year would be returned to each taxpayer. The payroll tax would be integrated with the income tax, serving a withholding function. Social security benefits would therefore come completely from general revenues because the payroll tax would generate no revenues. An alternative method would be simply to abolish the payroll tax and fund social security directly from general revenues.

[4]Pechman, Aaron, and Taussig, *Social Security: Perspectives for Reform.*

Those who advance these proposals still support calculating social security benefits on the basis of past earnings so that those with higher earnings would receive higher benefits, even though they may not have paid more into the program than those receiving lower benefits.

To analyze this reform, one needs to focus on political factors such as the attitudes of voters toward the program and how these will be changed by general-revenue financing. There are two reasonable ways to look at this reform proposal on this basis.

From one point of view, this proposal has serious shortcomings. First, it is not consistent with the original intent of the program. As we saw in chapter 2, the drafting committee that wrote the original bill expected the program would eventually be financed partly from general revenues many years in the future. President Roosevelt, however, strongly objected to this feature of the original draft and refused to send it to Congress until the committee rewrote it to provide for a fully self-supporting system, financed entirely from the payroll tax without subsidy from general revenues. Congress passed the bill consistent with Roosevelt's intent. The original intent of those who passed the Social Security Act, President Roosevelt and the Congress, was that it be permanently self-supporting with all funds generated through the payroll tax and none through general revenues.

Second, this proposal has the ring of deception to it. Congressman Burke advocates that the program be financed one-third by the employee, one-third by the employer, and one-third by the government. But who, we must ask, pays the government's share? The intent behind this proposal seems to be to hide the real costs of the program, to make voters think they are getting something for nothing, to fool them into thinking they are getting benefits paid for by someone else.

If the real costs of the program are hidden through general-revenue financing, voters may be led to support higher benefits and a greater expansion of the program than if they were aware of the full costs. This would be especially true if they continue to perceive their benefits as earned, even though they are not paying for them directly. Political pressures to increase benefits and further raid the general treasury could become dominant, resulting in a heavy general tax burden to finance runaway benefit promises. If Congress could increase benefits without increasing payroll taxes, a significant restraint imposing fiscal responsibility would be removed, and

Congress might legislate ever higher social security benefits financed from general revenues.

Hiding the true costs of the program may also make it more difficult for people to see the superior private investment alternatives to social security and what they are really losing by forgoing these alternatives. If people believe they are paying only two-thirds of the actual cost of the program, they will believe their returns are actually higher than they really are and fail to realize that private investment alternatives would provide them with a greater return on what they are really paying. Financing through general revenues does not change the pay-as-you-go nature of the program. It merely changes the distribution of the burden of the costs. Individuals and society are still losing the higher returns from the invested alternatives. Paying retirement benefits from general revenues to everyone and thereby allowing them to forgo making productive investments on their own is analogous to paying welfare benefits to everyone and thereby allowing them to forgo working, with the same detrimental effects on the nation's output and well-being.

Financing social security through general revenues is a form of welfare. Why should everyone be entitled to payments from the general treasury once they pass a certain age regardless of whether they are rich or poor or whether they need the money or not? This proposal is like George McGovern's 1972 presidential campaign proposal to grant $1,000 to everyone. The voters quite rightly viewed this suggestion as nonsense and rejected him resoundingly. Financing social security through general revenues is not any better.

Finally, if we are going to continue the concept of social security benefits based on earned entitlement, rather than need, and if we are going to strengthen the link between earnings and benefits, so that benefits received are to equal a fair return on past payments into the system, then the payroll tax is the correct way to finance the system. General-revenue financing would make it impossible to pay benefits based on past payments into the program. There would be no way to determine how much was paid for social security, and the amounts paid in taxes would bear no relation to what the person is to receive in benefits. To build a strong link between taxes and benefits, a payroll tax is necessary. With such a tax the amount each individual had paid into the program would be clear, and the amount of benefits each individual was to receive could be calculated on the basis of these tax payments. Unlike general-revenue taxes, the level of payroll taxes would be set at the level necessary to finance the desired amount of benefits. The level of general-revenue taxation is set independently of the amount of social security benefits desired.

Furthermore, if the entitlement to social security is to be earned, then all must pay the same price for what they get. One can earn a right to something only by paying its true cost. Otherwise he is receiving welfare, which is paid on the basis of charity, not earned entitlement. Since there is only one price or cost for a good or service, all would have to be paying that same price to be truly earning their benefits. This is what the payroll tax does: It charges everyone the same price for social security protection. It is true that this means that those with lower incomes pay a higher percentage of their incomes for this protection than those with higher incomes, but the same is true for the purchase of all goods or services. When individuals are purchasing a good or service, like insurance, everyone should in fairness be charged the same price. Individuals who walk into a supermarket should not be charged higher prices for their groceries because they have earned higher incomes. This would constitute an unfair penalty for success. It would deny individuals who had earned or produced higher incomes the benefits of their labor. It would in effect confiscate their higher incomes.

It is only fair that each person receive back in benefits what he paid into the program, plus a fair return on his tax money. Those who have paid more into the program should receive more in benefits. Individuals should not be charged a higher price for the same benefits, as would occur with general-revenue financing. To do so would mean that some people would not receive a fair return on their tax dollars. All would not receive the same return, and therefore all would not be treated equally.

If social security is to be an insurance program, therefore, with earned entitlements to benefits and with the amount of benefits based on how much was paid into the program in the past, the payroll tax is the only sensible way to finance the program. If social security is to provide a good or service, rather than welfare, it should charge each individual the same price for that protection, as it would do with the payroll tax.

Thus if general-revenue financing were to be the only reform of the program, it would be inappropriate. By itself, general-revenue financing is a bad idea. However, there is another way of looking at this proposal that suggests it would inevitably lead to additional desirable reforms and therefore would not be the only reform of the program.

In this view, general-revenue financing would destroy the concept of earned entitlement that currently underlies social security benefits. Since the public would realize that they are not paying directly for their benefits, they would not feel that anyone has really earned them or is really entitled to them. They would instead begin to see social security as one big welfare program financed by general revenues.

It is likely, therefore, that if social security is financed by general revenues there would be political pressure to stop payments to the elderly rich. Why should general revenues be used to give benefit payments to the wealthy? Political pressure is also likely to develop to impose a means test on the receipt of benefits so that benefits will go only to the elderly who are truly in need. Why should working people already struggling under the general tax burden be forced to pay general revenue benefits to those who are not in need? Why should we forgo other programs to use general revenues to pay such unnecessary benefits? General-revenue financing is likely to turn social security into another welfare program like SSI. Its insurance function would be completely eliminated and in effect privatized, which would achieve the ultimate ideal reform of the program.

With the link between taxes and benefits broken, the insurance analogy destroyed, and the earned entitlement concept eliminated, the true costs of the program may become apparent rather than hidden. As long as people think that their social security taxes are purchasing a good or service for them directly and individually, such as insurance, they will not perceive them as taxes at all. Instead of believing that their income has been reduced, as by taxes, they will believe only that the form of their income has been changed. Instead of receiving all cash, they will have received part cash and part insurance, which constitutes income in kind. As Carl Patton writes in *The Crisis in Social Security*, "Buying insurance after all does not reduce a person's wealth, it merely changes the form of wealth, substituting future benefit for present benefit, like putting money in the bank."[5]

As long as social security is perceived in this way, when benefits are increased the recipients will see a gain and support the move. When taxes are increased to finance these benefit increases, taxpayers will see no cost. They will merely think that they are becom-

5Institute for Contemporary Studies, *The Crisis in Social Security* (San Francisco: Institute for Contemporary Studies, 1977), p. 155.

ing entitled to more future benefits. As a result, when benefits and taxes are raised, the benefits are clearly perceivable but the costs are hidden. No opposition arises, therefore, to increases in benefits. As Patton writes, "Because people perceive payroll taxes as equivalent to insurance premiums, they believe that unlike all other public expenditures, social security spending is free — costless to taxpayers."[6]

With the payroll tax gone, this illusion of costless financing would also disappear. The cost of social security benefits would become immediately apparent. Voters would no longer believe that the taxes to finance their benefits are gaining them something directly in return, and people would become less willing to pay the tax. Direct opposition to increased benefits and taxes would develop.

Without the payroll tax, social security would have to compete for general revenues just like any other government program. Its true costs would become apparent in the heat of political controversy. If it still won out over other financing proposals, it would be taking revenues from these other programs, and the result would be cuts in other forms of government spending. The ultimate effect of abolishing the payroll tax may then be to take one revenue source away from the government, resulting in lower total taxes and government expenditures.

The possibility of the government spending less is why Milton Friedman supports general-revenue financing for social security and opposes the payroll tax, and it is also why many who support social security believe that the payroll tax must be kept despite its regressivity. The Social Security Administration also steadfastly supports payroll tax financing for this reason.

If reduced expenditures were the actual result of general-revenue financing, then this reform would be quite positive. It would have split the welfare function of social security from the insurance function and in effect privatized the latter by abolishing it as a government function, thus eliminating all of the shortcomings of the program that we have discussed. Social security would become just another welfare program with benefits limited to the poor, and it might then eventually be overhauled as part of a general welfare reform.

Whether or not general-revenue financing is a worthy reform depends on one's evaluation of how it will affect the political perceptions and attitudes of voters. If it helps them to see the true nature of

[6]Ibid.

social security and this perception leads them to reform it appropriately, then it would be an extremely positive reform. If it hides the true nature and costs of the program and blocks needed reform, it would be negative. Although evaluation of these political factors is tricky, it appears that those who believe that general-revenue financing would be only the first step in an inevitable reform of the program are the most persuasive. If that is so, then any cut in payroll taxes with a shift to general-revenue financing should be supported.

The Feldstein Proposals

As we saw in chapter 3, Martin Feldstein, professor of economics at Harvard University and head of the National Bureau of Economic Research, has demonstrated that pay-as-you-go financing has many serious, negative effects on the economy. To solve these problems, Feldstein suggests that social security taxes be saved and invested by the government in a trust fund. The assets and accumulated earned interest in this fund would then finance the future benefits of today's taxpayers. The program would then be run as most people believe it is actually run and as it was originally intended to be. Feldstein advocates investing the trust fund assets in outstanding government bonds.

Feldstein's proposal would require immediate and substantial tax increases because tax revenues would have to be high enough to pay current benefits as well as accumulate enough in the trust fund to pay for the future retirement of current workers. In the long run, however, taxes would be much lower because with the much higher-yielding investments in the trust fund the same retirement incomes as are promised now could be achieved with much lower tax rates.

Feldstein also advocates changing the current wage-indexing system to price indexing, as discussed above. He further advocates paying benefits only on the basis of past taxes paid into the program, with the welfare elements of the program transferred to SSI. He proposes the elimination of the earnings test and opposes general-revenue financing.[7]

---

[7]Feldstein has presented his reform proposals in numerous publications and articles. See Martin Feldstein, "Toward a Reform of Social Security" *The Public Interest,* Summer 1975; Martin Feldstein, "Facing the Social Security Crisis," *Harvard Institute of Economic Research,* Discussion Paper No. 492, July 1976; Martin Feldstein, "Social Insurance," *Harvard Institute of Economic Research,* Discussion Paper No. 477, May 1976; Martin Feldstein, "The Optimal Financing of Social Security," *Harvard In-*

Feldstein suggested a somewhat different approach toward trust fund financing in a 1974 paper.[8] Under this proposal, Feldstein recommended accumulating a fund large enough to pay all future benefits forever, instead of one merely large enough to pay currently earned benefits to current workers and recipients. After the accumulation of such a fund, the payroll tax could be abolished instead of having workers continue to pay into the program to finance their benefits. Feldstein calculated that in 1971 a trust fund of $600 billion would have been sufficient to finance all future social security benefits forever out of the before-tax returns on its investments. Since net income to the fund would equal only the after-tax return, Feldstein recommended an annual transfer to the fund from general revenues equal to the additional tax revenue generated by the fund's investments.

To accumulate this fund, Feldstein advocated an immediate increase in tax rates from 10% to between 20% to 25% for five or six years. At the time of his study this increase would have created a fund sufficiently large to allow the abolition of the payroll tax at the end of this period. Feldstein noted that the fund could instead be accumulated more slowly over time, if that method were deemed preferable. But by his calculations, present welfare would be increased the most by accumulating the fund at this rapid rate.

Whether a fund large enough to pay all future benefits was accumulated or one large enough to pay only currently earned benefits, Feldstein's reforms would either way be a substantial improvement over the current system. The extra investment would increase capital spending and national income, with the country benefiting from the increased productivity of the higher-yielding invested system. The distorting effects of the payroll tax on the labor supply would also be eliminated because workers would perceive the tax as part of their incomes, or, if a large enough fund were accumulated, the tax would be abolished. The distorting effects of the earnings test on the labor supply would also be eliminated. The individual would receive the higher returns available from the invest-

stitute of Economic Research, Discussion Paper No. 388, 1974; Martin Feldstein, "Strengthening Social Security," testimony to the Subcommittee on Social Security, Ways and Means Committee, House of Representatives, 15 May 1977; Martin Feldstein, Summary of Testimony on Social Security, Subcommittee on Fiscal Policy, Joint Economic Committee, 27 May 1976.

[8] Martin Feldstein, "The Optimal Financing of Social Security," *Harvard Institute of Economic Research*, Discussion Paper No. 388, 1974.

ment alternatives to pay-as-you-go financing, as discussed in chapter 4. The existence of a true trust fund would solve the bankruptcy problem discussed in chapter 5 by guaranteeing future benefits. Many of the problems concerning minorities discussed in chapter 6 would also be solved.

One possible objection to Feldstein's proposal is that accumulating such a large fund would lower the interest rate so greatly that the return on the invested funds would not be worthwhile, but Feldstein has already made the calculations necessary to counter this objection. He has found that a fund of the necessary size would reduce the real rate of return by less than two percentage points, making the invested system still far superior to a pay-as-you-go system.[9] His calculation of the necessary trust fund to finance future benefits forever without further taxation was based on this lower interest rate.

Another objection to Feldstein's trust fund proposal is that a social security surplus would produce excess savings and cause a recession or depression. This objection is based on Keynesian macroeconomic theory, which contends that a high level of demand is necessary to maintain national income and economic growth and that savings may decrease this demand, causing declines in income and growth. To accept this argument one has to accept the underlying Keynesian analysis, which has seemed more and more inadequate to explain modern economic events. Furthermore, even on Keynesian grounds, savings do not reduce demand as long as they are invested. Himself a Keynesian, Feldstein is not deterred by this argument. He writes:

> These concerns have inappropriately been carried from the Great Depression into the present decade. Now the capital market would have no difficulty in adjusting to an increasing rate of savings. With more capital available for investment, the cost of capital would fall; firms would introduce more capital intensive techniques of production, and would provide more good jobs in capital intensive industries. There is no reason why the United States cannot absorb savings at the same high rate that other developed countries can.[10]

Another objection is that holding the trust fund assets in government bonds would not add to real capital accumulation because the

[9]Ibid., pp. 26–29. See also, Martin Feldstein, "National Saving in the United States," *Harvard Institute of Economic Research*, Discussion Paper No. 506, October 1976, pp. 31–32.

[10]Martin Feldstein, "Toward a Reform of Social Security," *The Public Interest*, Summer 1975, p. 90.

government bonds do not represent an investment in real productive assets. Instead, the money invested in the bonds is used by the government for current expenditures. The interest on the bonds is not earned through increased production but is paid instead by increased general-revenue taxes in the future, which is very much like the current pay-as-you-go system. Investing the trust fund assets in government bonds has been likened to an individual spending money and claiming it is really invested in an IOU to himself.

Feldstein argues, however, that this objection is valid only if the trust fund is invested in newly created government bonds, but not if it is invested in outstanding government bonds. In the latter case the investment in such bonds displaces private funds invested in these bonds which would then be invested in private productive capital assets. Investment in productive assets would increase by the total amount of the investment in government bonds. Furthermore, the interest payments on these bonds would then be paid to the social security system rather than private holders of the bonds. Taxation would not have to be increased to meet the obligations of the bonds, and the interest would be earned in the same way that it would be earned by private holders of these bonds.

Although these objections to Feldstein's proposal may not be valid, there are nevertheless some serious problems with it, the most important of which is that it would give the government widespread ownership or control over large portions of the American economy. To meet this objection, Feldstein advocates investing the funds in outstanding government bonds. Yet there may not be enough outstanding bonds available to fully finance the fund. Even if the government purchased only a substantial portion of these bonds, the government's power to control the money supply would be seriously hampered.[11] The money supply is currently controlled through the buying and selling of government bonds by the Federal Reserve Board. If all or most of these bonds were already owned by the government, this method of control would be seriously curtailed or eliminated altogether. While many might consider this to be a very beneficial development, it is doubtful that it would be a politically viable option. Feldstein's proposal would therefore inevitably result in substantial investment by the government in the private economy.

[11]Alicia H. Munnell, *The Future of Social Security* (Washington D.C.: Brookings Institution, 1977), p. 131.

To the extent that the trust fund's investments were made outside of government bonds, these investments would become highly politicized, with politicians or other groups seeking to use the financial power behind these investments to reward or punish various other groups and individuals. This would be a serious problem even if the trust fund were limited to nonequity investments that would not involve management or ownership control. Labor unions, for example, might bring political pressure to use this financial power to punish recalcitrant employers and reward compliant ones. Civil rights groups might demand that this power be used to impose further affirmative action plans on firms and employers and to give special aid to minority enterprises. Legislative logrolling may lead these investments to be made on an inefficient political basis as individual legislators seek to gain additional funds for their districts. Conceivably the fund's investments could be used to award supporters of powerful politicians.

The fund's investments are also likely to be used as the basis for substantial government regulation of business and industry. As experience with other government programs should teach, government money never comes without strings attached. The trust fund's investments might be used to impose new labor or employment policies on firms and employers. They might be used to regulate pricing policies, especially as part of an antiinflation strategy. They might also be used to regulate the investment and expansion policies of private companies. In short, trust fund investments in the private economy would give the government a new and powerful means of imposing new thickets of regulation on the private economy.

Feldstein's proposal also does not solve all of the problems with the program. One of the most important of these is that the government's operation of a social security trust fund would still leave the program subject to all of the political instabilities noted in chapter 7. What would stop politicians from raiding the trust fund as they did in the past to hand out free benefits? It seems that the temptation to do so would be inevitable because politicians could buy votes in the short run and the negative consequences would not appear until years after they had gone. It would seem that history has shown that the government cannot be trusted to maintain such a fund.

Politicians would also still be able to abuse the program in other ways to advance their own short-term political interests. Powerful special interest groups could also still use their power to gain special privileges in the program for themselves at the expense of others. Or these groups may seek ideological gains by commandeering the trust fund to serve philosophical interests. They might advocate that the trust fund be used to finance new welfare benefits, to nationalize certain industries, or to put a man on Mars. Individuals would also still have to assert their needs and preferences and their desires for change through the political process. Government officials would still lack the incentives to structure and change the program to serve the public's needs adequately. As a result, the program is again likely to be poorly structured to the needs of taxpayers and beneficiaries and to be rigid and inflexible to change.

Furthermore, Feldstein's proposal would not do anything about solving the need for individually tailored insurance and investment plans to match the widely varying needs and preferences of individual Americans. With the government running the program there would still be one particular plan of insurance protection imposed on everyone, single or married, with children or not, rich or poor, black or white. Yet, as we have seen in earlier chapters, no one plan of insurance protection can adequately satisfy the diverse needs and preferences of all Americans. The result is that many Americans, particularly politically less powerful groups such as minorities and those who follow alternative lifestyles, will find that the plan of insurance of protection they are forced to accept is poorly suited to their actual circumstances and characteristics.

Finally, Feldstein's proposal still remains subject to the moral objections expressed in chapter 8. His plan is still compulsory and based on the use of force. It would still substantially restrict the liberty of American citizens, who would lose control over their own lives and a substantial portion of their own incomes.

These objections apply to both variants of the Feldstein proposal described above, and there are two additional objections to the proposal to accumulate a trust fund large enough to pay all benefits for all time. The first is that this would impose on the current generation the entire burden of financing all benefits forever. There seems to be no reason why this generation should have to bear this heavy burden, and to require them to do so seems extremely unfair.

Second, once this fund was accumulated, on what basis would benefits be paid out? Such benefit payments would certainly not be based on past contributions into the system because future generations would not be making such contributions. Benefit payments could conceivably be based on past earnings, but these payments would not be earned by the recipients in the sense that they have been paid for. The future recipients of these benefits would not have paid anything for them and therefore these benefits would simply constitute pure welfare. Why should the current generation be taxed to pay welfare to all future generations? Why should welfare, free benefits, be paid to those who are not in need or poor? It would seem then that the accumulation of such a fund would lead to inevitable pressures to impose a means test and limit payments to the poor and needy, as with general-revenue financing. The rest of the fund might well be used to follow other national purposes, such as further alleviating poverty, improving national defense, or financing other social projects. If this were the result, the welfare function of the program would have been separated from the insurance function with a privatization of the latter, but this method seems a rather roundabout way of achieving that result.

While Feldstein's proposal would substantially improve the current system, therefore, there would still be many problems with it. These problems could almost all be solved by going one step further and privatizing the insurance function of the program. The investments would then be made by private institutions in the private sector rather than through the government. This privatization would avoid the many problems associated with Feldstein's proposal and eliminate many of the shortcomings of the program, which Feldstein's proposal will not. With the investments held in private hands, there would be no problem concerning where the government would invest the trust fund assets. There would be no concern over whether the Federal Reserve Board could continue to control the money supply and pursue monetary policy. There would also be no concern over whether the government could be trusted to maintain the trust funds. All the political instabilities and difficulties discussed in chapter 7 would be eliminated. Individuals would be allowed to tailor their insurance protection to their own individual needs and preferences by choosing from a diverse and varied mixture of options offered in the private market. Competition in the marketplace might lead to the development of new options or the improvement of existing ones. Privatization would also eliminate much of the compulsion and coercion discussed in chapter 8. Although individuals would still be required to do some saving, they would be free to choose their own plans and exercise their own preferences. Individual liberty would therefore be increased.

If it is desirable to shift from the pay-as-you-go system of financing to an invested system, as Feldstein has demonstrated, then there is no reason not to go one step further and privatize the insurance function of the program. Even Feldstein admits that he would have no objection to such a privatized system where all individuals were required to invest a certain portion of their incomes in government-approved, moderate-risk private investments and insurance purchases.[12] This would solve all the problems that Feldstein's solution would by shifting the program from a pay-as-you-go basis to an invested system. Yet it would also solve most of the rest of the problems of the program while not entailing any of the additional problems which Feldstein's proposal raises. Once the superiority of the invested program over pay-as-you-go financing is established and the desirability of obtaining a trust fund is shown, there is no reason not to privatize the insurance function of the current pay-as-you-go program.

If such privatization is not immediately feasible for political reasons, Feldstein's proposal would nevertheless be a useful reform that would help to make such privatization easier in the future. The major difficulty in any privatization proposal is how to provide enough funding for future benefits while still paying current benefits or paying off the current liabilities of the program. Feldstein's proposal would eliminate this problem. Once social security is fully funded with a self-supporting trust fund, the current liabilities of the program will be paid off. Current benefit obligations will be funded and current taxpayers will have to worry only about providing for their own retirement benefits. It would then be easy to allow individuals who have made adequate alternative arrangements to drop out of the program. If some individuals opted out of the fully-funded system, the program would not go bankrupt. Because each individual would be paying his own way, the program could continue no matter how many dropped out. The adoption of Feldstein's proposal would make it much easier to eventually privatize the system or make it voluntary.

Feldstein's proposals seem like very sensible reforms that will greatly improve the social security program despite some difficulties. However, once it is admitted that these reforms are desirable, there is no reason not to go one step further and privatize the insurance function. This privatization will be discussed in more detail in the next chapter.

---

[12]Interview with Martin Feldstein, Harvard University, April 1978.

The Laffer-Ranson Proposals

Arthur Laffer, professor of business economics at the University of Southern California and Dr. David Ranson, a Boston consultant, offer another set of reform proposals.[13] These proposals are similar in many respects to those advanced by former Secretary of the Treasury William Simon.[14]

Laffer and Ranson first suggest a number of minor changes to stem the long-term growth of benefits. First, they suggest indexing benefits to prices rather than wages, as discussed above. Second, they advocate subjecting half of all social security benefits to the federal income tax. In private pension plans, either the benefits or contributions are taxed. Currently, only the employee share of social security taxes is treated as pretax income received and therefore subject to the income tax; the employer share goes untaxed. Also, all social security benefits are currently tax exempt. Taxing half of all social security benefits would, therefore, put them on the same footing as private alternatives. Such taxation would in effect lower benefit payments. If the general tax revenues generated in this way were paid into social security, the result would in reality be a tax cut rather than a tax increase because the payroll tax would not have to be raised to the level necessary to pay the unreduced benefits. Since the income tax is progressive with low rates and exemptions for the poor, the burden of benefit reductions effected in this way would fall almost entirely on those with higher incomes, including "double-dippers." The poor and those in need would lose little or nothing in benefits.

The third short-run adjustment is to very gradually raise the retirement age. This reform should be phased in slowly over time so those close to retirement with plans already made would not have their plans disturbed beyond their ability to compensate for the change. Laffer and Ranson suggest raising the retirement age to sixty-six for those now aged fifty, to sixty-seven for those now aged forty, and to sixty-eight for those now aged thirty.

In the long run, Laffer and Ranson advocate accumulating a trust fund to finance social security benefits on an invested rather than on

[13]Arthur B. Laffer and R. David Ranson, "A Proposal for Reforming Social Security," H.C. Wainwright and Co., May 19, 1977; Arthur B. Laffer and R. David Ranson, *The Social Security Problem*, unpublished manuscript.

[14]William Simon, "How to Rescue Social Security," *Wall Street Journal*, 8 November 1976.

a pay-as-you-go basis, much like Feldstein. They also advocate paying benefits strictly on the basis of past taxes, with all beneficiaries receiving what they have paid in plus interest. This would require the elimination of all current welfare elements in the program, including the abolition of the earnings test. The current welfare objective would be fully served by the SSI program. Once a trust fund is established with benefits related strictly to past taxes, Laffer and Ranson suggest that participation in social security be made voluntary if individuals could demonstrate that they had provided for their old age by alternative means. This would result in the gradual privatization of the system.

This reform proposal would essentially solve all of the major shortcomings of the current program once its final, long-run goal had been achieved. The only remaining coercive element would be the requirement that individuals make some provision for their old age. The short-range reforms would be useful in reducing the heavy tax burden of the program and making the long-range reforms more feasible. It may be better, however, to extend the preferred tax status of social security to private savings and investment programs rather than taxing social security benefits. The only major objection to this entire set of reform proposals is that it may take longer to reach the ideal system than necessary. Laffer and Ranson would require complete funding of the trust fund before voluntary privatization would be allowed. Such an accumulation could take decades. The reason for this delay is that Laffer and Ranson believe that financial soundness must be achieved before voluntary privatization could take place. If individuals were allowed to voluntarily leave the program before full funding, the system would go bankrupt because in a pay-as-you-go system those currently paying into the program are needed to finance current benefits.

A more direct way to privatize the system would be to finance current benefit obligations out of general revenues. Current taxpayers could leave the program if they made alternative arrangements or could stay in and continue to pay payroll taxes that could be invested and returned with interest upon retirement. This would make the continuing program just like a purchase of government bonds, and there would then be no threat of bankruptcy from individuals opting out of the program because it would no longer be financed on a pay-as-you-go basis from the payroll taxes of current workers. It is true that general taxes may have to be raised to meet benefit obligations, but the accumulation of a trust fund under the

Laffer-Ranson proposal would require increases in payroll taxes to finance both the fund and current benefits. The chief difference is that voluntary participation could begin now instead of decades hence, after the full accumulation of a trust fund.

The reforms advocated by Laffer and Ranson would constitute a major improvement over the present system and would eventually lead to an ideal system, although it may take longer than necessary.

The Hobbs-Powlesland Proposal

Charles D. Hobbs, former California Director of Social Welfare, and Stephen C. Powlesland of the Institute for Liberty and Community have advanced another reform proposal that would phase out the current social security system and replace it with a partially privatized voluntary system.[15]

The first step in this proposal is to abolish the payroll tax for both employees and employers. The employer share of the tax would be passed on to employees through a mandatory, across-the-board pay increase equal to the current employer share of the tax for each worker. The greatest percentage of these pay increases would accrue to low- and middle-income workers.

The second step would be to provide each worker currently covered by social security with U.S. retirement bonds in lieu of currently earned benefits. The amount of the bonds would equal the actuarial present value of the benefits each individual has earned under current legislation with the amount he has paid in taxes until now. Each present social security beneficiary would also receive these bonds in lieu of future benefit payments. The amount of these bonds would equal the actuarial present value of the future benefits each is entitled to under current law.

The value of these bonds would grow until maturity at the highest of three alternative rates: (a) the interest rate on U.S. Treasury bonds; (b) the growth rate of nominal GNP; or (c) the growth rate of the Consumer Price Index. The bonds would mature when the holder reached sixty-five or any older age at which the holder declared himself retired. At maturity the bonds would provide a guaranteed annuity income for life based upon the accumulated value of the bonds and actuarially determined average life expectan-

[15]Charles D. Hobbs and Stephen L. Powlesland, *Retirement Security Reform: Restructuring the Social Security System* (Concord, Vt.: Institute for Liberty and Community, 1975).

cies. If the bondholder died before or during retirement, a widow or widower and the worker's children would receive an adjusted annuity based upon the value of the bonds at the time of death. This annuity would last until the death of the widow or widower or until the children reached adulthood. During retirement the income would be adjusted annually to grow at the highest of the three alternative rates mentioned above. The authors would allow the bonds to be transferred only through inheritance upon the holder's death.

The third step would be to require that each employed person over twenty-five contribute either 10% of his gross income or $2,500, whichever is less, to his retirement fund. This fund would be invested in individual or group pension programs, IRA or Keogh accounts, or other government-approved investment programs. If a person did not invest in one of these alternatives, he or she would be required to invest the above amount in the purchase of additional retirement bonds structured like those discussed above. Individuals could purchase additional retirement bonds if they desired. These bonds could be invested in other private alternatives, presumably allowing the investing firms to cash them to get the assets to make their own investments, but otherwise these bonds could not be transferred except through inheritance. The authors advocate that the private alternatives be closely regulated and insured by the recently created Federal Pension Benefit Guaranty Corporation.

The final step would be to pay off the bonds as they matured through the current sale of retirement bonds and the use of general revenues to make up any deficit. The money received through the sale of retirement bonds is likely to fall far short of current benefit obligations, and the subsidy needed from general revenues will, therefore, probably be quite substantial.

At first this proposal may seem like a substantial improvement on the present system, but a closer analysis of the nature of the retirement bonds reveals that many of these improvements may be illusory.

One of the benefits of this reform is supposed to be that it makes participation in social security voluntary, but whether such participation is truly voluntary depends on the rate of return paid on the bonds as compared to private rates and government taxation of those private rates. For example, assume that the government promises to pay a 25% tax-free return on such bonds, and the real return in the private sector is 15% before taxes and 7% after taxes. Participation under these circumstances is hardly voluntary. Individuals are already forced to participate by paying the high returns promised on the bonds through general-revenue taxation. These same taxes make private alternatives unattractive. The individual would in effect be forced to participate in the purchase of bonds to get back the money he is forced to contribute to the system in general revenues.

Any return paid on the bonds that is above the after-tax rate of return available in the market would destroy the voluntary nature of the system. One must also ask why the government should be offering bonds with rates of return above market interest rates. Since the return on the bonds would have to be financed by general revenues, this above-market rate of return would constitute welfare for everybody.

If the government bonds could not guarantee rates of return above market rates, why should they be sold at all? Individuals could purchase private bonds at market rates, and the government already issues government bonds at these rates to finance the national debt. Individuals could therefore already purchase these bonds for their retirement. Encouraging individuals to finance their retirement by the purchase of new, additional government bonds would simply increase the national debt and place the future retirement security of individuals on the backs of future taxpayers instead of relying on self-supporting, productive investments. Furthermore, if the return on these bonds was below market rates, encouraging the public to buy them would simply serve to delude the gullible, innocent, and uninformed into making bad investments.

Similarly, depending on the rate of return offered on the bonds, financing social security benefits in this way would really not change the pay-as-you-go nature of the system. If the bonds offered higher than market rates, most individuals would continue to participate in the program. Current benefits would then be paid by a combination of unusually expensive current borrowing through the sale of government retirement bonds and general revenue taxation. The program would still be like a Ponzi scheme, with shortfalls in current revenues made up from general taxes. There would be no real investment anywhere as would occur under the proposals of Feldstein, and Laffer and Ranson. Benefits under this proposal would not be financed by the purchase of outstanding government bonds that would result in additional investment, as we saw in the discussion of Feldstein's proposal. They would instead by financed by the issuance of new government bonds, which results in no additional investment. The purchase of these government bonds generates no additional productivity to pay off the promised returns. If above-market returns are paid through unusually expensive borrowing and general taxation, the program would then constitute welfare for everybody.

If returns on the bonds were at market rates the same problems would exist, although to a lesser extent because some individuals would withdraw from the program. For those who remain, however, the program would still operate on a pay-as-you-go basis. If the returns were below market rates, many more people would withdraw, but under these circumstances there is really no reason to offer the bonds at all. People would simply be encouraged to buy poor investments. The poor, uninformed, and vulnerable would be fooled most.

Depending on the rate of return offered on the bonds, then, this proposal as presently constituted would solve very few of the shortcomings of the program we have discussed in earlier chapters. It would eliminate some of the distortions in the labor supply and many of the inequities discussed in chapter 6. But if the rate of return offered on the bonds was too high, the economy would still lose the production from additional capital investment discussed in chapter 3, and individuals would still be prevented from enjoying the higher investment returns discussed in chapter 4, although they may be fooled by the payment of high welfare returns on the bonds. The bankruptcy issue would be solved only to the extent that taxpayers are more willing to pay general-revenue taxes than payroll taxes. As the recent fiscal experiences of New York City and Cleveland indicate, however, there is no ironclad guarantee that they are. Although the system may be subject to less political instability because of the contractual nature of the bonds, the program would still be vulnerable in this regard. Finally, if the rate of return on the bonds was set too high, the program would not be voluntary.

If the rate of return were set low enough to avoid these problems, however, there would be no reason to offer the bonds at all. Given the rates suggested by Hobbs and Powlesland, private alternative investments would probably be able to pay higher returns, but, as we have seen, at any rate of return encouraging individuals to continue to purchase these bonds is a bad idea.

The proposal might be modified, however, to eliminate most of these difficulties. The bonds could still be issued to current participants and beneficiaries to represent current benefit promises that must be paid. For current taxpayers, the bonds would grow at a rate such that at maturity they would equal the value of currently earned benefits or the same proportion of currently promised benefits that each individual has paid of his lifetime tax bill. For current beneficiaries, the bonds would equal the present value of currently promised benefits. Individuals might still be required to save and invest a certain portion of their incomes in private alternative investments, but no additional retirement bonds would be sold. If individuals wanted to invest in government bonds at market rates they could purchase outstanding and currently issued local, state, and federal bonds. If it was thought necessary that individuals have some last-chance government investment alternative, social security bonds could be offered which would give each individual his money back with no rate of return except perhaps an adjustment for the rate of inflation. They would thus receive their money back in real terms. Bonds paid out to redeem currently promised benefits would be paid at maturity from general revenues.

This would solve most of the defects of the proposal and virtually all of the defects of the social security program which we have discussed. The program would be truly voluntary except for the requirement that some provision be made for retirement. Pay-as-you-go financing would be eliminated and the program would be run on an invested basis. The welfare function of the current program would have been separated from the insurance program and the latter would have been privatized. If modified in this way, this proposal would be a vast improvement over the current system.

The Buchanan Proposal

The Hobbs-Powlesland proposal is a modification of a proposal made by James Buchanan, professor of economics at the University of Virginia, in an article published in 1968.[16] This proposal was in turn a further refinement of a proposal presented by Buchanan and Colin Campbell, professor of economics at Dartmouth College, in the *Wall Street Journal* in 1966.[17]

This proposal also begins with the elimination of the payroll tax. Individuals would then be required to save and invest a certain portion of their incomes for retirement. This investment would be made

[16]James Buchanan, "Social Insurance in a Growing Economy: A Proposal for Radical Reform," National Tax Journal 386, 21 December 1968.

[17]James Buchanan and Colin Campbell, "Voluntary Social Security," *Wall Street Journal*, 20 December 1966.

in social insurance bonds that would have a return equal to the higher of (1) the rate of interest on long-term U.S. treasury bonds or (2) the rate of growth in GNP. Individuals would be allowed to invest in private alternatives instead, if they desired. The social insurance bonds would mature at the holder's retirement at sixty-five, entitling him to an actuarial annuity equal in value to the matured amount of the bonds. This annuity would pay individuals a certain amount each month for life. Individuals could purchase more than the required amount of bonds if they desired. However, all bonds would be nontransferable. The matured bonds would be paid off by proceeds from current bond sales and from general revenues.

For those currently in the program, Buchanan suggests that bonds be issued to them in lieu of their currently promised benefits. The amount of these bonds would be equal to the amount they would have accumulated if they had been participating in the new system all of their lives, purchasing with their social security taxes bonds that would grow in face value at the above rates. Benefits to current beneficiaries would be calculated as if their taxes had been used to purchase these bonds all of their lives and these bonds had grown at the above rates. If benefits to anyone, either current beneficiaries or current taxpayers, were less under the new system than the amounts they would have received under the current system, the difference would be paid to the participants out of general revenues.

This proposal has the same shortcomings as the Hobbs-Powlesland proposal. Buchanan sees it as a way of maintaining the advantages of a pay-as-you-go system while allowing individuals the freedom to leave the program if they desire. While the full shortcomings of pay-as-you-go financing may not have been apparent in 1968, there are no advantages to this form of financing, and it is wholly inadequate as compared to fully funded financing. Similarly, as noted earlier, Buchanan's proposal does not really make the system voluntary as long as the social insurance bonds yield above-market rates of return. If they paid market rates or less, there is no reason to have them since government bonds at market rates are already available. Buchanan's proposal, of course, can be modified in the same way as suggested for the Hobbs-Powlesland proposal.

The Shore Proposal

Warren Shore, author of *Social Security: The Fraud in Your Future,* has advanced another proposal meant to phase out the current system and replace it with a voluntary, partially privatized system.[18] Shore calls his proposal the New Generation Compact.

The first step in Shore's plan is to announce that private companies will be allowed to offer a combined package of life, retirement, and disability insurance to young Americans about to enter the work force. These individuals could then choose either the private plans or social security. If they chose a private plan, then their social security taxes would go to the insurance company as insurance premiums under a contract, rather than to the government. For every young worker that an insurance company signs up, the company will have to agree to pay the benefits the government owes to one newly retired worker beginning one year later. Ideally, higher income workers would be matched up with higher benefit retirees and lower income workers with lower benefit retirees. The portion of premiums paid for retirement insurance would be fully deductible for income tax purposes, as is currently the case for IRA and Keogh plans. Benefits to workers remaining in the system would continue to be financed by payroll taxes. The health insurance portion of social security would be financed by general revenues.

As time went on, more and more current workers would be covered by the private system rather than social security as young workers chose the superior private alternatives. Similarly, more and more current beneficiaries would be provided for through the private system. The government's tax revenues and benefit obligations would both decline. Eventually current beneficiaries under social security would be completely phased out.

Shore provides an example of how his plan would work. He assumes 100 new workers matched with 100 retirees. After five years, there would remain 99 young workers and only 81 of the new retirees because of deaths in that period. After ten years, the ratio would be 98 to 61, after fifteen years, 97 to 39, after twenty years, 95 to 20. He contends that such a plan would produce net income to the company after seven or eight years and a profit after eleven years. He argues that existing insurance contracts usually do not show a profit in their early years because of the expenses of acquiring a business and the need to acquire legal reserves, so the wait for net income would not be unusual. Furthermore, he contends, the expenses of acquiring this business would be minimal because workers would be required to buy insurance. The requirement to

[18]Warren Shore, *Social Security: The Fraud in Your Future* (New York: Macmillan, 1975).

buy insurance would also save another major cost to insurance companies—cancellation of policies in early years. Shore contends that the insurance company can make a profit, leave the individual worker with more than he would get under social security, and finance the benefits of one retiree for every young worker.

The key concept behind this reform is that allowing young workers out of social security to take advantage of higher yielding private alternatives would make these young workers so much better off that benefits could be paid to a retiree out of the increased returns and still leave the young worker with more than under social security. As we saw in chapter 9, because social security makes all future generations worse off, phasing out the program could make them better off. We also saw that although at any time the current working generation would have been better off if social security had never been started, it would not pay that generation to end the program itself because, if the system were ended now, the current working generation would have to pay for both its own retirement and that of the current retired generation. Shore's plan attempts to transfer some of the benefits that would accrue to future generations from ending the program to the current working generation to compensate the current generation for the burden of having to pay for two retirements. This occurs by shifting the burden of paying for some of the benefit entitlements of the current retired generation to the next working generation as it comes into the work force, thus allowing the system to be phased out without making the current working generation worse off.

The concept behind this reform is theoretically valid. It is based on the idea that social security is an inefficient way of providing for old age, and if a more productive, efficient method were used there would be more benefits for everybody.

The question about Shore's proposal is whether there is enough additional productivity from the invested system to make his reforms feasible. The private system may not be so much more productive after taxes than social security that there will be enough left over after paying for the retirement of an elderly person out of the premiums of a young person to still leave the young person better off than he would have been under social security. Although all future generations will surely be made better off by ending social security than the current working generation would be made worse off by paying the cost of doing so, this method of reform may not capture enough of these future benefits for the current generation to fully compensate it for the cost of phasing out the system.

The workability of this proposal thus depends on an empirical question. The benefit payments that must be made to one retiree will surely be much greater than the young person's taxes in each year. In 1979 the maximum tax was $2,807.54, while the retirement benefit for a maximum income worker was $6,256 for a single worker and $9,384 for a worker with a spouse. Thus the insurance company would have to advance the difference until the retiree's death. A person at sixty-five has a life expectancy of sixteen years. If a worker entered the system at twenty-two, the company would, on average, have to advance the difference between his taxes and the required benefits until he was thirty-eight. At that point, the worker would have to accumulate enough to pay back the company's advances with interest and still have enough remaining for himself to do better than under social security. It seems unlikely that this would be possible.

Perhaps this proposal could be modified to match two young persons with every retiree or perhaps more, although this might not leave enough workers in the social security system to pay sufficient taxes to support benefits to retirees remaining in the system. Alternatively, some of the retiree's benefits might be subsidized from general revenues. If that were done there might be more direct methods of phasing out the system, as we will see below.

It seems that this proposal needs more empirical investigation. If it could be shown to have a sound basis, this reform would be quite worthwhile. One of the chief advantages of this proposal is that, unlike all the others, it faces up to the question of how to phase out the enormous unfunded liability of the program. Others advocate meeting it from increased payroll taxes or general revenues without considering whether it would be politically feasible to raise the necessary taxes or cut other government expenditures. One might argue, however, that even if it is workable, this proposal provides an indirect roundabout method of privatization that might take substantially longer than more direct proposals. On the other hand, the gradualism of this proposal, and the fact that, if it works properly, there would be no substantial additional costs imposed on any one generation, might make it more politically feasible than more direct alternatives.

The Friedman Proposal

The final proposal we will consider has been advanced by Milton Friedman. Friedman advocates shifting the welfare function of the program to a negative income tax plan and completely privatizing the insurance function without the retention of a voluntary social security option.[19]

The first step in Friedman's plan is to abolish the payroll tax. The second step is to terminate any further accumulation of benefits. Third, Friedman would enact a negative income tax to serve the welfare function of the present program. This negative income tax would pay a subsidy to all those with incomes under a certain level, a subsidy that would be higher for those with lower incomes. This would in effect extend the current progressive income tax structure into the negative range. The progressive rates of taxation would fall from high levels for high incomes to zero at some income point and become progressively more negative for income below that point. The end result would be a guaranteed minimum income for all.

Fourth, Friedman would continue to pay all existing beneficiaries the amounts that they are entitled to under current law, except that benefits would be price indexed rather than wage indexed. He would also give beneficiaries the option to accept a capital sum equal to the present value of all future benefits instead of waiting for them to be paid over a period of time.

Fifth, Friedman would give every worker who has earned coverage under present law a commitment to the retirement and survivor's benefits that he would be entitled to under present law, given his present tax payments and earnings record. This commitment would be in the form of either a promise to pay the specified annual sum at the date when under present law he would be entitled to the sum, or government bonds equal in market value to the present value of those benefits, at the option of the worker.

Sixth, Friedman would give everyone who has not earned benefits but has paid taxes a capital sum equal to the accumulated value of those taxes.

Seventh, he would finance payments under steps four, five, and six out of general revenues.

Friedman notes that this reform simply recognizes explicitly current government debt obligations. It does not add to government debt but does terminate accumulation of further obligations. The ultimate effect of the reform would be to shift the welfare function of the current program to the negative income tax. The insurance

19Wilbur J. Cohen and Milton Friedman, *Social Security: Universal or Selective?* (Washington D.C.: American Enterprise Institute, 1972).

function would be entirely phased out through privatization with no remaining role for government in the insurance business.

This proposal would solve all of the problems with the current program discussed in earlier chapters, including the question of coercion and individual liberty discussed in chapter 8.

Friedman advocates a wide-ranging reform of the entire welfare system as part of this proposal, replacing all current welfare programs, including the welfare elements of social security, with a negative income tax that guarantees a minimum annual income to everyone. The chief objection to the negative income tax is that politically it is unlikely that it would replace all other welfare programs, as Friedman advocates, but is more likely to be added to all current welfare programs. Friedman would agree that in this case the negative income tax would make things worse, although if it did replace all other welfare programs it would probably be an improvement. Another objection to the negative income tax is its effect on incentives. It would seriously discourage from working all those with incomes below or near the guaranteed level who could quit work and receive the welfare payments even if they were able to work. To the extent that most current welfare programs deny welfare to those able to work, the negative income tax would worsen incentives. Finally, with a guaranteed annual income for all, political pressure might develop to raise the minimum income level frequently, increasing welfare payments beyond reasonable levels.

Given these problems, it may be better to transfer all of the welfare functions of the current social security program to the SSI program instead of instituting a negative income tax. It is also possible that private arrangements for charity would be superior to both these alternatives, but the question of the appropriate welfare program for a free society is beyond the scope of this book.

11

Social Security: The Ideal System

By now the need for fundamental reform of the social security program should be absolutely clear. The shortcomings of the program are numerous, and the negative impacts from these defects are powerful and severe. As recognition of these problems has become more widespread, many have advanced reform proposals to restructure the entire program. The reforms discussed in chapter 10 would improve the current system tremendously, but we need to go further than most of them to achieve the ideal system.

An ideal system to replace social security would serve both functions of the current program far better than social security serves either function now. This system would preserve individual liberty while at the same time improving economic performance and material well-being and ensuring adequate care for the poor and needy.

Not only can such a system be devised, it can be attained feasibly within a decade without major sacrifice and undue hardship, despite the enormous liabilities built up by the current program. This ideal system and a proposal for attaining it are the topics of this chapter.

The Ideal System

We have seen throughout this book that the current social security program seeks to serve two functions, a welfare and an insurance function. Through the welfare function, the program provides funds to those in poverty based on their need and regardless of how much they have paid into the system. Through the insurance function, the program provides individuals with income when certain contingencies occur, depending on how much they have paid into the program in the past and regardless of their need. As we have seen, these two functions are inherently contradictory, and the conflict between the two has produced all of the major shortcomings of the current program. The result is bad insurance and bad welfare.

The guiding principle behind social security reform should be to split the two functions into separate programs. The ideal system would continue to serve both functions but through entirely separate institutions.

The insurance function of the current program can be served by private institutions in the free market. People could use the money they are currently paying in social security taxes to buy packages of insurance and investment plans that would cover all of the major insurance contingencies covered by social security. We will discuss below how the private system could cover each of these contingencies.

Retirement insurance is basically a savings vehicle by which an individual accumulates a reserve to be consumed when he retires. Individuals could save the money they are currently paying into social security and accumulate it in such a reserve or retirement account instead. The money in this retirement account could then be invested in numerous private investment alternatives that would be economically productive and earn a rate of return to the reserve, increasing the fund to an amount far greater than the same individual could receive under social security.

The investment alternatives open to individuals for their retirement accounts are so numerous and varied that another book would be required to discuss them in detail. Perhaps the most important point to note is that individuals would not have to make these investments directly themselves. Instead, these investments could be made through banks, insurance companies, trust companies, and other market institutions that have the information and expertise to make such investments wisely. Information and transaction costs would therefore remain low. A company could sell a retirement plan to a person, who would agree to pay a certain amount annually to the company out of his account. When the person retired, the company would then return the money increased by a certain rate of accumulated interest earned by the company's investment of the funds.

Companies would take the money paid to them under such a contract and invest it in productive assets to earn the rate of return promised to the customer. The money could be invested in a diversified portfolio of stocks, bonds, notes, and other financial instruments. It could be invested in mortgages, providing new housing, in business loans, providing more jobs and material goods, or in loans to develop new energy sources. These contracts would be especially valuable to the companies because the money paid under them would be committed to the investment program for long periods of time. It could therefore be used for long-term investments without worrying about maintaining a high degree of liquidity for sudden withdrawals by customers. Banks are already willing to pay substantial premiums for funds committed to long-term deposits. Also, by diversifying their investments in a wide variety of alternatives, these companies could minimize risk. By selling these plans to reasonably large numbers of customers, they could also take advantage of any other economies of scale in investment.

The rate of return paid to individuals under such plans could be made to vary depending on how well the underlying investments did, or it could be fixed, putting the risk of loss on the companies. The amounts paid by each individual into his plan over the course of his life could be allowed to vary depending on specific needs and preferences. Those who are young and trying to start careers and families could pay less, agreeing to increase their payments later in life. Arrangements could also be made to allow withdrawal of the funds if the individual needed them, although a higher rate of return might be attainable if they were committed until retirement.

Individuals could use other vehicles besides banks and other financial intermediaries to invest the money they accumulate in their retirement accounts. One of these vehicles could be a group pension plan. Almost two-thirds of all workers in the United States are already involved in such plans. These plans could be expanded by allowing individuals to use the money they are saving in their retirement accounts to invest in the plans in addition to the amounts they are currently contributing. Under most pension plans today, a certain amount is deducted from the worker's paycheck each week with a matching amount donated by the employer. These amounts are then accumulated in a pension fund that is invested in much the same way as a bank or insurance company would invest the funds described above. Workers could add to the amounts they are paying into these pension funds by making payments from their retirement accounts. If workers were able to make such additional payments, firms that do not have such pension plans now might be more likely to institute them.

Instead of investing through a group pension plan or through a financial institution, the individual might want to invest alone, which can be done through an Individual Retirement Account (IRA). The law allows each individual to save a certain percentage of his income up to a maximum dollar amount in his own IRA. The amount of income saved in an IRA is not subject to the income tax when received. The funds in an IRA can then be turned over to a bank or trustee for investment, or the individual can invest the funds himself. The earnings of the investments in these accounts are also tax exempt. When an individual retires, however, he is taxed on the full amount of income received from these accounts. Under the new system being advanced here, those who wished to invest on their own instead of through a financial institution or pension plan could simply designate their retirement accounts as IRAs.

Today there are severe restrictions on the types of investments that can be made through an IRA, but these restrictions could be eased to allow people more freedom of choice. In addition to the more traditional investments discussed above, individuals could be free to make more personalized investments. A person may want to use his IRA funds to invest in his own business venture or to buy or develop real estate. This would be especially important to those with low incomes who might not otherwise be able to get funds to take advantage of these opportunities. An old and wise saying goes, you need money to make money. Individuals could take the money they are now paying in social security taxes and set themselves up in business with special tax breaks of their own. Another example of a personalized investment is an individual using the money in his IRA to build his own home. If he could set himself up in a home free of mortgage or rent payments, he would have a great deal of old-age security. Although this proposal may sound radical at first, it is really just like allowing the individual to lend a mortgage to himself.

The investment opportunities available to people are limitless. The point here is that the ideal retirement system could be structured to allow people to take advantage of these opportunities with the huge sums they are currently wasting in social security taxes. People could then use this money in ways that will most benefit themselves both before and after retirement according to their own personal needs, preferences, opportunities, and circumstances.

Another individual investment alternative is a savings account at a bank or savings and loan association. Individuals could use the funds in their retirement accounts to make deposits in these accounts. Through simple, long-term certificates of deposit, individuals can earn much higher returns than they could get through social security, especially if they were not taxed on the interest.

Whether the money individuals save in their retirement accounts is invested through insurance companies and other financial institutions, through group pension plans, or through a plan of individual investments, a new system of tax rules and exemptions should be devised for these accounts. These new retirement accounts should have at least the same tax exemptions as IRAs. Individuals should not have to pay any income tax on the portion of their incomes that they pay into these accounts each year. The annual amounts they are allowed to pay into such accounts should be at least as high as the amounts they would have paid in social security taxes under the current system. In addition, the returns earned by these accounts should be tax exempt. Individuals should not have to pay any income tax on the amounts earned by the investments in their retirement accounts. Any dividends paid on stock held by a retirement account should be tax exempt, as should any interest paid on mortgages, bonds, and notes. Any capital gains made from the sale of assets held by these accounts should also be free of tax. For example, if the assets in these accounts were invested in apartment buildings, land, hotels, or other real estate and this property was sold for a profit, this profit should be returned to the account tax free. The same rule should apply to capital gains from the sale of any other good or commodity the account may hold, including capital gains from the sale of stocks, bonds, notes, or other financial instruments.

In addition to the traditional types of tax exemptions that are available through IRAs, new, innovative exemptions could be devised to allow individuals to enjoy the production from the investments held by their retirement accounts. The income of any business or venture owned outright by these accounts should be tax exempt. If the account held an apartment house, for example, the net income from the rents would be credited to the account tax free. Similarly, the profits of any business corporation or company held outright by the account would be credited to the account for further investment tax free. This principle should be extended to investment in stocks, bonds, and notes of existing companies. A corporation whose stock had been completely purchased by these retirement accounts should have all of its profits free from tax because they are all ultimately earned by the accounts. If the corporation had half of its stock held by these accounts, half of its profits should be tax exempt, etc. The same should apply to both debt securities and equity instruments. If an account loans money to a corporation and the corporation has to pay half of whatever it earns with that money in taxes, the corporation will not be willing to pay as high an interest rate for that money as it would if it had to pay no tax. The corporation should therefore be tax exempt on whatever it earns with money borrowed from one of these retirement accounts. As corporations bid for these loans, the interest rates they have to pay would rise and the retirement accounts would ultimately receive the full benefits of the tax exemption. In the end, therefore, a corporation or company that had derived half of its funds from stocks, bonds, notes, loans, or other investments from these retirement accounts should have half of its profits tax exempt. A corporation would have the same proportion of its profits tax exempt as the proportion of its assets that were derived from the retirement accounts, whether through debt or equity. The same rule should apply to noncorporate businesses.

Each individual's account would thus become safe for saving, investment, and growth, allowing individuals the maximum freedom to earn their way to retirement security. The money paid into these accounts would be automatically tagged with a special tax exempt status, and anywhere that money went it would carry that status with it as long as the money was ultimately committed to retirement protection. Investments made with this money would not be taxed at any point.

These tax rules would allow investors to receive the full value of the extra production produced by their investments. They would receive the full real rate of return on capital investment, which is estimated by Feldstein at 12% or more. At these rates individual investors would do even better with their private sector investments than we saw in chapter 4. Furthermore, if the amount that each person could pay into these retirement accounts each year was limited to the amount he would have paid in social security taxes, these tax exemptions would result in no decrease in federal revenues. These provisions would merely exempt from taxation the additional production created by the investment of social security taxes, production that is not taxed now because it doesn't exist. Individuals would receive the full value created by the investments they make for their retirement. The entire $400 billion a year that Feldstein estimates would be created by the investment of social security taxes would go into the retirement accounts of individuals rather than into the coffers of the federal government.[1]

People would use these funds to provide for their retirement, and therefore there is no reason why these tax exemptions should not be allowed. They are fully consistent with our national policy of aiding the elderly. In fact, this system of tax exemptions would be the most efficient, effective, and fair aid program for the elderly possible. It would require no massive bureaucracy to administer it. At rates of 12% or more, the benefits would be enormous, yet they would not constitute a burden to society, as welfare does, because they would be financed entirely from the increased production resulting from the investments of each individual for his retirement. Unlike welfare, these benefits would be earned because they were created or produced by these investments. The benefits under this system would constitute the most that all individuals could receive in retirement benefits for a given amount of sacrifice earlier in life because these benefits would constitute all the increased production resulting from the provisions that had been made for retirement. Since a government tax and transfer payment scheme adds nothing to production, it could not pay individuals any greater benefits than this, and to the extent that it resulted in decreased production it would inevitably have to pay individuals less. This tax exemption system would simply allow individuals to receive all that had been produced without the government taking a share. It would simply

[1]The only negative impact on federal revenues from this system of tax exemptions results from the exemption of the portion of each person's regular ordinary income that he saves in his retirement account. Half of the amount paid in social security taxes is now subject to income taxation. If the amount that people are allowed to save each year in their tax exempt retirement accounts is limited to the amount they would have payed in social security taxes, the new system will provide for an exemption from the income tax of an amount equal to half of all social security taxes. Federal revenues will therefore decrease by the amount of tax revenues that would result from subjecting this amount of income to the income tax. But this exemption is already allowed for IRAs, so we have already decided as a matter of public policy to accept this tax loss in order to allow people to achieve greater retirement security. Under the new system we are describing here, more people will be able to take advantage of this IRA-type of exemption because they will be able to use the money they are currently paying in social security taxes to set up their own retirement accounts. But since we have already accepted the principle behind this type of exemption, the loss of revenue resulting from the greater use of this opportunity should not be considered unjustified. This same loss could occur under present law if more people took full advantage of IRA opportunities. It is true that the maximum tax exempt amount that could be saved each year will be higher under the new system than for IRAs today, but the effect on tax revenues from this difference is not decisive. In 1980 the total tax revenue loss from this exemption would have been only $10 to $20 billion, less than the size of the tax cut that was being considered to stimulate the economy.

remove all the barriers the government is currently placing in the
way of individuals trying to achieve retirement security. If the
government is really committed to helping the elderly, it should not
place extra burdens on the achievement of retirement security. It
should not tax those who are attempting to provide for their retirement.

Although this new system of tax exemption might at first appear
complex, it is actually relatively simple and straightforward compared to the many other types of special exemptions in the tax code.
The new system is simply a modified version of the IRA account,
which is already provided for in the current tax code. The only new
issue raised by the new system is to what extent a particular investment or business venture was financed with funds from retirement
accounts, but this is a straightforward issue that could be resolved
by reference to the ordinary records of financial transactions. It
would be one of the simplest issues presented by the tax code, not
one of the most complex. It would be far simpler than determining
the applicability of special tax provisions for investments made for
particular purposes, such as the provisions for the investment tax
credit or for energy saving investments or purchases or a host of
others. It would be far easier than the issues presented by the rules
for recaptured depreciation or even the issue of whether a lunch was
for business purposes, and therefore deductible, or for entertain-
ment purposes, and therefore not. The new system of tax exemptions
would present no novel or complex issues that would make the administration of our tax laws more difficult in any particular way.
The new system should greatly simplify the tax code because it
would replace the many varying types of special exemptions for different types of retirement and pension plans that now exist.

Once a person has reached retirement, he will have accumulated
a large retirement fund through investing in one or more of the
alternative investment methods described above. For the average
American family, this fund could easily exceed $0.5 million in real
terms. The amounts that people take out of these funds in retirement
benefits should also be tax exempt, as social security benefits currently are. The government should not seize and reallocate the assets
individuals have set aside for their retirement. The government
should not put barriers in the way of those trying to attain retirement security. If the amount that individuals could place in their tax
exempt retirement funds each year was limited to the amount that
each would have paid in social security taxes, then this exemption

would also not reduce federal revenues because social security benefits are not now taxed, and the higher benefits of the private system represent income that is not being produced now and is therefore also not now being taxed. Of course, the special system of tax exemptions we have described should continue to apply to investments made by these accounts, even after retirement.

With this retirement fund a person could now pursue an almost limitless array of alternative options to provide himself with retirement benefits. He could live off of the interest on the fund for the rest of his life and leave the fund to his children. He could use the fund to purchase an annuity contract that would guarantee him a certain income for the rest of his life. The seller of the annuity would then invest the fund to earn the amounts he is committed to pay to the retiree. The individual could also keep the fund and vary the amount of income he drew from it over his retirement years. He could use some of the money in the account to give lifetime gifts. For example, he might want to help his son or daughter get started in a business or career or help his grandchild through school. Each person would have complete control over the money to spend as he wished. In addition, he would not lose the money through any disqualifying act such as marriage, divorce, or work, as can happen now under social security. His life would be free from government restrictions and the money therefore worth far more to him than the same money under social security.

The survivor's insurance function of social security can also be served by private market institutions. Survivor's insurance is nothing more than term life insurance. Each person can use some of the money he would have paid in social security taxes to purchase term life insurance. If the individual dies before retirement, he can leave his wife and children both the life insurance amount and the amount in his retirement fund. These funds could then be used to finance the benefits to replace the survivor's benefits social security would have paid. Any investments made by these funds to finance these benefits should also be eligible for the special tax exemptions we have described for the retirement account.

A person, therefore, needs only to purchase a life insurance policy in an amount equal to the amount of desired insurance protection minus the amount in his retirement account. Over the years, as his retirement account grows, the amount of term life insurance he needs to buy will decline. This amount will reach zero when his retirement account is greater than the desired amount of survivor's protection. If the desired amount of survivor's protection is the same as is currently provided by social security, then for most people the fund alone will be enough to provide these benefits without the purchase of additional term life insurance sometime around the age of forty, assuming the individual enters the work force now and invests in his private package of insurance protection all that he would have paid in social security taxes under the current system. In the early years of life, when the amount of life insurance needed is higher, the rates are low because the chance of dying young is low. As the individual gets older and the rates rise, the amount needed will decline, so this expense will remain low.

If the individual dies before retirement these private alternatives will enable him to leave his family an amount equal to or greater than what social security provides. Furthermore, this private arrangement will be far superior to social security because the family will be left in complete control of the assets, which they can use as they please for the rest of their lives. In addition, if an individual is not married and has no dependents he need not purchase life insurance, as social security requires him to do, but if he does the amount purchased will be left to his heirs along with his retirement account. Individuals are thus free to vary the amount of survivor's insurance protection according to their needs.

People can also purchase disability insurance from private insurance companies with some of the money they are paying into social security. They can also use some of the money in their retirement accounts for support in the event of disability. As the fund grows, the person can again decrease the amount of disability insurance he is purchasing so that the amount of insurance plus the amount in his fund will be enough at any one time to pay him all the benefits social security would have paid him in event of disability, including retirement benefits. Ideally, these retirement benefits would be paid regardless of whether the individual recovered, as under the system described in chapter 4, so that the worker would be assured of getting at least as much in retirement benefits as under social security. The amount of disability insurance purchased under this arrangement would again fall to zero for workers currently entering the work force sometime in their forties, depending, of course, on the amounts they saved each year in their retirement accounts. Another source of income in the event of disability would be workmen's compensation. If a disabled worker currently receives workmen's compensation, social security will pay no more than the amount of benefits needed to supplement these workmen's compensation benefits until the total equals 80% of what he was earning while he was working.

Private insurance companies selling disability insurance would charge a premium each year to their customers based on the probability of disability, the probable length of disability, and the amount that would have to be paid to each individual worker in the event of disability. It could charge greater premiums to individuals with characteristics that tend to lead to disability more often and who therefore impose greater risks. Those in high-risk occupations would pay more than those in low-risk occupations. Similarly, the company would charge different premiums to individuals depending on the amount of benefits each would want in the event of disability. Those with large families would want more in benefits, so they would have to pay higher premiums. Those who were single or married but without children would want less in benefits, so they would pay less in premiums. Each year the company would collect all these premiums and invest them to fund the benefits to be paid to customers who had become disabled during the year. The premiums would have been set high enough so that all the benefit promises to disabled workers would be fully funded. That is, the company would invest the accumulated premium payments and use the earnings on these investments as well as the original funds to pay all the benefits in future years that had to be paid to those who had become disabled during the year. The company would aim to set premiums just high enough so that the total fund resulting from these premium payments would be completely used up by the time all the workers who had become disabled during the year had died or recovered. Any investments made by the insurance company with these premium payments to finance disability benefits should also be eligible for the system of tax exemptions we have described. A retirement account used to finance disability benefits would also continue to be eligible for these exemptions.

Finally, social security also provides health insurance for those over sixty-five, but the HI payroll tax rate is set at less than half of the amount required to finance the program after 1990. There is, therefore, talk of funding this program from general revenues and using the HI tax for the OASDI program. If this is done, then the program can continue to be financed in this way, while the rest of the program is privatized. (Of course, this would make the HI program welfare for everybody in it, which makes little sense.)

Alternatively, individuals could buy health insurance from private insurance companies that would provide the same coverage for those over sixty-five that social security does now. If they signed up for such health insurance plans early in life, even though coverage would not begin until after sixty-five, they could pay a very small premium each month. The insurance company would use these premiums to fund future benefits by making investments, and the income from these investments would allow the premiums to be even lower. Again, these investments could be eligible for the system of tax exemptions we have described. Individuals early in life present relatively equal risks of being sick after age sixty-five, so those who did become sick later in life would not have to worry about being unable to obtain health insurance. People could purchase this insurance when they start work as part of an overall package of life, disability, health, and retirement insurance. Individuals could also use the higher benefits from their private retirement accounts to pay for some of their medical expenses.

There is again no reason why private insurance companies could not provide this insurance at least as well as the federal government. In fact, given the lack of incentives in the government program for individuals to hold costs down, the private companies could probably provide this insurance much more cheaply. The only way the government could provide this insurance more cheaply is by subsidizing it from general revenues, in which case individuals would be paying for it indirectly. Still, if it was thought necessary to subsidize health insurance from general revenues, this could be done by allowing individuals to buy private health insurance and providing them with subsidy payments to meet the premiums.

We now turn to the second function served by social security—the welfare function. The poorest members of society, those who do not have regular employment, also do not have sufficient funds to save for an adequate retirement. All of their funds are needed for current necessities. These individuals do not now pay social security taxes because they are not regularly employed. Those individuals who do work regularly and pay social security taxes, but receive low wages, can receive substantial retirement benefits at adequate levels merely by using the money they are now paying in social security taxes to invest in private alternatives, as we saw in chapter 4. Still, even these individuals may need some income supplementation in their retirement years. Through its welfare function, social security now seeks to provide these individuals with benefits so that they can have adequate retirement incomes even though these benefits have not been earned or paid for.

This welfare function can be served by institutions, governmental or private, entirely separate and apart from the institutions that serve the insurance function. These institutions would provide the elderly poor with welfare subsidies so that all would have a minimum, adequate retirement income. These benefits would be paid subject to a means test so that only those who were truly poor and in need would receive payments. The money to finance these benefits would come from general revenues when the benefits were being provided through government institutions and from voluntary donations when the benefits were being provided through private institutions.

The most immediate vehicle for serving this function would be the SSI program, which was discussed in chapter 2. Under this program the elderly poor are given welfare benefits financed through general revenues and subject to a means test. If social security was replaced by the system described here, the welfare function of the program would be automatically picked up by SSI. Those who were in need could apply for benefits under the means-tested SSI program. As part of a general reform of the entire social security program, it would seem best to use the SSI program to serve this welfare function, at least initially. The program is already operating and is well-suited to serve the welfare function. Its adoption of this welfare role would ease the transition to the new system. Ultimately the SSI program might be replaced by a negative income tax that would provide funds to all those in need, including the elderly. Another alternative is to provide the poor with charity through private institutions.

Any welfare program raises the problem of potential abuse. While the means test will ensure that benefits are paid only to the poor, some people may take advantage of the program by failing to provide for their retirement years if they know that the government will provide them with benefits. There are two ways to eliminate this problem. The first is to require all able individuals to make some provision for their old age during their working years through the purchase of retirement insurance or other savings vehicles. Individuals could be required to use the amounts they are currently paying in social security taxes, or suitably lesser amounts because of the superiority of the private alternatives, to make provisions for the contingencies covered by social security. The second method is to make welfare payments only to those elderly individuals who are not able to continue working. Most sixty-five-year-old individuals are able to continue working, and there is no reason to provide benefits to those who were capable of providing for their retirement earlier in life but failed to do so in expectation of receiving welfare benefits. The problem of abuse, however, may not be severe enough to require either of these responses. As long as there is a means test and as long as the minimum income level is not set too high, the percentage of the population seeking benefits under such a welfare program for the elderly is not likely to be any higher than the percentage of the general population on welfare. This is true for the SSI program today.

The perfect welfare program for the poor is a topic for another book. The point is that the welfare function of social security can be served in a far superior fashion through one or more of these alternative institutions entirely separated from those serving the insurance function. These alternatives would provide benefits only to those in need, and not waste welfare benefits on those who are not. These benefits could also be provided by general revenues or voluntary donations, unlike social security, which finances its welfare benefits through the regressive payroll tax.

The system described here can serve both the welfare and insurance functions better than the current program serves either. Private market institutions can cover all the insurance contingencies currently covered by social security, preserving individual liberty and at the same time providing superior coverage in material terms. The welfare function can be served by alternative government or private institutions in ways that will make the poor better off financially and eliminate many inequities and hardships imposed on them by the current social security program.

Objections

There are three possible major objections to this system, all of which can be met by slight modifications of the system. Even with these modifications, the system described here would be vastly superior to social security.

The first objection is that if people are left free to decide for themselves how much to save for retirement, as they are in the system described above, many will not save anything. When they become old they will either live in misery and poverty or become welfare recipients. Both for their own good and for the good of society they must be forced to save for their old age.

This is the paternalistic justification for social security discussed in chapter 9. Although this argument does not justify forcing individuals to save for their old age, given the current state of public opinion, it may not be possible to reform social security toward an ideal system without a compromise on this issue. Therefore, as a compromise, the government could require everyone to save a certain percentage of his income up to some limit for a package of retirement, survivor's, disability, and health insurance protection. The amounts required for each type could be allowed to vary depending on the circumstances of each individual. For example, single people should not be required to buy as much term life insurance as married people with children. A person might also be allowed to vary the amount saved over his life according to his needs and preferences. A person might save less than the required amount during a specific period if he made up for it by saving more later.

Even with this requirement people would have far more freedom to control their own lives than they have now. The current social security system has three separate coercive elements: (a) the requirement that people purchase some insurance protection, (b) the requirement that this insurance protection be a specific plan—social security, and (c) the requirement that this plan be purchased from a specific seller—the federal government. The compromise requirement discussed here would eliminate (b) and (c), and individuals would then have more freedom and opportunity to control their own lives. Even with coercive element (a) remaining, individuals would still have all the options of the system discussed above for their insurance protection. The only option foreclosed would be to have no insurance protection at all.

A second objection is that if allowed to invest in whatever they want, many people would choose ventures that are too risky and unusual and end up losing all their money. As a result, they will be poor in old age despite their investments and live in misery or on welfare. Those making personalized, nontraditional investments, such as putting their money in their own small businesses, may be particularly subject to this risk. If these businesses fail, such individuals will be left with nothing in retirement. Individuals must therefore be forced to make safe investments for their retirement.

The underlying basis for this criticism is again paternalism: Individuals must be forced for their own good to take fewer risks than they might prefer. Ideally, however, individuals should be allowed to take risks. If they fail they will bear the losses, just as if they succeed they will reap the gains. If the losses are severe as to leave them in poverty, then welfare can alleviate their suffering. Preventing individuals from taking risks protects them not only from losses, but also from success. Investments with low risks have lower returns than investments with high risks.

Nevertheless, it may be politically necessary to compromise on this issue as well. One way of compromising would be to require individuals to choose investment alternatives from a list of low-risk, government-approved options. Companies willing to offer investment plans to individuals would apply to the government to be put on the list. If the companies agreed to follow certain traditional investment strategies with moderate risks, the government would include them. A person would have to choose one of the options on the list for his retirement investment. This requirement would apply only to that portion of each person's income that he is required to save under the first compromise. If a person failed to choose an option, the government would take the required amount of savings in social security taxes, as it does now, and return it at retirement increased at the rate of inflation.

Another way to solve the problem of risky investments would be for the government to guarantee retirement investments in the same way that it currently guarantees bank deposits under the Federal Deposit Insurance Corporation or pensions under the Federal Pension Benefit Guaranty Corporation. The government could guarantee any investment made with a company on the list described above; if the company failed, the government would pay the benefits promised by the company under its contract with the individual customer. This guarantee would again be only for the amount of investment required annually by the government.

Both variants of this compromise proposal as well as the first compromise could be phased out simply by reducing the annual amounts that the government requires to be invested. Alternatively, the government guarantees could be kept even with the elimination of the saving requirement. The government could offer individuals a guarantee of all benefits under contracts chosen from a list of investment alternatives approved by the government, although individuals would not be required to invest in these alternatives if they were willing to forgo the guarantee.

A third possible objection to the system we are proposing is that individuals should have the option to stay in social security and not be required to invest in the private sector. Some people may fear the risks of private investment or lack knowledge of the alternatives offered, and they may feel more secure with the government program.

If people had the option to leave the program, however, those who remained could not be given the same benefits as before because the program relies on pay-as-you-go financing. Their tax payments could be used to finance the remaining obligations of the program, but they would earn no rate of return through increased productivity. Giving these individuals any more than they pay in would require general-revenue financing, which is undesirable because it would amount to welfare for the recipients, regardless of whether they were truly in need. Furthermore, it would prevent the program from being truly voluntary because all taxpayers would have to participate through payment of general-revenue taxes. Such a return would suffer from all the drawbacks of the social insurance bonds advocated under the Hobbs-Powlesland proposal and the Buchanan proposal discussed in chapter 10.

People could, however, be allowed to buy social security bonds that would return their money to them in real terms when they retire. In other words, their money would be returned increased by a rate of return equal to the rate of inflation. This option has the undesirable feature of keeping the government in the insurance business, but it might be useful as a transitional mechanism. People might feel more secure with social security reform if they knew that those who wanted to could remain in the program. Furthermore, this compromise proposal would have the positive feature of automatically phasing itself out over time.

Although these compromise proposals make the system proposed here less attractive from a libertarian viewpoint, this system is still far superior to social security. These compromise reforms could eventually be phased out without much difficulty. The difficult major reforms of social security will have already been accomplished.

Two additional objections to the ideal system we are proposing should be noted, even though they are not valid. First, government officials have focused heavily on the fact that social security benefits are indexed to rise with the rate of inflation and have contended that this inflation-proof feature of the program cannot be matched by private alternatives. This is simply not true. As prices increase with inflation, the value of the assets that individuals hold in their invested retirement accounts will, on average, increase at the same rate. The prices charged for the goods and services produced by these investments will also, on average, increase at the rate of inflation. The profit or rate of return on those investments will therefore remain the same in real terms. During periods of inflation the profits of businesses are neither eliminated nor sharply reduced by the rise in prices. On the contrary, it is businesses that raise the prices on the goods and services their investments produce during the inflationary period. These price increases will not result in any long-term rise in profits for these businesses because they are merely increasing their prices in response to excess demand, which will percolate throughout the economy and increase their costs. The result will be to maintain long-term profit margins in real terms.

In chapter 4 we saw the real rates of return that individuals could expect on their retirement investments in the long run. The actual nominal rate of return will be higher, on average, by an amount equal to the rate of inflation. Private investments can pay these real rates of return because the value of the assets held by those investments will increase to compensate for inflation, and so will the prices of the goods and services produced by those investments, resulting in a stable, constant real rate of return. The higher private sector benefits discussed in chapter 4 were calculated on the basis of these expected real rates of return, and they were presented in real terms. Thus these benefits will not be depreciated by inflation.

While a person is working and accumulating his retirement fund, therefore, the future benefits that this fund will be able to pay will be increasing at the rate of inflation because of this automatic adjustment process. If a person chooses to live off the interest in this fund in retirement, his benefits will continue to increase at the rate of inflation because the interest rate generally increases with the rate of inflation so that the same real interest is paid, and the value of the assets in the fund will also tend to increase with inflation. Thus the individual will be able to attain his same expected benefits in real terms regardless of inflation. Similarly, if an individual purchases an annuity it will be possible for the seller of the annuity to agree to pay benefits in real terms, adjusted for inflation, because of the automatic adjustment process in the investments that would support the annuity. The same is true for benefits paid under life, disability, and health insurance policies. The superior private benefits discussed in chapter 4 were all based on the assumption that the seller of the private policies had agreed to increase benefits at the rate of inflation.

Furthermore, if it were true that the benefits offered under private alternatives could not be made inflation-proof as those offered through social security, it would simply mean that social security was offering individuals higher than market returns. Since these higher returns would be paid for through increased taxes rather than increased production, they would simply constitute welfare. The higher than market returns would only serve to obscure the superiority of the private system, which makes everyone better off by increasing production. Inflation-proof social security benefits under these circumstances would be just like offering social insurance bonds with higher than market returns (as discussed under the Hobbs-Powlesland and Buchanan proposals in chapter 10). As we have seen, there is no reason why the government should be pursuing this policy under these circumstances.

But most importantly, it is simply not true that the private, ideal system described here cannot match the inflation-proof benefits of social security. The private system can pay benefits automatically adjusted for inflation so that they will remain constant in real terms.

A second possible invalid objection to this ideal system is that the substantial additional capital investment that would result would decrease the return to capital to such an extent that private investment alternatives to social security would not be worthwhile. But any potential reduction in the return to capital due to this effect would not change the vast superiority of the private system over social security. Martin Feldstein has calculated that if everyone saved and invested enough to completely replace their social security benefits, the real rate of return on capital investments would fall by two percentage points or less from its current level of 12% or more.[2] This decline would not occur until sufficient investments had been accumulated to replace social security completely, which would take decades.

However, there are several reasons to believe that this decline would not occur at all. First, Feldstein's calculations assume that technology is constant, yet new improved technologies increase the productivity of capital. We are now in an era of particularly rapid technological advancement, and the new technologies that are now available and that may become available in the next few decades may well be expected to completely offset any decline in the rate of return due to increased investment.

---

[2]Martin Feldstein, "National Saving in the United States," *Harvard Institute of Economic Research*, Discussion Paper No. 506, October 1976, pp. 31–32; Martin Feldstein, "The Optimal Financing of Social Security," *Harvard Institute of Economic Research*, Discussion Paper No. 388, 1974.

This is especially probable in light of the energy crisis that now dominates the world economy. The solution to this crisis, whether through nuclear power, synthetic fuels, more difficult recovery processes of conventional fuels, or more efficent use of existing resources, will require enormous capital outlays. The dissipation of easily obtainable fossil fuels means that the return on the capital intensive technologies that will replace these fuels has soared dramatically. The "return" on these investments will be the elimination of the energy crisis, and that is a very high and valuable return indeed.

There are numerous other technological advancements not directly related to energy that promise to forestall any decline in the return to capital. New developments in electronics, computers, communications, space exploitation, and genetic engineering, to name but a few fields, could remake the American economy if the necessary capital becomes available. The returns on the capital investments implementing these new developments will be enormous.

A second reason to doubt that any decline in the return to capital investment will occur is the low rate of saving in the United States in recent decades. This low savings rate has meant very little capital accumulation during this period and, more recently, actual capital disaccumulation. This disaccumulation has been exacerbated by the combination of inflation and inadequate accounting and tax conventions for depreciation. These problems have meant delays in the introduction of available technologies, in additions to the housing stock, and in the replacement of outmoded capital plants. Much of the additional capital investment from a private retirement system, therefore, would go to replace the recently consumed capital and to embark on these delayed projects. Without this additional investment to reverse recent trends, the return on such investment will undoubtedly increase in future years. Much of the additional investment from a private retirement system is therefore likely merely to avert this increase in capital returns rather than lead to a decline in returns.

A third factor tending to offset any decline in capital returns due to increased investment is the recently developed trend of federal regulation requiring large capital outlays by businesses to solve real or perceived environmental and safety problems. These regulations divert funds away from productive capital investments and into numerous federally mandated alternative projects. If these diverted funds are not replaced by additional capital investment, the return on productive capital investments will increase. Much of the additional capital investment from a private retirement system, therefore, will simply replace the lost capital diverted by these regulations. This new capital investment will simply avert a rise in capital returns rather than cause a decline in those returns.

A fourth and final factor likely to offset any decline in capital returns is the increasing opportunities for capital investment in the developing third world countries. The economies of many of these countries are growing rapidly, and they present many opportunities for lucrative capital investment that were not possible when the countries were backward and undeveloped. Capital knows no nationality, and it is possible that substantial amounts of American capital will be diverted from investment in this country to investment in these developing economies. Some of the increased investment from a private retirement system will therefore merely replace this lost capital and again avert a rise in capital returns in this country.

The United States is now suffering from capital starvation. Many of our most severe problems—energy, housing, declining worker productivity, increased foreign competition, and sluggish or non-existent economic growth—require enormous amounts of capital for their solution. There will be no substantial decline in the return to capital until these problems are solved. With these problems, and the budding availability of many new, and even revolutionary, capital-intensive technologies, our economy should be quite capable of absorbing the additional capital investment from a private retirement system without any significant decline in capital investment returns. If the additional capital generated by the social security reform advocated here would cause such a decline, which would mean that it would lead to the solution of the problems we have mentioned, then it is clear that such reform would be more than worthwhile.

A Proposal for Reform

The chief difficulty in reforming the present social security program is the problem of paying off the current benefit obligations of the program while still saving for a reserve fund to pay for future benefits. The current social security program has an unfunded net liability of about $4 trillion, which represents the present value of currently accrued future benefit obligations. These benefits must be paid off at the same time that current workers are saving to finance their own future benefits. The difficult question is how to do this without imposing undue hardship on the current working generation.

Although this obstacle may seem insuperable at first glance, we will see that it can be solved with minimal hardship. The key to the problem is to find ways to capture some of the advantages of social security reform that will benefit future generations and use these captured benefits to pay off the current liabilities of the program.

We will examine first a set of short-term proposals, which will improve the system in the immediate future, and then a set of long-term proposals, which will lead to the establishment of the ideal system. Most of these short-term proposals are seriously being considered today as possible reforms of the program and they therefore raise important public questions of current interest. These proposals will, in general, not only improve the program in the short run but make long-term reform of the program easier and more feasible.

Short-Term Reform Perhaps the most important of these short-term reforms is the elimination of the welfare elements in the present social security benefit structure and the transfer of the welfare function to the SSI program. The elimination of all the welfare elements in the current program will result in a system that gives each person retirement benefits equal to the amount he has paid in past taxes, increased by an implicit rate of accumulated interest. A portion of each individual's taxes would be considered a premium for survivor's insurance, and another portion would be considered a premium for disability insurance. The amount of survivor's or disability benefits paid would depend solely on the amount of these premiums paid in the past, just as in private life and disability insurance. An equal dollar amount of each person's taxes would be considered a premium for health insurance benefits.

The elimination of the welfare benefit provisions in the current program does not mean that benefits would be cut. Total taxes collected would still be distributed to all recipients, but the basis for distribution would be different. If this meant that any individuals fell below a minimum standard of living, the SSI program would supplement their benefits to bring them back up to a decent level.

One of the current welfare elements is the progressivity of the benefit formula. As we saw in chapter 2, the benefit formula is weighted so that those with relatively lower incomes will get a higher percentage of their past taxes paid in benefits than those with higher incomes. This progressivity should be replaced with a strictly proportional formula, a proposal also advanced by Alicia Munnell in *The Future of Social Security*.[3] Munnell supports this reform because, by paying welfare benefits to those who are not poor, the current progressive formula wastes funds meant to help the poor. This change would also mean that the welfare benefits would be provided by the progressive income tax through the SSI program rather than the regressive payroll tax.

A similar reform would be to eliminate the additional benefits that retired and disabled workers receive for spouses and dependents. This benefit provision is one of the chief sources of the many inequities between families and individuals. Munnell endorses this proposal too, arguing that the current provision is an extremely inefficient way to channel money to low-income families because relatively few husband-wife families are poor.[4] She also argues that it is no longer reasonable to design the program on the basis of the presumed dependency of a married woman on the male head of household. The 1975 Social Security Advisory Council called for gradually reducing the 50% supplementary benefit for spouses of retired and disabled workers to 40% in six years, 30% in the next six years, 20% six years later, and so on until the secondary retirement benefits are completely eliminated in 2006.

Another welfare provision that should be eliminated is the minimum benefit, which provides a minimum monthly benefit regardless of the amount calculated through the benefit formula. Munnell also supports the elimination of this provision, as do many others, because it channels funds to people who are not poor but who nevertheless qualify for benefits under its terms.[5]

A fourth welfare provision that could be eliminated is the maximum family benefit, which puts a limit on the amount that can be received regardless of the amount calculated through the benefit formula. This provision should be eliminated so that all would receive the same proportion of past tax payments regardless of how high the benefits are.

A fifth welfare provision is the earnings test, which reduces benefits if a person earns more than a certain amount. This provi-

---

[3]Alicia H. Munnell, *The Future of Social Security* (Washington D.C.: Brookings Institution, 1977), pp. 38–44.
[4]Ibid., pp. 44–51.
[5]Ibid., pp. 51–52.

sion should also be eliminated so that people will receive benefits based on their past tax payments no matter how much they earn apart from the system.

The elimination of these and other welfare provisions in the social security benefit structure would separate the welfare and insurance portions of the program and allow the welfare function to be more adequately served by alternative means, which would also allow the insurance portion of the program to be improved by further reform. These reforms should probably be phased in slowly over time to give people time to adjust to the changes. It should be noted that there has been no suggestion that current benefits now paid to the elderly should be changed.

A second desirable short-term reform is the Hsiao proposal, discussed in chapter 10, which, by indexing benefits in the future to prices rather than to wages, would slow the growth of benefits in future years while still maintaining them at a more than adequate level. It would allow the program to avoid the future tax increases that will be necessary to finance the tremendous expansion of benefits under the current wage-indexing scheme. Most importantly, it would make long-term reform of the program easier because it would hold down the growth of the program's unfunded liabilities, which must be paid off in a shift from the current pay-as-you-go program to an invested system.

A third short-term reform is to phase in a gradual delay of the retirement age from sixty-five to sixty-eight. This proposal has been widely advocated by numerous groups and individuals including the Brookings Institution, the 1975 Social Security Advisory Council, and the Carter administration. As the work force continues to improve in health and to live longer, it makes sense to delay retirement and encourage individuals to remain productive, active members of society. Doing so would also slow the future growth of benefits, taxes, and liabilities, making long-term reform easier.

A fourth possible reform is general-revenue financing. By itself, this reform would not be a positive step, but, as we have seen, it is likely to lead to positive changes. If the program is financed from general revenues, its true cost will become more apparent because it will have to compete with other spending proposals for available funds. The reform will remove one additional tax source—the payroll tax—from federal control, probably leading to lower taxes and federal spending in the future. With the program financed by general revenues, political pressure is likely to lead to the imposition of a means test that would allow the program's benefits to be paid only to the poor, thus turning social security into a pure welfare program and leaving the insurance function to the private sector.

Furthermore, as we shall soon see, abolishing the payroll tax and meeting current benefit obligations from general revenues is the first step in the long-term reform proposals discussed below. Any shift toward general-revenue financing will be a start toward long-term reform and will begin to phase out the current liabilities of the program.

Any proposal to cut payroll taxes and use general-revenue financing should be supported, despite the deceptive intention of many of the proposal's advocates and the uninformed arguments generally advanced in its support. Many different methods of financing the program through general revenues have been suggested. Whatever the form of the ultimate proposal adopted, however, the reform is likely to be a desirable one because of its long-term political implications and its probable effects on the program.

A final short-term reform proposal is to abolish Regulation Q, which currently sets limits on the amount of interest small depositors can receive for their money at banks and other financial institutions. This reform would allow small depositors to get a fair market return on their money and begin to open up private alternatives to social security. The restrictive regulations on investments by banks and savings and loan institutions that created the need for Regulation Q should also be eased as part of this reform.

Long-Term Reform The short-term proposals discussed above will separate the welfare function from the insurance function of social security. The goal of the long-term proposals is to privatize the insurance function of the program and establish the ideal system described earlier.

The first step in this long-term reform proposal is to remove a tremendous burden on current taxpayers by abolishing the payroll tax. Abolishing the payroll tax would also stop the accrual of further benefit obligations and liabilities. The second step would be to give private institutions the opportunity to apply to the government to be put on a list of investment alternatives to social security. These firms would offer individuals packages of retirement, survivor's, disability, and perhaps hospital insurance like those described above for the ideal system. The government would grant approval to those firms that could demonstrate that they could handle their customer's funds fairly and honestly and that they would abide by traditional principles of sound insurance and responsible trust management. The government would expect the firms to take the money their customers paid in premiums and invest it in ways that would not involve undue risk. All companies that met these qualifications and received approval would be put on the government list. The government could then guarantee the investments, paying any benefits promised to individuals under contracts with these companies if the companies failed to do so.

The next step would be to calculate the age at which individuals could still receive more in retirement benefits investing in the private sector than they could through social security. As individuals get older, the amount they can accumulate for retirement by saving and investing outside of social security is reduced. Eventually, each will reach a point where the amount he can accumulate on his own outside of the program is less than what he could get if he continued in social security. In a recent paper Feldstein calculates that all those at least under the age of thirty-five could still do better with an invested system than through social security, assuming a low constant real rate of return of 3%.[6] In an article in 1966, Buchanan and Campbell calculated the cutoff age to be thirty-nine, at that time.[7]

If we assume higher rates of return, then these figures will be higher, especially if we institute the tax breaks for retirement investment that we have discussed and therefore it does not seem unreasonable to assume that this cutoff age would be at least forty years. In fact, with the high rates of return that would be earned by tax-free investments, the age may well be even higher.

All people in the age group below the cutoff age would be required to save a certain percentage of their incomes for retirement and insurance protection, although not necessarily through social security. This percentage could be made equal to what each person would have paid in social security taxes if the current program had been continued, although if each person invests this entire amount in private alternatives each will have a lot more in retirement benefits than what he would have had under social security. It is

[6]Martin Feldstein and Anthony Pellechio, "Social Security Wealth: The Impact of Alternative Inflation Adjustments," *Conference on Financing Social Security*, American Enterprise Institute, 1977.

[7]James M. Buchanan and Colin D. Campbell, "Voluntary Social Security," *Wall Street Journal*, 20 December 1966.

probably unnecessary to require everyone to make such lavish provisions for his retirement years. The amounts individuals are required to save, therefore, should probably be reduced so that with the higher returns from the private, invested alternatives individuals will have about the same retirement benefits as they would have had under social security, assuming that they save and invest no more than the required amounts. This would give working people a break by allowing them to use some of the money they are currently paying in social security taxes for current consumption.

The amount a person is required to save could be allowed to vary over his lifetime according to his needs and preferences. For example, individuals could save less in their twenties, when they are starting families, if they make it up in their thirties.

All those below the cutoff age will then be given the option of using the funds they are required to save to purchase one of the private alternatives on the government approved list. People will, in effect, be using the money they would have paid in social security taxes under the current system to purchase private alternatives. These private alternatives will provide individuals with a complete package of insurance protection covering all the major contingencies that social security does now. People who take this option will look to the private alternative chosen for all future benefits and will receive nothing from social security.

Those who choose this option will receive no social security benefits for their past tax payments. Since those who choose the private alternatives will be better off than if they had stayed in social security, they have no cause to complain about the loss of currently accrued social security benefits. This is a modification of the Friedman proposal discussed in chapter 10. Friedman would pay off all currently earned benefits, even for those in this group. The difference between his proposal and this one is simply one of political viability. It may simply be more politically feasible to reform the program if the benefits earned by those who can still do better outside the system are denied, thereby lowering the cost of the reform that has to be met from general revenues.

Those in this age group who stay in social security will receive benefits equal to their tax payments increased by the rate of inflation, instead of currently legislated social security benefits. If individuals are allowed to withdraw from the program, it cannot continue to pay currently promised benefits because it operates on a pay-as-you-go basis. Since the money paid into social security is not invested, it does not result in any increased production that can be used to pay a rate of return on past tax payments. The program can, therefore, return to the individual only what he has paid into it in the past. If his past tax payments are accumulated and increased at the rate of inflation, he will merely receive back what he has paid in real terms. The only way a rate of return can be paid on these past social security taxes without the payroll tax is if general revenues are used to finance it. As we saw in our discussion of the Hobbs-Powlesland and Buchanan proposals in chapter 10, however, there is no reason why such general revenue subsidies should be paid because they prevent the program from being truly voluntary.

To effectuate this new approach, those in this age group who stay in the program will receive social security bonds equal in value to their past tax payments into the program accumulated and increased by the rate of inflation. These bonds will continue to grow at the rate of inflation until the person holding them retires at age sixty-five or sixty-eight, but they will be redeemable at that age only if the individual has continued to pay social security taxes into the program all his life. As he continues to pay taxes into the program he will receive bonds with a face value equal to the amount of his taxes, and these bonds will grow with the annual rate of inflation. These bonds, however, can be redeemed at any time, and the individual will then receive back in real terms what he has paid in taxes. This provision allows those who have decided to stay in the program to opt out later if they choose and receive back the money they have paid since the new system was instituted. This redemption rule will not apply to the initial bonds paid to individuals in this age group who decide to stay in the program, however. These bonds represent taxes paid into the program before the adoption of the new system. These bonds will therefore not be redeemable if a person who originally decided to stay in the program later decides to drop out because those in this age group who decided to opt for the private alternatives initially and not stay in the program receive nothing for their past tax payments and therefore those who initially decide to stay in and later decide to drop out should also receive nothing. Otherwise, all will stay in the program until they get the redeemable bonds for their past tax payments and then opt out. This would frustrate our original policy decision to deny currently accrued benefits and grant nothing for past tax payments to those in this age group who decided to opt out of the program and were thereby made better off.

Once a person reaches retirement, the accumulated value of his bonds will support a certain level of retirement benefits. If the individual dies or becomes disabled, he or his survivors will be paid benefits based on the accumulated value of his bonds at that time. Once the individual has received back in benefits his accumulated taxes increased by the rate of inflation, these benefits will cease.

Ultimately the requirement that individuals in this age group must save a certain portion of their incomes to invest in one of the private alternatives or in social security bonds could be phased out. As people become more aware of and used to dealing with market institutions and as stable institutions developed, these people should be allowed to make their own decisions concerning whether and how much they want to save for retirement. As they saw how well these market institutions worked, they would be less apprehensive about making their own decisions. The savings requirement could therefore be phased out slowly. It might be reduced by 20% of the original amount every five years, for example. This would also phase out the requirement that an investment program have government approval to qualify as an acceptable alternative to social security and the government guarantee of investments for retirement because both apply only to the portion of each individual's income that the government requires be saved.

Even with the elimination of these requirements, however, some continued government guaranteed investment options would remain for those who wanted them. Savings accounts, government bonds, and pension plans are all guaranteed by the federal government. Those who thought such guarantees necessary and desirable could invest in these alternatives for their retirement.

A different set of rules would apply for those between the cut-off age, estimated at age forty, and age sixty. These individuals could not accumulate as much as they have been promised in social security benefits if they started saving and investing in the private sector at this late age. Those in this age group would therefore be given social security bonds that reach maturity on retirement. At maturity these bonds will equal what these individuals are currently promised in benefits under social security *minus* what they could get in the private sector if they now began saving and investing what they would otherwise pay in social security taxes. These individuals would then be required, starting now, to save a percentage of their incomes each year equal to the full amounts they would have paid in social security taxes if the current program had been continued.

They will, however, be allowed to use these funds to purchase one of the alternatives on the government-approved list. Those who choose one of these options will again be protected by an entire package of insurance services covering all of the major contingencies now covered by social security. The amount of retirement benefits received through these private alternatives will be supplemented by benefits from the initial social security bonds that these individuals are granted at the start of the reform. The benefits paid under these initial bonds would be designed so that those who choose one of the private alternatives would receive in retirement about what they would have received under social security if the current program had been continued. Similarly, if one of these individuals died or became disabled, the bonds would be structured to supplement the private alternative chosen so that the total amount of benefits received would be the same as would have been paid under the current social security program if it had been continued.

People in this age group who choose to remain in the program would use the funds they are required to save to purchase additional social security bonds. These bonds would be equal in face value to the amount paid to purchase them, and this value would grow until maturity on retirement at the annual rate of inflation. These individuals will therefore again just receive back in real terms the money they have paid to purchase these bonds. At retirement, therefore, they will receive less than they would have under the current social security program. If one of these individuals dies or becomes disabled before retirement, he will first receive benefits under his purchased bonds until he has received back in real terms all he had paid to purchase them. He would then receive the amount of benefits to which he was entitled under the initial bonds. The total amount of benefits would again be less than this individual would have received under the current social security program.

Nevertheless, because people in this age group could always choose one of the private alternatives, they will be left at least as well off as before the reform. They will be able to receive as much in retirement and insurance benefits as they would have received if the current program had been continued. Since they will not be made worse off, they should not oppose the reform. The requirement that these individuals save a certain percentage of their incomes each year could be phased out along with the same requirement for younger individuals.

To all those over sixty, the government would continue to pay what they are currently promised in social security benefits. These benefits, and all those that must be paid when the social security bonds of those who are younger are redeemed, would be paid from general revenues.

The final long-term reform is to institute the system of tax exemptions discussed above for the ideal system. This tax system is really an expansion of the treatment provided today for IRA and Keogh accounts, although it takes some of the tax principles applied to these accounts much farther than they have ever been taken before. The goal of this tax system is to allow individuals to receive the full value of the increased production created by the investments they make for retirement and insurance protection, free from taxation. This would allow them to receive the full 12% or more real rate of return earned by capital investments.

Since the private alternatives in this reform proposal are superior to social security for all those under sixty, virtually all individuals below this age will choose the private alternatives. Eventually all those who were sixty and over when the reform was instituted will die, and the government will be responsible only for paying off the initial amount of social security bonds paid to those who were between forty and sixty when the reform began. Once those in this age group have died, virtually all those who were in the younger group when the reform began will be relying primarily on private alternatives. Those who were still in the program for whatever reason will be paying for their own benefits directly. The government will then have no more obligations to meet from general revenues, and the system will have become completely privatized.

At any point in this process the requirement that individuals save some portion of their incomes for retirement and other insurance contingencies could be phased out along with the other remaining restrictive elements, if doing so was thought desirable. Alternatively, only the requirement that these savings be used to purchase private options from a government-approved list could be phased out while maintaining the savings requirement, thus allowing individuals to take advantage of the wider range of investments described under the ideal system. The program of government guarantees could also be phased out independently of the other elements in the reform. Once the current program has been privatized and fully funded, any of these further reforms could be quite easily instituted.

The end result of the short-term and long-term proposals advanced here is to separate the welfare function from the insurance function of the current program and to fully privatize the insurance function. These reforms will lead to the establishment of the ideal system we have described. The reforms we are proposing would leave a tremendous deficit in federal revenues. We have eliminated the payroll tax, but the burden of current benefit obligations remains to be funded from general revenues. Where will the general revenues to fund this deficit come from?

The Congress could merely raise general taxes to cover the deficit, but this would place the entire burden of the reform on the current working generation and might make the benefits of the reform too costly. It also seems unfair to make the current generation bear the entire burden of the cost of reform. Ideally, then, we should try to meet this burden without raising general taxes by using some of the benefits of the reform to the current and future generations to pay it off. The total to be paid is about $4 trillion, which represents the total unfunded liability of the program.

A major portion of this deficit will be eliminated by letting out of the program all those under the cut-off age estimated at forty without paying them their currently accrued benefits. Doing so is feasible because, considering the benefits of the reform, these individuals will still be better off after investing in the private sector even without their currently accrued social security benefits. They still have enough working years left so that if they use the money they would pay in social security taxes over the rest of their lives to invest in the private sector, they will still have more in retirement benefits than if they had continued in the social security program.

Another way of using these benefits to pay off the program's liabilities is to pay in social security benefits those aged forty to sixty the difference between (a) what they could earn in private sector investments in their remaining years with the money they would have paid in social security taxes and (b) what they have been promised in social security benefits. These individuals are left monetarily at least as well off as before the reform, and part of the monetary benefits of the reform is used to pay off the accrued liabilities of the program by reducing the benefits that must be paid.

After these reforms, we will be left with annual deficits in each of the next five years equal to the projected amount of benefit payments in each of those years. The annual deficit will decline steadily from projected benefits in each year after that, however, as the individuals retiring in those years will have their benefits reduced by the amounts they have earned through investment of their social security taxes in the private sector. Fifteen years after the reform was instituted, benefit payments will have been reduced sharply from projected levels because individuals who will retire in that year will have their benefits reduced by the amounts they have accumulated through fifteen years of investment. Those retiring in the years after that will require very little in benefits from general revenues as we approach the cut-off age when people are able to accumulate almost as much in private investments as they were promised in social security benefits. The projected benefit expenditures for these years will therefore decline drastically. Twenty-five years after the reform is instituted, those retiring will require no social security benefits, and the program will be completely phased out when the last individual who retired with some social security benefits dies. The amounts paid under the program will have become relatively small, however, long before that.

The burden of this phase-out stage could have been reduced further if the short-term reforms described above had been instituted before the long-term reform was started. Price-indexed benefits and a delayed retirement age could sharply reduce the burden that must be met from general revenues during this phase-out period. The impact from price indexing is greatest in the future, and any delay in the retirement age has to be phased in slowly, so the reduction in liabilities from these reforms would not be that great if they were adopted at the same time as the long-term reform. It may take many years to institute the long-term reform, but short-term reforms are on the political agenda now. If they are adopted, by the time the long-term reforms are adopted in several years these short-term reforms will have had a significant effect in reducing liabilities, thus making the long-term reforms more feasible.

There is an additional way in which some of the benefits of the reform can be captured to meet the general revenue deficit caused by the reform. We can delay the adoption of the tax exemption system we have described and continue to require all individuals to save and invest all that they would have paid in social security taxes. As the economy grows because of these investments, general revenue taxes will also grow. Some of the increased production generated by the saving and investment of social security taxes will then go into general revenues. This increase in general revenues can then be used to help pay off the liabilities of the program as it is phased out.

The reform will increase general revenues in another important

way. As we saw in chapter 3, the social security payroll tax constitutes a wedge between what the employer pays and what the
employee receives. This wedge reduces the employee's compensation
for working and thus discourages such work, leading to less employment, less economic activity, and a reduced national output. By
abolishing the payroll tax, the reform will eliminate the wedge and
lead to an increase in the compensation of employees, resulting in increased employment, increased economic activity, and increased
national output. These increases will result in increased general tax
revenues that will further narrow the deficit caused by the reform.

Even though under our reform proposal workers will be required
to save and invest the amounts they would have paid in social security taxes, this increase in general revenues will still occur. Employees
will now perceive these saved and invested amounts as part of their
income, and not as a tax, since these amounts directly benefit each
employee personally, just like the portion of each employee's compensation that is saved in a bank. Employees will therefore perceive
their compensation as increasing as much as if the payroll tax were
simply abolished with no continuing savings requirement. This savings requirement will lower the perceived compensation received by
employees to the extent that it requires workers to save and invest
more in retirement and insurance protection than they want. Then
workers would not be able to use this portion of their income to buy
the goods and services they really want, and it will not be worth as
much to them as if they could spend it without restrictions. But, as
an empirical matter, the reduction in perceived compensation due
to this effect is not likely to be substantial or to have a substantial
impact on general revenues.

It should be noted that the two impacts on tax revenue that we
have described here correspond to the two general categories of
social security's impacts on the economy discussed in chapter 3. We
shall refer to the impact on tax revenues resulting from the removal
of the payroll tax as the "payroll tax effect" and the impact on general revenues from the increased investments as the "investment
effect."

Over time, therefore, as individuals begin to accumulate bigger
and bigger investment accounts, the increased taxes generated by
these accounts will grow to larger and larger amounts. At the same
time, the increased economic activity resulting from the removal of
the payroll tax burden will also increase general revenues. Mean-
while, the liabilities that have to be met will be shrinking every year

after the first five years, as we have seen. Eventually, these two trends will converge, and the deficit will then be completely eliminated. After the deficit is safely phased out, the system of tax exemptions can be instituted and the amount of required savings can be reduced.

We can derive a very rough estimate of the magnitude of this deficit and its probable duration as a significant factor. We may assume that 1980 is the first year of the reform and that about half of the increased production due to investments is taxed away, or 6.25% out of an estimated 12.5% real rate of return before taxes, leaving a 6.25% real rate of return on investments after taxes. Let us focus on the OASDI program alone and assume that individuals will invest each year the full amount that they would have paid in OASDI taxes. By calculating the amount of general revenue taxes that will be generated each year by these investments and subtracting this amount from projected benefit expenditures, we can discover the annual deficit that will result each year, considering only the investment effect of the reform on general revenues. These totals are presented in table 58 under the column headed "annual deficit."

An estimate of the effect on general revenues from removing the payroll tax burden has been provided by economists Arthur Laffer and David Ranson. In a recent study, these economists estimated that if either the employer's or the employee's share of the social security payroll tax had been eliminated in 1977, general revenues would have increased in 1978 by $53 billion a year due to the resulting increase in employment, economic activity, and production.[8] To be conservative, we will consider this $53 billion as an estimate of the effect of eliminating the entire payroll tax in our reform, even though it is an estimate only of the impact from eliminating one-half of the payroll tax. We will also conservatively assume that this figure will remain the same after 1980, although it would undoubtedly continue to grow with the economy. The resulting annual deficit from the reform, after taking into account this impact on general revenues as well as the investment effect, is shown in table 58 under the heading "remaining deficit."

We can see in table 58 that the final resulting deficit in each year, after taking into account both effects on general revenues, is sub-

8Arthur B. Laffer and R. David Ranson, *The Prototype Wedge Model: A Tool for Supply-Side Economics*, Report to the Board of Directors, American Council for Capital Formation, Center for Policy Research, 1979.

stantial only in the early years of the reform, falling from $60 billion to about $50 billion over the first four years. After that the deficit declines steadily as the taxes generated by increased investment and economic activity expand rapidly to meet benefit obligations. The deficit falls to easily manageable amounts of $35 to $25 billion in the sixth and seventh years of the reform and falls to negligible amounts in the ninth year. These deficit amounts are all less than some of the federal budget deficits we have experienced in recent years.

After the first five years of the reform the annual benefit obligations that must be met will begin to decline from the projected amounts because those who retire in that year will have their benefits reduced by the amounts they have been able to earn through private investments for five years. The actual benefit obligations will decline further and more quickly each year as more individuals with reduced benefits made up for by investments retire and as these individuals will have invested for more years. The deficits shown in table 58 after the first five years are higher than the actual deficits will be. We can therefore expect the deficit to fall to an insignificant amount by the seventh or eighth year of the reform.

Even if we consider only the impact on tax revenues resulting from the investment effect, the resulting deficits are not overwhelming, although much more difficult to manage in the early years of the reform. As table 58 indicates, these deficits would remain just over $100 billion in each of the first four years. After that, however, the deficits would decline steadily, falling to $25.6 billion by the eleventh year of the reform, a comparatively minor and easily affordable amount. In the next year, the total deficit would be virtually eliminated, falling to $7.8 billion. Again, after the first five years these deficits are higher than the actual deficits will be because individuals retiring at that time will be relying on the private alternatives to supply a large portion of their benefits. Thus these deficits can be expected to fall to minor amounts as a result of this effect in the ninth or tenth year of the reform.

It should be reiterated that the deficits shown in table 58 would be reduced even further if some of the short-term reforms discussed above are adopted. Even if enacted at the same time as the long-term reform, price indexing and a delayed retirement age may make some significant dents in these deficits in the second five years of the reform.

These deficits should be seen in perspective. One can only expect reform of the enormous social security system to require large subsidies from general revenues in the early years. It is in fact quite encouraging that the huge unfunded liability of the program can be phased out so quickly and at such little cost. We have reduced this liability to the relatively small deficit amounts shown in table 58 by absolutely painless measures that will make no one worse off and most people better off. These measures have used the benefits of the reform to finance the accrued liabilities of the program, phasing them out while hurting no one. The only costs of the reform that remain to be met are these relatively small deficit amounts. Financing these deficits will be a significant problem for only six to eight years.

Furthermore, paying the amounts necessary to finance these deficits now will allow individuals to avoid the future tax increases that will be necessary under the current social security program. If the program is to meet its future benefit obligations, large tax increases above currently legislated tax rates will be necessary. The amounts that must be raised by these future tax increases are much greater than the amounts necessary to finance the deficits under our long-term reform proposal. If this reform is enacted, however, once the deficit is paid off the system of tax exemptions described above can be phased in and the amounts individuals are required to save can be sharply reduced below the amounts they would have paid in social security taxes, which will result in a significant increase in current disposable income.

In addition, the current trend among economists seems to favor changing social security over to a fully funded, invested basis, whether the investments are made through the government or through the private sector. These reform schemes, including those advocated by professors Feldstein and Friedman, all face the problem of financing current benefits while accumulating a fund. They will thus all face the problem of financing similar deficits either through increased taxes or other methods. Meeting these deficits is a manageable short-term problem whose solution will lead to enormous long-term benefits.

These deficits in fact do not even represent extremely difficult or unheard of amounts for the government to meet from general revenues. They are in about the same range, if not less, as the realistic cost estimates for some of the more ambitious national health insurance plans advanced by such highly respected national leaders as Senator Edward Kennedy. Given the enormous benefits of social security reform, and the severe problems of the current program, such reform would seem to warrant these costs far more than a new, enormous national health insurance program. Social security reform would seem to be a far more urgent national priority. The government should clean up the messes it has already before it makes new messes.

Thus we should think of social security reform as a new government program, and we should think of the resulting deficits as the cost of this new program to be financed from general revenues. This will put the cost of the reform in perspective and allow us to compare it more easily with alternative general revenue expenditures.

There are actually many ways that we can meet the costs of this reform, paying off the resulting deficits, in a relatively painless manner. Ideally, we should strive to gather the funds to pay these costs without increasing general tax rates.

First, eventually total general taxes collected increase as the economy grows, even though general tax rates have not been increased. The increased economic activity resulting from economic growth will yield a higher absolute amount of taxes. As the economy grows wages increase, and some people are pushed into higher tax brackets. As taxes increase through this process new government programs are added to spend the new funds. There are already many new government programs on the political agenda that might consume these tax increases. It would seem, however, that the enormous benefits of social security reform would outweigh the benefits of any of these other new programs. The addition of any other new programs could be delayed, therefore, so that the government can finance social security reform.

If the economy generated a mere $30 billion a year in discretionary funds to be spent in this way, the deficit from social security reform could be eliminated after one year. If the available funds totaled $20 billion a year, the deficit could be eliminated after two years. If the total was only $10 billion a year, the deficit could be virtually eliminated after only three years. Even if we focus on the deficits left after considering the investment effect of the reform on tax revenues alone, with $30 billion a year generated in discretionary funds the deficit would be eliminated after three years. With only an additional $20 billion a year the deficit would be eliminated after four years. With only an additional $10 billion a year the deficit would be virtually eliminated after six years.

Besides delaying new spending proposals to finance social security reform, we could also delay new tax cut proposals. For example, the Kemp-Roth bill would cut federal income tax rates by one-third over a three-year period. Our proposal for social security reform, however, eliminates the payroll tax, and it is therefore like a Kemp-Roth bill for social security taxes. We could thus delay the Kemp-Roth bill for a few years and enact this social security reform first, using the general revenues that would have been lost through the Kemp-Roth bill to finance the deficits created by social security reform.

Another possible method of raising general revenues to meet these deficits is to freeze the growth of existing government programs. Before Gerald Ford left office he left a budget proposal for the following year that was $30 billion less than the budget actually enacted under Jimmy Carter. This suggests that it is quite possible to restrain the growth in existing government programs to yield an extra $20 to $30 billion a year for social security reform. In a federal budget approaching $600 billion a year we should be able to find enough wasteful, marginal, or questionable government programs whose growth could be restrained to yield an additional $20 billion a year for a project as important as social security reform.

Ultimately, we could cut other government programs whose benefits are not as great as the benefits from social security reform. If we could find enough wasteful or marginal programs in the federal budget to cut $10 to $20 billion each year, another major step toward eliminating the deficit will have been achieved.

Another way of paring down the deficit would be to eliminate the payment of social security benefits to the wealthy or those who are not in need. Double-dippers who have qualified for the minimum social security pension in addition to their other government pensions and who have benefited from the welfare provisions in the program meant to help the poor could have their benefits cut. Those with high investment incomes or large asset holdings who are receiving social security benefits could also have their benefits cut. There are many retired doctors, lawyers, and business executives in this country with a million dollars in the bank who are drawing the maximum in social security benefits. There is no reason why working people struggling with average incomes to support their families should be taxed to pay benefits to those who do not need them. If we modestly estimate that out of $120 billion in benefits in 1980, $5 billion could be saved by cutting benefits of this nature, we could reduce our projected deficits by this amount each year.

Adding up the revenues from all these sources, we find that we could raise an additional $60 billion a year by conservative estimates to finance social security reform. This would be enough to entirely eliminate the deficit, all without raising tax rates. Even if we focus on the deficit resulting from a consideration of the investment effect of the reform alone, these additional funds would be enough to eliminate all of the deficit except for $54 billion in the first year. With a government that spends $600 billion a year, a $50 billion deficit for one year can be taken in stride and met from traditional financing sources. This deficit amount is well within the range of federal budget deficits that we have experienced in recent years.

We should note an alternative method of financing these deficits suggested by Roger MacBride, the 1976 Libertarian Party presidential candidate. MacBride suggests that the government sell off some of its assets to raise the funds to finance the deficits resulting from a social security reform measure along these lines. In particular, the government owns about half of the land in the western regions of the United States. Some of these holdings could easily be sold off to finance the social security deficits. If these sales were made in the first year of the reform, the government could probably raise enough to match the present value of the future deficits. The government would still retain large holdings of western lands even after these sales, and the deficit would have been paid off without increasing taxes. The government could raise additional funds by the accelerated sale of other assets such as off-shore drilling rights.

This proposal is a good one, but it is likely to encounter skepticism and opposition because it is such an unusual and novel way of accomplishing government financing. It also raises other issues, such as conservation and protection of the environment, that are complicated enough on their own, at least in a political sense, without bringing them into the debate over social security reform. Nevertheless, this alternative method of at least partially financing the social security reform deficit should be given serious consideration.

The specific numbers presented here on the absolute magnitude of the deficit and its probable duration are not important. What is important is that this discussion leads to the reasonable conclusion that the long-term reform proposal advanced in this chapter is entirely feasible. The annual deficits resulting from the reform that must be met from general revenues will dwindle to insignificant amounts six to eight years after the proposal is first adopted. Yet, even over this period, these deficits could be met from general revenues without raising general revenue tax rates. We may conclude, therefore, that this long-term reform proposal is not only feasible on an economic basis but is attainable without undue hardship or unreasonable financial strain on government resources.

Peace and Prosperity

The benefits of this long-term reform are remarkable to contemplate. All the problems we discussed in earlier chapters will be solved, and there will be several additional benefits as well. Everyone in society will benefit from this proposal and no one will be made worse off. Consequently, all should support it.

To begin with, the reform will have several extremely beneficial effects on the economy. National income will increase significantly as the funds that would have been spent in social security taxes are saved and invested in productive capital assets that will increase production and output. As we have seen, if we had invested enough to guarantee future social security benefits we would now have an extra $400 billion a year in GNP, or more than $5,000 per family. Without the discouraging effects of the payroll tax and the earnings test, employment will grow, increasing national income even more. The special skills and experience of the elderly will again be brought into productive use instead of being wasted in the idleness imposed by social security restrictions. The additional capital investment will create a large number of new jobs, lower unemployment, increase wages, and upgrade existing jobs, thereby creating more good jobs.

In the meantime, we will have gone a long way toward solving the capital shortage problems currently facing the economy. The new capital investment will modernize our factories, improving their efficiency and making them more competitive with foreign producers. It will provide more money for mortgages, thereby increasing and improving the currently inadequate housing supply. It will provide the necessary funds to search out, discover, and develop new energy supplies. The new capital can be used to finance new hospital equipment, which will save lives. It can be used to develop new and innovative technologies which will improve the quality of our lives. It will be used to create all the additional goods and services which Americans need and desire.

The reform will also allow today's young workers to earn far greater returns on the money they are currently paying in payroll taxes than they will ever receive under social security. They will be able to accumulate enormous trust funds for their old age, and the retirement incomes financed by these funds will be much greater than those that social security can pay. Even for average families these funds could climb to well over $0.5 million in today's dollars. Because of the much higher returns available in private investments, individuals could pay less than they are currently paying in social security taxes and still have much more in retirement. This would provide more disposable income for young people who are trying to start families, buy homes, and build careers.

These young people will also be able to buy insurance and investment plans that are suited to their particular needs. They will no longer be required to pay for insurance protection that they do not need or cannot receive. Furthermore, the money individuals save and invest under the new plan will be theirs to use and spend as they desire and their financial and personal freedom will thus be greatly increased. They can count on the new system to deal with each of them in a fair and equitable manner, paying each a fair and substantial return on what they have paid into the program. They will no longer be subject to the numerous inequities of the current program.

The reform will also eliminate the real and serious threat of bankruptcy that still haunts the current social security program. Even after the recent massive tax increases the program is still subject to enormous deficits projected into the future. These deficits will require tax increases to levels that will consume 25% to 33% of the wage incomes of most Americans if the benefits promised to current workers are to be met. Each year the reports of the Social Security Administration indicate that recent economic performance and social trends are only making these long-term projections worse. The long-term unfunded net liability of the program currently stands at $4 trillion.

Under the new system, future benefits to be paid will be backed by currently saved investments. There will be enough money already on hand to pay out what has been promised. Beneficiaries will no longer be subject to the vagaries of political fortune and the whims of current taxpayers. Their benefits will no longer be hostage to the fertility rate, the unemployment rate, and the inflation rate.

The reform will also include major benefits for many of the nation's most vulnerable minority groups. One of the groups benefiting the most from this reform would be the poor. The reduced unemployment, the increase in wages and in the availability of good jobs, the increased supplies of housing, energy, medical care, and other goods will all benefit the poor. The poor and those with low incomes are also in greater need of the higher returns available to them in the private invested system. These higher returns will enable them to secure decent and adequate retirement incomes.

The discrimination against the poor in the current system will also be eliminated because they will be able to buy insurance and retirement protection that is suited to their particular needs and circumstances. The oppressive payroll tax that now bears most harshly on the poor will also have been eliminated. Welfare benefits will no longer be financed by this regressive, counterproductive tax. Benefits available to help the poor will no longer be wasted by being paid to those who are not poor.

Blacks, a large percentage of whom are poor, will also enjoy these benefits. They also stand to benefit from a decrease in unemployment and from expanded mobility through improved economic performance. Women, especially those who are single, or childless, or who work, will benefit from the end of the discrimination against them in the current system. Women will be freer to lead the lives they desire. They will no longer be penalized for following new and uncommon patterns of living and forced to subsidize those who choose the more traditional modes.

The elderly will also benefit greatly. Their employment opportunities will no longer be restricted by the earnings test. They will have more substantial retirement incomes because of the higher returns from private investments. The money they do have, furthermore, will belong to them to be spent as they please. They will no longer be subject to government restrictions on their lives in order to qualify for benefits. They will be free to use their funds to pursue numerous options and opportunities that are now closed to them.

In fact, all minority groups and individuals who follow alternative lifestyles are likely to benefit because they will be able to purchase plans of insurance and retirement protection that are more suited to their particular needs and circumstances than social security, which is likely to be best suited to the needs and characteristics of politically powerful majorities.

The reformed system will not be subject to the political instabilities and difficulties associated with the current government program. Politicians will no longer be able to abuse the system for their own gain at the expense of the public. Politically powerful special interest groups will no longer be able to seek special privileges for personal or ideological gain. The private system will not be subject to corrupting political influences. Individuals will no longer have to use cumbersome political channels to get the kind of protection they want or to make the changes they desire. They can simply arrange their own affairs as they desire or choose the plan they want from the diverse options offered in the marketplace by companies with an incentive to keep their products competitive. Each person's personal affairs will no longer be a political issue whose final resolution is in the hands of the government. Individuals will no longer have to institute national political campaigns to deal with their retirement and insurance concerns.

The reform will also end the coercive elements of the current program. Under the new system, Americans will have greater individual liberty and greater freedom to control their own lives and their own incomes. The new system will be based on voluntary consent and free exchange instead of compulsion and force. Furthermore, federal taxes and expenditures will have been reduced by about one-fourth. A large portion of the insurance industry will have been denationalized and returned to the private sector where it belongs.

One of the most important benefits of this reform is that it will result in more widespread ownership of America's business and industry. Every individual will be accumulating a trust fund that will represent his ownership interest in the country's productive assets. The reform will thus be a way for average workers to capture a large portion of the profits of the nation's private enterprises and to use these profits to support their retirement. More fundamentally, workers will at last achieve a large degree of direct control over business enterprises, but through entirely fair and honest means: The workers will have simply bought out the businesses. Although such worker control has historically had appeal primarily for those on the left side of the political spectrum, there is no real conservative objection to such control achieved through these means. The workers would have simply become full-fledged capitalists in their own right. One clear direct result of this more widespread ownership will be a more equal distribution of wealth. In addition, with a large portion of the country's business sector owned by the common man, unnecessary government regulation and oppressive business taxation is more likely to be eliminated. There will also be less opportunity for political demagogues to manipulate antibusiness sentiment. The end result is thus likely to be a more efficient and fair economy. These important benefits of the reform proposal advocated here should not be overlooked.

Finally, this reform is likely to lead to the development of new options and alternatives in insurance and retirement protection. Companies competing for business will have an incentive to develop new innovations that will benefit their customers. They will be led to offer diverse and varied options to win the business of individuals with different needs, circumstances, and preferences. Competition will also lead to changes to match new social trends and needs.

These beneficial effects will all be achieved without the new, additional problems that would be created by having the government save and invest an enormous trust fund. There would be no concern over where the government could invest the funds without unduly interfering in the private economy. Such a government trust fund could serve as a new and powerful source of control over the free market. Many special interest groups would try to use the fund's investments for personal or ideological gain. The government would inevitably use these investments to impose a whole new set of regulations and controls on private industry. There would also be the constant political temptation to raid the trust funds to pass out free benefits. There would be no end to proposals to commandeer the trust fund for some so-called urgent national priority.

The private invested system would completely avoid these problems and solve several problems that a government investment program would not. It would provide a much more varied and diverse system of insurance and investment options, giving people a greater opportunity to choose a plan of protection suited to their needs. The private system would have a better incentive structure than the government program because the income and financial success of private firms would be entirely dependent on their ability to suit the desires of consumers. The political instabilities inherent in a government investment program would be eliminated. Individuals would have greater control over their own lives and incomes, and most of the force and coercion associated with a government program would be avoided. Once the superiority of an invested system over a pay-as-you-go program is established, there is no reason why investments should not be made through private market institutions rather than through the government.

Given all these numerous and powerful beneficial effects, it would seem that this reform proposal is well worthwhile. Its only costs are transitional—the need to pay off the resulting deficits in the first ten years of the reform. But the sacrifices necessary to meet these deficits are minor, especially compared with the benefits. The problems and negative impacts of the current program have become too severe to continue to be tolerated. Social security today is just no longer working. The outdated program must be fundamentally reformed to suit the needs of modern America.

Considering these benefits, and the fact that no group in society will be made worse off while all will to some extent be made better off, this reform proposal should be supported by everyone. Welfare state liberals should favor it because it abolishes the regressive payroll tax and funds the program from general revenues. It provides more funds for the poor by eliminating the current wasteful payment of welfare benefits to those who are not poor. It also helps the poor and other minority groups in the many ways described above. Finally, it results in a more equal distribution of wealth and income.

Conservatives should also favor the reform because it reduces taxes and government spending. It denationalizes a large portion of the insurance industry, relying instead on the private market forces generally favored by conservatives. It improves economic efficiency, increases the role of individual responsibility, and bases benefit payments on what has been earned and paid for rather than welfare criteria.

Labor unions have until now been staunch supporters of ever expanding social security, but this position should surely be reexamined because the reform proposal advanced here has enormous benefits for labor union members. It would provide workers, particularly young workers, with the opportunity to receive higher benefits for lower payments than they are currently receiving and to accumulate large amounts of wealth through the high-yielding private alternatives. It would eliminate the bankruptcy problem that threatens the future financial security of these workers. It would greatly improve the economy in which these workers earn their living. It would even result in higher wages and more jobs and employment, the chief goals of labor unions. It would also remove a burdensome tax on labor union members and in the long run allow them more currently disposable income. It would provide workers with a large ownership stake in America's business and industry.

Labor unions thus have several good reasons to support this reform and to stop their unquestioning support for the current structure of social security. In the past, labor unions may have perceived social security as the most feasible way of getting a basic pension plan for their workers, but given the fact that a superior alternative now exists for the provision of these pension benefits, it no longer makes sense for labor unions to support forcing workers to forgo this superior alternative and remain in the present program. If labor unions continue their unqualified support for the current social security program they will not be pursuing the best interests of their members.

Business should support this reform because it provides more capital for investment, improves the economic climate, and increases economic growth. It allows businesses to hire more workers and expand in the growing economy. It allows many businesses a new opportunity to provide insurance, savings, and investment plans to new customers.

Everyone should support the reform because everyone will be made better off by it. How can this be possible? It is possible because the reform replaces the current system with a more efficient, productive system that leads to increased production and output. The benefits from this new wealth can therefore be used to make everyone better off. The reform also makes all better off by providing costless benefits that result from the system's improved design, including increased individual liberty, improved financial solvency, and a wider range of investment choices.

Considering the impact this reform will have on various groups in society, it should be politically as well as economically feasible. No doubt individuals must be educated to see the tremendous benefits of this reform. Political leaders must have the courage to advance these controversial reforms, which will greatly benefit the entire nation. As long as individuals can be expected to follow their own self-interest in the long run, this proposal has excellent potential for political success. With the severe problems of the current program, the present state of public dissatisfaction, and the enormous benefits that would result, this reform proposal is politically practical in the real world today.

12

Epilogue

The last time fundamental social security reform was seriously considered on a national level was in the 1964 presidential campaign. Barry Goldwater, the Republican presidential nominee, suggested that social security be made voluntary and that individuals be allowed to make alternative arrangements in the private sector if they desired. He was denounced as an enemy of the elderly and the poor.

In Arizona there is a popular joke about Barry Goldwater. An old panhandler says, "You know, in 1964 they told me that if I voted for Barry Goldwater there would be a long and bloody war in southeast Asia, high inflation and unemployment, urban decay and economic stagnation, and riots in the cities and on the nation's campuses. And you know something? They were right. I voted for Barry Goldwater and all those things happened."

Can we really expect any fundamental and radical reform of social security to have a serious chance in the real world of politics, given the tremendous popularity of the program in the past? The answer is that fundamental and radical reform of the current social security program is not only possible but inevitable. Economist Arthur Laffer has compared social security to a red Maserati racing toward a brick wall at 100 miles an hour. It will be stopped; the only question is in what shape. We will either reform social security now, or we will restructure the program out of the salvaged wreckage.

Basic and fundamental reform of social security is inevitable because the program cannot continue as it is. The Social Security Administration's own projections of the future financial status of the program indicate that further large tax increases will be necessary to meet the program's benefit obligations. To pay the benefits currently being promised to young workers entering the work force today, tax rates will have to be raised to between 25% to 33% of the taxable payroll, as compared with 12% today. The government's own projections also indicate that cash flow problems will develop in portions of the program throughout the next decade, despite the continuing tax increases over this period already legislated by the 1977 amendments. By early 1980, this recession was still expected by most economists, against a backdrop of an inflation rate that was at least twice as high as expected.

To make matters worse, the economy is likely to continue to perform even more badly than expected. Inflation will continue to run much higher than under the government's projections, and the recession could easily develop into a far worse economic dip than projected. There is likely to be another substantial recession in the middle of the 1980–84 presidential term, along with continued high inflation. This probable economic performance will almost certainly throw the whole system into bankruptcy in the mid-1980s unless there are additional tax increases.

Even if the economic performance is not this bad, given the current climate of public opinion taxpayers will probably not be willing to pay the enormous tax increases necessary to bail out the program. Taxpayers are already complaining loudly about the 1977 tax increases, and they are not generally aware that further tax increases are already legislated. There is already considerable talk of a tax rollback, and legislators have even begun to advance schemes like using a windfall profits tax on oil to finance social security. If economic problems lead to the need for further tax increases in the 1980s, these tax increases will almost surely be denied.

In response to opposition to further payroll tax increases, Congress will end up subsidizing the program from general revenues. Once this occurs, political pressure will develop to increase reliance on the progressive income tax and decrease reliance on the regressive payroll tax. A larger and larger portion of the program will then be financed from general revenues.

Once this occurs political pressure will develop to put a means test on the receipt of these general revenue financed benefits. People will ask why benefits should be paid out of general revenues to those who are not poor or in need. The concept of earned entitlement to social security benefits will have been destroyed. The program will have become no more than a vehicle for making payments to people to not save for their retirement. General revenue financing will thus inevitably lead to the imposition of a means test that will cause social security's benefits to be paid only to the poor. Social security will then have become just another overlapping welfare program.

This is the inevitable result of continuing social security on its current course. The welfare function will become separated from the insurance function, and the latter will be privatized. Social security's days are numbered. The program as currently structured is unstable. It will be basically and fundamentally reformed. The only question is whether it will be done in a haphazard, unplanned, unintentional way, which will waste valuable time and unnecessarily prolong several of the program's negative impacts, or whether it will be done in a planned, orderly way.

Fortunately, there are several important factors indicating that the planned approach to reform is itself highly likely, if not inevitable. The most important of these is that the program is just now entering the mature phase after about forty years in the relatively worry-free start-up phase. As a result, the traditional popularity of the program is likely to dissipate quickly. Now the focus shifts from passing out free benefits to raising taxes to meet ever accelerating benefit obligations. The heavy tax burden imposed in recent years is already turning taxpayers against the program. Many consider current tax levels intolerable. As they begin to realize the magnitude of tax increases planned for the future, as they become aware of the enormous taxes necessary to pay the benefits promised to today's young workers, the traditional popularity of the program may be preserved only in history books. The spectre of these haunting tax increases and ultimate taxpayer rejection may lead to the institution of planned, orderly reform.

Furthermore, as the program matures its possible bankruptcy becomes a serious issue. Once a pay-as-you-go program reaches the mature stage, anything that threatens the delicate balance between current receipts and current obligations threatens to throw the entire program into bankruptcy. Without a trust fund to guarantee benefits, there is nothing to protect the program from any of the possible factors that may disrupt this balance. A sudden increase in unemployment or inflation, a decline in the growth of wages, a general recession, a decline in the fertility rate, all can threaten a pay-as-you-go program with bankruptcy. As these factors continue to threaten the periodic destruction of the program, public confidence in the security of the system will decline, and this will undermine continued support for the program, which will lead to political pressure for planned, orderly reform.

Also, as the program matures, the apparent returns an individual receives on his tax dollars will decline dramatically. The free benefits passed out in the start-up phase make social security appear to be able to pay higher returns than private alternatives, but when these free benefits cease in the mature stage the returns paid under social security will be far less than the returns available from the private sector. As the loss of this opportunity becomes apparent to voters, the popularity of the program is likely to dissipate, resulting in pressure for reform.

As the returns in the social security program fall, the inequities of the system are likely to become more apparent. When everyone is receiving far more than he has paid in taxes, no one is likely to object if some seem to receive more than others for no good reason. But when recipients are already receiving lower returns than they could get elsewhere, they are likely to become quite disturbed if some are receiving an inequitable share of the already inadequate benefits. The inequities of the program will therefore become more disturbing and political support for it will be further undermined.

The truth is that the current system is not working. It has many serious shortcomings, and is the source of many powerfully negative effects both on the economy and on the individual American citizens who participate in the program. These shortcomings and negative effects are entirely unnecessary and can be removed by the feasible and practical reforms that we have discussed. As more Americans become aware of these facts, political support for the program will further dwindle.

In addition, current political trends suggest that in the near future those groups that are likely to support social security reform will have greater political power and those that may oppose such reform will have less. The surprising and sudden power of the tax revolt is the most obvious example of this shift in power. From Proposition 13 to the Constitutional Convention to balance the budget and limit taxes to the Kemp-Roth bill, taxpayer objections to runaway taxes and government spending are beginning to have an impact. This impact is likely to be no less powerful for social security taxes, especially considering the heavy tax increases that will continue to occur.

There is also a trend of healthy skepticism toward and mistrust of government programs and government officials. Due in large part to Watergate, most voters realize that public officials cannot be blindly trusted, and voters are no longer surprised to find out that they have been misled. Due in large part to the shattering failures of

Great Society programs, voters also no longer take for granted the ability of government programs to solve social problems and accomplish their legislated goals. Consequently, voters are less likely to believe the misleading statements they have heard about the program and the rosy projections that have been advanced in the past. They will be more open to the suggestion that the program is not working well and that there may be a better way.

Finally, there is growing opposition to big government and the social domination and control implied by big government programs. Organizations and groups emphasizing individual liberty and a greater reliance on private-market institutions are gaining power at the expense of those who advocate more big government controls, programs, taxes, and spending. This is likely to strengthen the opposition to social security, which is big government at its best. Continued gains in political power by these groups will make fundamental social security reform even more likely.

The combination of these factors could easily lead one to the conclusion that planned yet fundamental social security reform is not only quite politically possible but inevitable. When taxpayers finally will tolerate no more, when the program threatens to collapse into bankruptcy, when voters finally learn the truth, basic and fundamental changes in the program will have to be made. It seems that sooner or later one or more of these events will occur, and when they do social security will fall.

But political events are entirely unpredictable. All that can be predicted is our willingness to fight for changes that will result not only in material improvements but in the establishment of a free society. We can be certain only of our courage to fight for ideals no matter how large, powerful, and established the opposition may be. We can be confident only in the enduring value of revealing the truth.

We will be aided in this fight, however, by recognition of the stark reality that the current program is simply not working and that, as the public has already been warned in the words of the *Wall Street Journal*, "The social security problem will return like Banquo's ghost until really serious and courageous efforts are made to solve it."

Appendix A:

The Incidence
of the Payroll Tax

In this appendix we will present, in a graph format commonly used by economists, the argument in chapter 2 concerning the incidence of the payroll tax.

In each graph the supply curve for labor is labeled S and the demand curve for labor is labeled D (MPL) to indicate that at each point along the curve the wage equals the marginal productivity of labor (MPL). The curve labeled D^1 is the demand for labor net of tax, which is the amount of labor demanded by the employer at each after-tax wage if the employer in addition has to pay a payroll tax to the government. The after-tax wage at each point along this curve is less than the MPL, or the original wage on the curve D (MPL), by precisely the amount of the tax, so the full amount the employer pays at each point, the after-tax wage plus the tax, is still equal to the MPL.

The vertical axis of each diagram denominates the wage in dollars, with W_0 equal to the original wage before the tax is imposed, W equal to the before-tax wage after the tax is imposed, and W^1 equal to the after-tax wage after the tax is imposed. In each case the tax T is equal to $W - W^1$. The horizontal axis denominates labor supply in hours of work with N_0 equal to the original labor supply before the tax is imposed and N equal to the labor supply after the tax is imposed.

As noted in the text, a substitution effect occurs in response to reduced wages because at the lower wage some workers no longer feel it is worth forgoing leisure in favor of work, and they therefore reduce their labor supply. An income effect also occurs in response to the reduced wage, however, because at the lower wage some workers are no longer able to earn enough money at the same amount of work as before to purchase the goods or services they need or want. These workers, therefore, increase their labor supply so that their total income at the reduced wage will approximate what it was before the reduction in wages.

GRAPH 1

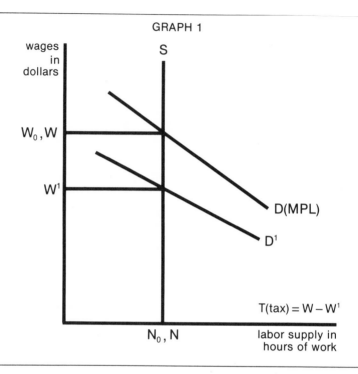

In graph 1 the substitution effect exactly equals the income effect. In technical economic terms the elasticity of labor supply equals zero. In this case, when the payroll tax is imposed on the original wage, W_0, the demand for labor by employers falls from D (MPL) to D^1. As graph 2 shows, the labor supply remains the same, $N = N_0$, and the after-tax wage that employees receive falls to W^1. This is less than the original wage W_0, which is now equal to the before-tax wage, W, by the full amount of the tax, T, and the employees will thus bear the full burden of the tax.

The employees bear this burden because in response to the reduced demand for labor, employees attempting to maintain their employment levels bid the wage down. In this case, however, employees do not reduce their labor supply in response to the declining wage. While some employees reduce their labor supply because of the substitution effect, others increase it because of the income effect, and since in this case these two effects are assumed to be equal, they cancel each other out, leaving the labor supply unchanged. Thus employees will continue to bid the wage down until employers are willing to hire as much labor as before—the entire unreduced labor supply $N = N_0$. This will result when the full amount employers have to pay, W^1 plus the tax, or W_1 is equal to the original wage W_0. The employees will therefore bid down the after-tax wage W^1 by the full amount of the tax T so that $W^1 + T = W = W_0$. At this point, employers will hire the same amount of labor as before, $N = N_0$, and the after-tax wage W^1 will be less than the original wage W_0 by the full amount of the tax T. When the substitution effect equals the income effect, therefore, the employees will bear the full burden of the payroll tax.

This analysis is based on the assumption that workers think of the payroll tax as a tax that reduces their compensation, and not as a part of their compensation that they are using to purchase insurance protection. If employees see the tax as a part of their compensation, then they will not perceive the tax as reducing their wages, and neither the income effect nor the substitution effect will occur.

Nevertheless, even if employees think of the tax in this way they will still bear the full burden of the payroll tax because when the tax is imposed and employers reduce their demand for labor, employees thinking of the tax as part of their income will still bid down the wage in an attempt to maintain their employment levels. Employees will also still not reduce their labor supply in response to the declining wage, but not in this case because the substitution effect equals the income effect. Instead, they will not reduce their labor supply because they will not perceive the wage as falling. They will merely see part of their compensation, the tax T, as going to purchase a good or service they need or want—insurance protection. In terms of graph 1, employees will perceive the wage as remaining at W_0, even after the tax is imposed, and therefore their labor supply will remain equal to N_0. Because the labor supply will not decrease in response to the tax, employees will again bid the after-tax wage down by the full amount of the tax so that employers will again hire the same amount of labor as before the tax was imposed.

The result under these circumstances therefore will be the same as in graph 1. The labor supply after the tax is imposed, N, will be the same as before the tax is imposed, N_0. The before-tax wage after the tax is imposed, W, will be the same as the original wage before the tax was imposed, W_0. The after-tax wage W^1 will be less than the original wage W_0 by the full amount of the tax. Thus the employees will again bear the full burden of the tax.

It is significant, however, that the reason for this result will not be

the same as the reason suggested by graph 1—that the income effect
equals the substitution effect, totally eliminating any reduction in
the labor supply. The reason will be that workers think of the tax as
part of their compensation and therefore do not perceive their wages
as falling, again resulting in no change in the labor supply. This
distinction is important because it suggests a second, totally independent set of circumstances under which the employees will bear
the full burden of the payroll tax. It is clear that the employees will
bear the full tax burden when there is no reduction in the labor supply in response to the tax, and there will be no such reduction, apart
from when the income effect equals the substitution effect, when
employees think of the tax as part of their compensation and
therefore do not see their wages as reduced. This set of circumstances is not included in any of the graphs, as we shall see. It should
be remembered, however, that regardless of the assumptions concerning the income and substitution effects that underlie these
graphs, there is an entirely independent set of circumstances under
which the employees will bear the full burden of the payroll tax.

In graph 2 the income effect is greater than the substitution effect
or, in more technical terms, the elasticity of labor supply is negative.

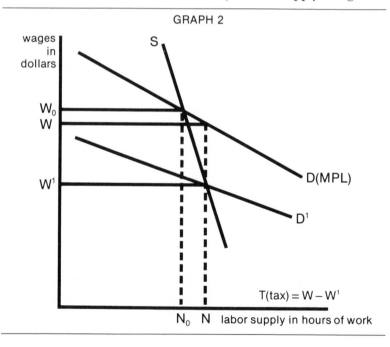

GRAPH 2

This is the case of the backward-bending labor supply curve: In response to the lower wage caused by the tax, the labor supply actually increases. When the payroll tax is imposed on the original wage, W_0, the demand for labor by employers again falls from D (MPL) to D^1. The labor supply then actually increases from N_0 to N. As a result, the after-tax wage W^1 falls from the original wage W_0 by more than the full amount of the tax, with the before-tax wage falling from W_0 to W. Thus the employee still bears the full burden of the payroll tax.

This occurs because, in response to the reduced demand for labor by employers, employees will again bid down the wage in their attempt to maintain their employment levels. In response to this declining wage, some employees will decrease their labor supply because of the substitution effect, and some will increase their labor supply because of the income effect, but since in this case the income effect is assumed to be stronger than the substitution effect, the end result is that the labor supply is actually increased. Employees will continue to bid down the wage until the employers are willing to hire even more labor than before the tax was imposed. This will occur when the before-tax wage to employers, W^1 plus T, or W, is less than the original wage W_0 by an amount sufficient to induce employers to hire the full increased labor supply N. Employees will therefore bid down the after-tax wage W^1 by even more than the full amount of the tax T so that the full before-tax wage to the employers, W, will be sufficiently less than W_0. The employees will again bear the full burden of the payroll tax.

It should again be noted that this analysis is based on the assumption that workers think of the payroll tax as a tax reducing their compensation. If they instead think of the tax as a part of their compensation that they are using to pay for insurance protection, they will not think of their wages as reduced by the tax, and neither the income effect nor the substitution effect will occur, and thus the labor supply will not increase in response to the tax but remain the same. In the terms of graph 2, since workers perceive their wage as remaining at W_0, their labor supply will remain at N_0. In this case, as noted above, the employees will still bear the full burden of the tax. Thus, as also noted above, although this case is not included in graph 2, it constitutes a separate, independent set of circumstances under which employees will bear the full burden of the payroll tax, regardless of assumptions concerning the income and substitution effects.

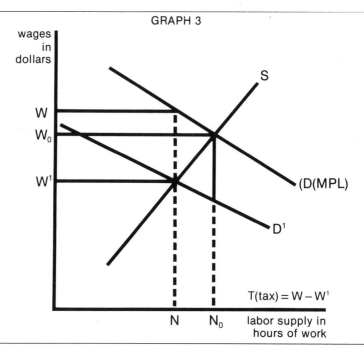

GRAPH 3

Finally, graph 3 presents the instance in which the substitution effect is greater than the income effect, or where the elasticity of labor supply is positive. In this case, when the payroll tax is imposed, the demand for labor again falls from D (MPL) to D^1. The labor supply then falls from N_0 to N and the before-tax wage increases from W_0 to W. Although the after-tax wage W^1 is less than W by the full amount of the tax, W^1 is less than the original wage W_0 by an amount smaller than the tax. It may thus appear that the employee in this case only bears $W_0 - W^1$ of the tax while the employer bears $W - W_0$ of the tax.

But graph 3 also shows that W, which is the full amount employers pay, is still equal to the MPL, while W^1, the amount the employees receive, is less than the MPL, or W, by the full amount of the tax. Thus the value of what the employees receive, W^1, is still less than the value of what the employees are producing, W = MPL, by the full amount of the tax T. The entire tax, therefore, is still coming out of what the employees are producing. The employers are not bearing any part of this tax because the productive value they are receiving from the workers, the new, higher MPL, is sufficient to compensate them fully for the higher wage. No part of what the employers produce is lost to the tax. The employees still bear the full burden of the payroll tax. This analysis indicates that the real reason that employers will never bear any part of the tax is that although employers will never pay any wage greater than the MPL, as clearly shown on all three graphs, employees will accept a wage less than the MPL, and therefore the employees end up bearing the wedge created by the payroll tax.

The process by which this result occurs is basically the same as the process described for the first two graphs. When the tax is imposed and the demand for labor falls, employees bid down the wage in an attempt to maintain their employment levels. This time, however, in response to the declining wage, the substitution effect overwhelms the income effect, and the labor supply decreases. Employees will not, therefore, bid the wage W^1 down by the full amount of the tax to induce employers to hire the full labor supply, N_0, which existed before the tax. They will instead only bid the wage W^1 down by a sufficient amount to get employers to hire the full reduced labor supply N. The full amount which employers pay, W^1 plus the tax, or W, will therefore be greater than W_0. But the employees will still bear the full burden of the tax because the full amount that employers pay, W, is still equal to the MPL, while the amount the employees receive, W^1, is less than the MPL by the full amount of the tax.

As noted in the text, this does not mean that there are no negative effects on the employer from the increase in wages. The tax imposes additional inefficiency costs beyond its mere monetary costs, and employers share these costs with employees, unlike the direct monetary costs. Thus in response to the new, higher wage and reduced labor supply, employers will substitute capital for the lost labor. This new capital-labor mix will not be as efficient, however, as the old capital-labor mix. If employers could pay employees their full value, the MPL, directly, employers could, given the higher labor supply induced at this wage and the smaller amount of necessary capital, produce the same output at lower cost. The higher cost of producing this output after the tax is imposed is therefore a simple inefficiency cost beyond the direct costs of the tax. The additional expense resulting from this inefficiency is not offset by any compensatory increase in value, as in the case of the increase in wages discussed earlier. Unless the employer can pass along all of this additional cost to other workers or consumers, which is unlikely, the employer will bear at least part of these costs. In fact, if the tax is raised high enough these inefficiency costs could become so great that the employer would be driven out of business.

Nevertheless, the full monetary cost of the payroll tax, apart from these inefficiency costs, is still borne by the employee. In considering who bears the burden of financing social security, the question of who bears these direct, monetary costs is the important issue. The burden of the inefficiency costs of the tax is an important separate question, discussed in chapter 3.

We should note again, in reference to graph 3, that neither the substitution effect nor the income effect, and consequently the increase in the labor supply, will occur if the employees think of the tax as a part of their compensation rather than as a tax. In this case they will perceive their wage as remaining at W_0, even after the imposition of the tax, and their labor supply will remain at N_0. As noted above, in this case the employees will still bear the full burden of the payroll tax. The employees will bear the full tax burden, regardless of the assumptions concerning the income and substitution effects, whenever employees think of the tax as a part of their compensation that they are using to purchase insurance protection rather than as a tax that is reducing their compensation.

Appendix B:

Tabular Data on Social Security

TABLE 1

TAX RATES
(percent of taxable payroll)

| | EMPLOYEE & EMPLOYER COMBINED | | | | | SELF-EMPLOYED | | | | |
	OASI	DI	HI	OASDI	OASDHI	OASI	DI	HI	OASDI	OASDHI
1937	2.00	—	—	—	—	—	—	—	—	—
1938	2.00	—	—	—	—	—	—	—	—	—
1939	2.00	—	—	—	—	—	—	—	—	—
1940	2.00	—	—	—	—	—	—	—	—	—
1941	2.00	—	—	—	—	—	—	—	—	—
1942	2.00	—	—	—	—	—	—	—	—	—
1943	2.00	—	—	—	—	—	—	—	—	—
1944	2.00	—	—	—	—	—	—	—	—	—
1945	2.00	—	—	—	—	—	—	—	—	—
1946	2.00	—	—	—	—	—	—	—	—	—
1947	2.00	—	—	—	—	—	—	—	—	—
1948	2.00	—	—	—	—	—	—	—	—	—
1949	2.00	—	—	—	—	—	—	—	—	—
1950	3.00	—	—	—	—	—	—	—	—	—
1951	3.00	—	—	—	—	2.25	—	—	—	—
1952	3.00	—	—	—	—	2.25	—	—	—	—
1953	3.00	—	—	—	—	2.25	—	—	—	—
1954	4.00	—	—	—	—	3.00	—	—	—	—
1955	4.00	—	—	—	—	3.00	—	—	—	—
1956	4.00	—	—	—	—	3.00	—	—	—	—
1957	4.00	0.50	—	4.50	—	3.00	0.375	—	3.375	—
1958	4.00	0.50	—	4.50	—	3.00	0.375	—	3.375	—
1959	4.50	0.50	—	5.00	—	3.375	0.375	—	3.75	—
1960	5.50	0.50	—	6.00	—	4.125	0.375	—	4.50	—
1961	5.50	0.50	—	6.00	—	4.125	0.375	—	4.50	—
1962	5.75	0.50	—	6.25	—	4.325	0.375	—	4.70	—
1963	6.75	0.50	—	7.25	—	5.025	0.375	—	5.40	—
1964	6.75	0.50	—	7.25	—	5.025	0.375	—	5.40	—
1965	6.75	0.50	—	7.25	—	5.025	0.375	—	5.40	—
1966	7.00	0.70	0.70	7.70	8.40	5.275	0.525	0.35	5.80	6.15
1967	7.10	0.70	1.00	7.80	8.00	5.375	0.525	0.50	5.90	6.40
1968	6.65	0.95	1.20	7.60	8.80	5.0875	0.7125	0.60	5.80	6.40
1969	7.45	0.95	1.20	8.40	9.60	5.5875	0.7125	0.60	6.30	6.90
1970	7.30	1.10	1.20	8.40	9.60	5.475	0.825	0.60	6.30	6.90
1971	8.10	1.10	1.20	9.20	10.40	6.075	0.825	0.60	6.9]	7.50
1972	8.10	1.10	1.20	9.20	10.40	6.075	0.825	0.60	6.90	7.50
1973	8.60	1.10	2.00	9.70	11.70	6.205	0.795	1.00	7.00	8.00
1974	8.75	1.15	1.80	9.90	11.70	6.185	0.815	0.90	7.00	7.90
1975	8.75	1.15	1.80	9.90	11.70	6.185	0.815	0.90	7.00	7.90
1976	8.75	1.15	1.80	9.90	11.70	6.185	0.815	0.90	7.00	7.90
1977	8.75	1.15	1.80	9.90	11.70	6.185	0.815	0.90	7.00	7.90
1978	8.55	1.55	2.00	10.10	12.10	6.01	1.09	1.00	7.10	8.10
1979	8.66	1.50	2.10	10.16	12.26	6.01	1.04	1.05	7.05	8.10
1980	8.66	1.50	2.10	10.16	12.26	6.01	1.04	1.05	7.05	8.10

SOURCE: 1979 Annual Report of the Board of Trustees of the Federal Old-Age and Survivors Insurance and Disability Insurance Trust Funds; 1979 Annual Report of the Board of Trustees of the Federal Hospital Insurance Trust Fund.

TABLE 2

SOCIAL SECURITY TAXES

	MAXIMUM TAXABLE INCOME[1]	MAXIMUM TAX[1] OASI	OASDI	OASDHI	TOTAL TAX COLLECTIONS[2] OASI	OASDI	OASDHI
1937	3,000	60	—	—	0.8	—	—
1938	3,000	60	—	—	0.4	—	—
1939	3,000	60	—	—	0.6	—	—
1940	3,000	60	—	—	0.3	—	—
1941	3,000	60	—	—	0.8	—	—
1942	3,000	60	—	—	1.0	—	—
1943	3,000	60	—	—	1.2	—	—
1944	3,000	60	—	—	1.3	—	—
1945	3,000	60	—	—	1.3	—	—
1946	3,000	60	—	—	1.3	—	—
1947	3,000	60	—	—	1.6	—	—
1948	3,000	60	—	—	1.7	—	—
1949	3,000	60	—	—	1.7	—	—
1950	3,000	90	—	—	2.7	—	—
1951	3,600	108	—	—	3.4	—	—
1952	3,600	108	—	—	3.8	—	—
1953	3,600	108	—	—	3.9	—	—
1954	3,600	144	—	—	5.2	—	—
1955	4,200	168	—	—	5.7	—	—
1956	4,200	168	—	—	6.2	—	—
1957	4,200	168	189	—	6.8	7.5	—
1958	4,200	168	189	—	7.6	8.5	—
1959	4,800	216	240	—	8.1	8.9	—
1960	4,800	264	288	—	10.9	11.9	—
1961	4,800	264	288	—	11.3	12.3	—
1962	4,800	276	300	—	12.1	13.1	—
1963	4,800	324	348	—	14.5	15.6	—
1964	4,800	324	348	—	15.7	16.8	—
1965	4,800	324	348	—	16.0	17.2	—
1966	6,600	462	508.20	554.20	20.6	22.6	24.5
1967	6,600	468.60	514.80	580.80	23.1	25.4	28.6
1968	7,800	518.70	592.80	686.40	23.7	27.0	31.2
1969	7,800	581.10	655.20	748.80	27.9	31.5	36.0
1970	7,800	569.40	655.20	748.80	30.3	34.7	39.7
1971	7,800	631.80	717.60	811.20	33.7	38.3	43.3
1972	9,000	729.00	828.00	936.00	37.8	42.9	48.7
1973	10,800	928.80	1047.60	1263.60	46.0	51.9	61.9
1974	13,200	1155.00	1306.80	1544.40	52.1	58.9	69.9
1975	14,100	1233.75	1395.90	1649.70	56.8	64.3	75.9
1976	15,300	1338.75	1514.70	1790.10	63.4	71.6	84.3
1977	16,500	1443.78	1633.50	1930.50	69.6	78.7	92.8
1978	17,700	1513.35	1787.70	2141.70	75.5	88.9	106.2
1979	22,900	1983.14	2326.64	2807.54	88.2[3]	103.5[3]	124.6[3]
1980	25,900	2242.94	2631.44	3175.34	100.4[3]	117.8[3]	141.8[3]

SOURCE: 1979 Annual Report of the Board of Trustees of the Federal Old-Age and Survivors Insurance and Disability Insurance Trust Funds; 1979 Annual Report of the Board of Trustees of the Federal Hospital Insurance Trust Fund; Social Security Bulletin Annual Statistical Supplement 1975.

[1]Figures in dollars.

[2]Figures in billions.

[3]Projections based on Social Security Administration Assumptions, Alternative II.

TABLE 3

Social Security Taxes and Other Federal Taxes[1]

	Total Federal Government Receipts	Personal Tax Receipts	Corporate Profits Tax and Indirect Business Tax and Non-Tax Accruals	Other Social Insurance Taxes	Social Security Taxes OASI	OASDI	OASDHI	As a Percent of Total Federal Taxes
1937	7.0	1.7	3.7	0.8	0.8	—	—	11.4%
1938	6.5	1.6	3.1	1.3	0.4	—	—	6.2%
1939	6.7	1.2	3.6	1.3	0.6	—	—	9.0%
1940	8.6	1.4	5.3	1.7	0.3	—	—	3.5%
1941	15.4	2.0	10.9	1.7	0.8	—	—	5.2%
1942	22.9	4.7	15.1	2.2	1.0	—	—	4.4%
1943	39.3	16.5	18.6	3.0	1.2	—	—	3.1%
1944	41.0	17.5	18.7	3.5	1.3	—	—	3.2%
1945	42.5	19.4	17.4	4.5	1.3	—	—	3.1%
1946	39.1	17.2	16.4	4.2	1.3	—	—	3.3%
1947	43.2	19.6	18.5	3.5	1.6	—	—	3.7%
1948	43.2	19.0	19.7	2.8	1.7	—	—	3.9%
1949	38.7	16.1	17.6	3.2	1.7	—	—	4.4%
1950	50.0	18.1	26.0	3.2	2.7	—	—	5.4%
1951	64.3	26.1	31.0	3.7	3.4	—	—	5.3%
1952	67.3	31.0	28.9	3.6	3.8	—	—	5.6%
1953	70.0	32.2	30.4	3.5	3.9	—	—	5.6%
1954	63.7	29.0	26.6	3.0	5.2	—	—	8.2%
1955	72.6	31.4	31.8	3.7	5.7	—	—	7.9%
1956	78.0	35.2	32.1	4.4	6.2	—	—	7.9%
1957	81.9	37.4	32.2	4.8	6.8	7.5	—	9.2%
1958	78.7	36.8	29.5	3.9	7.6	8.5	—	10.8%
1959	89.8	39.9	35.0	6.0	8.1	8.9	—	9.9%
1960	96.1	43.6	34.8	5.7	10.9	11.9	—	12.4%
1961	98.1	44.7	35.1	6.0	11.3	12.3	—	12.5%
1962	106.2	48.6	37.1	7.4	12.1	13.1	—	12.3%
1963	114.4	51.5	39.9	7.5	14.5	15.6	—	13.6%
1964	114.9	48.6	42.3	7.2	15.7	16.8	—	14.6%
1965	124.3	53.9	45.4	7.8	16.0	17.2	—	13.8%
1966	141.8	61.7	47.0	8.6	20.6	22.6	24.5	17.3%
1967	150.5	67.5	46.3	8.1	23.1	25.4	28.6	19.0%
1968	174.7	79.6	54.3	9.6	23.7	27.0	31.2	17.9%
1969	197.0	94.8	55.2	11.0	27.9	31.5	36.0	18.3%
1970	192.1	92.2	50.1	10.0	30.3	34.7	39.7	20.7%
1971	198.6	89.9	53.9	11.6	33.7	38.3	43.3	21.8%
1972	227.5	108.2	56.6	14.1	37.8	42.9	48.7	21.4%
1973	258.3	114.6	64.2	17.5	46.0	51.9	61.9	24.0%
1974	288.6	131.1	67.6	20.0	52.1	58.9	69.9	24.2%
1975	286.2	125.4	66.7	18.3	56.8	64.3	75.9	26.5%
1976	331.4	146.8	78.2	22.1	63.4	71.6	84.3	25.4%
1977	374.5	169.4	86.3	25.9	69.6	78.7	92.8	24.8%
1978	431.6	193.2	99.6	32.5	75.5	88.9	106.2	24.6%

Source: 1979 Economic Report of the President, National Income and Product Accounts, 1929–1974; Social Security Bulletin Annual Statistical Supplement 1975; 1979 Annual Report of the Board of Trustees of the Federal Old-Age and Survivors Insurance and Disability Insurance Trust Funds; 1979 Annual Report of the Board of Trustees of the Federal Hospital Insurance Trust Fund.

[1]All figures are in billions.

TABLE 4

FUTURE TAX RATES
(percent of taxable payroll)

| | EMPLOYEE & EMPLOYER COMBINED | | | | | SELF-EMPLOYED | | | | |
	OASI	DI	HI	OASDI	OASDHI	OASI	DI	HI	OASDI	OASDHI
1980	8.66	1.5	2.10	10.16	12.26	6.01	1.04	1.05	7.05	8.1
1981	9.05	1.65	2.60	10.70	13.30	6.7625	1.2375	1.30	8.00	9.30
1982	9.15	1.65	2.60	10.80	13.40	6.8125	1.2375	1.30	8.05	9.35
1983	9.15	1.65	2.60	10.80	13.40	6.8125	1.2375	1.30	8.05	9.35
1984	9.15	1.65	2.60	10.80	13.40	6.8125	1.2375	1.30	8.05	9.35
1985	9.50	1.90	2.70	11.40	14.10	7.125	1.425	1.35	8.55	9.9
1986	9.50	1.90	2.90	11.40	14.30	7.125	1.425	1.45	8.55	10.00
1987	9.50	1.90	2.90	11.40	14.30	7.125	1.425	1.45	8.55	10.00
1988	9.50	1.90	2.90	11.40	14.30	7.125	1.425	1.45	8.55	10.00
1989	9.50	1.90	2.90	11.40	14.30	7.125	1.425	1.45	8.55	10.00
1990 and later	10.20	2.20	2.90	12.40	15.30	7.650	1.650	1.45	9.30	10.75

SOURCE: 1979 Annual Report of the Board of Trustees of the Federal Old-Age and Survivors Insurance and Disability Insurance Trust Funds; 1979 Annual Report of the Board of Trustees of the Federal Hospital Insurance Trust Fund.

TABLE 5

FUTURE SOCIAL SECURITY TAXES[1]
(1980 constant dollars)

	MAXIMUM TAXABLE INCOME (1980 DOLLARS)	MAXIMUM TAX (1980 DOLLARS)		
		OASI	OASDI	OASDHI
1980	25,900	2,243	2,631	3,175
1981	28,232	2,555	3,021	3,755
1982	28,867	2,641	3,118	3,868
1983	29,609	2,709	3,198	3,968
1984	30,473	2,788	3,291	4,083
1985	31,093	2,954	3,545	4,384
1986	31,693	3,011	3,613	4,532
1987	32,304	3,069	3,683	4,619
1988	32,929	3,128	3,754	4,709
1989	33,547	3,187	3,824	4,797
1990	34,206	3,489	4,242	5,234
1995	37,516	3,827	4,652	5,740
2000	40,907	4,173	5,072	6,259
2005	44,459	4,535	5,513	6,802
2010	48,335	4,930	5,994	7,395
2015	52,543	5,359	6,515	8,039
2020	57,113	5,826	7,082	8,738
2025	62,087	6,333	7,699	9,499
2030	67,483	6,883	8,368	10,325
2035	73,360	7,483	9,097	11,224
2040	79,741	8,134	9,888	12,200
2045	86,677	8,841	10,748	13,262
2050	94,223	9,611	11,684	14,416

SOURCE: 1978 Annual Report of the Board of Trustees of the Federal Old-Age and Survivors Insurance and Disability Insurance Trust Funds; 1978 Annual Report of the Board of Trustees of the Federal Hospital Insurance Trust Fund.

[1]All figures are projections based on Alternative II, Intermediate Assumptions of the Social Security Administration.

TABLE 6

FUTURE TAX COLLECTIONS[1,2,3]

	OASI	OASDI	OASDHI
1979	88.2	103.5	124.6
1980	100.4[1]	117.8[1]	141.8[1]
1981	108.9	128.7	159.4
1982	115.5	136.4	170.4
1983	120.3	142.0	177.1
1985	133.5	160.2	198.1
1990	164.2	199.6	246.3
1995	185.0	224.9	277.5
2000	206.4	250.9	309.6
2005	232.8	283.0	349.2
2010	257.0	312.5	385.5
2015	285.7	347.3	428.5
2020	311.7	379.0	467.6
2025	339.9	413.3	509.9
2030	372.6	452.9	558.8
2035	410.5	499.0	615.7
2040	453.4	551.2	680.1
2045	499.9	607.8	749.9
2050	550.5	669.2	825.7

Source: Social Security Administration, 1979 Annual Report of the Board of Trustees of the Federal Old-Age and Survivors and Disability Insurance Trust Funds; 1979 Annual Report of the Board of Trustees of the Federal Hospital Insurance Trust Funds.

[1]All figures for 1980 and beyond are in constant 1980 dollars.

[2]All figures are projections based on Alternative II, Intermediate Assumptions of the Social Security Administration.

[3]All figures are in billions.

TABLE 7

Workers Covered by Social Security

	Total Number of Workers in Paid Employment'	Total Number of Workers in Covered Employment'	Covered Employment as Percent of Paid Employment'
1940	46.4	26.8	57.8
1941	50.4	31.3	62.1
1942	55.8	36.3	65.1
1943	60.8	42.0	69.1
1944	62.6	44.0	70.3
1945	61.0	42.0	68.9
1946	56.2	36.4	64.8
1947	57.7	37.3	64.6
1948	59.0	38.5	65.3
1949	58.4	37.4	64.0
1950	60.0	38.7	64.5
1951	62.5	49.5	79.5
1952	63.3	50.5	79.8
1953	63.8	51.1	80.1
1954	62.8	49.8	79.3
1955	64.5	55.0	85.3
1956	66.0	57.2	86.7
1957	66.0	57.4	87.0
1958	64.9	56.8	87.5
1959	66.6	58.5	87.8
1960	67.5	59.4	88.0
1961	67.9	59.7	87.9
1962	69.3	61.0	88.0
1963	70.2	61.9	88.2
1964	71.7	63.3	88.3
1965	73.6	65.6	89.1
1966	76.0	68.0	89.5
1967	76.9	68.9	89.6
1968	78.6	70.7	89.9
1969	80.5	72.7	90.3
1970	80.6	72.1	89.5
1971	81.5	72.9	89.4
1972	83.5	74.9	89.6
1973	85.9	77.3	90.0
1974	87.1	78.4	90.0
1975	86.2	77.6	90.0
1976	89.0	79.7	89.6
1977	92.2	82.2	89.2

Source: Social Security Bulletin Annual Statistical Supplement, 1975, Social Security Administration.
'Figures in millions.

TABLE 8

AGED COVERED BY SOCIAL SECURITY

	PERCENT OF AGED RECEIVING OASDHI BENEFITS	PERCENT OF AGED RECEIVING SSI BENEFITS	PERCENT OF AGED RECEIVING BOTH OASDHI OR SSI	PERCENT OF AGED RECEIVING OASDHI, OR SSI, OR BOTH	PERCENT OF OASDHI BENEFICIARIES RECEIVING SSI	PERCENT OF SSI BENEFICIARIES RECEIVING OASDHI
1940	0.7	21.7	0.1	22.3	14.3	0.5
1945	6.2	19.4	0.5	25.1	8.1	2.6
1950	16.4	22.4	2.2	36.6	12.6	9.8
1955	39.4	17.9	3.4	53.9	8.6	19.2
1960	61.6	14.1	4.1	71.6	6.6	28.5
1965	75.2	11.7	5.2	81.7	7.0	44.7
1966	77.0	11.3	5.5	82.8	7.1	48.7
1967	82.6	11.0	5.8	87.7	7.0	53.1
1968	83.7	10.5	6.0	88.2	7.1	57.2
1969	84.9	10.4	6.1	89.3	7.1	58.2
1970	85.5	10.4	6.3	89.6	7.4	60.4
1971	84.9	10.2	6.2	88.8	7.3	61.4
1972	85.6	9.6	6.1	89.1	7.1	63.3
1973	86.7	8.9	5.6	90.0	6.4	62.5
1974	88.3	9.6	6.8	91.1	7.7	70.8
1975	89.2	10.1	7.1	92.2	8.0	70.3
1976	89.7	10.4	7.2	93.3	7.5	65.9
1977	90.4	9.9	6.9	94.3	7.6	69.9

SOURCE: Social Security Bulletin Annual Statistical Supplement, 1975, Social Security Administration.

TABLE 9

GENERAL BENEFIT PROVISIONS
(monthly amounts)

	MINIMUM RETIREMENT BENEFIT	MAXIMUM RETIREMENT BENEFIT[4]	MAXIMUM FAMILY BENEFIT
1940	10.00	41.20	85.00
1941	10.00	41.60	85.00
1942	10.00	42.00	85.00
1943	10.00	42.40	85.00
1944	10.00	42.80	85.00
1945	10.00	43.20	85.00
1946	10.00	43.60	85.00
1947	10.00	44.00	85.00
1948	10.00	44.40	85.00
1949	10.00	44.80	85.00
1950	10.00	45.20	150.00
1951	20.00	68.50	150.00
1952	20.00	68.50	150.00
1953	25.00	85.00	168.75
1954	25.00	85.00	168.75
1955	30.00	98.50	200.00
1956	30.00	103.50	200.00
1957	30.00	108.50	200.00
1958	30.00	108.50	200.00
1959	33.00	116.00	254.00
1960	33.00	119.00	254.00
1961	33.00	120.00	254.00
1962	40.00	121.00	254.00
1963	40.00	122.00	254.00
1964	40.00	123.00	254.00
1965	44.00	131.70	368.00
1966	44.00	132.70	368.00
1967	44.00	135.90	368.00
1968	55.00	156.00	434.40
1969	55.00	160.00	434.40
1970	64.00	189.80	434.40
1971	70.40	213.10	517.00
1972	70.40	216.10	517.00
1973	84.50	266.10	707.90
1974	84.50	274.60	820.80
1975	93.80	316.30	847.70[1]
1976	101.40	364.00	949.90[2]
1977	107.90	412.70	1,045.80[3]
1978	114.30	459.80	—
1979	121.80	503.40	—

SOURCE: Social Security Bulletin Annual Statistical Supplement, 1975, Social Security Administration.

[1]Figure is for January, June, 1975 = 914.80.
[2]Figure is for January, June, 1976 = 1,010.70.
[3]Figure is for January.
[4]Single worker retired at age 65. Worker with spouse receives a 50% increase.

TABLE 10

TOTAL BENEFIT PAYMENTS[1]

	OASI	DI	HI	OASDI	OASDHI	OAA-SSI
1937	1	—	—	—	—	244
1938	10	—	—	—	—	360
1939	14	—	—	—	—	418
1940	35	—	—	—	—	450
1941	88	—	—	—	—	505
1942	131	—	—	—	—	569
1943	166	—	—	—	—	617
1944	209	—	—	—	—	679
1945	274	—	—	—	—	702
1946	378	—	—	—	—	762
1947	466	—	—	—	—	910
1948	556	—	—	—	—	1,038
1949	667	—	—	—	—	1,259
1950	961	—	—	—	—	1,454
1951	1,885	—	—	—	—	1,428
1952	2,194	—	—	—	—	1,463
1953	3,006	—	—	—	—	1,513
1954	3,670	—	—	—	—	1,498
1955	4,968	—	—	—	—	1,488
1956	5,715	—	—	—	—	1,529
1957	7,347	57	—	7,404	—	1,609
1958	8,327	249	—	8,576	—	1,647
1959	9,842	457	—	10,298	—	1,621
1960	10,677	568	—	11,245	—	1,626
1961	11,862	887	—	12,749	—	1,569
1962	13,356	1,105	—	14,461	—	1,566
1963	14,217	1,210	—	15,427	—	1,610
1964	14,914	1,309	—	16,223	—	1,607
1965	16,737	1,573	—	18,311	—	1,594
1966	18,267	1,781	891	20,048	20,939	1,630
1967	19,468	1,939	3,353	21,406	24,759	1,698
1968	22,642	2,294	4,179	24,936	29,115	1,673
1969	24,209	2,542	4,739	26,751	31,490	1,747
1970	28,796	3,067	5,124	31,863	36,987	1,866
1971	33,143	3,758	5,751	37,171	42,922	1,920
1972	37,122	4,473	6,318	41,595	47,913	1,894
1973	45,741	5,718	7,057	51,459	58,516	1,749
1974	51,618	6,903	9,099	58,521	67,620	2,414
1975	58,509	8,414	11,315	66,923	78,238	2,517
1976	65,699	9,966	13,340	75,665	89,005	2,420
1977	73,133	11,463	15,737	84,576	100,313	2,364
1978	80,352	12,513	17,682	92,865	110,547	2,342

SOURCE: Social Security Bulletin Annual Statistical Supplement, 1975; 1979 Annual Report of the Board of Trustees of the Federal Hospital Insurance Trust Fund; 1979 Annual Report of the Board of Trustees of the Federal Old-Age and Survivors Insurance and Disability Trust Funds, Department of Health, Education and Welfare.

[1]Figures in millions.

TABLE 11
SOCIAL SECURITY EXPENDITURES AND OTHER FEDERAL EXPENDITURES[1]

	TOTAL FEDERAL GOVERNMENT EXPENDITURE	NON-SOCIAL SECURITY TRANSFER PAYMENTS	FEDERAL PURCHASES OF GOODS AND SERVICES	TOTAL SOCIAL SECURITY EXPENDITURES			
				OASI	OASDI	OASDHI	AS A PERCENT OF TOTAL FED. EXPENDITURES
1937	7.4	0.9	4.7	0.001	—	—	0.01%
1938	8.6	1.2	5.5	0.010	—	—	0.12%
1939	8.9	1.3	5.2	0.014	—	—	0.16%
1940	10.0	1.4	6.1	0.062	—	—	0.62%
1941	20.5	1.3	16.9	0.114	—	—	0.56%
1942	56.1	1.4	52.0	0.159	—	—	0.28%
1943	85.8	1.0	81.3	0.195	—	—	0.23%
1944	95.5	1.5	89.4	0.238	—	—	0.25%
1945	84.6	4.4	74.6	0.304	—	—	0.36%
1946	35.6	11.0	17.6	0.418	—	—	1.17%
1947	29.8	10.3	12.7	0.512	—	—	1.72%
1948	34.9	10.9	16.7	0.607	—	—	1.74%
1949	41.3	13.1	20.4	0.721	—	—	1.75%
1950	40.8	13.4	18.7	1.022	—	—	2.50%
1951	57.8	9.7	38.3	1.966	—	—	3.40%
1952	71.1	8.6	52.4	2.282	—	—	3.21%
1953	77.1	8.3	57.5	3.094	—	—	4.01%
1954	69.8	9.6	47.9	3.741	—	—	5.36%
1955	68.1	9.3	44.5	5.079	—	—	7.46%
1956	71.9	9.5	45.9	5.841	—	—	8.12%
1957	79.6	9.9	50.0	7.507	7.567	—	9.51%
1958	88.9	12.5	53.9	8.646	8.907	—	10.02%
1959	91.0	11.1	53.9	10.308	10.793	—	11.86%
1960	93.1	11.7	53.7	11.198	11.798	—	12.67%
1961	101.9	13.7	57.4	12.432	13.388	—	13.14%
1962	110.4	12.6	63.7	13.973	15.156	—	13.73%
1963	114.2	13.0	64.6	14.920	16.217	—	14.20%
1964	118.2	13.1	65.2	15.613	17.020	—	14.40%
1965	123.8	13.3	67.3	17.501	19.187	—	15.50%
1966	143.6	13.9	78.8	18.967	20.913	21.912	15.26%
1967	163.7	16.4	90.9	20.382	22.471	25.901	15.82%
1968	180.6	17.8	98.0	23.557	26.015	30.292	16.77%
1969	188.4	20.0	97.5	25.176	27.892	32.749	17.38%
1970	204.2	25.1	95.6	29.848	33.108	38.389	18.80%
1971	220.6	30.9	96.2	34.542	38.542	44.442	20.15%
1972	244.7	33.4	102.1	38.522	43.281	49.784	20.34%
1973	265.0	35.4	102.2	47.175	53.148	60.437	22.81%
1974	299.3	47.6	111.1	53.397	60.593	69.965	23.38%
1975	356.8	68.3	123.1	60.395	69.184	80.765	22.64%
1976	385.2	69.7	129.9	67.876	78.242	91.921	23.86%
1977	422.6	69.4	145.1	75.309	87.254	103.273	24.44%
1978	461.0	71.1	154.0	83.064	96.018	114.196	24.77%

SOURCE: 1979 Economic Report of the President, National Income and Product Accounts, 1929–1974; Social Security Bulletin Annual Statistical Supplement 1975; 1979 Annual Report of the Board of Trustees of the Federal Old-Age and Survivors Insurance and Disability Insurance Trust Funds; 1979 Annual Report of the Board of Trustees of the Federal Hospital Insurance Trust Fund.

[1]All figures in billions.

TABLE 12

TOTAL FUTURE EXPENDITURES[1,2,3]

	OASI	DI	HI	OASDI	OASDHI
1979	93.1	14.4	21.5	107.6	129.1
1980	105.4	16.1	24.8	121.5	146.3
1981	110.2	16.6	26.9	126.8	153.7
1982	115.1	17.2	29.4	132.4	161.8
1983	120.0	17.9	32.3	137.9	170.2
1985	128.1	19.4	38.2	147.5	185.9
1990	149.2	22.9	56.5	172.3	228.8
1995	165.6	27.9	77.4	193.5	271.0
2000	180.1	35.2	99.6	215.5	315.1
2005	202.9	44.5	—	247.2	—
2010	238.4	53.4	—	291.8	—
2015	296.1	62.2	—	358.2	—
2020	368.0	68.8	—	436.7	—
2025	449.6	72.7	—	522.2	—
2030	524.1	76.0	—	600.5	—
2035	584.7	82.5	—	667.2	—
2040	631.6	92.0	—	724.1	—
2045	686.2	103.9	—	790.1	—
2050	756.7	115.0	—	871.6	—

SOURCE: 1979 Annual Report of the Board of Trustees of the Federal Old-Age and Survivors Insurance and Disability Insurance Trust Funds; 1979 Annual Report of the Board of Trustees of the Federal Old-Age Hospital Insurance Trust Fund.

[1]Figures in billions.
[2]All figures for 1980 and beyond are in constant 1980 dollars.
[3]All figures are projections based on Alternative II, Intermediate Assumptions of the Social Security Administration.

TABLE 13

OLD-AGE AND SURVIVORS INSURANCE BENEFICIARIES[1,2]

	RETIRED WORKERS AND DEPENDENTS			SURVIVORS OF DECEASED WORKERS			
	TOTAL	WORKERS	WIVES & HUSBANDS	CHILDREN	MOTHERS / FATHERS	CHILDREN	WIDOWS & WIDOWERS	PARENTS
1970	22,619	13,066	2,651	535	514	2,673	3,151	29
1971	23,416	13,604	2,673	556	523	2,745	3,287	28
1972	24,308	14,181	2,706	578	536	2,847	3,433	27
1973	25,273	14,880	2,756	602	548	2,887	3,575	25
1974	26,217	15,589	2,806	619	565	2,908	3,706	24
1975	26,998	16,210	2,836	633	568	2,905	3,823	22
1976	27,740	16,789	2,867	638	576	2,911	3,939	21
1977	28,428	17,380	2,899	670	573	2,843	4,042	19
1978	29,062	17,924	2,942	662	569	2,800	4,147	18
1979	29,923	18,662	2,988	664	575	2,760	4,257	17
1980	30,593	19,266	3,004	656	572	2,729	4,351	15
1985	33,976	22,305	3,068	616	560	2,606	4,811	10
1990	36,060	25,106	3,124	466	489	2,216	4,652	7
1995	37,834	27,007	3,085	359	538	2,230	4,608	7
2000	38,908	28,136	2,992	359	568	2,308	4,538	7
2005	40,488	29,865	2,923	391	571	2,323	4,408	7
2010	43,972	33,288	3,009	463	558	2,284	4,363	7
2015	49,297	38,564	3,085	570	545	2,235	4,291	7
2020	55,985	45,035	3,180	670	539	2,239	4,315	7
2025	62,618	51,436	3,235	733	530	2,261	4,416	7
2030	66,898	55,645	3,201	740	521	2,265	4,519	7
2035	68,463	57,307	3,083	714	518	2,254	4,580	7
2040	68,016	57,092	2,915	683	519	2,236	4,564	7
2045	67,921	57,107	2,849	691	521	2,231	4,515	7
2050	68,916	58,120	2,891	724	520	2,245	4,409	7
2055	70,475	59,637	2,992	753	515	2,247	4,324	7

SOURCE: 1979 Annual Report of the Board of Trustees of the Federal Old-Age and Survivors Insurance and Disability Insurance Trust Fund.

[1]Figures in thousands.
[2]All figures for 1979 and after are projections based on Alternative II, Intermediate Assumptions of the Social Security Administration.

TABLE 14

DISABILITY INSURANCE BENEFICIARIES[1,2]

	WORKERS	WIVES & HUSBANDS	CHILDREN	TOTAL
1970	1,436	271	861	2,568
1971	1,561	293	934	2,788
1972	1,737	327	1,028	3,092
1973	1,925	364	1,127	3,416
1974	2,098	391	1,203	3,692
1975	2,363	429	1,333	4,125
1976	2,602	468	1,462	4,532
1977	2,755	482	1,496	4,733
1978	2,858	491	1,512	4,861
1979	2,895	489	1,497	4,881
1980	2,942	486	1,486	4,914
1985	3,335	496	1,484	5,315
1990	3,862	644	1,465	5,971
1995	4,457	705	1,603	6,765
2000	5,209	781	1,829	7,819
2005	6,061	874	2,070	9,005
2010	6,777	961	2,277	10,015
2015	7,180	1,001	2,425	10,606
2020	7,260	1,008	2,538	10,806
2025	7,042	987	2,540	10,569
2030	6,766	956	2,446	10,168
2035	6,744	956	2,397	10,097
2040	6,950	979	2,438	10,367
2045	7,206	1,010	2,538	10,754
2050	7,316	1,024	2,606	10,946
2055	7,325	1,030	2,619	10,974

SOURCE: 1979 Annual Report of the Board of Trustees of the Federal Old-Age and Survivors Insurance and Disability Insurance Trust Funds.

[1]Figures in thousands.

[2]All figures for 1979 and later are projections based on Alternative II, Intermediate Assumptions of the Social Security Administration.

TABLE 15

AVERAGE MONTHLY BENEFIT PAYMENTS

	RETIRED WORKERS			SURVIVORS			
	TOTAL	MEN	WOMEN	WORKER AND SPOUSE	AGED WIDOW	WIDOW WITH ONE CHILD	WIDOW WITH TWO CHILDREN	WIDOW WITH THREE OR MORE CHILDREN
1940	$ 22.10	$ 22.80	$ 18.40	$ 36.40	$ 20.30	$ 33.90	$ 47.10	$ 51.30
1941	22.20	22.90	18.50	36.30	20.20	33.70	46.60	51.00
1942	22.50	23.30	18.70	36.80	20.20	33.90	46.50	50.70
1943	22.90	23.80	19.10	37.50	20.20	34.20	46.90	50.40
1944	23.00	24.10	19.30	37.90	20.20	34.40	47.30	50.10
1945	23.50	24.50	19.50	38.50	20.20	34.10	47.70	50.40
1946	23.90	24.90	19.60	39.00	20.20	34.60	48.20	51.40
1947	24.20	25.30	19.90	39.60	20.40	35.40	48.80	52.20
1948	24.60	25.80	20.10	40.40	20.60	36.00	49.80	53.00
1949	25.30	26.50	20.60	41.40	20.80	36.50	50.40	54.00
1950	42.20	44.60	34.80	71.70	36.50	76.90	93.90	92.40
1951	40.30	43.20	33.00	70.20	36.00	77.30	93.80	92.00
1952	47.10	50.70	39.10	81.60	40.70	87.50	106.00	101.30
1953	48.80	52.90	40.60	85.00	40.90	90.10	111.90	109.00
1954	56.50	61.60	47.00	99.10	46.30	103.90	130.50	126.80
1955	59.10	64.60	49.80	103.50	48.70	106.80	135.40	133.20
1956	59.90	66.10	51.10	105.90	50.10	109.90	141.00	138.70
1957	60.90	68.30	52.20	108.40	51.10	114.30	146.30	144.80
1958	62.60	70.70	53.50	111.20	51.90	117.00	151.70	150.70
1959	68.70	78.00	58.70	121.60	56.70	129.70	170.70	178.60
1960	69.90	79.90	59.60	123.90	57.70	131.70	188.00	181.70
1961	71.90	81.20	62.00	126.60	64.90	135.00	189.30	182.80
1962	72.50	81.80	62.60	127.90	65.90	137.30	190.70	186.80
1963	73.30	82.60	63.40	129.40	66.90	139.40	192.50	190.40
1964	73.90	83.60	64.30	130.70	67.90	141.60	193.40	192.10
1965	80.10	90.50	70.00	141.50	73.90	153.00	219.80	218.10
1966	80.60	91.20	70.70	142.50	74.30	154.30	221.90	218.80
1967	81.70	92.50	71.90	144.20	75.20	155.90	224.40	221.70
1968	95.00	107.10	84.20	166.30	86.80	179.00	257.10	253.40
1969	96.60	109.00	85.70	168.90	87.80	182.20	255.80	253.60
1970	114.20	128.70	101.60	198.90	102.40	213.00	291.10	289.90
1971	127.40	143.70	113.30	222.30	114.40	238.30	320.00	315.60
1972	157.10	177.00	140.20	272.50	138.30	290.00	383.10	376.10
1973	161.60	180.10	146.00	276.70	158.40	297.80	391.00	377.90
1974	183.10	204.20	164.60	312.30	178.80	335.00	438.40	421.90
1975	201.60	225.50	181.80	343.90	195.90	367.20	468.60	461.80
1976	218.80	245.10	197.10	373.10	211.00	399.80	503.40	499.70
1977	236.80	265.90	213.10	404.40	226.50	436.80	546.60	538.60

SOURCE: Social Security Bulletin, Annual Statistical Supplement, 1975, Social Security Administration.

TABLE 15 (Continued)

AVERAGE MONTHLY BENEFIT PAYMENTS

| | | | | DISABLED | |
| | | | | WORKER, WIFE & ONE CHILD | WORKER, WIFE & TWO CHILDREN |
	TOTAL	MEN	WOMEN		
1940					
1941					
1942					
1943					
1944					
1945					
1946					
1947					
1948					
1949					
1950					
1951					
1952					
1953					
1954					
1955					
1956					
1957	$ 72.80	$ 73.50	$ 69.80		
1958	81.70	84.70	70.60	$170.10	$165.50
1959	87.90	91.90	76.10	182.80	188.30
1960	87.90	91.90	76.90	184.70	192.20
1961	87.70	91.50	77.70	186.50	193.80
1962	88.00	92.10	78.10	185.80	194.70
1963	88.60	92.90	78.80	186.70	196.10
1964	89.20	93.80	79.30	187.70	197.10
1965	95.40	100.70	85.00	201.00	216.30
1966	95.80	101.20	85.20	202.00	217.80
1967	96.20	101.80	85.50	202.90	217.30
1968	109.20	115.60	97.20	229.70	242.00
1969	109.90	116.60	97.60	230.70	241.30
1970	128.10	136.30	113.10	264.10	273.20
1971	142.70	152.60	124.90	290.20	296.70
1972	175.00	188.20	151.80	356.30	362.80
1973	178.20	192.80	153.20	364.80	367.20
1974	200.00	217.80	170.60	409.90	411.30
1975	218.90	240.00	185.00	441.00	454.00
1976	237.40	261.40	199.40	482.20	495.70
1977	265.50	283.80	213.80	525.80	538.10

TABLE 16

ANNUAL BENEFIT AMOUNTS FOR SINGLE RETIRED WORKERS, 1953–2050
(figures after 1978 in constant 1978 dollars)

	AVERAGE ANNUAL BENEFIT[1] (single retirees)		
	LOW INCOME WORKER ($4600 in 1978)	AVERAGE INCOME WORKER ($9779 in 1978)	MAXIMUM INCOME WORKER ($16,500 in 1978)
1953	680	908	1,020
1954	708	962	1,074
1955	757	1,003	1,182
1956	769	1,117	1,242
1957	786	1,151	1,302
1958	803	1,189	1,302
1959	864	1,284	1,392
1960	876	1,296	1,428
1961	888	1,320	1,440
1962	888	1,332	1,452
1963	900	1,344	1,464
1964	900	1,368	1,476
1965	977	1,477	1,580
1966	977	1,490	1,592
1967	989	1,502	1,631
1968	1,122	1,711	1,854
1969	1,147	1,757	1,926
1970	1,337	2,056	2,278
1971	1,471	2,296	2,557
1972	1,587	2,488	2,766
1973	1,832	2,863	3,193
1974	2,005	3,144	3,565
1975	2,182	3,450	3,973
1976	2,385	3,820	4,531
1977	2,624	4,189	5,123
1978	2,880	4,595	5,727
1979	2,920	4,728	5,909
1980	2,992	4,855	6,122
1981	3,069	5,042	6,370
1982	2,745	4,441	5,652
1983	2,777	4,492	5,770
1984	2,838	4,593	5,953
1985	2,914	4,709	6,152
1986	2,974	4,807	6,327
1987	3,042	4,909	6,511
1988	3,122	5,038	6,722
1989	3,180	5,132	6,889
1990	3,241	5,229	7,058
1995	3,561	5,744	7,959
2000	3,899	6,288	9,045

TABLE 16 (Continued)

ANNUAL BENEFIT AMOUNTS FOR SINGLE RETIRED WORKERS, 1953-2050
(figures after 1978 in constant 1978 dollars)

	AVERAGE ANNUAL BENEFIT[1] (single retirees)		
	LOW INCOME WORKER ($4600 in 1978)	AVERAGE INCOME WORKER ($9779 in 1978)	MAXIMUM INCOME WORKER ($16,500 in 1978)
2005	4,243	6,842	10,202
2010	4,612	7,440	11,415
2015	5,012	8,085	12,635
2020	5,448	8,789	13,768
2025	5,923	9,554	14,968
2030	6,439	10,386	16,273
2035	6,999	11,290	17,690
2040	7,608	12,271	19,230
2045	8,269	13,340	20,902
2050	8,989	14,500	22,720

SOURCE: Social Security Administration.

[1]All figures are for single workers retiring at 65; those retiring with spouse receive a 50% increase.

TABLE 17

TOTAL CASH BENEFITS PAID TO INDIVIDUALS, OASI[1]

	TOTAL	TOTAL MONTHLY BENEFITS	TOTAL RETIRED WORKERS AND DEPENDENTS	TOTAL RETIRED WORKERS	TOTAL WIVES AND HUSBANDS	TOTAL CHILDREN
1940	32	24	17	15	2	—
1941	88	75	51	44	7	1
1942	131	116	76	65	10	1
1943	166	148	93	79	13	1
1944	209	187	113	97	16	1
1945	274	248	148	126	21	2
1946	378	350	222	189	31	2
1947	466	437	288	245	40	3
1948	556	524	352	300	49	4
1949	667	634	437	373	60	5
1950	961	928	651	557	88	6
1951	1,885	1,828	1,321	1,135	175	11
1952	2,194	2,131	1,539	1,328	200	12
1953	3,006	2,919	2,175	1,884	275	16
1954	3,670	3,578	2,698	2,340	338	21
1955	4,968	4,855	3,748	3,253	466	29
1956	5,715	5,605	4,361	3,793	536	33
1957	7,347	7,209	5,688	4,888	756	43
1958	8,327	8,194	6,474	5,567	851	56
1959	9,842	9,670	7,607	6,548	982	77
1960	10,677	10,512	8,196	7,053	1,051	92
1961	11,862	11,690	9,032	7,802	1,124	106
1962	13,356	13,173	10,162	8,813	1,216	134
1963	14,217	14,011	10,795	9,391	1,258	146
1964	14,914	14,698	11,281	9,854	1,277	150
1965	16,737	16,521	12,542	10,984	1,383	175
1966	18,266	18,030	13,372	11,727	1,429	216
1967	19,468	19,215	14,049	12,372	1,456	221
1968	22,642	22,373	16,204	14,278	1,673	253
1969	24,208	23,917	17,395	15,385	1,750	260
1970	28,797	28,503	20,770	18,438	2,029	303
1971	33,413	33,107	24,219	21,544	2,323	352
1972	37,122	36,802	27,057	24,143	2,532	382
1973	45,742	45,412	32,801	29,345	2,999	457
1974	51,618	51,291	37,218	33,377	3,308	533
1975	58,509	58,172	42,431	38,078	3,719	634
1976	65,699	65,367	47,894	43,057	4,115	722
1977	73,113	72,801	53,434	48,134	4,554	746
1978[2]	80,351	79,865	59,159	53,255	4,983	921

SOURCE: Social Security Bulletin Annual Statistical Supplement, 1975, Social Security Administration.

[1]Figures in millions.

[2]Preliminary.

TABLE 17 (Continued)

TOTAL CASH BENEFITS PAID TO INDIVIDUALS, OASI[1]

	TOTAL SURVIVORS BENEFITS	CHILDREN	WIDOWED MOTHERS	WIDOWS & WIDOWERS	PARENTS	SPECIAL AGE-72 BENEFICIARY	LUMP-SUM DEATH PAYMENTS
1940	6	3	2	—	–	—	9
1941	24	13	8	2	—	—	13
1942	40	21	13	5	—	—	15
1943	55	29	16	9	1	—	18
1944	73	39	20	14	1	—	22
1945	100	52	27	20	1	—	26
1946	128	66	32	28	1	—	28
1947	149	77	34	37	2	—	29
1948	172	86	36	48	2	—	32
1949	197	95	39	60	2	—	33
1950	277	135	49	89	3	—	33
1951	507	260	82	156	9	—	57
1952	592	298	92	191	10	—	63
1953	744	369	114	248	12	—	87
1954	880	430	133	304	13	—	92
1955	1,108	532	163	396	16	—	113
1956	1,244	581	177	469	17	—	109
1957	1,521	651	198	653	19	—	139
1958	1,720	720	223	757	20	—	133
1959	2,063	855	263	921	25	—	171
1960	2,316	945	286	1,057	28	—	164
1961	2,659	1,080	316	1,232	31	—	171
1962	3,011	1,171	336	1,470	34	—	183
1963	3,216	1,222	348	1,612	34	—	206
1964	3,416	1,275	354	1,754	33	—	216
1965	3,979	1,515	388	2,041	35	—	217
1966	4,613	1,812	415	2,351	35	44	237
1967	4,854	1,855	420	2,545	34	313	252
1968	5,839	2,207	478	3,117	37	330	269
1969	6,219	2,322	490	3,371	36	303	291
1970	7,428	2,760	574	4,055	39	305	294
1971	8,602	3,168	630	4,763	41	286	306
1972	9,481	3,433	679	5,326	43	264	320
1973	12,347	4,002	801	7,496	48	265	329
1974	13,836	4,399	898	8,490	49	237	327
1975	15,543	4,888	1,009	9,596	50	198	337
1976	17,298	5,384	1,113	10,750	51	174	332
1977	19,210	5,914	1,189	12,055	52	157	312
1978[2]	20,706	6,093	1,284	13,278	51	142	344

[1]Figures in millions.
[2]Preliminary.

TABLE 18

TOTAL CASH BENEFITS PAID TO INDIVIDUALS, DI[1]

	TOTAL	DISABLED WORKERS	WIVES AND HUSBANDS	CHILDREN
1957	57	57	—	—
1958	249	246	1	1
1959	457	390	29	38
1960	568	489	32	48
1961	887	724	54	109
1962	1,105	888	68	149
1963	1,210	965	73	172
1964	1,309	1,044	79	186
1965	1,573	1,246	95	232
1966	1,781	1,394	108	280
1967	1,939	1,519	113	307
1968	2,294	1,804	131	360
1969	2,542	2,014	139	389
1970	3,067	2,448	165	454
1971	3,758	3,028	192	539
1972	4,473	3,626	224	623
1973	5,718	4,676	281	760
1974	6,903	5,662	320	920
1975	8,414	6,908	385	1,121
1976	9,966	8,190	447	1,328
1977	11,463	9,456	503	1,503
1978[2]	12,513	10,315	541	1,657

SOURCE: Social Security Bulletin Annual Statistical Supplement, 1975, Social Security Administration.

[1]Figures in millions.
[2]Preliminary.

TABLE 19

THE SOCIAL SECURITY TRUST FUNDS
(figures in millions)

	OASI TRUST FUND TOTAL ASSETS	OASI TOTAL EXPEN-DITURES	RATIO	OASDI TRUST FUND TOTAL ASSETS	OASDI TOTAL EXPEN-DITURES	RATIO	OASDHI TRUST FUND TOTAL ASSETS	OASDHI TOTAL EXPEN-DITURES	RATIO
1937	766	1	76,600%	—	—	—	—	—	—
1938	1,132	10	11,320%	—	—	—	—	—	—
1939	1,724	14	12,314%	—	—	—	—	—	—
1940	2,031	6	3,276%	—	—	—	—	—	—
1941	2,762	114	2,423%	—	—	—	—	—	—
1942	3,688	159	2,319%	—	—	—	—	—	—
1943	4,820	195	2,472%	—	—	—	—	—	—
1944	6,005	238	2,523%	—	—	—	—	—	—
1945	7,121	304	2,342%	—	—	—	—	—	—
1946	8,150	418	1,950%	—	—	—	—	—	—
1947	9,360	512	1,828%	—	—	—	—	—	—
1948	10,722	607	1,766%	—	—	—	—	—	—
1949	11,816	721	1,639%	—	—	—	—	—	—
1950	13,721	1,022	1,343%	—	—	—	—	—	—
1951	15,540	1,966	790%	—	—	—	—	—	—
1952	17,442	2,282	764%	—	—	—	—	—	—
1953	18,707	3,094	605%	—	—	—	—	—	—
1954	20,576	3,741	550%	—	—	—	—	—	—
1955	21,663	5,079	427%	—	—	—	—	—	—
1956	22,519	5,841	386%	—	—	—	—	—	—
1957	22,393	7,507	298%	23,042	7,567	305%	—	—	—
1958	21,864	8,646	253%	23,243	8,907	261%	—	—	—
1959	20,141	10,308	195%	21,966	10,793	204%	—	—	—
1960	20,324	11,198	181%	22,613	11,798	192%	—	—	—
1961	19,725	12,432	159%	22,162	13,388	166%	—	—	—
1962	18,337	13,973	131%	20,705	15,156	137%	—	—	—
1963	18,480	14,920	124%	20,715	16,217	128%	—	—	—
1964	19,125	15,613	122%	21,172	17,020	124%	—	—	—
1965	18,235	17,501	104%	19,841	19,187	103%	—	—	—
1966	20,570	18,967	108%	22,308	20,913	107%	23,252	21,912	106%
1967	24,222	20,382	119%	26,250	22,471	117%	27,323	25,901	105%
1968	25,704	23,557	109%	28,729	26,015	110%	30,812	30,292	102%
1969	30,082	25,176	119%	34,182	27,892	123%	36,687	32,749	112%
1970	32,454	29,848	109%	38,068	33,108	115%	41,270	38,389	108%
1971	33,789	34,542	98%	40,434	38,542	105%	43,468	44,442	98%
1972	35,318	38,522	92%	42,775	43,281	99%	45,710	49,784	92%
1973	36,487	47,175	77%	44,414	53,148	84%	50,881	60,437	84%
1974	37,777	53,397	71%	45,886	60,593	76%	55,005	69,965	79%
1975	36,987	60,395	61%	44,342	69,184	64%	54,859	80,765	68%
1976	35,388	67,876	52%	41,133	78,242	53%	51,738	91,921	56%
1977	32,491	75,309	43%	35,861	87,254	41%	46,303	103,273	45%
1978	27,520	83,064	33%	31,746	96,018	33%	43,223	114,196	38%

SOURCE: 1979 Annual Report of the Board of Trustees of the Federal Old-Age and Survivors Insurance and Disability Insurance Trust Funds; 1979 Annual Report of the Board of Trustees of the Federal Hospital Insurance Trust Fund; Social Security Bulletin Annual Statistical Supplement, 1975.

TABLE 20

FUTURE TRUST FUNDS[2]

	OASI TRUST FUND AS A PERCENTAGE OF EXPENDITURES	OASDI TRUST FUND AS A PERCENTAGE OF EXPENDITURES
1979	30%	30%
1980	24%	25%
1981	19%	22%
1982	18%	23%
1983	18%	26%
1984	19%	29%
1985	19%	32%
1986	22%	40%
1987	26%	48%
1988	30%	56%
1989	34%	64%
1990	37%	70%
1991	46%	85%
1992	56%	100%
1993	66%	116%
1994	77%	131%
1995	88%	147%
1996	100%	163%
1997	112%	179%
1998	126%	195%
1999	139%	211%
2000	154%	228%
2005	225%	299%
2010	268%	335%
2015	258%	323%
2020	194%	263%
2025	89%	170%
2028	[1]	—
2032	—	[1]

SOURCE: 1979 Annual Report of the Board of Trustees of the Federal Old-Age and Survivors Insurance and Disability Insurance Trust Funds.

[1]Trust fund projected to be exhausted.

[2]Based on Alternative II, Intermediate Assumptions of the Social Security Administration.

TABLE 21

UNFUNDED LIABILITY AND THE TRUST FUNDS[1]

	UNFUNDED LIABILITY FOR THE OASDI PROGRAM	OASDI TRUST FUNDS	TRUST FUNDS AS A PERCENT OF THE UNFUNDED LIABILITY
1978	3,971	31.7	0.80%
1977	5,362	35.9	0.67%
1976	4,148	41.1	0.99%
1975	2,710	44.3	1.63%
1974	2,460	45.9	1.87%
1973	2,118	44.4	2.10%
1972	1,865	42.8	2.29%
1971	435	40.4	9.29%
1970	415	38.1	9.18%
1969	330	34.2	10.36%
1968	414	28.7	6.93%
1967	350	26.3	7.51%

SOURCE: Statement of Liabilities and Other Financial Commitments of the United States Government (Saltonstall Report), U.S. Treasury Department, 1967–1978.

[1]Figures in billions.

TABLE 22

WELFARE COMPONENT OF RETIREMENT BENEFITS[1]

	VALUE OF TAXES	VALUE OF BENEFITS	WELFARE SUBSIDY	WELFARE AS A PERCENT OF TOTAL BENEFIT	RATIO OF BENEFITS TO TAXES
1940	68.36	2,962.09	2,873.73	97.7%	43.3
1941	91.87	3,065.83	2,973.96	97.0%	33.4
1942	117.47	3,366.60	3,249.13	96.5%	28.7
1943	146.82	3,802.64	3,655.81	96.1%	25.9
1944	181.13	4,220.22	4,039.09	95.7%	23.3
1945	218.68	4,641.41	4,422.72	95.3%	21.2
1946	265.04	4,674.09	4,409.05	94.3%	17.6
1947	309.51	5,056.13	4,746.62	93.9%	16.3
1948	373.88	5,467.84	5,093.96	93.2%	14.6
1949	422.23	5,978.50	5,556.27	92.9%	14.2
1950	485.12	7,967.16	7,482.04	93.9%	16.4
1951	605.79	9,793.02	9,187.22	93.8%	16.2
1952	693.24	7,611.72	6,918.46	90.9%	11.0
1953	798.89	7,836.81	7,037.92	89.8%	9.8
1954	902.73	8,449.77	7,547.04	89.3%	9.4
1955	1,029.31	9,078.98	8,049.66	88.7%	8.8
1956	1,168.70	9,730.04	8,561.25	88.0%	8.3
1957	1,336.43	10,227.88	8,941.44	87.4%	7.7
1958	1,509.38	11,299.69	9,790.31	86.6%	7.5
1959	1,705.78	11,427.99	9,722.21	85.1%	6.7
1960	1,960.49	11,936.84	9,976.35	83.6%	6.1
1961	2,291.32	12,227.14	9,935.82	81.3%	5.3
1962	2,603.37	12,991.82	10,388.45	80.0%	5.0
1963	3,689.58	14,057.98	10,368.41	73.8%	3.8
1964	3,370.66	15,083.91	11,713.25	77.7%	4.5
1965	3,893.22	9,451.80	5,558.58	58.8%	2.4
1966	4,460.10	17,236.58	12,776.48	74.1%	3.9
1967	5,134.15	18,610.00	13,475.85	72.4%	3.6
1968	5,821.77	17,775.80	11,954.04	67.2%	3.1
1969	6,623.45	21,943.70	15,320.25	69.8%	3.3
1970	7,660.55	24,265.95	16,605.40	68.4%	3.2
1971	8,668.61	25,935.63	17,267.02	66.6%	3.0

SOURCE: Douglas Munro, "Welfare Component and Labor Supply Effects of OASDHI Benefits." Ohio State University, 1976.

[1]Males with median earnings retiring at age 65.

TABLE 23

Total Benefit Payments under the ssi Program[1]

	Total ssi Benefits	ssi Benefits to the Aged	ssi Benefits to the Blind	ssi Benefits to the Disabled
1978	6,372	2,342	148	3,882
1977	6,134	2,364	142	3,628
1976	5,900	2,420	134	3,346
1975	5,716	2,517	127	3,072
1974	5,097	2,414	126	2,557

Source: Department of Health, Education and Welfare.
[1]Figures in millions.

TABLE 24

Maximum Income, Alternative III
Benefits Which Can Be Paid by Private System[1]

Real Rates of Return	Retirement Trust Fund Accumulated at Age 65	Perpetual Annuity	Life Annuity Single Worker	Life Annuity, Couple — Both Spouses Alive	Life Annuity, Couple — One Spouse Alive
3.0%	478,746	14,362 (31%)	43,648 (95%)	36,377 (79%)	24,251 (53%)
3.5%	541,403	18,949 (41%)	51,307 (111%)	43,015 (93%)	28,677 (62%)
4.0%	612,459	24,498 (53%)	60,264 (130%)	50,811 (110%)	33,874 (73%)
4.5%	693,437	31,205 (68%)	70,769 (153%)	59,993 (130%)	39,996 (87%)
5.0%	786,233	39,312 (85%)	83,138 (180%)	70,846 (153%)	47,231 (102%)
5.5%	892,792	49,104 (106%)	97,720 (211%)	83,686 (181%)	55,791 (121%)
6.0%	1,015,403	60,924 (132%)	114,932 (248%)	98,895 (214%)	65,930 (143%)
6.5%	1,156,709	75,186 (162%)	135,270 (292%)	116,925 (253%)	77,950 (168%)
7.0%	1,319,891	92,392 (200%)	159,333 (344%)	138,325 (299%)	92,217 (199%)
7.5%	1,508,361	113,127 (244%)	187,800 (405%)	163,718 (353%)	109,145 (236%)
8.0%	1,726,449	138,116 (298%)	221,521 (478%)	193,884 (418%)	129,256 (279%)

Social Security Pays: Single Worker—12,525 (27%)
　　　　　　　　　　Couple, Both Spouses Alive—18,787 (41%)
　　　　　　　　　　Couple, One Spouse Alive—12,525 (27%)

[1]All figures in constant 1980 dollars, replacement ratios in parentheses.

TABLE 25

Average Income, Alternative III
Benefits Which Can Be Paid by Private System[']

Real Rates of Return	Retirement Trust Fund Accumulated at Age 65	Perpetual Annuity	Life Annuity Single Worker	Life Annuity, Couple Both Spouses Alive	Life Annuity, Couple One Spouse Alive
3.0%	209,519	6,286 (31%)	19,102 (94%)	15,920 (78%)	10,613 (52%)
3.5%	243,337	8,517 (42%)	23,060 (113%)	19,333 (95%)	12,889 (63%)
4.0%	280,379	11,215 (55%)	27,588 (135%)	23,261 (114%)	15,507 (76%)
4.5%	322,025	14,491 (71%)	32,864 (161%)	27,860 (137%)	18,574 (91%)
5.0%	369,574	18,479 (91%)	39,080 (191%)	33,302 (163%)	22,201 (109%)
5.5%	424,423	23,343 (114%)	46,455 (227%)	39,783 (195%)	26,522 (130%)
6.0%	488,008	29,281 (143%)	55,237 (270%)	47,530 (232%)	31,686 (155%)
6.5%	561,834	36,519 (179%)	65,703 (321%)	56,793 (278%)	37,862 (185%)
7.0%	647,797	45,346 (222%)	78,200 (382%)	67,889 (332%)	45,260 (221%)
7.5%	747,945	56,096 (274%)	93,124 (454%)	81,182 (397%)	54,122 (264%)
8.0%	864,844	69,188 (338%)	110,968 (541%)	97,124 (474%)	64,749 (316%)

Social Security Pays: Single Worker—8,172 (40%)
Couple, Both Spouses Alive—12,258 (60%)
Couple, One Spouse Alive—8,172 (40%)

'All figures in constant 1980 dollars, replacement ratios in parentheses.

TABLE 26

LOW INCOME, ALTERNATIVE III
BENEFITS WHICH CAN BE PAID BY PRIVATE SYSTEM[1]

REAL RATES OF RETURN	RETIREMENT TRUST FUND ACCUMULATED AT AGE 65	PERPETUAL ANNUITY	LIFE ANNUITY SINGLE WORKER	LIFE ANNUITY, COUPLE	
				BOTH SPOUSES ALIVE	ONE SPOUSE ALIVE
3.0%	113,592	3,408 (34%)	10,356 (103%)	8,631 (86%)	5,754 (57%)
3.5%	136,050	4,762 (48%)	12,893 (128%)	10,809 (108%)	7,206 (72%)
4.0%	160,270	6,411 (64%)	15,770 (156%)	13,297 (132%)	8,864 (88%)
4.5%	187,407	8,433 (84%)	19,126 (190%)	16,214 (161%)	10,809 (107%)
5.0%	218,608	10,930 (109%)	23,116 (229%)	19,698 (195%)	13,132 (130%)
5.5%	254,961	14,023 (139%)	27,906 (276%)	23,899 (237%)	15,933 (158%)
6.0%	297,609	17,857 (177%)	33,686 (333%)	28,986 (287%)	19,324 (192%)
6.5%	347,900	22,613 (224%)	40,685 (403%)	35,167 (348%)	23,445 (232%)
7.0%	407,362	28,515 (282%)	49,175 (487%)	42,692 (423%)	28,461 (282%)
7.5%	477,806	35,835 (355%)	59,490 (589%)	51,861 (513%)	34,574 (342%)
8.0%	561,387	44,911 (444%)	72,032 (713%)	63,045 (624%)	42,030 (416%)

Social Security Pays: Single Worker—5,270 (53%)
                    Couple, Both Spouses Alive—7,905 (79%)
                    Couple, One Spouse Alive—5,270 (53%)

[1] All figures in constant 1980 dollars, replacement ratios in parentheses.

TABLE 27

Maximum Income, Alternative II
Benefits Which Can Be Paid by Private System[1]

Real Rates of Return	Retirement Trust Fund Accumulated at Age 65	Perpetual Annuity	Life Annuity Single Worker	Life Annuity, Couple	
				Both Spouses Alive	One Spouse Alive
3.0%	471,291	14,139 (25%)	42,968 (75%)	35,810 (63%)	23,874 (42%)
3.5%	534,491	18,707 (33%)	50,652 (88%)	42,466 (74%)	28,311 (49%)
4.0%	604,579	24,183 (42%)	59,489 (103%)	50,158 (87%)	33,439 (58%)
4.5%	683,728	30,768 (54%)	69,778 (121%)	59,153 (103%)	39,436 (69%)
5.0%	773,905	38,695 (67%)	81,834 (142%)	69,735 (121%)	46,490 (81%)
5.5%	877,072	48,239 (84%)	95,999 (166%)	82,213 (143%)	54,808 (95%)
6.0%	995,320	59,719 (104%)	112,659 (195%)	96,939 (168%)	64,626 (112%)
6.5%	1,131,319	73,536 (127%)	132,300 (229%)	114,359 (198%)	76,239 (132%)
7.0%	1,287,924	90,155 (156%)	155,474 (269%)	134,975 (234%)	89,983 (156%)
7.5%	1,468,488	110,137 (191%)	182,836 (316%)	159,390 (276%)	106,260 (184%)
8.0%	1,677,025	134,162 (232%)	215,179 (372%)	188,334 (326%)	125,556 (217%)

Social Security Pays: Single Worker—15,551 (27%)
　　　　　　　　　　　Couple, Both Spouses Alive—23,326 (41%)
　　　　　　　　　　　Couple, One Spouse Alive—15,551 (27%)

[1]All figures in constant 1980 dollars, replacement ratios in parentheses.

TABLE 28

AVERAGE INCOME, ALTERNATIVE II
BENEFITS WHICH CAN BE PAID BY PRIVATE SYSTEM[1]

REAL RATES OF RETURN	RETIREMENT TRUST FUND ACCUMULATED AT AGE 65	PERPETUAL ANNUITY	LIFE ANNUITY SINGLE WORKER	LIFE ANNUITY, COUPLE	
				BOTH SPOUSES ALIVE	ONE SPOUSE ALIVE
3.0%	192,998	5,790 (23%)	17,596 (69%)	14,665 (58%)	9,776 (39%)
3.5%	229,526	8,033 (32%)	21,752 (85%)	18,236 (72%)	12,157 (48%)
4.0%	268,202	10,728 (42%)	26,390 (103%)	22,251 (87%)	14,834 (58%)
4.5%	309,887	13,945 (55%)	31,626 (124%)	26,810 (105%)	17,873 (70%)
5.0%	356,349	17,817 (70%)	37,681 (147%)	32,110 (126%)	21,407 (84%)
5.5%	409,107	22,501 (88%)	44,778 (175%)	38,348 (150%)	25,565 (100%)
6.0%	469,662	28,180 (110%)	53,160 (208%)	45,743 (179%)	30,495 (119%)
6.5%	539,738	35,083 (137%)	63,119 (247%)	54,559 (213%)	36,373 (142%)
7.0%	621,077	43,475 (170%)	74,974 (293%)	65,089 (254%)	43,393 (170%)
7.5%	715,586	53,669 (210%)	89,095 (348%)	77,670 (304%)	51,780 (202%)
8.0%	825,688	66,055 (258%)	105,944 (413%)	92,727 (362%)	61,818 (241%)

Social Security Pays: Single Worker—10,272 (40%)
Couple, Both Spouses Alive—15,408 (60%)
Couple, One Spouse Alive—10,272 (40%)

[1]All figures in constant 1980 dollars, replacement ratios in parentheses.

TABLE 29

Low Income, Alternative II
Benefits Which Can Be Paid by Private System[1]

Real Rates of Return	Retirement Trust Fund Accumulated at Age 65	Perpetual Annuity	Life Annuity Single Worker	Life Annuity, Couple Both Spouses Alive	Life Annuity, Couple One Spouse Alive
3.0%	101,927	3,058 (24%)	9,293 (73%)	7,745 (61%)	5,163 (41%)
3.5%	125,802	4,403 (35%)	11,922 (93%)	9,995 (78%)	6,663 (52%)
4.0%	152,231	6,089 (48%)	14,979 (117%)	12,630 (99%)	8,420 (66%)
4.5%	180,365	8,116 (63%)	18,407 (143%)	15,605 (122%)	10,403 (81%)
5.0%	211,436	10,572 (82%)	22,358 (174%)	19,052 (148%)	12,701 (99%)
5.5%	246,801	13,574 (106%)	27,013 (210%)	23,134 (180%)	15,423 (120%)
6.0%	287,798	17,268 (134%)	32,575 (253%)	28,030 (218%)	18,687 (145%)
6.5%	335,798	21,827 (170%)	39,269 (305%)	33,944 (264%)	22,629 (176%)
7.0%	392,233	27,456 (213%)	47,349 (368%)	41,106 (319%)	27,404 (213%)
7.5%	458,906	34,418 (267%)	57,137 (443%)	49,810 (387%)	33,207 (258%)
8.0%	537,734	43,019 (334%)	68,997 (535%)	60,389 (469%)	40,259 (313%)

Social Security Pays: Single Worker—6,720 (53%)
                   Couple, Both Spouses Alive—10,080 (79%)
                   Couple, One Spouse Alive—6,720 (53%)

[1]All figures in constant 1980 dollars, replacement ratios in parentheses.

TABLE 30

MAXIMUM INCOME, ALTERNATIVE I
BENEFITS WHICH CAN BE PAID BY PRIVATE SYSTEM[1]

REAL RATES OF RETURN	RETIREMENT TRUST FUND ACCUMULATED AT AGE 65	PERPETUAL ANNUITY	LIFE ANNUITY SINGLE WORKER	LIFE ANNUITY, COUPLE	
				BOTH SPOUSES ALIVE	ONE SPOUSE ALIVE
3.0%	482,833	14,485 (21%)	44,020 (62%)	36,687 (52%)	24,458 (34%)
3.5%	550,283	18,260 (27%)	52,149 (73%)	43,721 (62%)	29,147 (41%)
4.0%	623,119	24,925 (35%)	61,313 (86%)	51,696 (73%)	34,464 (48%)
4.5%	703,826	31,672 (45%)	71,829 (100%)	60,892 (85%)	40,595 (57%)
5.0%	794,909	39,745 (56%)	84,055 (117%)	71,628 (100%)	47,752 (67%)
5.5%	898,546	49,420 (69%)	98,349 (137%)	84,225 (118%)	56,150 (79%)
6.0%	1,016,981	61,019 (85%)	115,111 (161%)	99,049 (138%)	66,033 (92%)
6.5%	1,152,743	74,928 (105%)	134,806 (188%)	116,524 (163%)	77,683 (108%)
7.0%	1,308,685	91,608 (128%)	157,980 (220%)	137,151 (191%)	91,434 (128%)
7.5%	1,487,981	111,599 (156%)	185,263 (258%)	161,506 (225%)	107,671 (150%)
8.0%	1,694,603	135,568 (189%)	217,435 (303%)	190,308 (265%)	126,872 (177%)

Social Security Pays: Single Worker—19,076 (27%)
Couple, Both Spouses Alive—28,614 (41%)
Couple, One Spouse Alive—19,076 (27%)

[1] All figures in constant 1980 dollars, replacement ratios in parentheses.

TABLE 31

AVERAGE INCOME, ALTERNATIVE I
BENEFITS WHICH CAN BE PAID BY PRIVATE SYSTEM[1]

REAL RATES OF RETURN	RETIREMENT TRUST FUND ACCUMULATED AT AGE 65	PERPETUAL ANNUITY	LIFE ANNUITY SINGLE WORKER	LIFE ANNUITY, COUPLE BOTH SPOUSES ALIVE	LIFE ANNUITY, COUPLE ONE SPOUSE ALIVE
3.0%	184,241	5,527 (18%)	16,797 (54%)	13,999 (45%)	9,333 (30%)
3.5%	222,331	7,782 (25%)	21,070 (67%)	17,664 (57%)	11,776 (38%)
4.0%	264,549	10,582 (34%)	26,031 (83%)	21,948 (70%)	14,632 (47%)
4.5%	309,383	13,922 (45%)	31,574 (100%)	26,767 (85%)	17,844 (57%)
5.0%	357,535	17,877 (57%)	37,806 (120%)	32,217 (103%)	21,478 (68%)
5.5%	410,964	22,603 (72%)	44,982 (143%)	38,522 (123%)	25,681 (82%)
6.0%	471,492	28,289 (90%)	53,367 (169%)	45,921 (146%)	30,614 (97%)
6.5%	540,865	35,156 (112%)	63,251 (201%)	54,673 (174%)	36,449 (116%)
7.0%	621,068	43,475 (138%)	74,973 (238%)	65,088 (207%)	43,392 (138%)
7.5%	714,027	53,552 (170%)	88,901 (282%)	77,501 (246%)	51,667 (164%)
8.0%	822,083	65,767 (209%)	105,482 (334%)	92,322 (293%)	61,548 (195%)

Social Security Pays: Single Worker—12,816 (40%)
Couple, Both Spouses Alive—19,224 (61%)
Couple, One Spouse Alive—12,816 (40%)

[1]All figures in constant 1980 dollars, replacement ratios in parentheses.

TABLE 32

Low Income, Alternative I
Benefits Which Can Be Paid by Private System[1]

Real Rates of Return	Retirement Trust Fund Accumulated at Age 65	Perpetual Annuity	Life Annuity Single Worker	Life Annuity, Couple	
				Both Spouses Alive	One Spouse Alive
3.0%	95,743	2,872 (18%)	8,729 (54%)	7,275 (46%)	4,850 (30%)
3.5%	119,755	4,191 (26%)	11,349 (71%)	9,515 (59%)	6,343 (40%)
4.0%	147,507	5,900 (37%)	14,514 (90%)	12,238 (76%)	8,158 (51%)
4.5%	178,725	8,043 (50%)	18,240 (113%)	15,463 (96%)	10,308 (64%)
5.0%	212,013	10,601 (66%)	22,419 (139%)	19,104 (119%)	12,736 (79%)
5.5%	248,522	13,669 (85%)	27,202 (168%)	23,295 (144%)	15,530 (96%)
6.0%	289,923	17,395 (108%)	32,816 (203%)	28,237 (175%)	18,825 (117%)
6.5%	337,848	21,960 (136%)	39,509 (244%)	34,151 (211%)	22,767 (141%)
7.0%	393,825	27,568 (171%)	47,541 (294%)	41,273 (255%)	27,515 (170%)
7.5%	459,628	34,472 (213%)	57,227 (354%)	49,888 (309%)	33,259 (206%)
8.0%	537,220	42,978 (266%)	68,931 (426%)	60,331 (373%)	40,221 (249%)

Social Security Pays: Single Worker—8,446 (53%)
Couple, Both Spouses Alive—12,669 (79%)
Couple, One Spouse Alive—8,446 (53%)

[1]All figures in constant 1980 dollars, replacement ratios in parentheses.

TABLE 33

U.S. Total Fertility Rate[1]
1800–1978

Year	Rate	Year	Rate	Year	Rate
1978	1.757	1933	2.17	1890	3.87
1977	1.78	1932	2.32	1889	3.99
1976	1.72	1931	2.40	1888	4.06
1975	1.77	1930	2.53	1887	4.06
1974	1.83	1929	2.53	1886	4.11
1973	1.87	1928	2.66	1885	4.23
1972	2.00	1927	2.82	1884	4.29
1971	2.25	1926	2.90	1883	4.29
1970	2.43	1925	3.01	1882	4.25
1969	2.42	1924	3.12	1881	4.25
1968	2.43	1923	3.10	1880	4.24
1967	2.53	1922	3.11	1879	4.23
1966	2.67	1921	3.33	1878	4.27
1965	2.88	1920	3.26	1877	4.37
1964	3.17	1919	3.07	1876	4.45
1963	3.30	1918	3.31	1875	4.55
1962	3.42	1917	3.33	1874	4.54
1961	3.56	1916	3.23	1873	4.57
1960	3.61	1915	3.25	1872	4.58
1959	3.64	1914	3.30	1871	4.55
1958	3.63	1913	3.35	1870	4.55
1957	3.68	1912	3.35	1869	4.57
1956	3.60	1911	3.34	1868	4.54
1955	3.50	1910	3.42	1867	4.56
1954	3.46	1909	3.46	1866	4.47
1953	3.35	1908	3.51	1865	4.34
1952	3.29	1907	3.52	1864	4.26
1951	3.20	1906	3.53	1863	4.38
1950	3.03	1905	3.50	1862	4.72
1949	3.04	1904	3.44	1861	5.07
1948	3.03	1903	3.41	1860	5.21
1947	3.18	1902	3.38	1859	5.21
1946	2.86	1901	3.38	1858	5.30
1945	2.42	1900	3.56	1857	5.30
1944	2.49	1899	3.57	1856	5.26
1943	2.64	1898	3.60	1855	5.31
1942	2.55	1897	3.64	1850	5.42
1941	2.33	1896	3.77	1840	6.14
1940	2.23	1895	3.83	1830	6.55
1939	2.17	1894	3.89	1820	6.73
1938	2.22	1893	3.98	1810	6.92
1937	2.17	1892	4.01	1800	7.04
1936	2.15	1891	3.93		
1935	2.19				
1934	2.23				

Source: 1800–1916: Ansley J. Coale & Melvin Zelnik, *New Estimates of Fertility and Population in the United States* (Princeton University Press, 1963); 1916–1969: National Center for Health Statistics; 1970–1978: 1979 Annual Report of the Board of Trustees of the Federal Old-Age and Survivors Insurance and Disability Insurance Trust Funds.

[1]Figures for 1800–1916 are for white population only; statistics for the entire population were unavailable.

TABLE 34

POPULATION AGED 65 AND OLDER AS A
PERCENTAGE OF THOSE AGED 20–64

	ACTUAL
1960	17.4%
1965	18.2%
1970	18.4%
1975	19.0%
1976	19.1%
1977	19.1%
1978	19.2%

	ALTERNATIVE I	ALTERNATIVE II	ALTERNATIVE III
1979	19.3%	19.3%	19.3%
1980	19.4%	19.4%	19.5%
1985	19.9%	20.1%	20.4%
1990	20.9%	21.2%	21.7%
1995	21.3%	21.8%	22.5%
2000	20.9%	21.6%	22.5%
2005	20.3%	21.3%	22.5%
2010	20.8%	22.2%	24.1%
2015	22.8%	24.9%	27.8%
2020	25.6%	28.5%	33.0%
2025	28.5%	32.6%	39.4%
2030	30.1%	35.7%	45.3%
2035	29.3%	36.1%	48.6%
2040	27.4%	35.1%	50.5%
2045	25.7%	34.1%	52.2%
2050	25.3%	34.2%	54.2%

SOURCE: 1979 Annual Report of the Board of Trustees of the Federal Old-Age & Survivors Insurance and Disability Insurance Trust Funds, Social Security Administration.

TABLE 35

OASDI BENEFICIARIES AS A
PERCENTAGE OF COVERED WORKERS
1945–2050

	ACTUAL		
1945	2%		
1950	6%		
1955	12%		
1960	20%		
1965	25%		
1970	28%		
1975	31%		
1978	31%		
	ALTERNATIVE I	ALTERNATIVE II	ALTERNATIVE III
1980	31%	31%	32%
1985	30%	31%	32%
1990	31%	32%	33%
1995	31%	33%	34%
2000	32%	33%	35%
2005	32%	34%	36%
2010	33%	36%	40%
2015	36%	40%	45%
2020	39%	44%	52%
2025	42%	48%	59%
2030	42%	50%	64%
2035	41%	50%	68%
2040	39%	50%	70%
2045	38%	49%	73%
2050	38%	49%	75%

SOURCE: 1979 Annual Report of the Board of Trustees of the Federal Old-Age & Survivors Insurance and Disability Insurance Trust Funds.

TABLE 36

MARRIAGES PER 1000 UNMARRIED WOMEN
15 YEARS AND OLDER 1963–1977

1963	73.4
1964	74.6
1965	75.0
1966	75.6
1967	76.4
1968	79.1
1969	80.0
1970	76.5
1971	76.2
1972	77.9
1973	76.0
1974	72.0
1975	66.9
1976	66.8
1977	68.0

SOURCE: National Center for Health Statistics, Marriage and Divorce Branch, U.S. Bureau of the Census.

TABLE 37

DIVORCES + ANNULMENTS PER 1000 MARRIED WOMEN
15 YEARS AND OLDER 1963–1977

1963	9.6
1964	10.0
1965	10.6
1966	10.9
1967	11.2
1968	12.5
1969	13.4
1970	14.9
1971	15.9
1972	17.0
1973	18.2
1974	19.3
1975	20.3
1976	21.1
1977	21.5

SOURCE: National Center for Health Statistics, Marriage and Divorce Branch, U.S. Bureau of the Census.

TABLE 38

LONG RUN DEFICITS CAUSED BY 1972 ERROR

| | PRE-1977 SYSTEM | EXPENDITURES AS A PERCENT OF TAXABLE EARNINGS | | PRE-1977 TAX RATES | PRE-1977 DEFICIT |
		WAGE INDEXING	PRICE INDEXING		
1976	10.8	10.8	10.8	9.9	0.9
1980	10.7	10.7	10.6	9.9	0.8
1990	12.1	11.8	10.5	9.9	2.2
2000	13.4	12.4	10.0	9.9	3.5
2010	16.0	13.4	10.0	9.9	6.1
2020	21.3	16.5	11.5	11.9	9.4
2030	26.0	18.9	12.5	11.9	14.1
2040	27.4	18.9	11.9	11.9	15.5
2050	28.6	18.8	11.3	11.9	16.7

SOURCE: *Financing Social Security: Issues for the Short and Long-Term,* Congressional Budget Office, July 1977.

TABLE 39

ASSUMPTIONS OF THE SOCIAL SECURITY ADMINISTRATION
IN THE 1979 ANNUAL REPORT

	ALTERNATIVE I				ALTERNATIVE II				ALTERNATIVE III			
	RATE OF GROWTH IN REAL WAGES	UNEMPLOY- MENT	INFLATION	FERTILITY	RATE OF GROWTH IN REAL WAGES	UNEMPLOY- MENT	INFLATION	FERTILITY	RATE OF GROWTH IN REAL WAGES	UNEMPLOY- MENT	INFLATION	FERTILITY
1979	− 1.0	6.0	9.3	1.831	− 1.1	6.0	9.4	1.793	− 1.1	6.3	10.3	1.737
1980	1.3	6.2	7.3	1.871	0.6	6.2	7.4	1.809	− 0.2	8.2	8.9	1.715
1981	2.2	5.7	6.5	1.911	2.5	6.0	6.6	1.824	1.9	7.4	7.3	1.693
1982	2.7	4.9	5.2	1.952	1.9	5.3	5.5	1.839	1.4	6.9	6.3	1.671
1983	1.8	4.2	4.0	1.992	1.5	5.0	4.5	1.855	1.2	6.4	6.0	1.649
1984	1.8	4.0	3.1	2.033	1.4	5.0	4.0	1.870	1.1	6.0	6.0	1.627
1985	2.0	4.0	3.0	2.074	1.3	5.0	4.0	1.887	1.2	6.0	6.0	1.606
1986	2.1	4.0	3.0	—	1.7	5.0	4.0	—	1.1	6.0	6.0	—
1987	2.4	4.0	3.0	—	2.0	5.0	4.0	—	1.3	6.0	6.0	—
1988	2.5	4.0	3.0	—	2.0	5.0	4.0	—	1.5	6.0	6.0	—
1989	2.5	4.0	3.0	—	2.0	5.0	4.0	—	1.5	6.0	6.0	—
1990	2.5	4.0	3.0	2.292	2.0	5.0	4.0	2.036	1.5	6.0	6.0	1.544
1995	2.4	4.0	3.0	2.443	1.9	5.0	4.0	2.075	1.4	6.0	6.0	1.524
2000	2.25	4.0	3.0	2.394	1.75	5.0	4.0	2.100	1.25	6.0	6.0	1.509
2005	2.25	4.0	3.0	2.500	1.75	5.0	4.0	2.100	1.25	6.0	6.0	1.500

SOURCE: 1979 Annual Report of the Board of Trustees of the Federal Old-Age and Survivors and Disability Insurance Trust Funds.

TABLE 40

ASSUMPTIONS OF THE SOCIAL SECURITY ADMINISTRATION IN THE 1978 ANNUAL REPORT

	ALTERNATIVE I				ALTERNATIVE II				ALTERNATIVE III			
	RATE OF GROWTH IN REAL WAGES	UNEMPLOY-MENT	INFLATION	FERTILITY	RATE OF GROWTH IN REAL WAGES	UNEMPLOY-MENT	INFLATION	FERTILITY	RATE OF GROWTH IN REAL WAGES	UNEMPLOY-MENT	INFLATION	FERTILITY
1977	1.2	7.0	6.5	1.789	1.2	7.0	6.5	1.789	1.2	7.0	6.5	1.789
1978	1.1	6.3	6.1	1.764	1.1	6.3	6.1	1.758	1.1	6.3	6.1	1.745
1979	2.4	5.9	6.0	1.793	1.8	5.9	6.1	1.775	1.4	6.0	6.8	1.737
1980	2.6	5.3	5.5	1.822	2.2	5.4	5.7	1.791	0.3	7.0	7.1	1.729
1981	2.6	4.9	5.0	1.852	2.2	5.0	5.2	1.808	1.0	7.0	7.0	1.720
1982	2.9	4.3	4.5	1.881	2.4	4.8	5.0	1.825	1.8	6.6	6.5	1.712
1983	3.1	4.0	4.0	1.910	2.4	4.6	4.7	1.841	2.0	6.2	6.0	1.704
1984	2.5	4.2	3.5	1.940	2.0	4.8	4.1	1.858	1.5	5.8	5.5	1.696
1985	2.5	4.5	3.0	1.970	2.0	5.0	4.0	1.876	1.5	5.5	5.0	1.689
1986	2.5	4.5	3.0	2.002	2.0	5.0	4.0	1.896	1.5	5.5	5.0	1.684
1987	2.5	4.5	3.0	2.036	2.0	5.0	4.0	1.918	1.5	5.5	5.0	1.682
1988	2.5	4.5	3.0	2.070	2.0	5.0	4.0	1.941	1.5	5.5	5.0	1.682
1989	2.5	4.5	3.0	2.104	2.0	5.0	4.0	1.964	1.5	5.5	5.0	1.684
1990	2.5	4.5	3.0	2.137	2.0	5.0	4.0	1.987	1.5	5.5	5.0	1.688
1991	2.5	4.5	3.0	2.168	2.0	5.0	4.0	2.009	1.5	5.5	5.0	1.693
1992	2.4	4.5	3.0	2.196	1.9	5.0	4.0	2.030	1.4	5.5	5.0	1.697
1993	2.4	4.5	3.0	2.220	1.9	5.0	4.0	2.047	1.4	5.5	5.0	1.701
1994	2.4	4.4	3.0	2.241	1.9	5.0	4.0	2.062	1.4	5.5	5.0	1.703
1995	2.4	4.5	3.0	2.257	1.9	5.0	4.0	2.073	1.4	5.5	5.0	1.705
1996	2.3	4.5	3.0	2.270	1.8	5.0	4.0	2.082	1.3	5.5	5.0	1.706
1997	2.3	4.5	3.0	2.280	1.8	5.0	4.0	2.089	1.3	5.5	5.0	1.707
1998	2.3	4.5	3.0	2.287	1.8	5.0	4.0	2.094	1.3	5.5	5.0	1.707

TABLE 40 (Continued)

ASSUMPTIONS OF THE SOCIAL SECURITY ADMINISTRATION IN THE 1978 ANNUAL REPORT

	ALTERNATIVE I				ALTERNATIVE II				ALTERNATIVE III			
	RATE OF GROWTH IN REAL WAGES	UNEMPLOY-MENT	INFLATION	FERTILITY	RATE OF GROWTH IN REAL WAGES	UNEMPLOY-MENT	INFLATION	FERTILITY	RATE OF GROWTH IN REAL WAGES	UNEMPLOY-MENT	INFLATION	FERTILITY
1999	2.3	4.5	3.0	2.292	1.8	5.0	4.0	2.097	1.3	5.5	5.0	1.706
2000	2.25	4.5	3.0	2.296	1.75	5.0	4.0	2.099	1.25	5.5	5.0	1.705
2001	2.25	4.5	3.0	2.298	1.75	5.0	4.0	2.100	1.25	5.5	5.0	1.704
2002	2.25	4.5	3.0	2.299	1.75	5.0	4.0	2.100	1.25	5.5	5.0	1.702
2003	2.25	4.5	3.0	2.299	1.75	5.0	4.0	2.100	1.25	5.5	5.0	1.701
2004	2.25	4.5	3.0	2.299	1.75	5.0	4.0	2.100	1.25	5.5	5.0	1.700
2005	2.25	4.5	3.0	2.300	1.75	5.0	4.0	2.100	1.25	5.5	5.0	1.700

SOURCE: 1978 Annual Report of the Board of Trustees of the Federal Old-Age and Survivors and Disability Insurance Trust Funds.

TABLE 41

Estimated Future Expenditures of OASDI
under Alternatives I, II & III, 1979–2005
as a Percent of Taxable Payroll
1979 Annual Report

	Scheduled Tax Rate	Expenditures Alternative I	Difference	Expenditures Alternative II	Difference	Expenditures Alternative III	Difference
1979	10.16	10.35	−0.19	10.36	−0.20	10.35	−0.19
1980	10.16	10.48	−0.32	10.56	−0.40	10.85	−0.69
1981	10.70	10.28	0.42	10.39	0.31	10.77	−0.07
1982	10.80	10.21	0.59	10.41	0.39	10.85	−0.05
1983	10.80	10.16	0.64	10.44	0.36	10.84	−0.04
1984	10.80	10.13	0.67	10.48	0.32	10.84	0.04
1985	11.40	10.09	1.31	10.50	0.90	10.87	0.53
1986	11.40	10.04	1.36	10.51	0.89	10.90	0.50
1987	11.40	9.97	1.43	10.51	0.89	10.93	0.47
1988	11.40	9.91	1.49	10.49	0.91	10.95	0.45
1989	11.40	9.98	1.42	10.60	0.80	11.10	0.30
1990	12.40	10.05	2.35	10.70	1.70	11.25	1.15
1991	12.40	10.02	2.38	10.69	1.71	11.28	1.12
1992	12.40	9.99	2.41	10.68	1.72	11.31	1.09
1993	12.40	9.97	2.43	10.68	1.72	11.33	1.07
1994	12.40	9.95	2.45	10.67	1.73	11.36	1.04
1995	12.40	9.94	2.46	10.67	1.73	11.39	1.01
1996	12.40	9.90	2.50	10.66	1.74	11.39	1.01
1997	12.40	9.87	2.53	10.64	1.76	11.39	1.01
1998	12.40	9.86	2.54	10.64	1.76	11.40	1.00
1999	12.40	9.84	2.56	10.64	1.76	11.42	0.98
2000	12.40	9.83	2.57	10.65	1.75	11.44	0.96
2005	12.40	9.85	2.55	10.83	1.57	11.91	0.49
2010	12.40	10.33	2.07	11.58	0.82	13.09	−0.69
2015	12.40	11.19	1.21	12.79	−0.39	14.90	−2.50
2020	12.40	12.24	0.16	14.29	−1.89	17.21	−4.81
2025	12.40	13.08	−0.68	15.67	−3.27	19.64	−7.24
2030	12.40	13.31	−0.91	16.44	−4.04	21.59	−9.19
2035	12.40	13.00	−0.60	16.58	−4.18	22.93	−10.53
2040	12.40	12.38	−0.02	16.29	−3.89	23.75	−11.35
2045	12.40	11.98	−0.42	16.12	−3.72	24.53	−12.13
2050	12.40	11.87	−0.53	16.15	−3.75	25.17	−12.77
2055	12.40	11.91	0.49	16.27	−3.87	25.65	−13.25
25-Year Averages							
1979–2003	11.76	10.01	1.75	10.59	1.17	11.16	0.60
2004–2028	12.40	11.48	0.92	13.26	−0.86	15.74	−3.34
2029–2053	12.40	12.45	−0.05	16.30	−3.90	23.74	−11.34
75-Year Averages							
1970–2055	12.19	11.31	0.88	13.38	−1.19	16.88	−4.69

Source: 1979 Annual Report of the Board of Trustees of the Federal Old-Age and Survivors Insurance and Disability Insurance Trust Funds.

TABLE 42

ESTIMATED FUTURE EXPENDITURES OF OASDI UNDER ALTERNATIVES I, II & III, 1979–2005 AS A PERCENT OF TAXABLE PAYROLL

1978 ANNUAL REPORT

	SCHEDULED TAX RATE	EXPENDITURES ALTERNATIVE I	DIFFERENCE	EXPENDITURES ALTERNATIVE II	DIFFERENCE	EXPENDITURES ALTERNATIVE III	DIFFERENCE
1979	10.16	10.41	−0.25	10.45	−0.29	10.46	−0.30
1980	10.16	10.26	−0.10	10.34	−0.18	10.69	−0.53
1981	10.70	10.06	0.64	10.17	0.53	10.70	0.00
1982	10.80	9.99	0.81	10.18	0.62	10.81	−0.01
1983	10.80	9.91	0.89	10.17	0.63	10.83	−0.03
1984	10.80	9.95	0.85	10.27	0.53	10.83	−0.03
1985	11.40	9.98	1.42	10.31	1.09	10.82	0.58
1986	11.40	9.99	1.41	10.36	1.04	10.87	0.53
1987	11.40	10.01	1.39	10.41	0.99	10.93	0.47
1988	11.40	10.03	1.37	10.46	0.94	11.00	0.40
1989	11.40	10.10	1.30	10.51	0.89	11.01	0.39
1990	12.40	10.17	2.23	10.58	1.82	11.03	1.37
1991	12.40	10.25	2.15	10.66	1.74	11.10	1.30
1992	12.40	10.33	2.07	10.73	1.67	11.17	1.23
1993	12.40	10.40	2.00	10.79	1.61	11.23	1.17
1994	12.40	10.45	1.95	10.84	1.56	11.27	1.13
1995	12.40	10.51	1.89	10.90	1.50	11.31	1.09
1996	12.40	10.52	1.88	10.91	1.49	11.33	1.07
1997	12.40	10.54	1.86	10.94	1.46	11.36	1.04
1998	12.40	10.56	1.84	10.96	1.44	11.39	1.01
1999	12.40	10.58	1.82	10.99	1.41	11.43	0.97
2000	12.40	10.61	1.79	11.02	1.38	11.46	0.94
2001	12.40	10.65	1.75	11.08	1.32	11.54	0.86
2002	12.40	10.70	1.70	11.14	1.26	11.62	0.78
2005	12.40	10.85	1.55	11.32	1.08	11.88	0.52
2010	12.40	11.50	0.90	12.08	0.32	12.88	−0.48
2015	12.40	12.54	−0.14	13.30	−0.90	14.43	−2.03
2020	12.40	13.79	−1.39	14.74	−2.34	16.34	−3.94
2025	12.40	14.85	−2.45	16.06	−3.66	18.22	−5.82
2030	12.40	15.29	−2.89	16.73	−4.33	19.54	−7.14
2035	12.40	15.16	−2.76	16.80	−4.40	20.22	−7.82
2040	12.40	14.71	−2.31	16.49	−4.09	20.42	−8.02
2045	12.40	14.39	−1.99	16.28	−3.88	20.61	−8.21
2050	12.40	14.33	−1.93	16.26	−3.86	20.84	−8.44
2055	12.40	14.35	−1.95	16.29	−3.89	20.98	−8.58
25-YEAR AVERAGES							
1978–2002	11.67	10.32	1.35	10.64	1.03	11.08	0.59
2003–2027	12.40	12.72	−0.32	13.51	−1.11	14.77	−2.37
2028–2052	12.40	14.76	−2.36	16.50	−4.10	20.30	−7.90
75-YEAR AVERAGES							
1978–2052	12.16	12.60	−0.44	13.55	−1.39	15.38	−3.22

SOURCE: 1978 Annual Report of the Board of Trustees of the Federal Old-Age and Survivors Insurance and Disability Insurance Trust Funds.

TABLE 43

ESTIMATED FUTURE EXPENDITURES OF HI
UNDER ALTERNATIVES I, II & III, 1979-2050
AS A PERCENT OF TAXABLE PAYROLL
1979 ANNUAL REPORT

	SCHEDULED HI TAX RATE	EXPENDITURES ALTERNATIVE I	DIFFERENCE	EXPENDITURES ALTERNATIVE II	DIFFERENCE	EXPENDITURES ALTERNATIVE III	DIFFERENCE
1979	2.10	2.03	0.07	2.03	0.07	2.03	0.07
1980	2.10	2.11	−0.01	2.12	−0.02	2.15	−0.05
1985	2.70	2.59	0.11	2.73	−0.03	2.94	−0.24
1990	2.90	3.06	−0.16	3.51	−0.61	4.13	−1.23
1995	2.90	3.40	−0.05	4.27	−1.37	5.50	−2.60
2000	2.90	3.58	−0.68	4.92	−2.02	6.98	−4.08
2025	2.90			7.44'	−4.54'		
2050	2.90			7.61'	−4.71'		
1979-2003	2.78			3.64	−0.86		
2002-2026	2.90			6.48'	−3.58'		
2027-2051	2.90			7.53'	−4.63'		
1977-2051	2.83'			5.87'	−3.04'		

SOURCE: 1979-2000: *1979 Annual Report of the Board of Trustees of the Federal Hospital Insurance Trust Fund;* 2000-2051: *The Financial Status of Social Security after the Social Security Amendments of 1977,* A. Haeworth Robertson, Chief Actuary, S.S.A.

'Figures based on the Robertson study.

TABLE 44

Estimated Future Expenditures of HI
under Alternatives I, II & III, 1979–2050
as a Percent of Taxable Payroll
1978 Annual Report

	Scheduled HI Tax Rate	Expenditures Alternative I	Difference	Expenditures Alternative II	Difference	Expenditures Alternative III	Difference
1979	2.10	2.07	0.03	2.09	0.01	2.10	0.00
1980	2.10	2.14	− 0.04	2.18	− 0.08	2.26	− 0.16
1985	2.70	2.62	0.08	2.86	− 0.16	3.04	− 0.34
1990	2.90	3.10	− 0.20	3.65	− 0.75	4.22	− 1.32
1995	2.90	3.49	− 0.59	4.47	− 1.57	5.58	− 2.68
2000	2.90	3.69	− 0.79	5.20	− 2.30	7.08	− 4.18
2025	2.90			7.44[1]	− 4.54[1]		
2050	2.90			7.61[1]	− 4.71[1]		
1978– 2002	2.74			3.67	− 0.93		
2002– 2026	2.90			6.48[1]	− 3.58[1]		
2027– 2051	2.90			7.53[1]	− 4.63[1]		
1977– 2051	2.83[1]			5.87[1]	− 3.04[1]		

Source: 1978–2000: *1978 Annual Report of the Board of Trustees of the Federal Hospital Insurance Trust Fund;* 2000–2051: *The Financial Status of Social Security after the Social Security Amendments of 1977,* A. Haeworth Robertson, Chief Actuary, S.S.A.

[1]Figures based on the Robertson study.

TABLE 45

ESTIMATED FUTURE EXPENDITURES OF OASDHI
UNDER ALTERNATIVES I, II & III, 1979-2050
AS A PERCENT OF TAXABLE PAYROLL
1979 ANNUAL REPORT

	SCHEDULED OASDHI HI TAX RATE	EXPENDITURES ALTERNATIVE I	DIFFERENCE	EXPENDITURES ALTERNATIVE II	DIFFERENCE	EXPENDITURES ALTERNATIVE III	DIFFERENCE
1979	12.26	12.38	-0.12	12.39	-0.13	12.38	-0.12
1980	12.26	12.59	-0.33	12.68	-0.42	13.00	-0.74
1985	14.10	12.68	1.42	12.23	0.87	13.81	0.29
1990	15.30	13.11	2.19	14.21	1.09	15.38	-0.08
1995	15.30	13.34	1.96	14.94	0.36	16.89	-1.59
2000	15.30	13.41	1.89	15.57	-0.27	18.42	-3.12
2025	15.30			23.11	-7.81		
2050	15.30			23.76	-8.46		

SOURCE: Compiled from tables 41 and 43.

TABLE 46

ESTIMATED FUTURE EXPENDITURES OF OASDHI
UNDER ALTERNATIVES I, II & III, 1979-2050
AS A PERCENT OF TAXABLE PAYROLL
1978 ANNUAL REPORT

	SCHEDULED OASDHI HI TAX RATE	EXPENDITURES ALTERNATIVE I	DIFFERENCE	EXPENDITURES ALTERNATIVE II	DIFFERENCE	EXPENDITURES ALTERNATIVE III	DIFFERENCE
1979	12.26	12.48	-0.22	12.54	-0.28	12.56	-0.30
1980	12.26	12.40	-0.14	12.52	-0.26	12.95	-0.69
1985	14.10	12.60	1.50	13.17	0.93	13.86	0.24
1990	15.30	13.27	2.03	14.23	1.07	15.25	0.05
1995	15.30	14.00	1.30	15.37	-0.07	16.89	-1.59
2000	15.30	14.30	1.00	16.22	-0.92	18.54	-3.24
2025	15.30			23.50	-8.20		
2050	15.30			23.87	-8.57		

SOURCE: Compiled from tables 42 and 44.

TABLE 47

OASDI AND OASDHI EXPENDITURES, 1979–2050
ALTERNATIVE II ASSUMPTIONS[1,2]
1979 ANNUAL REPORT

	OASDI EXPENDITURES	OASDI TAXES	DIFFERENCE	OASDHI EXPENDITURES	OASDHI TAXES	DIFFERENCE
1979	107.6	103.5	− 4.1	129.1	124.6	− 4.5
1980	121.5	117.8	− 3.7	146.3	141.8	− 4.5
1981	126.9	128.7	1.8	153.8	159.4	5.6
1982	132.4	136.4	4.0	161.7	170.4	8.7
1983	137.9	142.0	4.1	170.2	177.1	6.9
1985	147.5	160.2	12.7	185.9	198.1	12.2
1990	172.3	199.6	27.3	228.8	246.3	17.5
1995	193.5	224.9	31.4	271.0	277.5	6.5
2000	215.5	250.9	35.4	215.1	309.6	− 5.5
2005	247.2	283.0	35.8			
2010	291.8	312.5	20.7			
2015	358.2	247.3	− 10.9			
2020	436.7	379.0	− 57.7			
2025	522.2	413.3	− 108.9	770.2	509.9	− 260.3
2030	600.5	452.9	− 147.6			
2035	667.2	499.0	− 168.2			
2040	724.1	551.2	− 172.9			
2045	790.1	607.8	− 182.3			
2050	871.6	669.2	− 202.4	1282.3	825.7	−456.6

SOURCE: 1979 Annual Report of the Board of Trustees of the Federal Old-Age and Survivors Insurance and Disability Insurance Trust Funds, Social Security Administration.

[1]All figures are in billions.

[2]Figures for 1980 and after are in constant 1980 dollars.

TABLE 48

OASDI AND OASDHI EXPENDITURES, 1980–2050
ALTERNATIVE III ASSUMPTIONS[1,2]
1979 ANNUAL REPORT

	OASDI EXPENDITURES	OASDI TAXES	DIFFERENCE	OASDHI EXPENDITURES	OASDHI TAXES	DIFFERENCE
1980	123.0	115.2	− 7.8	147.8	141.1	− 6.7
1985	149.0	156.3	7.3	203.3	209.5	6.2
1990	173.0	190.6	17.6	236.4	235.2	− 1.2
1995	192.0	209.0	17.0	284.6	257.8	− 26.8
2000	209.7	227.3	17.6	337.7	280.5	− 57.2
2005	235.4	245.1	9.7			
2010	274.6	260.1	− 14.5			
2015	325.9	271.2	− 54.7			
2020	387.5	279.2	− 108.3			
2025	452.2	285.5	− 166.7	669.5	352.3	− 317.2
2030	507.9	291.7	− 216.2			
2035	551.6	298.3	− 253.3			
2040	584.1	304.9	− 279.2			
2045	615.5	311.1	− 304.4			
2050	643.8	317.2	− 326.6	889.6	391.3	− 498.3

SOURCE: 1979 Annual Report of the Board of Trustees of the Federal Old-Age and Survivors Insurance and Disability Insurance Trust Funds, Social Security Administration.

[1]All figures are in billions.

[2]Figures for 1980 and after are in constant 1980 dollars.

TABLE 49

EXPENDITURES AS A PERCENT OF TRUST FUND ASSETS,
OASI AND OASDI PROGRAMS, 1979–2040,
AS PROJECTED IN THE 1979 ANNUAL REPORT

	ALTERNATIVE I		ALTERNATIVE II		ALTERNATIVE III	
	OASI	OASDI	OASI	OASDI	OASI	OASDI
1979	30%	30%	30%	30%	30%	29%
1980	24%	25%	24%	25%	24%	25%
1981	20%	23%	19%	22%	16%	19%
1982	20%	25%	18%	23%	12%	17%
1983	22%	30%	18%	26%	8%	16%
1984	25%	36%	19%	29%	5%	15%
1985	29%	43%	19%	32%	2%	15%
1986	37%	56%	22%	40%	2%	19%
1987	45%	69%	26%	48%	2%	23%
1988	55%	83%	30%	56%	2%	26%
1989	64%	97%	34%	64%	2%	30%
1990	73%	110%	37%	70%	1%	31%
1991	89%	133%	46%	85%	5%	41%
1992	106%	156%	56%	100%	10%	50%
1993	124%	180%	66%	116%	14%	58%
1994	142%	204%	77%	131%	18%	67%
1995	161%	228%	88%	147%	22%	75%
1996	182%	253%	100%	163%	27%	84%
1997	203%	279%	112%	179%	32%	92%
1998	226%	305%	126%	195%	37%	100%
1999	249%	330%	139%	211%	43%	108%
2000	273%	357%	154%	228%	49%	116%
2005	393%	477%	225%	299%	77%	145%
2010	485%	563%	268%	335%	74%	136%
2015	521%	599%	258%	323%	20%	78%
2020	498%	586%	194%	263%	1%	1%
2025	440%	547%	89%	170%	1%	1%
2030	378%	510%	1%	59%	1%	1%
2035	330%	490%	1%	1%	1%	1%
2040	307%	496%	1%	1%	1%	1%
TRUST FUND TO BE EXHAUSTED IN:		2028	2032	2016	2018	

SOURCE: 1979 Annual Report of the Board of Trustees of the Federal Old-Age and Survivors Insurance and Disability Insurance Trust Funds.

TABLE 50

EXPENDITURES AS A PERCENT OF TRUST FUND ASSETS, OASI AND OASDI PROGRAMS, 1979–2040, AS PROJECTED IN THE 1978 ANNUAL REPORT

	ALTERNATIVE I		ALTERNATIVE II		ALTERNATIVE III	
	OASI	OASDI	OASI	OASDI	OASI	OASDI
1979	29%	28%	29%	28%	29%	28%
1980	24%	24%	24%	24%	23%	24%
1981	22%	22%	21%	21%	17%	18%
1982	25%	27%	23%	25%	15%	16%
1983	31%	34%	27%	30%	13%	15%
1984	39%	42%	32%	35%	12%	14%
1985	47%	50%	37%	40%	11%	14%
1986	59%	63%	44%	49%	13%	18%
1987	71%	77%	52%	58%	16%	22%
1988	82%	90%	59%	67%	17%	26%
1989	94%	102%	66%	75%	19%	29%
1990	105%	114%	73%	82%	21%	32%
1991	123%	135%	86%	98%	30%	43%
1992	141%	155%	99%	113%	38%	54%
1993	159%	174%	111%	127%	46%	63%
1994	176%	192%	124%	141%	53%	73%
1995	194%	211%	136%	154%	61%	81%
1996	212%	228%	148%	167%	68%	90%
1997	230%	246%	161%	179%	76%	98%
1998	249%	264%	174%	191%	84%	106%
1999	269%	281%	188%	203%	93%	113%
2000	288%	298%	201%	215%	101%	120%
2005	385%	372%	266%	262%	139%	145%
2010	453%	416%	303%	279%	149%	138%
2015	465%	416%	289%	253%	109%	88%
2020	422%	373%	221%	186%	17%	1%
2025	341%	302%	116%	87%	1%	1%
2030	246%	219%	1%	1%	1%	1%
2035	151%	135%	1%	1%	1%	1%
2040	63%	55%	1%	1%	1%	1%
TRUST FUND TO BE EXHAUSTED IN:	2043	2043	2029	2028	2020	2019

SOURCE: 1978 Annual Report of the Board of Trustees of the Federal Old-Age and Survivors Insurance and Disability Insurance Trust Funds.

TABLE 51

NET WORTH AND UNFUNDED LIABILITY OF
THE SOCIAL SECURITY PROGRAM[1]

	ACTUARIAL LIABILITIES (present value of future benefits)		ACTUARIAL ASSETS (present value of future taxes		ACTUARIAL NET WORTH (present value of future deficits)		UNFUNDED NET LIABILITY
	OASDI	OASDHI	OASDI	OASDHI	OASDI	OASDHI	OASDI
1978	10,343	11,370	9,414	10,181	− 929	− 1,189	3,971
1977	11,638	12,528	6,850	7,499	− 4,788	− 5,030	5,362
1976	10,510	11,216	6,333	6,924	− 4,177	− 4,292	4,148
1975	7,071	7,622	4,971	5,509	− 2,100	− 2,113	2,710
1974	6,533	6,998	5,220	5,693	− 1,312	− 1,304	2,460
1973	5,526	5,940	5,350	5,783	− 176	− 158	2,118
1972	4,717	4,989	4,857	5,142	+ 140	+ 153	1,865
1971	1,185	1,461	1,173	1,316	− 12	+ 145	435
1970	1,146	1,379	1,143	1,281	− 3	− 98	415
1969	1,067	1,220	1,129	1,257	+ 62	+ 38	330
1968	1,142	1,242	1,157	1,264	+ 15	+ 21	414
1967	968	1,042	1,060	1,139	+ 92	+ 96	350

SOURCE: Statement of Liabilities and Other Financial Commitments of the U.S. Government (Saltonstall Reports), 1967–1978, U.S. Treasury Department.

[1]All figures in billions.

TABLE 52

DISTRIBUTION OF TOTAL WEALTH
AND ITS COMPONENTS, 1962

TOTAL WEALTH CLASS	PERCENT OF FAMILIES	PERCENT OF FUNGIBLE WEALTH	PERCENT OF SOCIAL SECURITY WEALTH	PERCENT OF TOTAL WEALTH
LESS THAN 10,000	11.6	0.3	3.9	1.6
10,000– 24,999	39.6	8.4	36.5	18.2
25,000– 49,999	32.5	23.3	38.6	28.6
50,000– 74,999	9.3	15.9	11.9	14.5
75,000– 99,999	2.9	7.6	3.9	6.3
100,000– 199,999	2.6	11.9	3.5	8.9
200,000– 249,999	0.5	4.3	0.5	3.0
250,000 +	1.0	28.4	1.2	18.9

SOURCE: Martin Feldstein, "Social Security and the Distribution of Wealth," *Journal of the American Statistical Association,* December 1976.

TABLE 53

Women in Labor Force, 1940–1975

	Total[1] Women	Single[1] Women	Married[1] Women	Widowed, Divorced[1] Separated Women	Percent of Single Women Working	Percent of Married Women Working	Percent of Widowed, Divorced Separated Working
1940	13.8	6.7	4.2	2.9	48.1	14.7	—
1950	17.8	5.6	8.6	3.6	50.5	23.8	37.8
1960	22.5	5.4	12.3	4.9	44.1	30.5	40.0
1970	31.2	7.0	18.4	5.9	53.0	40.8	39.1
1975	36.5	8.5	21.1	6.9	56.7	44.4	40.7
1979	—	—	—	—	57.0	50.0	41.2

Source: U.S. Department of Commerce, Bureau of the Census, Current Population Reports, Series P-50; U.S. Department of Labor, Employment and Training Report of the President, from Marilyn M. Flowers, *Women and Social Security: An Institutional Dilemma* (Washington D.C.: American Enterprise Institute, 1977); and U.S. Labor Department.

[1]Totals in millions.

TABLE 54

PROJECTED OASDI EXPENDITURES UNDER
WAGE INDEXING + PRICE INDEXING

		EXPENDITURES AS A PERCENT OF TAXABLE PAYROLL				EXPENDITURES AS A PERCENT OF GNP	
	CURRENT TAX RATE	WAGE INDEXING	DEFICIT	PRICE INDEXING	DEFICIT	WAGE INDEXING	PRICE INDEXING
1979	10.16	10.9	− 0.74	10.9	− 0.74	4.5	4.5
1985	11.40	11.5	− 0.1	11.0	+ 0.40	4.7	4.5
1990	12.4	11.9	+ 0.5	11.0	+ 1.4	4.9	4.5
1995	12.4	12.2	+ 0.2	10.8	+ 1.6	5.0	4.4
2000	12.4	12.5	− 0.1	10.5	+ 1.9	5.1	4.3
2010	12.4	13.8	− 1.4	10.6	+ 1.8	5.7	4.3
2020	12.4	16.7	− 4.3	12.0	+ 0.4	6.9	4.9
2030	12.4	19.0	− 6.6	12.8	− 0.4	7.8	5.3
2040	12.4	18.4	− 6.0	11.8	+ 0.6	7.6	4.9
2050	12.4	17.8	− 5.4	10.9	+ 1.5	7.3	4.5

SOURCE: William C. Hsiao, Harvard University, "An Optimal Indexing Method for Social Security," Conference on Financial Social Security, American Enterprise Institute, 1977.

TABLE 55

PROJECTED OASDI EXPENDITURES UNDER
WAGE INDEXING AND PRICE INDEXING[1,2]

		PROJECTED TOTAL EXPENDITURES				WAGE INDEXING AS A PERCENTAGE OF PRICE INDEXING
	SCHEDULED TAXES	WAGE INDEXING	DEFICIT	PRICE INDEXING	DEFICIT	
1980	116.2	119.3	− 3.1	119.3	− 3.1	100%
1990	198.5	190.5	+ 8.0	176.1	+ 22.4	108%
2000	252.8	254.8	− 2.0	214.1	+ 38.7	119%
2010	316.6	352.4	− 35.8	270.7	+ 45.9	130%
2020	378.5	509.8	− 131.3	366.3	+ 12.2	139%
2030	450.9	690.8	− 239.9	465.4	− 14.5	148%
2040	547.0	811.7	− 264.7	520.6	+ 26.4	156%
2050	662.0	950.2	− 288.2	581.9	+ 80.1	163%

SOURCE: 1978 Annual Report of the Board of Trustees of the Federal Old-Age and Survivors Insurance Trust Funds, Social Security Administration.

[1] All figures in billions.
[2] Figures in constant 1980 dollars.

TABLE 56

REPLACEMENT RATIOS UNDER WAGE INDEXING AND PRICE INDEXING 1979–2055 PRE-TAX INCOME (SINGLE WORKER)

	WAGE INDEXING (Present Law)			PRICE INDEXING (Hsiao Proposal)		
	LOW INCOME	AVERAGE INCOME	HIGH INCOME	LOW INCOME	AVERAGE INCOME	HIGH INCOME
1979	63	48	35	63	48	35
1980	63	48	30	63	48	30
1985	54	41	23	54	42	23
1990	55	41	24	51	40	22
1995	55	42	25	47	37	21
2000	55	42	26	45	36	21
2005	55	42	27	44	34	21
2010	55	42	27	42	33	21
2015	55	42	28	41	31	21
2020	55	42	28	40	30	20
2025	55	42	28	39	28	20
2030	55	42	28	38	27	19
2035	55	42	28	37	26	19
2040	55	42	28	37	25	18
2045	55	42	28	36	24	18
2050	55	42	28	34	23	18
2055	55	42	28	33	22	17

SOURCE: Social Security Administration.

TABLE 57

REPLACEMENT RATIOS UNDER WAGE INDEXING
AND PRICE INDEXING 1979–2050
AFTER-TAX INCOME

	WAGE INDEXING (Present Law)			PRICE INDEXING (Hsiao Proposal)		
	LOW INCOME	AVERAGE INCOME	HIGH INCOME	LOW INCOME	AVERAGE INCOME	HIGH INCOME
SINGLE WORKER						
1979	70	58	45	73	58	44
1990	69	57	44	62	49	38
2000	69	57	45	55	44	37
2010	69	57	47	52	41	37
2020	69	57	47	49	39	36
2030	69	57	47	46	36	34
2040	69	57	47	43	35	33
2050	69	57	47	39	34	32
WORKER WITH SPOUSE						
1979	103	87	65	106	87	63
1990	101	85	63	90	74	55
2000	101	85	65	81	66	53
2010	101	85	67	76	62	53
2020	101	85	67	72	58	51
2030	101	85	67	67	54	50
2040	101	85	67	63	52	48
2050	101	85	67	58	50	46

SOURCE: William C. Hsiao, Harvard University, "An Optimal Indexing Method For Social Security," Conference on Financing Social Security, American Enterprise Institute, 1977.

TABLE 58

Deficits to Be Made Up by General Revenues[1,2,3] from Long-Term Reform Proposal

	Total Retirement Account	Annual Addition to Account	Taxes Generated by Account	Annual Return to Account	Annual Benefit Obligations	Annual Deficit	Other Additions to General Revenues	Remaining Deficit
1980	0	117.8	7.4	7.4	121.5	114.1	53.0	61.1
1981	125.2	128.7	15.9	15.9	126.8	110.9	53.0	57.9
1982	269.8	136.4	25.4	25.4	132.4	107.0	53.0	54.0
1983	431.6	142.0	35.9	35.9	137.9	102.0	53.0	49.0
1984	609.5	151.1	47.5	47.5	142.7	95.2	53.0	42.2
1985	808.1	160.2	60.5	60.5	147.5	87.0	53.0	34.0
1986	1028.8	168.1	74.8	74.8	152.5	77.0	53.0	24.7
1987	1271.7	176.0	90.5	90.5	157.5	67.0	53.0	14.0
1988	1538.2	183.9	107.6	107.6	162.5	54.9	53.0	1.9
1989	1829.7	191.8	126.3	126.3	167.5	41.2	53.0	—
1990	2147.8	199.6	146.7	146.7	172.3	25.6	53.0	—
1991	2494.1	204.7	168.7	168.7	176.5	7.8	53.0	—

Source: Calculated from tables 6 and 12.

[1] All figures are in billions.

[2] All figures are in constant 1980 dollars.

[3] All figures are projections based on Alternative II, Intermediate Assumptions of the Social Security Administration, 1979 Annual Report.

Author Index

Subject Index

476

CATO
INSTITUTE

The Cato Institute is named for the libertarian pamphlets *Cato's Letters*, which were inspired by the Roman Stoic Cato the Younger. Written by John Trenchard and Thomas Gordon, *Cato's Letters* were widely read in the American colonies in the early eighteenth century and played a major role in laying the philosophical foundation for the revolution that followed.

The erosion of civil and economic liberties in the modern world has occurred in concert with a widening array of social problems. These disturbing developments have resulted from a major failure to examine social problems in terms of the fundamental principles of human dignity, economic welfare, and justice.

The Cato Institute aims to broaden public policy debate by sponsoring programs designed to assist both the scholar and the concerned layperson in analyzing questions of political economy.

The programs of the Cato Institute include the sponsorship and publication of basic research in social philosophy and public policy; publication of major journals on the scholarship of liberty and commentary on political affairs; production of debate forums for radio; and organization of an extensive program of symposia, seminars, and conferences.